BULGARIAN
VOCABULARY

FOR ENGLISH SPEAKERS

ENGLISH-BULGARIAN

The most useful words
To expand your lexicon and sharpen
your language skills

9000 words

Bulgarian vocabulary for English speakers - 9000 words
By Andrey Taranov

T&P Books vocabularies are intended for helping you learn, memorize and review foreign words. The dictionary is divided into themes, covering all major spheres of everyday activities, business, science, culture, etc.

The process of learning words using T&P Books' theme-based dictionaries gives you the following advantages:

- Correctly grouped source information predetermines success at subsequent stages of word memorization
- Availability of words derived from the same root allowing memorization of word units (rather than separate words)
- Small units of words facilitate the process of establishing associative links needed for consolidation of vocabulary
- Level of language knowledge can be estimated by the number of learned words

T&P Books Publishing
www.tpbooks.com

ISBN: 978-1-78071-305-2

This book is also available in E-book formats.
Please visit www.tpbooks.com or the major online bookstores.

BULGARIAN VOCABULARY
for English speakers

T&P Books vocabularies are intended to help you learn, memorize, and review foreign words. The vocabulary contains over 9000 commonly used words arranged thematically.

- Vocabulary contains the most commonly used words
- Recommended as an addition to any language course
- Meets the needs of beginners and advanced learners of foreign languages
- Convenient for daily use, revision sessions, and self-testing activities
- Allows you to assess your vocabulary

Special features of the vocabulary

- Words are organized according to their meaning, not alphabetically
- Words are presented in three columns to facilitate the reviewing and self-testing processes
- Words in groups are divided into small blocks to facilitate the learning process
- The vocabulary offers a convenient and simple transcription of each foreign word

The vocabulary has 256 topics including:

Basic Concepts, Numbers, Colors, Months, Seasons, Units of Measurement, Clothing & Accessories, Food & Nutrition, Restaurant, Family Members, Relatives, Character, Feelings, Emotions, Diseases, City, Town, Sightseeing, Shopping, Money, House, Home, Office, Working in the Office, Import & Export, Marketing, Job Search, Sports, Education, Computer, Internet, Tools, Nature, Countries, Nationalities and more ...

T&P BOOKS' THEME-BASED DICTIONARIES

The Correct System for Memorizing Foreign Words

Acquiring vocabulary is one of the most important elements of learning a foreign language, because words allow us to express our thoughts, ask questions, and provide answers. An inadequate vocabulary can impede communication with a foreigner and make it difficult to understand a book or movie well.

The pace of activity in all spheres of modern life, including the learning of modern languages, has increased. Today, we need to memorize large amounts of information (grammar rules, foreign words, etc.) within a short period. However, this does not need to be difficult. All you need to do is to choose the right training materials, learn a few special techniques, and develop your individual training system.

Having a system is critical to the process of language learning. Many people fail to succeed in this regard; they cannot master a foreign language because they fail to follow a system comprised of selecting materials, organizing lessons, arranging new words to be learned, and so on. The lack of a system causes confusion and eventually, lowers self-confidence.

T&P Books' theme-based dictionaries can be included in the list of elements needed for creating an effective system for learning foreign words. These dictionaries were specially developed for learning purposes and are meant to help students effectively memorize words and expand their vocabulary.

Generally speaking, the process of learning words consists of three main elements:

- Reception (creation or acquisition) of a training material, such as a word list
- Work aimed at memorizing new words
- Work aimed at reviewing the learned words, such as self-testing

All three elements are equally important since they determine the quality of work and the final result. All three processes require certain skills and a well-thought-out approach.

New words are often encountered quite randomly when learning a foreign language and it may be difficult to include them all in a unified list. As a result, these words remain written on scraps of paper, in book margins, textbooks, and so on. In order to systematize such words, we have to create and continually update a "book of new words." A paper notebook, a netbook, or a tablet PC can be used for these purposes.

This "book of new words" will be your personal, unique list of words. However, it will only contain the words that you came across during the learning process. For example, you might have written down the words "Sunday," "Tuesday," and "Friday." However, there are additional words for days of the week, for example, "Saturday," that are missing, and your list of words would be incomplete. Using a theme dictionary, in addition to the "book of new words," is a reasonable solution to this problem.

The theme-based dictionary may serve as the basis for expanding your vocabulary.

It will be your big "book of new words" containing the most frequently used words of a foreign language already included. There are quite a few theme-based dictionaries available, and you should ensure that you make the right choice in order to get the maximum benefit from your purchase.

Therefore, we suggest using theme-based dictionaries from T&P Books Publishing as an aid to learning foreign words. Our books are specially developed for effective use in the sphere of vocabulary systematization, expansion and review.

Theme-based dictionaries are not a magical solution to learning new words. However, they can serve as your main database to aid foreign-language acquisition. Apart from theme dictionaries, you can have copybooks for writing down new words, flash cards, glossaries for various texts, as well as other resources; however, a good theme dictionary will always remain your primary collection of words.

T&P Books' theme-based dictionaries are specialty books that contain the most frequently used words in a language.

The main characteristic of such dictionaries is the division of words into themes. For example, the *City* theme contains the words "street," "crossroads," "square," "fountain," and so on. The *Talking* theme might contain words like "to talk," "to ask," "question," and "answer".

All the words in a theme are divided into smaller units, each comprising 3–5 words. Such an arrangement improves the perception of words and makes the learning process less tiresome. Each unit contains a selection of words with similar meanings or identical roots. This allows you to learn words in small groups and establish other associative links that have a positive effect on memorization.

The words on each page are placed in three columns: a word in your native language, its translation, and its transcription. Such positioning allows for the use of techniques for effective memorization. After closing the translation column, you can flip through and review foreign words, and vice versa. "This is an easy and convenient method of review – one that we recommend you do often."

Our theme-based dictionaries contain transcriptions for all the foreign words. Unfortunately, none of the existing transcriptions are able to convey the exact nuances of foreign pronunciation. That is why we recommend using the transcriptions only as a supplementary learning aid. Correct pronunciation can only be acquired with the help of sound. Therefore our collection includes audio theme-based dictionaries.

The process of learning words using T&P Books' theme-based dictionaries gives you the following advantages:

- You have correctly grouped source information, which predetermines your success at subsequent stages of word memorization
- Availability of words derived from the same root (lazy, lazily, lazybones), allowing you to memorize word units instead of separate words
- Small units of words facilitate the process of establishing associative links needed for consolidation of vocabulary
- You can estimate the number of learned words and hence your level of language knowledge
- The dictionary allows for the creation of an effective and high-quality revision process
- You can revise certain themes several times, modifying the revision methods and techniques
- Audio versions of the dictionaries help you to work out the pronunciation of words and develop your skills of auditory word perception

The T&P Books' theme-based dictionaries are offered in several variants differing in the number of words: 1.500, 3.000, 5.000, 7.000, and 9.000 words. There are also dictionaries containing 15,000 words for some language combinations. Your choice of dictionary will depend on your knowledge level and goals.

We sincerely believe that our dictionaries will become your trusty assistant in learning foreign languages and will allow you to easily acquire the necessary vocabulary.

TABLE OF CONTENTS

PRONUNCIATION GUIDE

Letter	Bulgarian example	T&P phonetic alphabet	English example
А а	кантар	[a]	shorter than in ask
Б б	бор	[b]	baby, book
В в	водач	[v]	very, river
Г г	година	[g]	game, gold
Д д	данък	[d]	day, doctor
Е е	елен	[ɛ]	man, bad
Ж ж	живот	[ʒ]	forge, pleasure
З з	зеле	[z]	zebra, please
И и	ивица	[i]	shorter than in feet
Й й	йод	[j]	yes, New York
К к	колиба	[k]	clock, kiss
Л л	локва	[l]	lace, people
М м	майка	[m]	magic, milk
Н н	намаление	[n]	name, normal
О о	одеяло	[o], [ɔ]	drop, baught
П п	пари	[p]	pencil, private
Р р	речник	[r]	rice, radio
С с	секира	[s]	city, boss
Т т	торба	[t]	tourist, trip
У у	утре	[u]	book
Ф ф	филия	[f]	face, food
Х х	храна	[ɦ], [x]	as in Scots loch
Ц ц	царевица	[ʦ]	cats, tsetse fly
Ч ч	чанта	[ʧ]	church, French
Ш ш	шал	[ʃ]	machine, shark
Щ щ	щъркел	[ʃ]	machine, shark
Ъ ъ	огън	[ı]	big, America
Ь ь	миньор	[ʲ]	soft sign - no sound
нь	треньор	[ɲ]	canyon, new
ль	бельо	[ʎ]	daily, million
ть	фотьойл	[t]	tune, student
Ю ю	ютия	[ju]	youth, usually
Я я	яхния	[ja]	young, yard

ABBREVIATIONS used in the vocabulary

ab.	-	about
adj	-	adjective
adv	-	adverb
anim.	-	animate
as adj	-	attributive noun used as adjective
e.g.	-	for example
etc.	-	et cetera
fam.	-	familiar
fem.	-	feminine
form.	-	formal
inanim.	-	inanimate
masc.	-	masculine
math	-	mathematics
mil.	-	military
n	-	noun
pl	-	plural
pron.	-	pronoun
sb	-	somebody
sing.	-	singular
sth	-	something
v aux	-	auxiliary verb
vi	-	intransitive verb
vi, vt	-	intransitive, transitive verb
vt	-	transitive verb

m	-	masculine noun
f	-	feminine noun
m pl	-	masculine plural
f pl	-	feminine plural
n pl	-	neuter plural
m, f	-	masculine, feminine

BASIC CONCEPTS

Basic concepts. Part 1

1. Pronouns

I, me	**аз**	[az]
you	**ти**	[ti]
he	**той**	[tɔj]
she	**тя**	[tʲa]
it	**то**	[tɔ]
we	**ние**	[ˈniɛ]
you (to a group)	**вие**	[ˈviɛ]
they	**те**	[tɛ]

2. Greetings. Salutations. Farewells

Hello! (fam.)	**Здравей!**	[zdraˈvɛj]
Hello! (form.)	**Здравейте!**	[zdraˈvɛjtɛ]
Good morning!	**Добро утро!**	[dɔbˈrɔ ˈutrɔ]
Good afternoon!	**Добър ден!**	[ˈdɔbır dɛn]
Good evening!	**Добър вечер!**	[ˈdɔbır ˈvɛʧər]
to say hello	**поздравявам**	[pɔzdraˈvʲavam]
Hi! (hello)	**Здрасти!**	[ˈzdrasti]
greeting (n)	**поздрав** (m)	[ˈpɔzdrav]
to greet (vt)	**приветствувам**	[priˈvɛʦtvuvam]
How are you?	**Как си?**	[kak si]
What's new?	**Какво ново?**	[kakˈvɔ ˈnɔvɔ]
Bye-Bye! Goodbye!	**Довиждане!**	[dɔˈviʒdanɛ]
See you soon!	**До скора среща!**	[dɔ ˈskɔra ˈsrɛʃta]
Farewell!	**Сбогом!**	[ˈzbɔgɔm]
to say goodbye	**сбогувам се**	[sbɔˈguvam sɛ]
So long!	**До скоро!**	[dɔ ˈskɔrɔ]
Thank you!	**Благодаря!**	[blagɔdaˈrʲa]
Thank you very much!	**Много благодаря!**	[ˈmnɔgɔ blagɔdaˈrʲa]
You're welcome	**Моля.**	[ˈmɔʎa]
Don't mention it!	**Няма нищо.**	[ˈɲama ˈniʃtɔ]
It was nothing	**Няма за какво.**	[ˈɲama za kakˈvɔ]

Excuse me! (fam.)	**Извинявай!**	[izvi'ɲavaj]
Excuse me! (form.)	**Извинявайте!**	[izvi'ɲavajtɛ]
to excuse (forgive)	**извинявам**	[izvi'ɲavam]
to apologize (vi)	**извинявам се**	[izvi'ɲavam sɛ]
My apologies	**Моите извинения.**	['mɔitɛ izvi'nɛnijɑ]
I'm sorry!	**Прощавайте!**	[prɔʃ'tavajtɛ]
please (adv)	**моля**	['mɔʎa]
Don't forget!	**Не забравяйте!**	[nɛ zab'rav'ajtɛ]
Certainly!	**Разбира се!**	[raz'bira sɛ]
Of course not!	**Разбира се, не!**	[raz'bira sɛ nɛ]
Okay! (I agree)	**Съгласен!**	[sɪg'lasɛn]
That's enough!	**Стига!**	['stiga]

3. How to address

mister, sir	**Господине**	[gɔspɔ'dinɛ]
ma'am	**Госпожо**	[gɔs'pɔʒɔ]
miss	**Госпожице**	[gɔs'pɔʒiʦə]
young man	**Младежо**	[mla'dɛʒɔ]
young man (little boy)	**Момче**	[mɔm'ʧə]
miss (little girl)	**Момиче**	[mɔ'miʧə]

4. Cardinal numbers. Part 1

0 zero	**нула** (f)	['nula]
1 one	**едно**	[ɛd'nɔ]
2 two	**две**	[dvɛ]
3 three	**три**	[tri]
4 four	**четири**	['ʧətiri]
5 five	**пет**	[pɛt]
6 six	**шест**	[ʃɛst]
7 seven	**седем**	['sɛdɛm]
8 eight	**осем**	['ɔsɛm]
9 nine	**девет**	['dɛvɛt]
10 ten	**десет**	['dɛsɛt]
11 eleven	**единадесет**	[ɛdi'nadɛsɛt]
12 twelve	**дванадесет**	[dva'nadɛsɛt]
13 thirteen	**тринадесет**	[tri'nadɛsɛt]
14 fourteen	**четиринадесет**	[ʧətiri'nadɛsɛt]
15 fifteen	**петнадесет**	[pɛt'nadɛsɛt]
16 sixteen	**шестнадесет**	[ʃɛs'nadɛsɛt]
17 seventeen	**седемнадесет**	[sɛdɛm'nadɛsɛt]
18 eighteen	**осемнадесет**	[ɔsɛm'nadɛsɛt]

19 nineteen	**деветнадесет**	[dɛvɛt'nadɛsɛt]
20 twenty	**двадесет**	['dvadɛsɛt]
21 twenty-one	**двадесет и едно**	['dvadɛsɛt i ɛd'nɔ]
22 twenty-two	**двадесет и две**	['dvadɛsɛt i dvɛ]
23 twenty-three	**двадесет и три**	['dvadɛsɛt i tri]
30 thirty	**тридесет**	['tridɛsɛt]
31 thirty-one	**тридесет и едно**	['tridɛsɛt i ɛd'nɔ]
32 thirty-two	**тридесет и две**	['tridɛsɛt i dvɛ]
33 thirty-three	**тридесет и три**	['tridɛsɛt i tri]
40 forty	**четиридесет**	[ʧə'tiridɛsɛt]
41 forty-one	**четиридесет и едно**	[ʧə'tiridɛsɛt i ɛd'nɔ]
42 forty-two	**четиридесет и две**	[ʧə'tiridɛsɛt i dvɛ]
43 forty-three	**четиридесет и три**	[ʧə'tiridɛsɛt i tri]
50 fifty	**петдесет**	[pɛtdɛ'sɛt]
51 fifty-one	**петдесет и едно**	[pɛtdɛ'sɛt i ɛd'nɔ]
52 fifty-two	**петдесет и две**	[pɛtdɛ'sɛt i dvɛ]
53 fifty-three	**петдесет и три**	[pɛtdɛ'sɛt i tri]
60 sixty	**шестдесет**	[ʃɛstdɛ'sɛt]
61 sixty-one	**шестдесет и едно**	[ʃɛstdɛ'sɛt i ɛd'nɔ]
62 sixty-two	**шестдесет и две**	[ʃɛstdɛ'sɛt i dvɛ]
63 sixty-three	**шестдесет и три**	[ʃɛstdɛ'sɛt i tri]
70 seventy	**седемдесет**	[sɛdɛmdɛ'sɛt]
71 seventy-one	**седемдесет и едно**	[sɛdɛmdɛ'sɛt i ɛd'nɔ]
72 seventy-two	**седемдесет и две**	[sɛdɛmdɛ'sɛt i dvɛ]
73 seventy-three	**седемдесет и три**	[sɛdɛmdɛ'sɛt i tri]
80 eighty	**осемдесет**	[ɔsɛmdɛ'sɛt]
81 eighty-one	**осемдесет и едно**	[ɔsɛmdɛ'sɛt i ɛd'nɔ]
82 eighty-two	**осемдесет и две**	[ɔsɛmdɛ'sɛt i dvɛ]
83 eighty-three	**осемдесет и три**	[ɔsɛmdɛ'sɛt i tri]
90 ninety	**деветдесет**	[dɛvɛtdɛ'sɛt]
91 ninety-one	**деветдесет и едно**	[dɛvɛtdɛ'sɛt i ɛd'nɔ]
92 ninety-two	**деветдесет и две**	[dɛvɛtdɛ'sɛt i dvɛ]
93 ninety-three	**деветдесет и три**	[dɛvɛtdɛ'sɛt i tri]

5. Cardinal numbers. Part 2

100 one hundred	**сто**	[stɔ]
200 two hundred	**двеста**	['dvɛsta]
300 three hundred	**триста**	['trista]
400 four hundred	**четиристотин**	['ʧətiris'tɔtin]
500 five hundred	**петстотин**	['pɛʦ'tɔtin]
600 six hundred	**шестстотин**	['ʃɛsʦ'tɔtin]
700 seven hundred	**седемстотин**	['sɛdɛms'tɔtin]

800 eight hundred	**осемстотин**	['ɔsɛms'tɔtin]
900 nine hundred	**деветстотин**	['dɛvɛʦ'tɔtin]
1000 one thousand	**хиляда** (f)	[hi'ʎada]
2000 two thousand	**две хиляди**	[dvɛ 'hiʎadi]
3000 three thousand	**три хиляди**	[tri 'hiʎadi]
10000 ten thousand	**десет хиляди**	['dɛsɛt 'hiʎadi]
one hundred thousand	**сто хиляди**	[stɔ 'hiʎadi]
million	**милион** (m)	[mili'ɔn]
billion	**милиард** (m)	[mili'ard]

6. Ordinal numbers

first (adj)	**първи**	['pɪrvi]
second (adj)	**втори**	['ftɔri]
third (adj)	**трети**	['trɛti]
fourth (adj)	**четвърти**	[ʧət'vɪrti]
fifth (adj)	**пети**	['pɛti]
sixth (adj)	**шести**	['ʃɛsti]
seventh (adj)	**седми**	['sɛdmi]
eighth (adj)	**осми**	['ɔsmi]
ninth (adj)	**девети**	[dɛ'vɛti]
tenth (adj)	**десети**	[dɛ'sɛti]

7. Numbers. Fractions

fraction	**дроб** (f)	[drɔb]
one half	**една втора**	[ɛd'na 'ftɔra]
one third	**една трета**	[ɛd'na 'trɛta]
one quarter	**една четвърта**	[ɛd'na ʧət'vɪrta]
one eighth	**една осма**	[ɛd'na 'ɔsma]
one tenth	**една десета**	[ɛd'na dɛ'sɛta]
two thirds	**две трети**	[dvɛ 'trɛti]
three quarters	**три четвърти**	[tri ʧət'vɪrti]

8. Numbers. Basic operations

subtraction	**изваждане** (n)	[iz'vaʒdanɛ]
to subtract (vi, vt)	**изваждам**	[iz'vaʒdam]
division	**деление** (n)	[dɛ'lɛniɛ]
to divide (vt)	**деля**	[dɛ'ʎa]
addition	**събиране** (n)	[sɪ'biranɛ]
to add up (vt)	**събера**	[sɪbɛ'ra]

to add (vi, vt)	**прибавям**	[pri'bavʲam]
multiplication	**умножение** (n)	[umnɔ'ʒɛniɛ]
to multiply (vt)	**умножавам**	[umnɔ'ʒavam]

9. Numbers. Miscellaneous

digit, figure	**цифра** (f)	['ʦifra]
number	**число** (n)	[ʧis'lɔ]
numeral	**числително име** (n)	[ʧis'litɛlnɔ 'imɛ]
minus sign	**минус** (m)	['minus]
plus sign	**плюс** (m)	[plys]
formula	**формула** (f)	['fɔrmula]
calculation	**изчисление** (n)	[isʧis'lɛniɛ]
to count (vt)	**броя**	[brɔ'jɑ]
to count up	**преброявам**	[prɛbrɔ'jɑvam]
to compare (vt)	**сравнявам**	[srav'ɲavam]
How much?	**Колко?**	['kɔlkɔ]
sum, total	**сума** (f)	['suma]
result	**резултат** (m)	[rɛzul'tat]
remainder	**остатък** (m)	[ɔs'tatık]
a few ...	**няколко**	['ɲakɔlkɔ]
few, little (adv)	**малко ...**	['malkɔ]
the rest	**остатък** (m)	[ɔs'tatık]
one and a half	**един и половина**	[ɛ'din i pɔlɔ'vina]
dozen	**дузина** (f)	[du'zina]
in half (adv)	**наполовина**	[napɔlɔ'vina]
equally (evenly)	**поравно**	[pɔ'ravnɔ]
half	**половина** (f)	[pɔlɔ'vina]
time (three ~s)	**път** (m)	[pıt]

10. The most important verbs. Part 1

to advise (vt)	**съветвам**	[sı'vɛtvam]
to agree (say yes)	**съгласявам се**	[sıgla'sʲavam sɛ]
to answer (vi, vt)	**отговарям**	[ɔtgɔ'varʲam]
to arrive (vi)	**пристигам**	[pris'tigam]
to ask (~ oneself)	**питам**	['pitam]
to ask (~ sb to do sth)	**моля**	['mɔʎa]
to be (vi)	**съм, бъда**	[sım], ['bıda]
to be afraid	**страхувам се**	[stra'huvam sɛ]
to be hungry	**искам да ям**	['iskam da jɑm]
to be interested in ...	**интересувам се**	[intɛrɛ'suvam sɛ]
to be needed	**трябвам**	['trʲabvam]

to be surprised	**удивлявам се**	[udiv'ʎavam sɛ]
to be thirsty	**искам да пия**	['iskam da 'pijɑ]
to begin (vt)	**започвам**	[za'pɔʧvam]
to belong to ...	**принадлежа ...**	[prinadlɛ'ʒa]
to boast (vi)	**хваля се**	['hvaʎa sɛ]
to break (split into pieces)	**чупя**	['ʧupʲa]
to call (for help)	**викам**	['vikam]
can (v aux)	**мога**	['mɔga]
to catch (vt)	**ловя**	[lɔ'vʲa]
to change (vt)	**сменям**	['smɛɲam]
to choose (select)	**избирам**	[iz'biram]
to come down	**слизам**	['slizam]
to come in (enter)	**влизам**	['vlizam]
to compare (vt)	**сравнявам**	[srav'ɲavam]
to complain (vi, vt)	**оплаквам се**	[ɔp'lakvam sɛ]
to confuse (mix up)	**обърквам**	[ɔ'bɪrkvam]
to continue (vt)	**продължавам**	[prɔdɪ'ʒavam]
to control (vt)	**контролирам**	[kɔntrɔ'liram]
to cook (dinner)	**готвя**	['gɔtvʲa]
to cost (vt)	**струвам**	['struvam]
to count (add up)	**броя**	[brɔ'jɑ]
to count on ...	**разчитам на ...**	[ras'ʧitam na]
to create (vt)	**създам**	[sɪz'dam]
to cry (weep)	**плача**	['plaʧa]

11. The most important verbs. Part 2

to deceive (vi, vt)	**лъжа**	['lɪʒa]
to decorate (tree, street)	**украсявам**	[ukra'sʲavam]
to defend (a country, etc.)	**защитавам**	[zaʃti'tavam]
to demand (request firmly)	**изисквам**	[i'ziskvam]
to dig (vt)	**ровя**	['rɔvʲa]
to discuss (vt)	**обсъждам**	[ɔb'sɪʒdam]
to do (vt)	**правя**	['pravʲa]
to doubt (have doubts)	**съмнявам се**	[sɪm'ɲavam sɛ]
to drop (let fall)	**изтървавам**	[istɪr'vavam]
to excuse (forgive)	**извинявам**	[izvi'ɲavam]
to exist (vi)	**съществувам**	[sɪʃtɛst'vuvam]
to expect (foresee)	**предвиждам**	[prɛd'viʒdam]
to explain (vt)	**обяснявам**	[ɔbʲas'ɲavam]
to fall (vi)	**падам**	['padam]
to find (vt)	**намирам**	[na'miram]

to finish (vt)	**приключвам**	[prik'lytʧvam]
to fly (vi)	**летя**	[lɛ'tʲa]
to follow ... (come after)	**вървя след ...**	[var'vʲa sled]
to forget (vi, vt)	**забравям**	[zab'ravʲam]
to forgive (vt)	**прощавам**	[prɔʃ'tavam]
to give (vt)	**давам**	['davam]
to give a hint	**намеквам**	[na'mɛkvam]
to go (on foot)	**вървя**	[vɪr'vʲa]
to go for a swim	**къпя се**	['kɪpʲa sɛ]
to go out (from ...)	**излизам**	[iz'lizam]
to guess right	**отгатна**	[ɔt'gatna]
to have (vt)	**имам**	['imam]
to have breakfast	**закусвам**	[za'kusvam]
to have dinner	**вечерям**	[vɛ'ʧərʲam]
to have lunch	**обядвам**	[ɔ'bʲadvam]
to hear (vt)	**чувам**	['ʧuvam]
to help (vt)	**помагам**	[pɔ'magam]
to hide (vt)	**крия**	['krijɑ]
to hope (vi, vt)	**надявам се**	[na'dʲavam sɛ]
to hunt (vi, vt)	**ловувам**	[lɔ'vuvam]
to hurry (vi)	**бързам**	['bɪrzam]

12. The most important verbs. Part 3

to inform (vt)	**информирам**	[infɔr'miram]
to insist (vi, vt)	**настоявам**	[nastɔ'jɑvam]
to insult (vt)	**оскърбявам**	[ɔskɪr'bʲavam]
to invite (vt)	**каня**	['kaɲa]
to joke (vi)	**шегувам се**	[ʃɛ'guvam sɛ]
to keep (vt)	**съхранявам**	[sɪhra'ɲavam]
to keep silent	**мълча**	[mɪl'ʧa]
to kill (vt)	**убивам**	[u'bivam]
to know (sb)	**познавам**	[pɔz'navam]
to know (sth)	**знам**	[znam]
to laugh (vi)	**смея се**	['smɛjɑ sɛ]
to liberate (city, etc.)	**освобождавам**	[ɔsvɔbɔʒ'davam]
to like (I like ...)	**харесвам**	[ha'rɛsvam]
to look for ... (search)	**търся**	['tɪrsʲa]
to love (sb)	**обичам**	[ɔ'biʧam]
to make a mistake	**греша**	[grɛ'ʃʌ]
to manage, to run	**ръководя**	[rɪkɔ'vɔdʲa]
to mean (signify)	**означавам**	[ɔzna'ʧavam]
to mention (talk about)	**споменавам**	[spɔmɛ'navam]

to miss (school, etc.)	**пропускам**	[prɔ'puskam]
to notice (see)	**забелязвам**	[zabɛ'ʎazvam]
to object (vi, vt)	**възразявам**	[vɪzra'zʲavam]
to observe (see)	**наблюдавам**	[nably'davam]
to open (vt)	**отварям**	[ɔt'varʲam]
to order (meal, etc.)	**поръчвам**	[pɔ'rɪʧvam]
to order (mil.)	**заповядвам**	[zapɔ'vʲadvam]
to own (possess)	**владея**	[vla'dɛjɑ]
to participate (vi)	**участвам**	[u'ʧastvam]
to pay (vi, vt)	**плащам**	['plaʃtam]
to permit (vt)	**разрешавам**	[razrɛ'ʃʌvam]
to plan (vt)	**планирам**	[pla'niram]
to play (children)	**играя**	[ig'rajɑ]
to pray (vi, vt)	**моля се**	['mɔʎa sɛ]
to prefer (vt)	**предпочитам**	[prɛtpɔ'ʧitam]
to promise (vt)	**обещавам**	[ɔbɛʃ'tavam]
to pronounce (vt)	**произнасям**	[prɔiz'nasʲam]
to propose (vt)	**предлагам**	[prɛd'lagam]
to punish (vt)	**наказвам**	[na'kazvam]
to read (vi, vt)	**чета**	[ʧə'tɪ]
to recommend (vt)	**съветвам**	[sɪ'vɛtvam]
to refuse (vi, vt)	**отказвам се**	[ɔt'kazvam sɛ]
to regret (be sorry)	**съжалявам**	[sɪʒa'ʎavam]
to rent (sth from sb)	**наемам**	[na'ɛmam]
to repeat (say again)	**повтарям**	[pɔf'tarʲam]
to reserve, to book	**резервирам**	[rɛzɛr'viram]
to run (vi)	**бягам**	['bʲagam]

13. The most important verbs. Part 4

to save (rescue)	**спасявам**	[spa'sʲavam]
to say (~ thank you)	**кажа**	['kaʒa]
to scold (vt)	**ругая**	[ru'gajɑ]
to see (vt)	**виждам**	['viʒdam]
to sell (vt)	**продавам**	[prɔ'davam]
to send (vt)	**изпращам**	[isp'raʃtam]
to shoot (vi)	**стрелям**	['strɛʎam]
to shout (vi)	**викам**	['vikam]
to show (vt)	**показвам**	[pɔ'kazvam]
to sign (document)	**подписвам**	[pɔt'pisvam]
to sit down (vi)	**сядам**	['sʲadam]
to smile (vi)	**усмихвам се**	[us'mihvam sɛ]
to speak (vi, vt)	**говоря**	[gɔ'vɔrʲa]
to steal (money, etc.)	**крада**	[kra'da]

to stop (please ~ calling me)	**прекратявам**	[prɛkra'tʲavam]
to stop (for pause, etc.)	**спирам се**	['spiram sɛ]
to study (vt)	**изучавам**	[izu'ʧavam]
to swim (vi)	**плувам**	['pluvam]
to take (vt)	**взимам**	['vzimam]
to think (vi, vt)	**мисля**	['misʎa]
to threaten (vt)	**заплашвам**	[zap'laʃvam]
to touch (with hands)	**пипам**	['pipam]
to translate (vt)	**превеждам**	[prɛ'vɛʒdam]
to trust (vt)	**доверявам**	[dɔvɛ'rʲavam]
to try (attempt)	**опитвам се**	[ɔ'pitvam sɛ]
to turn (~ to the left)	**завивам**	[za'vivam]
to underestimate (vt)	**недооценявам**	[nɛdɔ:ʦə'ɲavam]
to understand (vt)	**разбирам**	[raz'biram]
to unite (vt)	**обединявам**	[ɔbɛdi'ɲavam]
to wait (vt)	**чакам**	['ʧakam]
to want (wish, desire)	**искам**	['iskam]
to warn (vt)	**предупреждавам**	[prɛduprɛʒ'davam]
to work (vi)	**работя**	[ra'bɔtʲa]
to write (vt)	**пиша**	['piʃʌ]
to write down	**записвам**	[za'pisvam]

14. Colors

color	**цвят** (m)	[ʦvʲat]
shade (tint)	**оттенък** (m)	[ɔt'tɛnɪk]
hue	**тон** (m)	[tɔn]
rainbow	**небесна дъга** (f)	[nɛ'bɛsna dɪ'ga]
white (adj)	**бял**	[bʲal]
black (adj)	**черен**	['ʧərɛn]
gray (adj)	**сив**	[siv]
green (adj)	**зелен**	[zɛ'lɛn]
yellow (adj)	**жълт**	[ʒɪlt]
red (adj)	**червен**	[ʧər'vɛn]
blue (adj)	**син**	[sin]
light blue (adj)	**небесносин**	[nɛbɛsnɔ'sin]
pink (adj)	**розов**	['rɔzɔv]
orange (adj)	**оранжев**	[ɔ'ranʒɛv]
violet (adj)	**виолетов**	[viɔ'lɛtɔv]
brown (adj)	**кафяв**	[ka'fʲav]
golden (adj)	**златен**	['zlatɛn]
silvery (adj)	**сребрист**	[srɛb'rist]

beige (adj)	**бежов**	['bɛʒɔv]
cream (adj)	**кремав**	['krɛmaf]
turquoise (adj)	**тюркоазен**	[tyrkɔ'azɛn]
cherry red (adj)	**вишнев**	['viʃnɛv]
lilac (adj)	**лилав**	[li'laf]
crimson (adj)	**малинов**	[ma'linɔv]
light (adj)	**светъл**	['svɛtɪl]
dark (adj)	**тъмен**	['tɪmɛn]
bright, vivid (adj)	**ярък**	['jarɪk]
colored (pencils)	**цветен**	['tsvɛtɛn]
color (e.g., ~ film)	**цветен**	['tsvɛtɛn]
black-and-white (adj)	**черно-бял**	['tʃɛrnɔ b'al]
plain (one-colored)	**едноцветен**	[ɛdnɔts'vɛtɛn]
multicolored (adj)	**многоцветен**	[mnɔgɔts'vɛtɛn]

15. Questions

Who?	**Кой?**	[kɔj]
What?	**Какво?**	[kak'vɔ]
Where? (at, in)	**Къде?**	[kɪ'dɛ]
Where (to)?	**Къде?**	[kɪ'dɛ]
From where?	**Откъде?**	[ɔtkɪ'dɛ]
When?	**Кога?**	[kɔ'ga]
Why? (What for?)	**За какво?**	[za kak'vɔ]
Why? (reason)	**Защо?**	[zaʃ'tɔ]
What for?	**За какво?**	[za kak'vɔ]
How? (in what way)	**Как?**	[kak]
Which?	**Кой?**	[kɔj]
To whom?	**На кого?**	[na kɔ'gɔ]
About whom?	**За кого?**	[za kɔ'gɔ]
About what?	**За какво?**	[za kak'vɔ]
With whom?	**С кого?**	[s kɔ'gɔ]
How many? How much?	**Колко?**	['kɔlkɔ]
Whose?	**Чий?**	[tʃij]

16. Prepositions

with (accompanied by)	**с …**	[s]
without	**без**	[bɛz]
to (indicating direction)	**в, във**	[v], [vɪf]
about (talking ~ ...)	**за**	[za]
before (in time)	**преди**	[prɛ'di]
in front of ...	**пред …**	[prɛd]

under (beneath, below)	**под**	[pɔd]
above (over)	**над**	[nad]
on (atop)	**върху**	[vɪr'hu]
from (off, out of)	**от**	[ɔt]
of (made from)	**от**	[ɔt]
in (e.g., ~ ten minutes)	**след**	[slɛt]
over (across the top of)	**през**	[prɛs]

17. Function words. Adverbs. Part 1

Where? (at, in)	**Къде?**	[kɪ'dɛ]
here (adv)	**тук**	[tuk]
there (adv)	**там**	[tam]
somewhere (to be)	**някъде**	['ɲakɪdɛ]
nowhere (not anywhere)	**никъде**	['nikɪdɛ]
by (near, beside)	**до ...**	[dɔ]
by the window	**до прозореца**	[dɔ prɔ'zɔrɛtsa]
Where (to)?	**Къде?**	[kɪ'dɛ]
here (e.g., come ~!)	**тук**	[tuk]
there (e.g., to go ~)	**натам**	[na'tatɪk]
from here (adv)	**оттук**	[ɔt'tuk]
from there (adv)	**оттам**	[ɔt'tam]
close (adv)	**близо**	['blizɔ]
far (adv)	**далече**	[da'lɛʧə]
near (e.g., ~ Paris)	**до**	[dɔ]
nearby (adv)	**редом**	['rɛdɔm]
not far (adv)	**недалече**	[nɛda'lɛʧə]
left (adj)	**ляв**	[ʎav]
on the left	**отляво**	[ɔt'ʎavɔ]
to the left	**вляво**	['vʎavɔ]
right (adj)	**десен**	['dɛsɛn]
on the right	**отдясно**	[ɔt'dʲasnɔ]
to the right	**вдясно**	['vdʲasnɔ]
in front (adv)	**отпред**	[ɔtp'rɛd]
front (as adj)	**преден**	['prɛdɛn]
ahead (look ~)	**напред**	[nap'rɛd]
behind (adv)	**отзад**	[ɔt'zad]
from behind	**отзад**	[ɔt'zad]
back (towards the rear)	**назад**	[na'zad]
middle	**среда** (f)	[srɛ'da]

in the middle	**по средата**	[pɔ srɛ'data]
at the side	**встрани**	[fstra'ni]
everywhere (adv)	**навсякъде**	[nav'sʲakɪdɛ]
around (in all directions)	**наоколо**	[na'ɔkɔlɔ]
from inside	**отвътре**	[ɔt'vɪtrɛ]
somewhere (to go)	**някъде**	['ɲakɪdɛ]
straight (directly)	**направо**	[nap'ravɔ]
back (e.g., come ~)	**обратно**	[ɔb'ratnɔ]
from anywhere	**откъдето и да е**	[ɔtkɪ'dɛtɔ i da ɛ]
from somewhere	**отнякъде**	[ɔt'ɲakɪdɛ]
firstly (adv)	**първо**	['pɪrvɔ]
secondly (adv)	**второ**	['ftɔrɔ]
thirdly (adv)	**трето**	['trɛtɔ]
suddenly (adv)	**изведнъж**	[izvɛd'nɪʃ]
at first (adv)	**в началото**	[f na'ʧalɔtɔ]
for the first time	**за пръв път**	[za prɪv 'pɪt]
long before ...	**много време преди ...**	['mnɔgɔ 'vrɛmɛ prɛ'di]
anew (over again)	**наново**	[na'nɔvɔ]
for good (adv)	**завинаги**	[za'vinagi]
never (adv)	**никога**	['nikɔga]
again (adv)	**пак**	[pak]
now (adv)	**сега**	[sɛ'ga]
often (adv)	**често**	['ʧəstɔ]
then (adv)	**тогава**	[tɔ'gava]
urgently (quickly)	**срочно**	['srɔʧnɔ]
usually (adv)	**обикновено**	[ɔbiknɔ'vɛnɔ]
by the way, ...	**между другото ...**	['mɛʒdu 'drugɔtɔ]
possible (that is ~)	**възможно**	[vɪz'mɔʒnɔ]
probably (adv)	**вероятно**	[vɛrɔ'jatnɔ]
maybe (adv)	**може би**	['mɔʒɛ bi]
besides ...	**освен това, ...**	[ɔs'vɛn tɔ'va]
that's why ...	**затова**	[zatɔ'va]
in spite of ...	**въпреки че ...**	['vɪprɛki ʧə]
thanks to ...	**благодарение на ...**	[blagɔda'rɛniɛ na]
what (pron.)	**какво**	[kak'vɔ]
that (conj.)	**че**	[ʧə]
something	**нещо**	['nɛʃtɔ]
anything (something)	**нещо**	['nɛʃtɔ]
nothing	**нищо**	['niʃtɔ]
who (pron.)	**кой**	[kɔj]
someone	**някой**	['ɲakɔj]
somebody	**някой**	['ɲakɔj]
nobody	**никой**	['nikɔj]
nowhere (a voyage to ~)	**никъде**	['nikɪdɛ]

nobody's	**ничий**	['nitʃij]
somebody's	**нечий**	['nɛtʃij]
so (I'm ~ glad)	**така**	[ta'ka]
also (as well)	**също така**	['sɪʃtɔ ta'ka]
too (as well)	**също**	['sɪʃtɔ]

18. Function words. Adverbs. Part 2

Why?	**Защо?**	[zaʃ'tɔ]
for some reason	**кой знае защо**	[kɔj 'znaɛ zaʃ'tɔ]
because ...	**защото ...**	[zaʃ'tɔtɔ]
for some purpose	**кой знае защо**	[kɔj 'znaɛ zaʃ'tɔ]
and	**и**	[i]
or	**или**	[i'li]
but	**но**	[nɔ]
for (e.g., ~ me)	**за**	[za]
too (~ many people)	**прекалено**	[prɛka'lɛnɔ]
only (exclusively)	**само**	['samɔ]
exactly (adv)	**точно**	['tɔtʃnɔ]
about (more or less)	**около**	['ɔkɔlɔ]
approximately (adv)	**приблизително**	[pribli'zitɛlnɔ]
approximate (adj)	**приблизителен**	[pribli'zitɛlɛn]
almost (adv)	**почти**	[pɔtʃ'ti]
the rest	**остатък** (m)	[ɔs'tatɪk]
the other (second)	**друг**	[druk]
other (different)	**друг**	[druk]
each (adj)	**всеки**	['vsɛki]
any (no matter which)	**всеки**	['vsɛki]
many, much (a lot of)	**много**	['mnɔgɔ]
many people	**много**	['mnɔgɔ]
all (everyone)	**всички**	['vsitʃki]
in return for ...	**в обмяна на ...**	[v ɔb'mʲana na]
in exchange (adv)	**в замяна**	[v za'mʲana]
by hand (made)	**ръчно**	['rɪtʃnɔ]
hardly (negative opinion)	**едва ли**	[ɛd'va li]
probably (adv)	**вероятно**	[vɛrɔ'jɑtnɔ]
on purpose (adv)	**специално**	[spɛtsi'alnɔ]
by accident (adv)	**случайно**	[slu'tʃajnɔ]
very (adv)	**много**	['mnɔgɔ]
for example (adv)	**например**	[nap'rimɛr]
between	**между**	[mɛʒ'du]
among	**сред**	[srɛd]

so much (such a lot)	**толкова**	['tɔlkɔva]
especially (adv)	**особено**	[ɔ'sɔbɛnɔ]

Basic concepts. Part 2

19. Weekdays

Monday	**понеделник** (m)	[pɔnɛ'dɛlnik]
Tuesday	**вторник** (m)	['ftɔrnik]
Wednesday	**сряда** (f)	['srʲada]
Thursday	**четвъртък** (m)	[ʧət'vɪrtɪk]
Friday	**петък** (m)	['pɛtɪk]
Saturday	**събота** (f)	['sɪbɔta]
Sunday	**неделя** (f)	[nɛ'dɛʎa]
today (adv)	**днес**	[dnɛs]
tomorrow (adv)	**утре**	['utrɛ]
the day after tomorrow	**вдругиден**	[vdrugi'dɛn]
yesterday (adv)	**вчера**	['vʧəra]
the day before yesterday	**завчера**	['zavʧəra]
day	**ден** (m)	[dɛn]
working day	**работен ден** (m)	[ra'bɔtɛn dɛn]
public holiday	**празничен ден** (m)	['praznitʃən dɛn]
day off	**почивен ден** (m)	[pɔ'ʧivɛn 'dɛn]
weekend	**почивни дни** (m pl)	[pɔ'ʧivni dni]
all day long	**цял ден**	[ʦʲal dɛn]
next day (adv)	**на следващия ден**	[na 'slɛdvaʃtija dɛn]
two days ago	**преди два дена**	[prɛ'di dva 'dɛna]
the day before	**в навечерието**	[v navɛ'ʧəriɛtɔ]
daily (adj)	**всекидневен**	[vsɛkid'nɛvɛn]
every day (adv)	**всекидневно**	[vsɛkid'nɛvnɔ]
week	**седмица** (f)	['sɛdmiʦa]
last week (adv)	**през миналата седмица**	[prɛs 'minalata 'sɛdmiʦa]
next week (adv)	**през следващата седмица**	[prɛs 'slɛdvaʃtata sɛdmiʦa]
weekly (adj)	**седмичен**	['sɛdmiʧən]
every week (adv)	**седмично**	['sɛdmiʧnɔ]
twice a week	**два пъти на седмица**	[dva pɪ'ti na 'sɛdmiʦa]
every Tuesday	**всеки вторник**	['vsɛki 'vtɔrnik]

20. Hours. Day and night

morning	**сутрин** (f)	['sutrin]
in the morning	**сутринта**	[sutrin'ta]

noon, midday	**пладне** (n)	['pladnɛ]
in the afternoon	**следобед**	[slɛ'dɔbɛd]
evening	**вечер** (f)	['vɛʧər]
in the evening	**вечер**	['vɛʧər]
night	**нощ** (f)	[nɔʃt]
at night	**нощем**	['nɔʃtɛm]
midnight	**полунощ** (f)	[pɔlu'nɔʃt]
second	**секунда** (f)	[sɛ'kunda]
minute	**минута** (f)	[mi'nuta]
hour	**час** (m)	[ʧas]
half an hour	**половин час** (m)	[pɔlɔ'vin ʧas]
quarter of an hour	**четвърт** (f) **час**	['ʧətvɪrt ʧas]
fifteen minutes	**петнадесет минути**	[pɛt'nadɛsɛt mi'nuti]
24 hours	**денонощие** (n)	[dɛnɔ'nɔʃtiɛ]
sunrise	**изгрев слънце** (n)	['izgrɛv 'slɪnʦə]
dawn	**разсъмване** (n)	[raz'sɪmvanɛ]
early morning	**ранна сутрин** (f)	['rana 'sutrin]
sunset	**залез** (m)	['zalɛz]
early in the morning	**рано сутрин**	['ranɔ 'sutrin]
this morning	**тази сутрин**	['tazi 'sutrin]
tomorrow morning	**утре сутрин**	['utrɛ 'sutrin]
this afternoon	**днес през деня**	[dnɛs prɛs dɛ'ɲa]
in the afternoon	**следобед**	[slɛ'dɔbɛd]
tomorrow afternoon	**утре следобед**	['utrɛ slɛ'dɔbɛd]
tonight (this evening)	**довечера**	[dɔ'vɛʧəra]
tomorrow night	**утре вечер**	['utrɛ 'vɛʧər]
at 3 o'clock sharp	**точно в три часа**	['tɔʧnɔ v tri ʧa'sa]
about 4 o'clock	**около четири часа**	['ɔkɔlɔ 'ʧətiri ʧa'sa]
by 12 o'clock	**към дванадесет часа**	[kɪm dva'nadɛsɛt ʧa'sa]
in 20 minutes	**след двадесет минути**	[slɛt 'dvadɛsɛt mi'nuti]
in an hour	**след един час**	[slɛt ɛ'din ʧas]
on time (adv)	**навреме**	[nav'rɛmɛ]
a quarter of ...	**без четвърт ...**	[bɛs 'ʧətvɪrt]
within an hour	**в течение на един час**	[v tɛ'ʧəniɛ na ɛ'din ʧas]
every 15 minutes	**на всеки петнадесет минути**	[na 'vsɛki pɛt'nadɛsɛt mi'nuti]
round the clock	**цяло денонощие**	['ʦʲalɔ dɛnɔ'nɔʃtiɛ]

21. Months. Seasons

January	**януари** (m)	[janu'ari]
February	**февруари** (m)	[fɛvru'ari]

March	**март** (m)	[mart]
April	**април** (m)	[ap'ril]
May	**май** (m)	[maj]
June	**юни** (m)	['juni]
July	**юли** (m)	['juli]
August	**август** (m)	['avgust]
September	**септември** (m)	[sɛp'tɛmvri]
October	**октомври** (m)	[ɔk'tɔmvri]
November	**ноември** (m)	[nɔ'ɛmvri]
December	**декември** (m)	[dɛ'kɛmvri]
spring	**пролет** (f)	['prɔlɛt]
in spring	**през пролетта**	[prɛz prɔlɛt'ta]
spring (as adj)	**пролетен**	['prɔlɛtɛn]
summer	**лято** (n)	['ʎatɔ]
in summer	**през лятото**	[prɛz 'ʎatɔtɔ]
summer (as adj)	**летен**	['lɛtɛn]
fall	**есен** (f)	['ɛsɛn]
in fall	**през есента**	[prɛz ɛsɛn'ta]
fall (as adj)	**есенен**	['ɛsɛnɛn]
winter	**зима** (f)	['zima]
in winter	**през зимата**	[prɛz 'zimata]
winter (as adj)	**зимен**	['zimɛn]
month	**месец** (m)	['mɛsɛʦ]
this month	**през този месец**	[prɛs 'tɔzi 'mɛsɛʦ]
next month	**през следващия месец**	[prɛz 'slɛdvaʃtija 'mɛsɛʦ]
last month	**през миналия месец**	[prɛz 'minalija 'mɛsɛʦ]
a month ago	**преди един месец**	[prɛ'di ɛ'din 'mɛsɛʦ]
in a month	**след един месец**	[slɛt ɛ'din 'mɛsɛʦ]
in two months	**след два месеца**	[slɛt dva 'mɛsɛʦa]
the whole month	**цял месец**	[ʦʲal 'mɛsɛʦ]
all month long	**цял месец**	[ʦʲal 'mɛsɛʦ]
monthly (~ magazine)	**месечен**	['mɛsɛʧən]
monthly (adv)	**месечно**	['mɛsɛʧnɔ]
every month	**всеки месец**	['vsɛki 'mɛsɛʦ]
twice a month	**два пъти на месец**	[dva 'pɪti na 'mɛsɛʦ]
year	**година** (f)	[gɔ'dina]
this year	**тази година**	['tazi gɔ'dina]
next year	**през следващата година**	[prɛz 'slɛdvaʃtata gɔdina]
last year	**през миналата година**	[prɛz 'minalata gɔ'dina]
a year ago	**преди една година**	[prɛ'di ɛd'na gɔ'dina]
in a year	**след една година**	[slɛt ɛd'na gɔ'dina]

in two years	**след две години**	[slɛt dvɛ gɔ'dini]
the whole year	**цяла година**	['tsʲala gɔ'dina]
all year long	**цяла година**	['tsʲala gɔ'dina]
every year	**всяка година**	['vsʲaka gɔ'dina]
annual (adj)	**ежегоден**	[ɛʒɛ'gɔdɛn]
annually (adv)	**ежегодно**	[ɛʒɛ'gɔdnɔ]
4 times a year	**четири пъти годишно**	['tʃətiri 'pɪti gɔ'diʃnɔ]
date (e.g., today's ~)	**число** (n)	[tʃis'lɔ]
date (e.g., ~ of birth)	**дата** (f)	['data]
calendar	**календар** (m)	[kalɛn'dar]
half a year	**половин година**	[pɔlɔ'vin gɔ'dina]
six months	**полугодие** (n)	[pɔlu'gɔdiɛ]
season (summer, etc.)	**сезон** (m)	[sɛ'zɔn]
century	**век** (m)	[vɛk]

22. Time. Miscellaneous

time	**време** (n)	['vrɛmɛ]
instant (n)	**миг** (m)	[mig]
moment	**мигновение** (n)	[mignɔ'vɛniɛ]
instant (adj)	**мигновен**	[mignɔ'vɛn]
lapse (of time)	**отрязък** (m)	[ɔt'rʲazɪk]
life	**живот** (m)	[ʒi'vɔt]
eternity	**вечност** (f)	['vɛtʃnɔst]
epoch	**епоха** (f)	[ɛ'pɔha]
era	**ера** (f)	['ɛra]
cycle	**цикъл** (m)	['tsikɪl]
period	**период** (m)	[pɛ'riɔd]
term (short-~)	**срок** (m)	[srɔk]
the future	**бъдеще** (n)	['bɪdɛʃtɛ]
future (as adj)	**бъдещ**	['bɪdɛʃt]
next time	**следващия път**	['slɛdvaʃtija pɪt]
the past	**минало** (n)	['minalɔ]
past (recent)	**минал**	['minal]
last time	**миналия път**	['minalija pɪt]
later (adv)	**по-късно**	[pɔ 'kɪsnɔ]
after (prep.)	**след това**	[slɛd tɔ'va]
nowadays (adv)	**сега**	[sɛ'ga]
now (adv)	**сега**	[sɛ'ga]
immediately (adv)	**незабавно**	[nɛza'bavnɔ]
soon (adv)	**скоро**	['skɔrɔ]
in advance (beforehand)	**предварително**	[prɛdva'ritɛlnɔ]
a long time ago	**отдавна**	[ɔt'davna]
recently (adv)	**неотдавна**	[nɛɔt'davna]

destiny	**съдба** (f)	[sıd'ba]
memories (childhood ~)	**памет** (f)	['pamɛt]
archives	**архив** (m)	[ar'hiv]
during ...	**по времето на ...**	[pɔ 'vrɛmɛtɔ na]
long, a long time (adv)	**дълго**	['dılgɔ]
not long (adv)	**недълго**	[nɛ'dılgɔ]
early (in the morning)	**рано**	['ranɔ]
late (not early)	**късно**	['kısnɔ]
forever (for good)	**завинаги**	[za'vinagi]
to start (begin)	**започвам**	[za'pɔʧvam]
to postpone (vt)	**отложа**	[ɔt'lɔʒa]
at the same time	**едновременно**	[ɛdnɔv'rɛmɛnɔ]
permanently (adv)	**постоянно**	[pɔstɔ'janɔ]
constant (noise, pain)	**постоянен**	[pɔstɔ'janɛn]
temporary (adj)	**временен**	['vrɛmɛnɛn]
sometimes (adv)	**понякога**	[pɔ'ɲakɔga]
rarely (adv)	**рядко**	['rʲadkɔ]
often (adv)	**често**	['ʧəstɔ]

23. Opposites

rich (adj)	**богат**	[bɔ'gat]
poor (adj)	**беден**	['bɛdɛn]
ill, sick (adj)	**болен**	['bɔlɛn]
healthy (adj)	**здрав**	[zdrav]
big (adj)	**голям**	[gɔ'ʎam]
small (adj)	**малък**	['malık]
quickly (adv)	**бързо**	['bırzɔ]
slowly (adv)	**бавно**	['bavnɔ]
fast (adj)	**бърз**	[bırz]
slow (adj)	**бавен**	['bavɛn]
cheerful (adj)	**весел**	['vɛsɛl]
sad (adj)	**тъжен**	['tıʒɛn]
together (adv)	**заедно**	['zaɛdnɔ]
separately (adv)	**поотделно**	[pɔ:t'dɛlnɔ]
aloud (to read)	**на глас**	[na 'glas]
silently (to oneself)	**на ум**	[na 'um]
tall (adj)	**висок**	[vi'sɔk]
low (adj)	**нисък**	['nisık]

deep (adj)	**дълбок**	[dɪl'bɔk]
shallow (adj)	**плитък**	['plitɪk]
yes	**да**	[da]
no	**не**	[nɛ]
distant (in space)	**далечен**	[da'lɛʧən]
nearby (adj)	**близък**	['blizɪk]
far (adv)	**далече**	[da'lɛʧə]
nearby (adv)	**близо**	['blizɔ]
long (adj)	**дълъг**	['dɪlɪg]
short (adj)	**къс**	[kɪs]
good (kindhearted)	**добър**	[dɔ'bɪr]
evil (adj)	**зъл**	[zɪl]
married (adj)	**женен**	['ʒɛnɛn]
single (adj)	**ерген**	[ɛr'gɛn]
to forbid (vt)	**забранявам**	[zabra'ɲavam]
to permit (vt)	**разрешавам**	[razrɛ'ʃʌvam]
end	**край** (m)	[kraj]
beginning	**начало** (n)	[na'ʧalɔ]
left (adj)	**ляв**	[ʎav]
right (adj)	**десен**	['dɛsɛn]
first (adj)	**първи**	['pɪrvi]
last (adj)	**последен**	[pɔs'lɛdɛn]
crime	**престъпление** (n)	[prɛstɪp'lɛniɛ]
punishment	**наказание** (n)	[naka'zaniɛ]
to order (vt)	**заповядвам**	[zapɔ'vʲadvam]
to obey (vi, vt)	**подчиня се**	[pɔdʧi'ɲa sɛ]
straight (adj)	**прав**	[prav]
curved (adj)	**крив**	[kriv]
paradise	**рай** (m)	[raj]
hell	**ад** (m)	[ad]
to be born	**родя се**	[rɔ'dʲa sɛ]
to die (vi)	**умра**	[um'ra]
strong (adj)	**силен**	['silɛn]
weak (adj)	**слаб**	[slap]
old (adj)	**стар**	[star]
young (adj)	**млад**	[mlad]

old (adj)	**стар**	[star]
new (adj)	**нов**	[nɔv]
hard (adj)	**твърд**	[tvɪrd]
soft (adj)	**мек**	[mɛk]
warm (adj)	**топъл**	['tɔpɪl]
cold (adj)	**студен**	[stu'dɛn]
fat (adj)	**дебел**	[dɛ'bɛl]
thin (adj)	**слаб**	[slap]
narrow (adj)	**тесен**	['tɛsɛn]
wide (adj)	**широк**	[ʃi'rɔk]
good (adj)	**добър**	[dɔ'bɪr]
bad (adj)	**лош**	[lɔʃ]
brave (adj)	**храбър**	['hrabɪr]
cowardly (adj)	**страхлив**	[strah'lif]

24. Lines and shapes

square	**квадрат** (m)	[kvad'rat]
square (as adj)	**квадратен**	[kvad'ratɛn]
circle	**кръг** (m)	[krɪg]
round (adj)	**кръгъл**	['krɪgɪl]
triangle	**триъгълник** (m)	[tri'ɪgɪlnik]
triangular (adj)	**триъгълен**	[tri'ɪgɪlɛn]
oval	**овал** (m)	[ɔ'val]
oval (as adj)	**овален**	[ɔ'valɛn]
rectangle	**правоъгълник** (m)	[pravɔ'ɪgɪlnik]
rectangular (adj)	**правоъгълен**	[pravɔ'ɪgɪlɛn]
pyramid	**пирамида** (f)	[pira'mida]
rhombus	**ромб** (m)	[rɔmb]
trapezoid	**трапец** (m)	[tra'pɛʦ]
cube	**куб** (m)	[kub]
prism	**призма** (f)	['prizma]
circumference	**окръжност** (f)	[ɔk'rɪʒnɔst]
sphere	**сфера** (f)	['sfɛra]
ball (solid sphere)	**кълбо** (n)	[kɪl'bɔ]
diameter	**диаметър** (m)	[di'amɛtɪr]
radius	**радиус** (m)	['radius]
perimeter (circle's ~)	**периметър** (m)	[pɛ'rimɛtɪr]
center	**център** (m)	['ʦəntɪr]
horizontal (adj)	**хоризонтален**	[hɔrizɔn'talɛn]
vertical (adj)	**вертикален**	[vɛrti'kalɛn]

parallel (n)	**паралел** (f)	[para'lɛl]
parallel (as adj)	**паралелно**	[para'lɛlnɔ]
line	**линия** (f)	['linija]
stroke	**черта** (f)	[ʧər'ta]
straight line	**права** (f)	['prava]
curve (curved line)	**крива** (f)	['kriva]
thin (line, etc.)	**тънък**	['tɪnɪk]
contour (outline)	**контур** (m)	['kɔntur]
intersection	**пресичане** (n)	[prɛ'siʧanɛ]
right angle	**прав ъгъл** (m)	[prav 'ɪgɪl]
segment	**сегмент** (m)	[sɛg'mɛnt]
sector	**сектор** (m)	['sɛktɔr]
side (of triangle)	**страна** (f)	[stra'na]
angle	**ъгъл** (m)	['ɪgɪl]

25. Units of measurement

weight	**тегло** (n)	[tɛg'lɔ]
length	**дължина** (f)	[dɪʤi'na]
width	**широчина** (f)	[ʃirɔʧi'na]
height	**височина** (f)	[visɔʧi'na]
depth	**дълбочина** (f)	[dɪlbɔʧi'na]
volume	**обем** (m)	[ɔ'bɛm]
area	**площ** (f)	[plɔʃt]
gram	**грам** (m)	[gram]
milligram	**милиграм** (m)	[milig'ram]
kilogram	**килограм** (m)	[kilɔg'ram]
ton	**тон** (m)	[tɔn]
pound	**фунт** (m)	[funt]
ounce	**унция** (f)	['unʦija]
meter	**метър** (m)	['mɛtɪr]
millimeter	**милиметър** (m)	[mili'mɛtɪr]
centimeter	**сантиметър** (m)	[santi'mɛtɪr]
kilometer	**километър** (m)	[kilɔ'mɛtɪr]
mile	**миля** (f)	['miʎa]
inch	**дюйм** (m)	[dyjm]
foot	**фут** (m)	[fut]
yard	**ярд** (m)	[jard]
square meter	**квадратен метър** (m)	[kvad'ratɛn 'mɛtɪr]
hectare	**хектар** (m)	[hɛk'tar]
liter	**литър** (m)	['litɪr]
degree	**градус** (m)	['gradus]
volt	**волт** (m)	[vɔlt]

ampere	**ампер** (m)	[am'pɛr]
horsepower	**конска сила** (f)	['kɔnska 'sila]
quantity	**количество** (n)	[kɔ'litʃəstvɔ]
a little bit of ...	**малко ...**	['malkɔ]
half	**половина** (f)	[pɔlɔ'vina]
dozen	**дузина** (f)	[du'zina]
piece (item)	**брой** (m)	[brɔj]
size	**размер** (m)	[raz'mɛr]
scale (map ~)	**мащаб** (m)	[maʃ'tab]
minimal (adj)	**минимален**	[mini'malɛn]
the smallest (adj)	**най-малък**	[naj 'malık]
medium (adj)	**среден**	['srɛdɛn]
maximal (adj)	**максимален**	[maksi'malɛn]
the largest (adj)	**най-голям**	[naj gɔ'ʎam]

26. Containers

jar (glass)	**буркан** (m)	[bur'kan]
can	**тенекия** (f)	[tɛnɛ'kija]
bucket	**кофа** (f)	['kɔfa]
barrel	**бъчва** (f)	['bıtʃva]
basin (for washing)	**леген** (m)	[lɛ'gɛn]
tank (for liquid, gas)	**резервоар** (m)	[rɛzɛrvɔ'ar]
hip flask	**манерка** (f)	[ma'nɛrka]
jerrycan	**туба** (f)	['tuba]
cistern (tank)	**цистерна** (f)	[tsis'tɛrna]
mug	**чаша** (f)	['tʃaʃʌ]
cup (of coffee, etc.)	**чаша** (f)	['tʃaʃʌ]
saucer	**чинийка** (f)	[tʃi'nijka]
glass (tumbler)	**чаша** (f)	['tʃaʃʌ]
wineglass	**чаша** (f)	['tʃaʃʌ]
saucepan	**тенджера** (f)	['tɛndʒɛra]
bottle (~ of wine)	**бутилка** (f)	[bu'tilka]
neck (of the bottle)	**гърло** (n) **на бутилка**	['gırlɔ na bu'tilka]
carafe	**стъклена кана** (f)	['stıklɛna 'kana]
pitcher (earthenware)	**кана** (f)	['kana]
vessel (container)	**съд** (m)	[sıt]
pot (crock)	**гърне** (n)	[gır'nɛ]
vase	**ваза** (f)	['vaza]
bottle (~ of perfume)	**шишенце** (n)	[ʃi'ʃɛntsə]
vial, small bottle	**шишенце** (n)	[ʃi'ʃɛntsə]
tube (of toothpaste)	**тубичка** (f)	['tubitʃka]

sack (bag)	**чувал** (m)	[ʧu'val]
bag (paper ~, plastic ~)	**плик** (m)	[plik]
pack (of cigarettes, etc.)	**кутия** (f)	[ku'tijɑ]
box (e.g., shoebox)	**кутия** (f)	[ku'tijɑ]
crate	**щайга** (f)	['ʃtajga]
basket	**кошница** (f)	['kɔʃniʦa]

27. Materials

material	**материал** (m)	[matɛri'al]
wood	**дърво** (n)	[dɪr'vɔ]
wooden (adj)	**дървен**	['dɪrvɛn]
glass (n)	**стъкло** (n)	[stɪk'lɔ]
glass (as adj)	**стъклен**	['stɪklɛn]
stone (n)	**камък** (m)	['kamɪk]
stone (as adj)	**каменен**	['kamɛnɛn]
plastic (n)	**пластмаса** (f)	[plast'masa]
plastic (as adj)	**пластмасов**	[plast'masɔv]
rubber (n)	**гума** (f)	['guma]
rubber (as adj)	**гумен**	['gumɛn]
cloth, fabric (n)	**плат** (m)	[plat]
fabric (as adj)	**от плат**	[ɔt 'plat]
paper (n)	**хартия** (f)	[har'tijɑ]
paper (as adj)	**хартиен**	[har'tiɛn]
cardboard (n)	**картон** (m)	[kar'tɔn]
cardboard (as adj)	**картонен**	[kar'tɔnɛn]
polyethylene	**полиетилен** (m)	[pɔliɛti'lɛn]
cellophane	**целофан** (m)	[ʦəlɔ'fan]
plywood	**шперплат** (m)	[ʃpɛrp'lat]
porcelain (n)	**порцелан** (m)	[pɔrʦə'lan]
porcelain (as adj)	**порцеланов**	[pɔrʦə'lanɔf]
clay (n)	**глина** (f)	['glina]
clay (as adj)	**глинен**	['glinɛn]
ceramics (n)	**керамика** (f)	[kɛ'ramika]
ceramic (as adj)	**керамичен**	[kɛ'ramiʧən]

28. Metals

metal (n)	**метал** (m)	[mɛ'tal]
metal (as adj)	**метален**	[mɛ'talɛn]

alloy (n)	**сплав** (m)	[splav]
gold (n)	**злато** (n)	['zlatɔ]
gold, golden (adj)	**златен**	['zlatɛn]
silver (n)	**сребро** (n)	[srɛb'rɔ]
silver (as adj)	**сребърен**	['srɛbırɛn]
iron (n)	**желязо** (n)	[ʒɛ'ʎazɔ]
iron (adj), made of iron	**железен**	[ʒɛ'lɛzɛn]
steel (n)	**стомана** (f)	[stɔ'mana]
steel (as adj)	**стоманен**	[stɔ'manɛn]
copper (n)	**мед** (f)	[mɛd]
copper (as adj)	**меден**	['mɛdɛn]
aluminum (n)	**алуминий** (m)	[alu'minij]
aluminum (as adj)	**алуминиев**	[alu'miniɛv]
bronze (n)	**бронз** (m)	[brɔnz]
bronze (as adj)	**бронзов**	['brɔnzɔv]
brass	**месинг** (m)	['mɛsiŋg]
nickel	**никел** (m)	['nikɛl]
platinum	**платина** (f)	[pla'tina]
mercury	**живак** (m)	[ʒi'vak]
tin	**калай** (m)	[ka'laj]
lead	**олово** (n)	[ɔ'lɔvɔ]
zinc	**цинк** (m)	[ʦiŋk]

HUMAN BEING

Human being. The body

29. Humans. Basic concepts

human being	**човек** (m)	[ʧɔ'vɛk]
man (adult male)	**мъж** (m)	[mɪʒ]
woman	**жена** (f)	[ʒɛ'na]
child	**дете** (n)	[dɛ'tɛ]
girl	**момиче** (n)	[mɔ'miʧə]
boy	**момче** (n)	[mɔm'ʧə]
teenager	**тинейджър** (m)	[ti'nɛjʤɪr]
old man	**старец** (m)	['starɛʦ]
old woman	**старица** (f)	['stariʦa]

30. Human anatomy

organism	**организъм** (m)	[ɔrga'nizɪm]
heart	**сърце** (n)	[sɪr'ʦə]
blood	**кръв** (f)	[krɪv]
artery	**артерия** (f)	[ar'tɛrija]
vein	**вена** (f)	['vɛna]
brain	**мозък** (m)	['mɔzɪk]
nerve	**нерв** (m)	[nɛrv]
nerves	**нерви** (m pl)	['nɛrvi]
vertebra	**прешлен** (m)	['prɛʃlɛn]
spine	**гръбнак** (m)	[grɪb'nak]
stomach (organ)	**стомах** (m)	[stɔ'mah]
intestines, bowel	**стомашно-чревен тракт** (m)	[stɔ'maʃnɔ 'ʧrɛvɛn trakt]
intestine (e.g., large ~)	**черво** (n)	[ʧər'vɔ]
liver	**черен дроб** (m)	['ʧərɛn drɔb]
kidney	**бъбрек** (m)	['bɪbrɛk]
bone	**кост** (f)	[kɔst]
skeleton	**скелет** (m)	['skɛlɛt]
rib	**ребро** (n)	[rɛb'rɔ]
skull	**череп** (m)	['ʧərɛp]
muscle	**мускул** (m)	['muskul]

biceps	**бицепс** (m)	['biʦəps]
tendon	**сухожилие** (n)	[suhɔ'ʒiliɛ]
joint	**става** (f)	['stava]
lungs	**бели дробове** (m pl)	['bɛli 'drɔbɔvɛ]
genitals	**полови органи** (m pl)	['pɔlɔvi 'ɔrgani]
skin	**кожа** (f)	['kɔʒa]

31. Head

head	**глава** (f)	[gla'va]
face	**лице** (n)	[li'ʦə]
nose	**нос** (m)	[nɔs]
mouth	**уста** (f)	[us'ta]
eye	**око** (n)	[ɔ'kɔ]
eyes	**очи** (n pl)	[ɔ'ʧi]
pupil	**зеница** (f)	['zɛniʦa]
eyebrow	**вежда** (f)	['vɛʒda]
eyelash	**мигла** (f)	['migla]
eyelid	**клепач** (m)	[klɛ'paʧ]
tongue	**език** (m)	[ɛ'zik]
tooth	**зъб** (m)	[zɪb]
lips	**устни** (f pl)	['ustni]
cheekbones	**скули** (f pl)	['skuli]
gum	**венец** (m)	[vɛ'nɛʦ]
palate	**небце** (n)	[nɛb'ʦə]
nostrils	**ноздри** (f pl)	['nɔzdri]
chin	**брадичка** (f)	[bra'diʧka]
jaw	**челюст** (f)	['ʧəlyst]
cheek	**буза** (f)	['buza]
forehead	**чело** (n)	[ʧə'lɔ]
temple	**слепоочие** (n)	[slɛpɔ'ɔʧiɛ]
ear	**ухо** (n)	[u'hɔ]
back of the head	**тил** (m)	[til]
neck	**шия** (f)	['ʃijɑ]
throat	**гърло** (n)	['gɪrlɔ]
hair	**коса** (f)	[kɔ'sa]
hairstyle	**прическа** (f)	[pri'ʧəska]
haircut	**подстригване** (n)	[pɔʦt'rigvanɛ]
wig	**перука** (f)	[pɛ'ruka]
mustache	**мустаци** (m pl)	[mus'taʦi]
beard	**брада** (f)	[bra'da]
to have (a beard, etc.)	**нося**	['nɔsʲa]
braid	**коса** (f)	[kɔ'sa]
sideburns	**бакенбарди** (pl)	[bakɛn'bardi]

red-haired (adj)	**червенокос**	[ʧərvɛnɔ'kɔs]
gray (hair)	**беловлас**	[bɛlɔv'las]
bald (adj)	**плешив**	[plɛ'ʃiv]
bald patch	**плешивина** (f)	[plɛʃivi'na]
ponytail	**опашка** (f)	[ɔ'paʃka]
bangs	**бретон** (m)	[brɛ'tɔn]

32. Human body

hand	**китка** (f)	['kitka]
arm	**ръка** (f)	[rɪ'ka]
finger	**пръст** (m)	[prɪst]
thumb	**палец** (m)	['palɛʦ]
little finger	**кутре** (n)	[kut'rɛ]
nail	**нокът** (m)	['nɔkɪt]
fist	**юмрук** (m)	[jum'ruk]
palm	**длан** (f)	[dlan]
wrist	**китка** (f)	['kitka]
forearm	**предмишница** (f)	[prɛd'miʃniʦa]
elbow	**лакът** (m)	['lakɪt]
shoulder	**рамо** (n)	['ramɔ]
leg	**крак** (m)	[krak]
foot	**ходило** (n)	[hɔ'dilɔ]
knee	**коляно** (n)	[kɔ'ʎanɔ]
calf (part of leg)	**прасец** (m)	[pra'sɛʦ]
hip	**бедро** (n)	[bɛd'rɔ]
heel	**пета** (f)	[pɛ'ta]
body	**тяло** (n)	['tʲalɔ]
stomach	**корем** (m)	[kɔ'rɛm]
chest	**гърди** (f pl)	[gɪr'di]
breast	**гърди** (f pl)	[gɪr'di]
flank	**страна** (f)	[stra'na]
back	**гръб** (m)	[grɪb]
lower back	**кръст** (m)	[krɪst]
waist	**талия** (f)	['talijɑ]
navel	**пъп** (m)	[pɪp]
buttocks	**седалище** (n)	[sɛ'daliʃtɛ]
bottom	**задник** (m)	['zadnik]
beauty mark	**бенка** (f)	['bɛŋka]
birthmark	**родилно петно** (n)	[rɔ'dilnɔ pɛt'nɔ]
tattoo	**татуировка** (f)	[tatui'rɔvka]
scar	**белег** (m)	['bɛlɛg]

Clothing & Accessories

33. Outerwear. Coats

clothes	**облекло** (n)	[ɔblɛk'lɔ]
outer clothes	**горни дрехи** (f pl)	['gɔrni 'drɛhi]
winter clothes	**зимни дрехи** (f pl)	['zimni 'drɛhi]
overcoat	**палто** (n)	[pal'tɔ]
fur coat	**кожено палто** (n)	['kɔʒɛnɔ pal'tɔ]
fur jacket	**полушубка** (f)	[pɔlu'ʃupka]
down coat	**пухено яке** (n)	['puhɛnɔ 'jakɛ]
jacket (e.g., leather ~)	**яке** (n)	['jakɛ]
raincoat	**шлифер** (m)	['ʃlifɛr]
waterproof (adj)	**непромокаем**	[nɛprɔmɔ'kaɛm]

34. Men's & women's clothing

shirt	**риза** (f)	['riza]
pants	**панталон** (m)	[panta'lɔn]
jeans	**дънки, джинси** (pl)	['dɪŋki], ['ʤinsi]
jacket (of man's suit)	**сако** (n)	[sa'kɔ]
suit	**костюм** (m)	[kɔs'tym]
dress (frock)	**рокля** (f)	['rɔkʎa]
skirt	**пола** (f)	[pɔ'la]
blouse	**блуза** (f)	['bluza]
knitted jacket	**жилетка** (f)	[ʒi'lɛtka]
jacket (of woman's suit)	**сако** (n)	[sa'kɔ]
T-shirt	**тениска** (f)	['tɛniska]
shorts (short trousers)	**къси панталони** (m pl)	['kɪsi panta'lɔni]
tracksuit	**анцуг** (m)	['anʦug]
bathrobe	**хавлиен халат** (m)	[hav'lien ha'lat]
pajamas	**пижама** (f)	[pi'ʒama]
sweater	**пуловер** (m)	[pu'lɔvɛr]
pullover	**пуловер** (m)	[pu'lɔvɛr]
vest	**елек** (m)	[ɛ'lɛk]
tailcoat	**фрак** (m)	[frak]
tuxedo	**смокинг** (m)	['smɔkiŋg]
uniform	**униформа** (f)	[uni'fɔrma]

workwear	**работно облекло** (n)	[ra'bɔtnɔ ɔblɛk'lɔ]
overalls	**гащеризон** (m)	[gaʃtɛri'zɔn]
coat (e.g., doctor's smock)	**бяла престилка** (f)	['bʲala prɛs'tilka]

35. Clothing. Underwear

underwear	**бельо** (n)	[bɛ'lɜ]
undershirt (A-shirt)	**потник** (m)	['pɔtnik]
socks	**чорапи** (m pl)	[ʧɔ'rapi]
nightgown	**нощница** (f)	['nɔʃnitsa]
bra	**сутиен** (m)	[suti'ɛn]
knee highs	**чорапи три четвърт** (m pl)	[ʧɔ'rapi tri 'ʧətvɪrt]
tights	**чорапогащник** (m)	[ʧɔrapɔ'gaʃtnik]
stockings (thigh highs)	**чорапи** (m pl)	[ʧɔ'rapi]
bathing suit	**бански** (m)	['banski]

36. Headwear

hat	**шапка** (f)	['ʃʌpka]
fedora	**шапка** (f)	['ʃʌpka]
baseball cap	**шапка** (f) **за голф**	['ʃʌpka za gɔlf]
flatcap	**каскет** (m)	[kas'kɛt]
beret	**барета** (f)	[ba'rɛta]
hood	**качулка** (f)	[ka'ʧulka]
panama hat	**панама** (f)	[pa'nama]
knitted hat	**плетена шапка** (f)	['plɛtɛna 'ʃʌpka]
headscarf	**кърпа** (f)	['kɪrpa]
women's hat	**шапка** (f)	['ʃʌpka]
hard hat	**каска** (f)	['kaska]
garrison cap	**пилотка** (f)	[pi'lɔtka]
helmet	**шлем** (m)	[ʃlɛm]
derby	**бомбе** (n)	[bɔm'bɛ]
top hat	**цилиндър** (m)	[tsi'lindɪr]

37. Footwear

footwear	**обувки** (f pl)	[ɔ'bufki]
ankle boots	**ботинки** (pl)	[bɔ'tiŋki]
shoes (low-heeled ~)	**обувки** (f pl)	[ɔ'bufki]
boots (cowboy ~)	**ботуши** (m pl)	[bɔ'tuʃi]

slippers	**чехли** (m pl)	['ʧəhli]
tennis shoes	**маратонки** (f pl)	[mara'tɔŋki]
sneakers	**кецове** (m pl)	['kɛʦɔvɛ]
sandals	**сандали** (pl)	[san'dali]
cobbler	**обущар** (m)	[ɔbuʃ'tar]
heel	**ток** (m)	[tɔk]
pair (of shoes)	**чифт** (m)	[ʧift]
shoestring	**връзка** (f)	['vrɪska]
to lace (vt)	**връзвам**	['vrɪzvam]
shoehorn	**обувалка** (f)	[ɔbu'valka]
shoe polish	**крем** (m) **за обувки**	[krɛm za ɔ'buvki]

38. Textile. Fabrics

cotton (n)	**памук** (m)	[pa'muk]
cotton (as adj)	**от памук**	[ɔt pa'muk]
flax (n)	**лен** (m)	[lɛn]
flax (as adj)	**от лен**	[ɔt lɛn]
silk (n)	**коприна** (f)	[kɔp'rina]
silk (as adj)	**копринен**	[kɔp'rinɛn]
wool (n)	**вълна** (f)	['vɪlna]
woolen (adj)	**вълнен**	['vɪlnɛn]
velvet	**кадифе** (n)	[kadi'fɛ]
suede	**велур** (m)	[vɛ'lur]
corduroy	**кадифе** (n)	[kadi'fɛ]
nylon (n)	**найлон** (m)	[naj'lɔn]
nylon (as adj)	**от найлон**	[ɔt naj'lɔn]
polyester (n)	**полиестер** (m)	[pɔli'ɛstɛr]
polyester (as adj)	**полиестерен**	[pɔli'ɛstɛrɛn]
leather (n)	**кожа** (f)	['kɔʒa]
leather (as adj)	**кожен**	['kɔʒɛn]
fur (n)	**кожа** (f)	['kɔʒa]
fur (e.g., ~ coat)	**кожен**	['kɔʒɛn]

39. Personal accessories

gloves	**ръкавици** (f pl)	[rɪka'viʦi]
mittens	**ръкавици** (f pl) **с един пърст**	[rɪka'viʦi s ɛ'din prɪst]
scarf (muffler)	**шал** (m)	[ʃʌl]
glasses	**очила** (pl)	[ɔʧi'la]
frame (eyeglass ~)	**рамка** (f) **за очила**	['ramka za ɔʧi'la]

umbrella	**чадър** (m)	[ʧa'dır]
walking stick	**бастун** (m)	[bas'tun]
hairbrush	**четка** (f) **за коса**	['ʧətka za kɔ'sa]
fan	**ветрило** (n)	[vɛt'rilɔ]
necktie	**вратовръзка** (f)	[vratɔv'rızka]
bow tie	**папийонка** (f)	[papi'joŋka]
suspenders	**тиранти** (pl)	[ti'ranti]
handkerchief	**носна кърпичка** (f)	['nɔsna 'kırpiʧka]
comb	**гребен** (m)	['grɛbɛn]
barrette	**шнола** (f)	['ʃnɔla]
hairpin	**фиба** (f)	['fiba]
buckle	**катарама** (f)	[kata'rama]
belt	**колан** (m)	[kɔ'lan]
shoulder strap	**ремък** (m)	['rɛmık]
bag (handbag)	**чанта** (f)	['ʧanta]
purse	**чантичка** (f)	['ʧantiʧka]
backpack	**раница** (f)	['ranitsa]

40. Clothing. Miscellaneous

fashion	**мода** (f)	['mɔda]
in vogue (adj)	**модерен**	[mɔ'dɛrɛn]
fashion designer	**моделиер** (m)	[mɔdɛli'ɛr]
collar	**яка** (f)	[jɑ'ka]
pocket	**джоб** (m)	[ʤɔb]
pocket (as adj)	**джобен**	['ʤɔbɛn]
sleeve	**ръкав** (m)	[rı'kav]
hanging loop	**закачалка** (f)	[zaka'ʧalka]
fly (on trousers)	**копчелък** (m)	[kɔpʧə'lık]
zipper (fastener)	**цип** (m)	[tsip]
fastener	**закопчалка** (f)	[zakɔp'ʧalka]
button	**копче** (n)	['kɔpʧə]
buttonhole	**илик** (m)	[i'lik]
to come off (ab. button)	**откъсна се**	[ɔt'kısna sɛ]
to sew (vi, vt)	**шия**	['ʃijɑ]
to embroider (vi, vt)	**бродирам**	[brɔ'diram]
embroidery	**бродерия** (f)	[brɔ'dɛrijɑ]
sewing needle	**игла** (f)	[ig'la]
thread	**конец** (m)	[kɔ'nɛts]
seam	**тегел** (m)	[tɛ'gɛl]
to get dirty (vi)	**изцапам се**	[is'tsapam sɛ]
stain (mark, spot)	**петно** (n)	[pɛt'nɔ]

to crease, crumple (vi)	**смачкам се**	['smatʃkam sɛ]
to tear (vt)	**скъсам**	['skɪsam]
clothes moth	**молец** (m)	[mɔ'lɛts]

41. Personal care. Cosmetics

toothpaste	**паста** (f) **за зъби**	['pasta za 'zɪbi]
toothbrush	**четка** (f) **за зъби**	['tʃətka za 'zɪbi]
to brush one's teeth	**мия си зъбите**	['mijɑ si 'zɪbitɛ]
razor	**бръснач** (m)	[brɪs'natʃ]
shaving cream	**крем** (m) **за бръснене**	[krɛm za 'brɪsnɛnɛ]
to shave (vi)	**бръсна се**	['brɪsna sɛ]
soap	**сапун** (m)	[sa'pun]
shampoo	**шампоан** (m)	[ʃʌmpɔ'an]
scissors	**ножица** (f)	['nɔʒitsa]
nail file	**пиличка** (f) **за нокти**	['pilitʃka za 'nɔkti]
nail clippers	**ножичка** (f) **за нокти**	['nɔʒitʃka za 'nɔkti]
tweezers	**пинсета** (f)	[pin'sɛta]
cosmetics	**козметика** (f)	[kɔz'mɛtika]
face mask	**маска** (f)	['maska]
manicure	**маникюр** (m)	[mani'kyr]
to have a manicure	**правя маникюр**	['pravʲa mani'kyr]
pedicure	**педикюр** (m)	[pɛdi'kyr]
make-up bag	**козметична чантичка** (f)	[kɔzmɛ'titʃna 'tʃantitʃka]
face powder	**пудра** (f)	['pudra]
powder compact	**пудриера** (f)	[pudri'ɛra]
blusher	**руж** (f)	[ruʃ]
perfume (bottled)	**парфюм** (m)	[par'fym]
toilet water (perfume)	**тоалетна вода** (f)	[tɔa'lɛtna vɔ'da]
lotion	**лосион** (m)	[lɔsi'ɔn]
cologne	**одеколон** (m)	[ɔdɛkɔ'lɔn]
eyeshadow	**сенки** (f pl) **за очи**	['sɛŋki za ɔ'tʃi]
eyeliner	**молив** (m) **за очи**	['mɔliv za ɔ'tʃi]
mascara	**спирала** (f)	[spi'rala]
lipstick	**червило** (n)	[tʃər'vilɔ]
nail polish, enamel	**лак** (m) **за нокти**	[lak za 'nɔkti]
hair spray	**лак** (m) **за коса**	[lak za kɔ'sa]
deodorant	**дезодорант** (m)	[dɛzɔdɔ'rant]
cream	**крем** (m)	[krɛm]
face cream	**крем** (m) **за лице**	[krɛm za li'tsə]
hand cream	**крем** (m) **за ръце**	[krɛm za rɪ'tsə]

anti-wrinkle cream	**крем** (m) **срещу бръчки**	[krɛm srɛʃ'tu 'brıʧki]
day (as adj)	**дневен**	['dnɛvɛn]
night (as adj)	**нощен**	['nɔʃtɛn]
tampon	**тампон** (m)	[tam'pɔn]
toilet paper	**тоалетна хартия** (f)	[tɔa'lɛtna har'tijɑ]
hair dryer	**сешоар** (m)	[sɛʃɔ'ar]

42. Jewelry

jewelry	**скъпоценности** (f pl)	[skıpɔ'ʦənɔsti]
precious (e.g., ~ stone)	**скъпоценен**	[skıpɔ'ʦənɛn]
hallmark	**проба** (f)	['prɔba]
ring	**пръстен** (m)	['prıstɛn]
wedding ring	**халка** (f)	[hal'ka]
bracelet	**гривна** (f)	['grivna]
earrings	**обеци** (f pl)	[ɔbɛ'ʦi]
necklace (~ of pearls)	**огърлица** (f)	[ɔgır'liʦa]
crown	**корона** (f)	[kɔ'rɔna]
bead necklace	**гердан** (m)	[gɛr'dan]
diamond	**диамант** (m)	[dia'mant]
emerald	**изумруд** (m)	[izum'rud]
ruby	**рубин** (m)	[ru'bin]
sapphire	**сапфир** (m)	[sap'fir]
pearl	**бисер** (m)	['bisɛr]
amber	**кехлибар** (m)	[kɛhli'bar]

43. Watches. Clocks

watch (wristwatch)	**часовник** (m)	[ʧa'sɔvnik]
dial	**циферблат** (m)	[ʦifɛrb'lat]
hand (of clock, watch)	**стрелка** (f)	[strɛl'ka]
metal watch band	**гривна** (f)	['grivna]
watch strap	**каишка** (f)	[ka'iʃka]
battery	**батерия** (f)	[ba'tɛrijɑ]
to be dead (battery)	**батерията се изтощи**	[ba'tɛrijɑta sɛ istɔʃ'ti]
to change a battery	**сменям батерия**	['smɛɲam ba'tɛrijɑ]
to run fast	**избързвам**	[iz'bırzvam]
to run slow	**изоставам**	[izɔs'tavam]
wall clock	**стенен часовник** (m)	['stɛnɛn ʧa'sɔvnik]
hourglass	**пясъчен часовник** (m)	['pʲasıʧən ʧa'sɔvnik]
sundial	**слънчев часовник** (m)	['slınʧəv ʧa'sɔvnik]
alarm clock	**будилник** (m)	[bu'dilnik]

watchmaker	**часовникар** (m)	[ʧasɔvni'kar]
to repair (vt)	**поправям**	[pɔp'ravʲam]

Food. Nutricion

44. Food

meat	**месо** (n)	[mɛ'sɔ]
chicken	**кокошка** (f)	[kɔ'kɔʃka]
young chicken	**пиле** (n)	['pilɛ]
duck	**патица** (f)	['patitsa]
goose	**гъска** (f)	['gɪska]
game	**дивеч** (f)	['divɛʧ]
turkey	**пуйка** (f)	['pujka]
pork	**свинско** (n)	['svinskɔ]
veal	**телешко месо** (n)	['tɛlɛʃkɔ me'sɔ]
lamb	**агнешко** (n)	['agnɛʃkɔ]
beef	**говеждо** (n)	[gɔ'vɛʒdɔ]
rabbit	**питомен заек** (m)	['pitɔmɛn 'zaɛk]
sausage (salami, etc.)	**салам** (m)	[sa'lam]
vienna sausage	**кренвирш** (m)	['krɛnvirʃ]
bacon	**бекон** (m)	[bɛ'kɔn]
ham	**шунка** (f)	['ʃuŋka]
gammon (ham)	**бут** (m)	[but]
pâté	**пастет** (m)	[pas'tɛt]
liver	**черен дроб** (m)	['ʧərɛn drɔb]
lard	**сланина** (f)	[sla'nina]
ground beef	**кайма** (f)	[kaj'ma]
tongue	**език** (m)	[ɛ'zik]
egg	**яйце** (n)	[jɑj'tsə]
eggs	**яйца** (n pl)	[jɑj'tsa]
egg white	**белтък** (m)	[bɛl'tɪk]
egg yolk	**жълтък** (m)	[ʒɪl'tɪk]
fish	**риба** (f)	['riba]
seafood	**морски продукти** (m pl)	['mɔrski prɔ'dukti]
caviar	**хайвер** (m)	[haj'vɛr]
crab	**морски рак** (m)	['mɔrski rak]
shrimp	**скарида** (f)	[ska'rida]
oyster	**стрида** (f)	['strida]
spiny lobster	**лангуста** (f)	[la'ŋgusta]
octopus	**октопод** (m)	[ɔktɔ'pɔd]
squid	**калмар** (m)	[kal'mar]
sturgeon	**есетра** (f)	[ɛ'sɛtra]

salmon	**сьомга** (f)	['sɜmga]
halibut	**палтус** (m)	['paltus]
cod	**треска** (f)	['trɛska]
mackerel	**скумрия** (f)	[skum'rijɑ]
tuna	**риба тон** (m)	['riba tɔn]
eel	**змиорка** (f)	[zmi'ɔrka]
trout	**пъстърва** (f)	[pɪs'tɪrva]
sardine	**сардина** (f)	[sar'dina]
pike	**щука** (f)	['ʃtuka]
herring	**селда** (f)	['sɛlda]
bread	**хляб** (m)	[hʎab]
cheese	**кашкавал** (m)	[kaʃka'val]
sugar	**захар** (f)	['zahar]
salt	**сол** (f)	[sɔl]
rice	**ориз** (m)	[ɔ'riz]
pasta	**макарони** (pl)	[maka'rɔni]
noodles	**юфка** (f)	[juf'ka]
butter	**краве масло** (n)	['kravɛ mas'lɔ]
vegetable oil	**олио** (n)	['ɔliɔ]
sunflower oil	**слънчогледово масло**	[slɪnʧɔg'ledɔvɔ 'maslɔ]
margarine	**маргарин** (m)	[marga'rin]
olives	**маслини** (f pl)	[mas'lini]
olive oil	**зехтин** (m)	[zɛh'tin]
milk	**мляко** (n)	['mʎakɔ]
condensed milk	**сгъстено мляко** (n)	[sgɪs'tɛnɔ 'mʎakɔ]
yogurt	**йогурт** (m)	['jogurt]
sour cream	**сметана** (f)	[smɛ'tana]
cream (of milk)	**каймак** (m)	[kaj'mak]
mayonnaise	**майонеза** (f)	[majo'nɛza]
buttercream	**крем** (m)	[krɛm]
flour	**брашно** (n)	[braʃ'nɔ]
canned food	**консерви** (f pl)	[kɔn'sɛrvi]
cornflakes	**царевичен флейкс** (m)	['ʦarɛviʧən flɛjks]
honey	**мед** (m)	[mɛd]
jam	**конфитюр** (m)	[kɔnfi'tyr]
chewing gum	**дъвка** (f)	['dɪfka]

45. Drinks

water	**вода** (f)	[vɔ'da]
drinking water	**питейна вода** (f)	[pi'tɛjna vɔ'da]

mineral water	**минерална вода** (f)	[minɛ'ralna vɔ'da]
still (adj)	**негазирана**	[nɛga'ziran]
carbonated (adj)	**газирана**	[ga'ziran]
sparkling (adj)	**газирана**	[ga'ziran]
ice	**лед** (m)	[lɛd]
with ice	**с лед**	[s lɛt]
non-alcoholic (adj)	**безалкохолен**	[bɛzalkɔ'hɔlɛn]
soft drink	**безалкохолна напитка** (f)	[bɛzalkɔ'hɔlna na'pitka]
cool soft drink	**разхладителна напитка** (f)	[rashla'ditɛlna na'pitka]
lemonade	**лимонада** (f)	[limɔ'nada]
liquor	**спиртни напитки** (f pl)	['spirtni na'pitki]
wine	**вино** (n)	['vinɔ]
white wine	**бяло вино** (n)	['bʲalɔ 'vinɔ]
red wine	**червено вино** (n)	[ʧər'vɛnɔ 'vinɔ]
liqueur	**ликьор** (m)	[li'kɜr]
champagne	**шампанско** (n)	[ʃʌm'panskɔ]
vermouth	**вермут** (m)	[vɛr'mut]
whisky	**уиски** (n)	[u'iski]
vodka	**водка** (f)	['vɔtka]
gin	**джин** (m)	[ʤin]
cognac	**коняк** (m)	[kɔ'ɲak]
rum	**ром** (m)	[rɔm]
coffee	**кафе** (n)	[ka'fɛ]
black coffee	**черно кафе** (n)	['ʧərnɔ ka'fɛ]
coffee with milk	**кафе** (n) **с мляко**	[ka'fɛ s 'mʎakɔ]
cappuccino	**кафе** (n) **със сметана**	[ka'fɛ sɪs smɛ'tana]
instant coffee	**разтворимо кафе** (n)	[rastvɔ'rimɔ ka'fɛ]
milk	**мляко** (n)	['mʎakɔ]
cocktail	**коктейл** (m)	[kɔk'tɛjl]
milk shake	**млечен коктейл** (m)	['mlɛʧən kɔk'tɛjl]
juice	**сок** (m)	[sɔk]
tomato juice	**доматен сок** (m)	[dɔ'matɛn sɔk]
orange juice	**портокалов сок** (m)	[pɔrtɔ'kalɔv sɔk]
freshly squeezed juice	**фреш** (m)	[frɛʃ]
beer	**бира** (f)	['bira]
light beer	**светла бира** (f)	['svɛtla 'bira]
dark beer	**тъмна бира** (f)	['tɪmna 'bira]
tea	**чай** (m)	[ʧaj]
black tea	**черен чай** (m)	['ʧərɛn ʧaj]
green tea	**зелен чай** (m)	[zɛ'lɛn ʧaj]

46. Vegetables

vegetables	**зеленчуци** (m pl)	[zɛlɛn'ʧuʦi]
greens	**зарзават** (m)	[zarza'vat]
tomato	**домат** (m)	[dɔ'mat]
cucumber	**краставица** (f)	['krastaviʦa]
carrot	**морков** (m)	['mɔrkɔf]
potato	**картофи** (pl)	[kar'tɔfi]
onion	**лук** (m)	[luk]
garlic	**чесън** (m)	['ʧəsɪn]
cabbage	**зеле** (n)	['zɛlɛ]
cauliflower	**карфиол** (m)	[karfi'ɔl]
Brussels sprouts	**брюкселско зеле** (n)	['bryksɛlskɔ 'zɛlɛ]
broccoli	**броколи** (n)	['brɔkɔli]
beetroot	**цвекло** (n)	[ʦvɛk'lɔ]
eggplant	**патладжан** (m)	[patla'ʤan]
zucchini	**тиквичка** (f)	['tikviʧka]
pumpkin	**тиква** (f)	['tikva]
turnip	**ряпа** (f)	['rʲapa]
parsley	**магданоз** (m)	[magda'nɔz]
dill	**копър** (m)	['kɔpɪr]
lettuce	**салата** (f)	[sa'lata]
celery	**целина** (f)	['ʦəlina]
asparagus	**аспержа** (f)	[as'pɛrʒa]
spinach	**спанак** (m)	[spa'nak]
pea	**грах** (m)	[grah]
beans	**боб** (m)	[bɔb]
corn (maize)	**царевица** (f)	['ʦarɛviʦa]
kidney bean	**фасул** (m)	[fa'sul]
pepper	**пипер** (m)	[pi'pɛr]
radish	**репичка** (f)	['rɛpiʧka]
artichoke	**ангинар** (m)	[aŋgi'nar]

47. Fruits. Nuts

fruit	**плод** (m)	[plɔt]
apple	**ябълка** (f)	['jabɪlka]
pear	**круша** (f)	['kruʃʌ]
lemon	**лимон** (m)	[li'mɔn]
orange	**портокал** (m)	[pɔrtɔ'kal]
strawberry	**ягода** (f)	['jagɔda]
mandarin	**мандарина** (f)	[manda'rina]
plum	**слива** (f)	['sliva]

peach	**праскова** (f)	['praskɔva]
apricot	**кайсия** (f)	[kaj'sijɑ]
raspberry	**малина** (f)	[ma'lina]
pineapple	**ананас** (m)	[ana'nas]
banana	**банан** (m)	[ba'nan]
watermelon	**диня** (f)	['diɲa]
grape	**грозде** (n)	['grɔzdɛ]
sour cherry	**вишна** (f)	['viʃna]
sweet cherry	**череша** (f)	[ʧə'rɛʃʌ]
melon	**пъпеш** (m)	['pɪpɛʃ]
grapefruit	**грейпфрут** (m)	['grɛjpfrut]
avocado	**авокадо** (n)	[avɔ'kadɔ]
papaya	**папая** (f)	[pa'pajɑ]
mango	**манго** (n)	['maŋgɔ]
pomegranate	**нар** (m)	[nar]
redcurrant	**червено френско грозде** (n)	[ʧər'vɛnɔ 'frɛnskɔ grɔzdɛ]
blackcurrant	**черно френско грозде** (n)	['ʧərnɔ 'frɛnskɔ grɔzdɛ]
gooseberry	**цариградско грозде** (n)	[ʦarig'raʦkɔ 'grɔzdɛ]
bilberry	**боровинки** (f pl)	[bɔrɔ'viŋki]
blackberry	**къпина** (f)	[kɪ'pina]
raisin	**стафиди** (f pl)	[sta'fidi]
fig	**смокиня** (f)	[smɔ'kiɲa]
date	**фурма** (f)	[fur'ma]
peanut	**фъстък** (m)	[fɪs'tɪk]
almond	**бадем** (m)	[ba'dɛm]
walnut	**орех** (m)	['ɔrɛh]
hazelnut	**лешник** (m)	['lɛʃnik]
coconut	**кокосов орех** (m)	[kɔ'kɔsɔv 'ɔrɛh]
pistachios	**шамфъстъци** (m pl)	[ʃʌmfɪs'tɪʦi]

48. Bread. Candy

confectionery (pastry)	**сладкарски изделия** (n pl)	[slad'karski iz'dɛlijɑ]
bread	**хляб** (m)	[hʎab]
cookies	**бисквити** (f pl)	[bisk'viti]
chocolate (n)	**шоколад** (m)	[ʃɔkɔ'lad]
chocolate (as adj)	**шоколадов**	[ʃɔkɔ'ladɔv]
candy	**бонбон** (m)	[bɔn'bɔn]
cake (e.g., cupcake)	**паста** (f)	['pasta]
cake (e.g., birthday ~)	**торта** (f)	['tɔrta]
pie (e.g., apple ~)	**пирог** (m)	[pi'rɔk]

filling (for cake, pie)	**плънка** (f)	['plıŋka]
whole fruit jam	**сладко** (n)	['sladkɔ]
marmalade	**мармалад** (m)	[marma'lat]
waffle	**вафли** (f pl)	['vafli]
ice-cream	**сладолед** (m)	[sladɔ'lɛd]

49. Cooked dishes

course, dish	**ястие** (n)	['jɑstiɛ]
cuisine	**кухня** (f)	['kuhɲa]
recipe	**рецепта** (f)	[rɛ'ʦəpta]
portion	**порция** (f)	['pɔrʦijɑ]
salad	**салата** (f)	[sa'lata]
soup	**супа** (f)	['supa]
clear soup (broth)	**бульон** (m)	[bu'ʎʲɔn]
sandwich (bread)	**сандвич** (m)	['sandviʧ]
fried eggs	**пържени яйца** (n pl)	['pırʒɛni jɑj'ʦa]
cutlet (croquette)	**кюфте** (n)	[kyf'tɛ]
hamburger (beefburger)	**хамбургер** (m)	['hamburgɛr]
beefsteak	**бифтек** (m)	[bif'tɛk]
stew	**задушено** (n)	[zadu'ʃɛnɔ]
side dish	**гарнитура** (f)	[garni'tura]
spaghetti	**спагети** (pl)	[spa'gɛti]
mashed potatoes	**картофено пюре** (n)	[kar'tɔfɛnɔ py'rɛ]
pizza	**пица** (f)	['piʦa]
porridge (oatmeal, etc.)	**каша** (f)	['kaʃʌ]
omelet	**омлет** (m)	[ɔm'lɛt]
boiled (e.g., ~ beef)	**варен**	[va'rɛn]
smoked (adj)	**пушен**	['puʃɛn]
fried (adj)	**пържен**	['pırʒɛn]
dried (adj)	**сушен**	[su'ʃɛn]
frozen (adj)	**замразен**	[zamra'zɛn]
pickled (adj)	**маринован**	[mari'nɔvan]
sweet (sugary)	**сладък**	['sladık]
salty (adj)	**солен**	[sɔ'lɛn]
cold (adj)	**студен**	[stu'dɛn]
hot (adj)	**горещ**	[gɔ'rɛʃt]
bitter (adj)	**горчив**	[gɔr'ʧiv]
tasty (adj)	**вкусен**	['vkusɛn]
to cook in boiling water	**готвя**	['gɔtvʲa]
to cook (dinner)	**готвя**	['gɔtvʲa]
to fry (vt)	**пържа**	['pırʒa]
to heat up (food)	**затоплям**	[za'tɔpʎam]

to salt (vt)	**соля**	[sɔ'ʎa]
to pepper (vt)	**слагам пипер**	['slagam pi'pɛr]
to grate (vt)	**стъргам**	['stɪrgam]
peel (n)	**кожа** (f)	['kɔʒa]
to peel (vt)	**беля**	['bɛʎa]

50. Spices

salt	**сол** (f)	[sɔl]
salty (adj)	**солен**	[sɔ'lɛn]
to salt (vt)	**соля**	[sɔ'ʎa]
black pepper	**черен пипер** (m)	['ʧərɛn pi'pɛr]
red pepper	**червен пипер** (m)	[ʧər'vɛn pi'pɛr]
mustard	**горчица** (f)	[gɔr'ʧiʦa]
horseradish	**хрян** (m)	[hrʲan]
condiment	**подправка** (f)	[pɔdp'ravka]
spice	**подправка** (f)	[pɔdp'ravka]
sauce	**сос** (m)	[sɔs]
vinegar	**оцет** (m)	[ɔ'ʦət]
anise	**анасон** (m)	[ana'sɔn]
basil	**босилек** (m)	[bɔ'silɛk]
cloves	**карамфил** (m)	[karam'fil]
ginger	**джинджифил** (m)	[ʤinʤi'fil]
cinnamon	**канела** (f)	[ka'nɛla]
sesame	**сусам** (m)	[su'sam]
bay leaf	**дафинов лист** (m)	[da'finɔv list]
paprika	**червен пипер** (m)	[ʧər'vɛn pi'pɛr]
caraway	**черен тмин** (m)	['ʧərɛn tmin]
saffron	**шафран** (m)	[ʃʌf'ran]

51. Meals

food	**храна** (f)	[hra'na]
to eat (vi, vt)	**ям**	[jɑm]
breakfast	**закуска** (f)	[za'kuska]
to have breakfast	**закусвам**	[za'kusvam]
lunch	**обяд** (m)	[ɔ'bʲad]
to have lunch	**обядвам**	[ɔ'bʲadvam]
dinner	**вечеря** (f)	[vɛ'ʧərʲa]
to have dinner	**вечерям**	[vɛ'ʧərʲam]
appetite	**апетит** (m)	[apɛ'tit]
Enjoy your meal!	**Добър апетит!**	[dɔ'bɪr apɛ'tit]

to open (~ a bottle)	**отварям**	[ɔt'varʲam]
to spill (liquid)	**излея**	[iz'lɛja]
to spill out (vi)	**излея се**	[iz'lɛja sɛ]
to boil (vi)	**вря**	[vrʲa]
to boil (vt)	**варя до кипване**	[va'rʲa dɔ 'kipvanɛ]
boiled (~ water)	**преварен**	[prɛva'rɛn]
to chill, cool down (vt)	**охладя**	[ɔhla'dʲa]
to chill (vi)	**изстудявам се**	[isstu'dʲavam sɛ]
taste, flavor	**вкус** (m)	[vkus]
aftertaste	**страничен вкус** (m)	[stra'nitʃən vkus]
to be on a diet	**отслабвам**	[ɔts'labvam]
diet	**диета** (f)	[di'ɛta]
vitamin	**витамин** (m)	[vita'min]
calorie	**калория** (f)	[ka'lɔrija]
vegetarian (n)	**вегетарианец** (m)	[vɛgɛtari'anɛts]
vegetarian (adj)	**вегетариански**	[vɛgɛtari'anski]
fats (nutrient)	**мазнини** (f pl)	[mazni'ni]
proteins	**белтъчини** (f pl)	[bɛltɪtʃi'ni]
carbohydrates	**въглехидрати** (m pl)	[vɪglɛhid'rati]
slice (of lemon, ham)	**резенче** (n)	['rɛzɛntʃə]
piece (of cake, pie)	**парче** (n)	[par'tʃə]
crumb (of bread)	**троха** (f)	[trɔ'ha]

52. Table setting

spoon	**лъжица** (f)	[lɪ'ʒitsa]
knife	**нож** (m)	[nɔʒ]
fork	**вилица** (f)	['vilitsa]
cup (of coffee)	**чаша** (f)	['tʃaʃʌ]
plate (dinner ~)	**чиния** (f)	[tʃi'nija]
saucer	**чинийка** (f)	[tʃi'nijka]
napkin (on table)	**салфетка** (f)	[sal'fɛtka]
toothpick	**клечка** (f) **за зъби**	['klɛtʃka za 'zɪbi]

53. Restaurant

restaurant	**ресторант** (m)	[rɛstɔ'rant]
coffee house	**кафене** (n)	[kafɛ'nɛ]
pub, bar	**бар** (m)	[bar]
tearoom	**чаен салон** (m)	['tʃaɛn sa'lɔn]
waiter	**сервитьор** (m)	[sɛrvi'tɜr]
waitress	**сервитьорка** (f)	[sɛrvi'tɜrka]

bartender	**барман** (m)	['barman]
menu	**меню** (n)	[mɛ'ny]
wine list	**карта** (f) **на виното**	['karta na 'vinɔtɔ]
to book a table	**резервирам масичка**	[rɛzɛr'viram 'masitʃka]
course, dish	**ядене** (n)	['jadɛnɛ]
to order (meal)	**поръчам**	[pɔ'rɪtʃam]
to make an order	**правя поръчка**	['pravʲa pɔ'rɪtʃka]
aperitif	**аперитив** (m)	[apɛri'tiv]
appetizer	**мезе** (n)	[mɛ'zɛ]
dessert	**десерт** (m)	[dɛ'sɛrt]
check	**сметка** (f)	['smɛtka]
to pay the check	**плащам сметка**	['plaʃtam 'smɛtka]
to give change	**връщам ресто**	['vrɪʃtam 'rɛstɔ]
tip	**бакшиш** (m)	[bak'ʃiʃ]

Family, relatives and friends

54. Personal information. Forms

name, first name	**име** (n)	['imɛ]
family name	**фамилия** (f)	[fa'milija]
date of birth	**дата** (f) **на раждане**	['data na 'raʒdanɛ]
place of birth	**място** (n) **на раждане**	['masto na 'raʒdanɛ]
nationality	**националност** (f)	[natsio'nalnost]
place of residence	**местожителство** (n)	[mɛsto'ʒitɛlstvo]
country	**страна** (f)	[stra'na]
profession (occupation)	**професия** (f)	[pro'fɛsija]
gender, sex	**пол** (m)	[pol]
height	**ръст** (m)	[rɪst]
weight	**тегло** (n)	[tɛg'lo]

55. Family members. Relatives

mother	**майка** (f)	['majka]
father	**баща** (m)	[baʃ'ta]
son	**син** (m)	[sin]
daughter	**дъщеря** (f)	[dɪʃtɛ'rʲa]
younger daughter	**по-малка дъщеря** (f)	[po 'malka dɪʃtɛ'rʲa]
younger son	**по-малък син** (m)	[po 'malɪk sin]
eldest daughter	**по-голяма дъщеря** (f)	[po go'ʎama dɪʃtɛ'rʲa]
eldest son	**по-голям син** (m)	[po go'ʎam sin]
brother	**брат** (m)	[brat]
sister	**сестра** (f)	[sɛst'ra]
cousin (masc.)	**братовчед** (m)	[bratov'tʃəd]
cousin (fem.)	**братовчедка** (f)	[bratov'tʃədka]
mom	**мама** (f)	['mama]
dad, daddy	**татко** (m)	['tatko]
parents	**родители** (m pl)	[ro'ditɛli]
child	**дете** (n)	[dɛ'tɛ]
children	**деца** (n pl)	[dɛ'tsa]
grandmother	**баба** (f)	['baba]
grandfather	**дядо** (m)	['dʲado]
grandson	**внук** (m)	[vnuk]

granddaughter	**внучка** (f)	['vnutʃka]
grandchildren	**внуци** (m pl)	['vnutsi]
uncle	**вуйчо** (m)	['vujtʃɔ]
aunt	**леля** (f)	['lɛʎa]
nephew	**племенник** (m)	['plɛmɛnik]
niece	**племенница** (f)	['plɛmɛnitsa]
mother-in-law (wife's mother)	**тъща** (f)	['tɪʃta]
father-in-law (husband's father)	**свекър** (m)	['svɛkɪr]
son-in-law (daughter's husband)	**зет** (m)	[zɛt]
stepmother	**мащеха** (f)	['maʃtɛha]
stepfather	**пастрок** (m)	['pastrɔk]
infant	**кърмаче** (n)	[kɪr'matʃə]
baby (infant)	**бебе** (n)	['bɛbɛ]
little boy, kid	**момченце** (n)	[mɔm'tʃəntsə]
wife	**жена** (f)	[ʒɛ'na]
husband	**мъж** (m)	[mɪʒ]
spouse (husband)	**съпруг** (m)	[sɪp'rug]
spouse (wife)	**съпруга** (f)	[sɪp'ruga]
married (masc.)	**женен**	['ʒɛnɛn]
married (fem.)	**омъжена**	[ɔ'mɪʒɛna]
single (unmarried)	**неженен**	[nɛ'ʒɛnɛn]
bachelor	**ерген** (m)	[ɛr'gɛn]
divorced (masc.)	**разведен**	[raz'vɛdɛn]
widow	**вдовица** (f)	[vdɔ'vitsa]
widower	**вдовец** (m)	[vdɔ'vɛts]
relative	**роднина** (m, f)	[rɔd'nina]
close relative	**близък роднина** (m)	['blizɪk rɔd'nina]
distant relative	**далечен роднина** (m)	[da'lɛtʃən rɔd'nina]
relatives	**роднини** (pl)	[rɔd'nini]
orphan (boy or girl)	**сирак** (m)	[si'rak]
guardian (of minor)	**опекун** (m)	[ɔpɛ'kun]
to adopt (a boy)	**осиновявам**	[ɔsinɔ'vʲavam]
to adopt (a girl)	**осиновявам момиче**	[ɔsinɔ'vʲavam mɔ'mitʃə]

56. Friends. Coworkers

friend (masc.)	**приятел** (m)	[pri'jatɛl]
friend (fem.)	**приятелка** (f)	[pri'jatɛlka]
friendship	**приятелство** (n)	[pri'jatɛlstvɔ]
to be friends	**дружа**	[dru'ʒa]

buddy (masc.)	**приятел** (m)	[pri'jatɛl]
buddy (fem.)	**приятелка** (f)	[pri'jatɛlka]
partner	**партньор** (m)	[part'nɜr]
chief (boss)	**шеф** (m)	[ʃɛf]
superior	**началник** (m)	[na'ʧalnik]
subordinate	**подчинен** (m)	[pɔdʧi'nɛn]
colleague	**колега** (m, f)	[kɔ'lɛga]
acquaintance (person)	**познат** (m)	[pɔz'nat]
fellow traveler	**спътник** (m)	['spɪtnik]
classmate	**съученик** (m)	[sɪuʧə'nik]
neighbor (masc.)	**съсед** (m)	[sɪ'sɛd]
neighbor (fem.)	**съседка** (f)	[sɪ'sɛdka]
neighbors	**съседи** (m pl)	[sɪ'sɛdi]

57. Man. Woman

woman	**жена** (f)	[ʒɛ'na]
girl (young woman)	**девойка** (f)	[dɛ'vɔjka]
bride	**годеница** (f)	[gɔdɛ'niʦa]
beautiful (adj)	**хубава**	['hubava]
tall (adj)	**висока**	[vi'sɔka]
slender (adj)	**стройна**	['strɔjna]
short (adj)	**невисок**	[nɛvi'sɔk]
blonde (n)	**блондинка** (f)	[blɔn'diŋka]
brunette (n)	**брюнетка** (f)	[bry'nɛtka]
ladies' (adj)	**дамски**	['damski]
virgin (girl)	**девственица** (f)	['dɛvstvɛniʦa]
pregnant (adj)	**бременна**	['brɛmɛna]
man (adult male)	**мъж** (m)	[mɪʒ]
blond (n)	**блондин** (m)	[blɔn'din]
brunet (n)	**брюнет** (m)	[bry'nɛt]
tall (adj)	**висок**	[vi'sɔk]
short (adj)	**невисок**	[nɛvi'sɔk]
rude (rough)	**груб**	[grub]
stocky (adj)	**едър**	['ɛdɪr]
robust (adj)	**як**	[jak]
strong (adj)	**силен**	['silɛn]
strength	**сила** (f)	['sila]
stout, fat (adj)	**пълен**	['pɪlɛn]
swarthy (adj)	**мургав**	['murgav]
well-built (adj)	**строен**	['strɔɛn]
elegant (adj)	**елегантен**	[ɛlɛ'gantɛn]

58. Age

age	**възраст** (f)	['vızrast]
youth (young age)	**младост** (f)	['mladɔst]
young (adj)	**млад**	[mlad]
younger (adj)	**по-малък**	[pɔ 'malık]
older (adj)	**по-голям**	[pɔ gɔ'ʎam]
young man	**младеж** (m)	[mla'dɛʒ]
teenager	**тийнейджър** (m)	[ti'nɛjʤır]
guy, fellow	**момък** (m)	['mɔmık]
old man	**старец** (m)	['starɛʦ]
old woman	**старица** (f)	['stariʦa]
adult	**възрастен**	['vızrastɛn]
middle-aged (adj)	**на средна възраст**	[na 'srɛdna 'vızrast]
elderly (adj)	**възрастен**	['vızrastɛn]
old (adj)	**стар**	[star]
retirement	**пенсия** (f)	['pɛnsija]
to retire (from job)	**пенсионирам се**	[pɛnsiɔ'niram sɛ]
retiree	**пенсионер** (m)	[pɛnsiɔ'nɛr]

59. Children

child	**дете** (n)	[dɛ'tɛ]
children	**деца** (n pl)	[dɛ'ʦa]
twins	**близнаци** (m pl)	[bliz'naʦi]
cradle	**люлка** (f)	['lylka]
rattle	**дрънкалка** (f)	[drı'ŋkalka]
diaper	**памперс** (m)	['pampɛrs]
pacifier	**биберон** (m)	[bibɛ'rɔn]
baby carriage	**детска количка** (f)	['dɛʦka kɔ'liʧka]
kindergarten	**детска градина** (f)	['dɛʦka gra'dina]
babysitter	**детегледачка** (f)	[dɛtɛglɛ'daʧka]
childhood	**детство** (n)	['dɛʦtvɔ]
doll	**кукла** (f)	['kukla]
toy	**играчка** (f)	[ig'raʧka]
construction set	**конструктор** (m)	[kɔnst'ruktɔr]
well-bred (adj)	**възпитан**	[vıs'pitan]
ill-bred (adj)	**невъзпитан**	[nɛvıs'pitan]
spoiled (adj)	**разглезен**	[razg'lɛzɛn]
to be naughty	**палувам**	[pa'luvam]

mischievous (adj)	**палав**	['palav]
mischievousness	**лудория** (f)	[ludɔ'rijɑ]
mischievous child	**палавник** (m)	['palavnik]
obedient (adj)	**послушен**	[pɔs'luʃɛn]
disobedient (adj)	**непослушен**	[nɛpɔs'luʃɛn]
docile (adj)	**благоразумен**	[blagɔra'zumɛn]
clever (smart)	**умен**	['umɛn]
child prodigy	**вундеркинд** (m)	['vundɛrkind]

60. Married couples. Family life

to kiss (vt)	**целувам**	[ʦə'luvam]
to kiss (vi)	**целувам се**	[ʦə'luvam sɛ]
family (n)	**семейство** (n)	[sɛ'mɛjstvɔ]
family (as adj)	**семеен**	[sɛ'mɛ:n]
couple	**двойка** (f)	['dvɔjka]
marriage (state)	**брак** (m)	[brak]
hearth (home)	**семейно огнище** (n)	[sɛ'mɛjnɔ ɔg'niʃtɛ]
dynasty	**династия** (f)	[di'nastijɑ]
date	**среща** (f)	['srɛʃta]
kiss	**целувка** (f)	[ʦə'luvka]
love (for sb)	**обич** (f)	['ɔbiʧ]
to love (sb)	**обичам**	[ɔ'biʧam]
beloved	**любим**	[ly'bim]
tenderness	**нежност** (f)	['nɛʒnɔst]
tender (affectionate)	**нежен**	['nɛʒɛn]
faithfulness	**вярност** (f)	['vʲarnɔst]
faithful (adj)	**верен**	['vɛrɛn]
care (attention)	**грижа** (f)	['griʒa]
caring (~ father)	**грижлив**	[griʒ'liv]
newlyweds	**младоженци** (m pl)	[mladɔ'ʒɛnʦi]
honeymoon	**меден месец** (m)	['mɛdɛn 'mɛsɛʦ]
to get married (ab. woman)	**омъжа се**	[ɔ'mɪʒa sɛ]
to get married (ab. man)	**женя се**	['ʒɛɲa sɛ]
wedding	**сватба** (f)	['svatba]
golden wedding	**златна сватба** (f)	['zlatna 'svadba]
anniversary	**годишнина** (f)	[gɔ'diʃnina]
lover (masc.)	**любовник** (m)	[ly'bɔvnik]
mistress	**любовница** (f)	[ly'bɔvniʦa]
adultery	**изневяра** (f)	[iznɛ'vʲara]
to cheat on ... (commit adultery)	**изневерявам**	[iznɛvɛ'rʲavam]

jealous (adj)	**ревнив**	[rɛv'niv]
to be jealous	**ревнувам**	[rɛv'nuvam]
divorce	**развод** (m)	[raz'vɔd]
to divorce (vi)	**развеждам се**	[raz'vɛʒdam sɛ]
to quarrel (vi)	**карам се**	['karam sɛ]
to be reconciled	**сдобрявам се**	[zdɔb'rʲavam sɛ]
together (adv)	**заедно**	['zaɛdnɔ]
sex	**секс** (m)	[sɛks]
happiness	**щастие** (n)	['ʃtastiɛ]
happy (adj)	**щастлив**	[ʃtast'liv]
misfortune (accident)	**нещастие** (n)	[nɛʃ'tastiɛ]
unhappy (adj)	**нещастен**	[nɛʃ'tastɛn]

Character. Feelings. Emotions

61. Feelings. Emotions

feeling (emotion)	**чувство** (n)	['ʧustvɔ]
feelings	**чувства** (n pl)	['ʧustva]
to feel (vt)	**чувствам**	['ʧuvstvam]
hunger	**глад** (m)	[glad]
to be hungry	**искам да ям**	['iskam da jɑm]
thirst	**жажда** (f)	['ʒaʒda]
to be thirsty	**искам да пия**	['iskam da 'pijɑ]
sleepiness	**сънливост** (f)	[sɪn'livɔst]
to feel sleepy	**искам да спя**	['iskam da spʲa]
tiredness	**умора** (f)	[u'mɔra]
tired (adj)	**изморен**	[izmɔ'rɛn]
to get tired	**уморя се**	[umɔ'rʲa sɛ]
mood (humor)	**настроение** (n)	[nastrɔ'ɛniɛ]
boredom	**скука** (f)	['skuka]
to be bored	**скучая**	[sku'ʧajɑ]
seclusion	**самота** (f)	[samɔ'ta]
to seclude oneself	**уединявам се**	[uədi'ɲavam sɛ]
to worry (make anxious)	**безпокоя**	[bɛspɔkɔ'jɑ]
to be worried	**безпокоя се**	[bɛspɔkɔ'jɑ sɛ]
worrying (n)	**безпокойство** (n)	[bɛspɔ'kɔjstvɔ]
anxiety	**тревога** (f)	[trɛ'vɔga]
preoccupied (adj)	**загрижен**	[zag'riʒɛn]
to be nervous	**нервирам се**	[ner'viram sɛ]
to panic (vi)	**паникьосвам се**	[pani'kɜsvam sɛ]
hope	**надежда** (f)	[na'dɛʒda]
to hope (vi, vt)	**надявам се**	[na'dʲavam sɛ]
certainty	**увереност** (f)	[u'vɛrɛnɔst]
certain, sure (adj)	**уверен**	[u'vɛrɛn]
uncertainty	**неувереност** (f)	[nɛu'vɛrɛnɔst]
uncertain (adj)	**неуверен**	[nɛu'vɛrɛn]
drunk (adj)	**пиян**	[pi'jɑn]
sober (adj)	**трезвен**	['trɛzvɛn]
weak (adj)	**слаб**	[slap]
happy (adj)	**щастлив**	[ʃtast'liv]
to scare (vt)	**изплаша**	[isp'laʃʌ]

fury (madness)	**бяс** (m)	[bʲas]
rage (fury)	**ярост** (f)	['jarɔst]
depression	**депресия** (f)	[dɛp'rɛsija]
discomfort	**дискомфорт** (m)	[diskɔm'fɔrt]
comfort	**комфорт** (m)	[kɔm'fɔrt]
to regret (be sorry)	**съжалявам**	[sɪʒa'ʎavam]
regret	**съжаление** (n)	[sɪʒa'lɛniɛ]
bad luck	**несполука** (f)	[nɛspɔ'luka]
sadness	**огорчение** (n)	[ɔgɔr'ʧəniɛ]
shame (remorse)	**срам** (m)	[sram]
gladness	**веселба** (f)	[vɛsɛl'ba]
enthusiasm, zeal	**ентусиазъм** (m)	[ɛntusi'azɪm]
enthusiast	**ентусиаст** (m)	[ɛntusi'ast]
to show enthusiasm	**ентусиазирам**	[ɛntusia'ziram]

62. Character. Personality

character	**характер** (m)	[ha'raktɛr]
character flaw	**недостатък** (m)	[nɛdɔs'tatɪk]
mind	**ум** (m)	[um]
reason	**разум** (m)	['razum]
conscience	**съвест** (f)	['sɪvɛst]
habit (custom)	**навик** (m)	['navik]
ability	**способност** (f)	[spɔ'sɔbnɔst]
can (e.g., ~ swim)	**умея**	[u'mɛja]
patient (adj)	**търпелив**	[tɪrpɛ'liv]
impatient (adj)	**нетърпелив**	[nɛtɪrpɛ'liv]
curious (inquisitive)	**любопитен**	[lybɔ'pitɛn]
curiosity	**любопитство** (n)	[lybɔ'piʦtvɔ]
modesty	**скромност** (f)	['skrɔmnɔst]
modest (adj)	**скромен**	['skrɔmɛn]
immodest (adj)	**нескромен**	[nɛsk'rɔmɛn]
laziness	**мързел** (m)	['mɪrzɛl]
lazy (adj)	**мързелив**	[mɪrzɛ'liv]
lazy person (masc.)	**мързеливец** (m)	[mɪrzɛ'livɛʦ]
cunning (n)	**хитрост** (f)	['hitrɔst]
cunning (as adj)	**хитър**	['hitɪr]
distrust	**недоверие** (n)	[nɛdɔ'vɛriɛ]
distrustful (adj)	**недоверчив**	[nɛdɔvɛr'ʧiv]
generosity	**щедрост** (f)	['ʃtɛdrɔst]
generous (adj)	**щедър**	['ʃtɛdɪr]
talented (adj)	**талантлив**	[talant'lif]

talent	**талант** (m)	[ta'lant]
courageous (adj)	**смел**	[smɛl]
courage	**смелост** (m)	['smɛlɔst]
honest (adj)	**честен**	['ʧəstɛn]
honesty	**честност** (f)	['ʧəstnɔst]
careful (cautious)	**предпазлив**	[prɛdpaz'liv]
brave (courageous)	**храбър**	['hrabɪr]
serious (adj)	**сериозен**	[sɛri'ɔzɛn]
strict (severe, stern)	**строг**	[strɔg]
decisive (adj)	**решителен**	[rɛ'ʃitɛlɛn]
indecisive (adj)	**нерешителен**	[nɛrɛ'ʃitɛlɛn]
shy, timid (adj)	**свенлив**	[svɛn'liv]
shyness, timidity	**свенливост** (f)	[svɛn'livɔst]
confidence (trust)	**доверие** (n)	[dɔ'vɛriɛ]
to believe (trust)	**вярвам**	['vʲarvam]
trusting (naïve)	**доверчив**	[dɔvɛr'ʧiv]
sincerely (adv)	**искрено**	['iskrɛnɔ]
sincere (adj)	**искрен**	['iskrɛn]
sincerity	**искреност** (f)	['iskrɛnɔst]
open (person)	**открит**	[ɔtk'rit]
calm (adj)	**тих**	[tih]
frank (sincere)	**откровен**	[ɔtkrɔ'vɛn]
naïve (adj)	**наивен**	[na'ivɛn]
absent-minded (adj)	**разсеян**	[ras'sɛjɑn]
funny (odd)	**смешен**	['smɛʃɛn]
greed	**алчност** (f)	['alʧnɔst]
greedy (adj)	**алчен**	['alʧən]
stingy (adj)	**стиснат**	['stisnat]
evil (adj)	**зъл**	[zɪl]
stubborn (adj)	**инат**	[i'nat]
unpleasant (adj)	**неприятен**	[nɛpri'jɑtɛn]
selfish person (masc.)	**егоист** (m)	[ɛgɔ'ist]
selfish (adj)	**егоистичен**	[ɛgɔis'tiʧən]
coward	**страхливец** (m)	[strah'livɛʦ]
cowardly (adj)	**страхлив**	[strah'lif]

63. Sleep. Dreams

to sleep (vi)	**спя**	[spʲa]
sleep, sleeping	**сън** (m)	[sɪn]
dream	**сън** (m)	[sɪn]
to dream (in sleep)	**сънувам**	[sɪ'nuvam]
sleepy (adj)	**сънен**	['sɪnɛn]

bed	**легло** (n)	[lɛg'lɔ]
mattress	**дюшек** (m)	[dy'ʃɛk]
blanket (comforter)	**одеяло** (n)	[ɔdɛ'jalɔ]
pillow	**възглавница** (f)	[vɪzg'lavnitsa]
sheet	**чаршаф** (m)	[ʧar'ʃʌf]
insomnia	**безсъние** (n)	[bɛs'sɪniɛ]
sleepless (adj)	**безсънен**	[bɛs'sɪnɛn]
sleeping pill	**приспивателно** (n)	[prispi'vatɛlnɔ]
to take a sleeping pill	**взимам приспивателно**	['vzimam prispi'vatɛlnɔ]
to feel sleepy	**искам да спя**	['iskam da spʲa]
to yawn (vi)	**прозявам се**	[prɔ'zʲavam sɛ]
to go to bed	**отивам да спя**	[ɔ'tivam da spʲa]
to make up the bed	**оправям легло**	[ɔp'ravʲam lɛg'lɔ]
to fall asleep	**заспивам**	[zas'pivam]
nightmare	**кошмар** (m)	[kɔʃ'mar]
snoring	**хъркане** (n)	['hɪrkanɛ]
to snore (vi)	**хъркам**	['hɪrkam]
alarm clock	**будилник** (m)	[bu'dilnik]
to wake (vt)	**събудя**	[sɪ'budʲa]
to wake up	**събуждам се**	[sɪ'buʒdam sɛ]
to get up (vi)	**ставам**	['stavam]
to wash up (vi)	**измивам се**	[iz'mivam sɛ]

64. Humour. Laughter. Gladness

humor (wit, fun)	**хумор** (m)	['humɔr]
sense of humor	**чувство** (f) **за хумор**	['ʧustvɔ za 'humɔr]
to have fun	**веселя се**	[vɛsɛ'ʎa sɛ]
cheerful (adj)	**весел**	['vɛsɛl]
merriment, fun	**веселба** (f)	[vɛsɛl'ba]
smile	**усмивка** (f)	[us'mifka]
to smile (vi)	**усмихвам се**	[us'mihvam sɛ]
to start laughing	**засмея се**	[zas'mɛja sɛ]
to laugh (vi)	**смея се**	['smɛja sɛ]
laugh, laughter	**смях** (m)	[smʲah]
anecdote	**виц** (m)	[vits]
funny (anecdote, etc.)	**смешен**	['smɛʃɛn]
funny (odd)	**смешен**	['smɛʃɛn]
to joke (vi)	**шегувам се**	[ʃɛ'guvam sɛ]
joke (verbal)	**шега** (f)	[ʃɛ'ga]
joy (emotion)	**радост** (f)	['radɔst]
to rejoice (vi)	**радвам се**	['radvam sɛ]
glad, cheerful (adj)	**радостен**	['radɔstɛn]

65. Discussion, conversation. Part 1

communication	**общуване** (n)	[ɔbʃtuvanɛ]
to communicate	**общувам**	[ɔbʃtuvam]
conversation	**разговор** (m)	['razgɔvɔr]
dialog	**диалог** (m)	[dia'lɔg]
discussion (discourse)	**дискусия** (f)	[dis'kusija]
debate	**спор** (m)	[spɔr]
to debate (vi)	**споря**	['spɔrʲa]
interlocutor	**събеседник** (m)	[sɪbɛ'sɛdnik]
topic (theme)	**тема** (f)	['tɛma]
point of view	**гледна точка** (f)	['glɛdna 'tɔʧka]
opinion (viewpoint)	**мнение** (n)	['mnɛniɛ]
speech (talk)	**слово** (n)	['slɔvɔ]
discussion (of report, etc.)	**обсъждане** (n)	[ɔb'sɪʒdanɛ]
to discuss (vt)	**обсъждам**	[ɔb'sɪʒdam]
talk (conversation)	**беседа** (f)	[bɛ'sɛda]
to talk (vi)	**беседвам**	[bɛ'sɛdvam]
meeting	**среща** (f)	['srɛʃta]
to meet (vi, vt)	**срещам се**	['srɛʃtam sɛ]
proverb	**пословица** (f)	[pɔs'lɔviʦa]
saying	**поговорка** (f)	[pɔgɔ'vɔrka]
riddle (poser)	**гатанка** (f)	['gataŋka]
to ask a riddle	**задавам гатанка**	[za'davam 'gataŋka]
password	**парола** (f)	[pa'rɔla]
secret	**секрет** (m)	[sɛk'rɛt]
oath (vow)	**клетва** (f)	['klɛtva]
to swear (an oath)	**заклевам се**	[zak'lɛvam sɛ]
promise	**обещание** (n)	[ɔbɛʃtaniɛ]
to promise (vt)	**обещавам**	[ɔbɛʃtavam]
advice (counsel)	**съвет** (m)	[sɪ'vɛt]
to advise (vt)	**съветвам**	[sɪ'vɛtvam]
to follow one's advice	**слушам**	['sluʃʌm]
news	**новина** (f)	[nɔvi'na]
sensation (news)	**сензация** (f)	[sɛn'zaʦija]
information (data)	**сведения** (n pl)	['svɛdɛnija]
conclusion (decision)	**извод** (m)	['izvɔd]
voice	**глас** (m)	[glas]
compliment	**комплимент** (m)	[kɔmpli'mɛnt]
kind (nice)	**любезен**	[ly'bɛzɛn]
word	**дума** (f)	['duma]
phrase	**фраза** (f)	['fraza]
answer	**отговор** (m)	['ɔtgɔvɔr]

truth	**истина** (f)	['istina]
lie	**лъжа** (f)	[lı'ʒa]
thought	**мисъл** (f)	['misıl]
idea (inspiration)	**идея** (f)	[i'dɛja]
fantasy	**измислица** (f)	[iz'mislitsa]

66. Discussion, conversation. Part 2

respected (adj)	**уважаем**	[uva'ʒaɛm]
to respect (vt)	**уважавам**	[uva'ʒavam]
respect	**уважение** (n)	[uva'ʒɛniɛ]
Dear ... (letter)	**Уважаем ...**	[uva'ʒaɛm]
to introduce (present)	**запозная**	[zapɔz'naja]
intention	**намерение** (n)	[namɛ'rɛniɛ]
to intend (have in mind)	**каня се**	['kaɲa sɛ]
wish	**пожелание** (n)	[pɔʒɛ'laniɛ]
to wish (~ good luck)	**пожелая**	[pɔʒɛ'laja]
surprise (astonishment)	**учудване** (n)	[u'ʧudvanɛ]
to surprise (amaze)	**удивлявам**	[udiv'ʎavam]
to be surprised	**удивлявам се**	[udiv'ʎavam sɛ]
to give (vt)	**дам**	[dam]
to take (get hold of)	**взема**	['vzɛma]
to give back	**върна**	['vırna]
to return (give back)	**върна**	['vırna]
to apologize (vi)	**извинявам се**	[izvi'ɲavam sɛ]
apology	**извинение** (n)	[izvi'nɛniɛ]
to forgive (vt)	**прощавам**	[prɔʃ'tavam]
to talk (speak)	**разговарям**	[razgɔ'varʲam]
to listen (vi)	**слушам**	['sluʃʌm]
to hear out	**изслушам**	[iss'luʃʌm]
to understand (vt)	**разбера**	[razbɛ'ra]
to show (display)	**покажа**	[pɔ'kaʒa]
to look at ...	**гледам**	['glɛdam]
to call (with one's voice)	**повикам**	[pɔ'vikam]
to disturb (vt)	**преча**	['prɛʧa]
to pass (to hand sth)	**предам**	[prɛ'dam]
demand (request)	**молба** (f)	[mɔl'ba]
to request (ask)	**моля**	['mɔʎa]
demand (firm request)	**изискване** (n)	[i'ziskvanɛ]
to demand (request firmly)	**изисквам**	[i'ziskvam]
to tease (nickname)	**дразня**	['draznʲa]
to mock (make fun of)	**присмивам се**	[pris'mivam sɛ]

mockery, derision	**подигравка** (f)	[pɔdig'rafka]
nickname	**прякор** (m)	['prʲakɔr]
allusion	**намек** (m)	['namɛk]
to allude (vi)	**намеквам**	[na'mɛkvam]
to imply (vt)	**подразбирам**	[pɔdraz'biram]
description	**описание** (n)	[ɔpi'saniɛ]
to describe (vt)	**опиша**	[ɔ'piʃʌ]
praise (compliments)	**похвала** (f)	[pɔh'vala]
to praise (vt)	**похваля**	[pɔh'vaʎa]
disappointment	**разочарование** (n)	[razɔʧarɔ'vaniɛ]
to disappoint (vt)	**разочаровам**	[razɔʧa'rɔvam]
to be disappointed	**разочаровам се**	[razɔʧa'rɔvam sɛ]
supposition	**предположение** (n)	[prɛdpɔlɔ'ʒɛniɛ]
to suppose (assume)	**предполагам**	[prɛtpɔ'lagam]
warning (caution)	**предпазване** (n)	[prɛd'pazvanɛ]
to warn (vt)	**предпазя**	[prɛt'pazʲa]

67. Discussion, conversation. Part 3

to talk into (convince)	**уговоря**	[ugɔ'vɔrʲa]
to calm down (vt)	**успокоявам**	[uspɔkɔ'jɑvam]
silence (~ is golden)	**мълчание** (n)	[mɪl'ʧaniɛ]
to keep silent	**мълча**	[mɪl'ʧa]
to whisper (vi, vt)	**шепна**	['ʃɛpna]
whisper	**шепот** (m)	['ʃɛpɔt]
frankly, sincerely (adv)	**откровено**	[ɔtkrɔ'vɛnɔ]
in my opinion ...	**според мен ...**	['spɔrɛt mɛn]
detail (of the story)	**подробност** (f)	[pɔd'rɔbnɔst]
detailed (adj)	**подробен**	[pɔd'rɔbɛn]
in detail (adv)	**подробно**	[pɔd'rɔbnɔ]
hint, clue	**подсказка** (f)	[pɔʦ'kaska]
to give a hint	**подскажа**	[pɔʦ'kaʒa]
look (glance)	**поглед** (m)	['pɔglɛd]
to have a look	**погледна**	[pɔg'lɛdna]
fixed (look)	**неподвижен**	[nɛpɔd'viʒɛn]
to blink (vi)	**мигам**	['migam]
to wink (vi)	**мигна**	['migna]
to nod (in assent)	**кимна**	['kimna]
sigh	**въздишка** (f)	[vɪz'diʃka]
to sigh (vi)	**въздъхна**	[vɪz'dɪhna]

to shudder (vi)	**стряскам се**	['strʲaskam sɛ]
gesture	**жест** (m)	[ʒɛst]
to touch (one's arm, etc.)	**докосна се**	[dɔ'kɔsna sɛ]
to seize (by the arm)	**хващам**	['hvaʃtam]
to tap (on the shoulder)	**тупам**	['tupam]
Look out!	**Внимавай!**	[vni'mavaj]
Really?	**Нима?**	[ni'ma]
Good luck!	**Късмет!**	[kɪs'mɛt]
I see!	**Ясно!**	['jɑsnɔ]
It's a pity!	**Жалко!**	['ʒalkɔ]

68. Agreement. Refusal

consent (agreement)	**съгласие** (n)	[sɪg'lasiɛ]
to agree (say yes)	**съгласявам се**	[sɪgla'sʲavam sɛ]
approval	**одобрение** (n)	[ɔdɔb'rɛniɛ]
to approve (vt)	**одобря**	[ɔdɔb'rʲa]
refusal	**отказ** (m)	['ɔtkaz]
to refuse (vi, vt)	**отказвам се**	[ɔt'kazvam sɛ]
Great!	**Отлично!**	[ɔt'litʃnɔ]
All right!	**Добре!**	[dɔb'rɛ]
Okay! (I agree)	**Дадено!**	['dadɛnɔ]
forbidden (adj)	**забранен**	[zabra'nɛn]
it's forbidden	**забранено**	[zabra'nɛnɔ]
incorrect (adj)	**грешен**	['grɛʃɛn]
to reject (~ a demand)	**отклоня**	[ɔtklɔ'ɲa]
to support (cause, idea)	**подкрепям**	[pɔtkrɛ'pʲam]
to accept (~ an apology)	**приема**	[pri'ɛma]
to confirm (vt)	**потвърдя**	[pɔtvɪr'dʲa]
confirmation	**потвърждение** (n)	[pɔtvɪrʒ'dɛniɛ]
permission	**разрешение** (n)	[razrɛ'ʃɛniɛ]
to permit (vt)	**разреша**	[razrɛ'ʃʌ]
decision	**решение** (n)	[rɛ'ʃɛniɛ]
to say nothing	**премълча**	[prɛmɪl'tʃa]
condition (term)	**условие** (n)	[us'lɔviɛ]
excuse (pretext)	**привидна причина** (f)	[pri'vidna pri'tʃina]
praise (compliments)	**похвала** (f)	[pɔh'vala]
to praise (vt)	**похваля**	[pɔh'vaʎa]

69. Success. Good luck. Failure

success	**успех** (m)	[us'pɛh]
successfully (adv)	**успешно**	[us'pɛʃnɔ]

successful (adj)	**успешен**	[us'pεʃεn]
good luck	**сполука** (f)	[spɔ'luka]
Good luck!	**Късмет!**	[kɪs'mεt]
lucky (e.g., ~ day)	**сполучлив**	[spɔlutʃ'lif]
lucky (fortunate)	**успешен**	[us'pεʃεn]
failure	**несполука** (f)	[nεspɔ'luka]
misfortune	**несполука** (f)	[nεspɔ'luka]
bad luck	**нещастие** (n)	[nεʃ'tastiε]
unsuccessful (adj)	**несполучлив**	[nεspɔlutʃ'liv]
catastrophe	**катастрофа** (f)	[katast'rɔfa]
pride	**гордост** (f)	['gɔrdɔst]
proud (adj)	**горд**	[gɔrd]
to be proud	**гордея се**	[gɔr'dεja sε]
winner	**победител** (m)	[pɔbε'ditεl]
to win (vi)	**победя**	[pɔbε'dʲa]
to lose (not win)	**загубя**	[za'gubʲa]
try	**опит** (m)	['ɔpit]
to try (vi)	**опитвам се**	[ɔ'pitvam sε]
chance (opportunity)	**шанс** (m)	[ʃʌns]

70. Quarrels. Negative emotions

shout (scream)	**вик** (m)	[vik]
to shout (vi)	**викам**	['vikam]
to start to cry out	**закрещя**	[zakrεʃ'tʲa]
quarrel	**караница** (f)	['karanitsa]
to quarrel (vi)	**карам се**	['karam sε]
fight (scandal)	**скандал** (m)	[skan'dal]
to have a fight	**правя скандали**	['pravʲa skan'dali]
conflict	**конфликт** (m)	[kɔnf'likt]
misunderstanding	**недоразумение** (n)	[nεdɔrazu'mεniε]
insult	**оскърбление** (n)	[ɔskɪrb'lεniε]
to insult (vt)	**оскърбявам**	[ɔskɪr'bʲavam]
insulted (adj)	**оскърбен**	[ɔskɪr'bεn]
resentment	**обида** (f)	[ɔ'bida]
to offend (vt)	**обидя**	[ɔ'bidʲa]
to take offense	**обидя се**	[ɔ'bidʲa sε]
indignation	**възмущение** (n)	[vɪzmuʃ'tεniε]
to be indignant	**възмущавам се**	[vɪzmuʃ'tavam sε]
complaint	**оплакване** (n)	[ɔp'lakvanε]
to complain (vi, vt)	**оплаквам се**	[ɔp'lakvam sε]
apology	**извинение** (n)	[izvi'nεniε]
to apologize (vi)	**извинявам се**	[izvi'ɲavam sε]

to beg pardon	**моля за прошка**	['mɔʎa za 'prɔʃka]
criticism	**критика** (f)	['kritika]
to criticize (vt)	**критикувам**	[kriti'kuvam]
accusation	**обвинение** (n)	[ɔbvi'nɛniɛ]
to accuse (vt)	**обвинявам**	[ɔbvi'ɲavam]
revenge	**отмъщение** (n)	[ɔtmɪʃ'tɛniɛ]
to revenge (vt)	**отмъщавам**	[ɔtmɪʃ'tavam]
to pay back	**отплатя**	[ɔtpla'tʲa]
disdain	**презрение** (n)	[prɛz'rɛniɛ]
to despise (vt)	**презирам**	[prɛ'ziram]
hatred, hate	**омраза** (f)	[ɔm'raza]
to hate (vt)	**мразя**	['mrazʲa]
nervous (adj)	**нервен**	['nɛrvɛn]
to be nervous	**нервирам се**	[ner'viram sɛ]
angry (mad)	**сърдит**	[sɪr'dit]
to make angry	**разсърдя**	[ras'sɪrdʲa]
humiliation	**унижение** (n)	[uni'ʒɛniɛ]
to humiliate (vt)	**унижавам**	[uni'ʒavam]
to humiliate oneself	**унижавам се**	[uni'ʒavam sɛ]
shock	**шок** (m)	[ʃɔk]
to shock (vt)	**шокирам**	[ʃɔ'kiram]
trouble (annoyance)	**неприятност** (f)	[nɛpri'jɑtnɔst]
unpleasant (adj)	**неприятен**	[nɛpri'jɑtɛn]
fear (dread)	**страх** (m)	[strah]
terrible (storm, heat)	**силен**	['silɛn]
scary (e.g., ~ story)	**страшен**	['straʃɛn]
horror	**ужас** (m)	['uʒas]
awful (crime, news)	**ужасен**	[u'ʒasɛn]
to begin to tremble	**затреперя**	[zatrɛ'pɛrʲa]
to cry (weep)	**плача**	['platʃa]
to start crying	**заплача**	[zap'latʃa]
tear	**сълза** (f)	[sɪl'za]
fault	**вина** (f)	[vi'na]
guilt (feeling)	**вина** (f)	[vi'na]
dishonor (disgrace)	**позор** (m)	[pɔ'zɔr]
protest	**протест** (m)	[prɔ'tɛst]
stress	**стрес** (m)	[strɛs]
to disturb (vt)	**безпокоя**	[bɛspɔkɔ'jɑ]
to be furious	**ядосвам се (на ...)**	[jɑ'dɔsvam sɛ na]
mad, angry (adj)	**зъл**	[zɪl]
to end (~ a relationship)	**прекъсвам**	[prɛ'kɪsvam]
to swear (at sb)	**карам се**	['karam sɛ]

to be scared	**плаша се**	['plaʃʌ sɛ]
to hit (strike with hand)	**ударя**	[u'darʲa]
to fight (vi)	**бия се**	['bijɑ sɛ]
to settle (a conflict)	**урегулирам**	[urɛgu'liram]
discontented (adj)	**недоволен**	[nɛdɔ'vɔlɛn]
furious (adj)	**яростен**	['jɑrɔstɛn]
It's not good!	**Това не е хубаво!**	[tɔ'va nɛ ɛ 'hubavɔ]
It's bad!	**Това е лошо!**	[tɔ'va ɛ 'lɔʃɔ]

Medicine

71. Diseases

sickness	**болест** (f)	['bɔlɛst]
to be sick	**боледувам**	[bɔlɛ'duvam]
health	**здраве** (n)	['zdravɛ]
runny nose (coryza)	**хрема** (f)	['hrɛma]
angina	**ангина** (f)	[a'ŋgina]
cold (illness)	**настинка** (f)	[nas'tiŋka]
to catch a cold	**настина**	[nas'tina]
bronchitis	**бронхит** (m)	[brɔn'hit]
pneumonia	**възпаление** (n) **на белите дробове**	[vɪspa'lɛniɛ na 'bɛlitɛ 'drɔbɔvɛ]
flu, influenza	**грип** (m)	[grip]
near-sighted (adj)	**късоглед**	[kɪsɔg'lɛd]
far-sighted (adj)	**далекоглед**	[dalɛkɔg'lɛd]
strabismus (crossed eyes)	**кривогледство** (n)	[krivɔg'lɛdstvɔ]
cross-eyed (adj)	**кривоглед**	[krivɔg'lɛd]
cataract	**катаракта** (f)	[kata'rakta]
glaucoma	**глаукома** (f)	[glau'kɔma]
stroke	**инсулт** (m)	[in'sult]
heart attack	**инфаркт** (m)	[in'farkt]
myocardial infarction	**инфаркт** (m) **на миокарда**	[in'farkt na miɔ'karda]
paralysis	**парализа** (f)	[pa'raliza]
to paralyze (vt)	**парализирам**	[parali'ziram]
allergy	**алергия** (f)	[a'lɛrgijɑ]
asthma	**астма** (f)	['astma]
diabetes	**диабет** (m)	[dia'bɛt]
toothache	**зъбобол** (m)	[zɪbɔ'bɔl]
caries	**кариес** (m)	['kariɛs]
diarrhea	**диария** (f)	[di'arijɑ]
constipation	**запек** (m)	['zapɛk]
stomach upset	**разстройство** (n) **на стомаха**	[rast'rɔjstvɔ na stɔ'maha]
food poisoning	**отравяне** (n)	[ɔt'ravʲanɛ]
to have a food poisoning	**отровя се**	[ɔt'rɔvʲa sɛ]
arthritis	**артрит** (m)	[art'rit]

rickets	**рахит** (m)	[ra'hit]
rheumatism	**ревматизъм** (m)	[rɛvma'tizɪm]
atherosclerosis	**атеросклероза** (m)	[atɛrɔsklɛ'rɔza]
gastritis	**гастрит** (m)	[gast'rit]
appendicitis	**апандисит** (m)	[apandi'sit]
ulcer	**язва** (f)	['jɑzva]
measles	**дребна шарка** (f)	['drɛbna 'ʃʌrka]
German measles	**шарка** (f)	['ʃʌrka]
jaundice	**жълтеница** (f)	[ʒɪltɛ'niʦa]
hepatitis	**хепатит** (m)	[hɛpa'tit]
schizophrenia	**шизофрения** (f)	[ʃizɔfrɛ'nijɑ]
rabies (hydrophobia)	**бяс** (m)	[bʲas]
neurosis	**невроза** (f)	[nɛv'rɔza]
concussion	**сътресение на мозъка** (n)	[sɪtrɛ'sɛniɛ na 'mɔzɪka]
cancer	**рак** (m)	[rak]
sclerosis	**склероза** (f)	[sklɛ'rɔza]
multiple sclerosis	**множествена склероза** (f)	['mnɔʒɛstvɛna sklɛrɔza]
alcoholism	**алкохолизъм** (m)	[alkɔhɔ'lizɪm]
alcoholic (n)	**алкохолик** (m)	[alkɔhɔ'lik]
syphilis	**сифилис** (m)	['sifilis]
AIDS	**СПИН** (m)	[spin]
tumor	**тумор** (m)	['tumɔr]
malignant (adj)	**злокачествен**	[zlɔ'kaʧəstvɛn]
benign (adj)	**доброкачествен**	[dɔbrɔ'kaʧəstvɛn]
fever	**треска** (f)	['trɛska]
malaria	**малария** (f)	[ma'larijɑ]
gangrene	**гангрена** (f)	[gaŋg'rɛna]
seasickness	**морска болест** (f)	['mɔrska 'bɔlɛst]
epilepsy	**епилепсия** (f)	[ɛpi'lɛpsijɑ]
epidemic	**епидемия** (f)	[ɛpi'dɛmijɑ]
typhus	**тиф** (m)	[tif]
tuberculosis	**туберкулоза** (f)	[tubɛrku'lɔza]
cholera	**холера** (f)	[hɔ'lɛra]
plague (bubonic ~)	**чума** (f)	['ʧuma]

72. Symptoms. Treatments. Part 1

symptom	**симптом** (m)	[simp'tɔm]
temperature	**температура** (f)	[tɛmpɛra'tura]
high temperature	**висока температура** (f)	[vi'sɔka tɛmpɛra'tura]

pulse	**пулс** (m)	[puls]
giddiness	**световъртеж** (m)	[svɛtɔvɪr'tɛʃ]
hot (adj)	**горещ**	[gɔ'rɛʃt]
shivering	**тръпки** (f pl)	['trɪpki]
pale (e.g., ~ face)	**бледен**	['blɛdɛn]
cough	**кашлица** (f)	['kaʃlitsa]
to cough (vi)	**кашлям**	['kaʃʎam]
to sneeze (vi)	**кихам**	['kiham]
faint	**припадък** (m)	[pri'padɪk]
to faint (vi)	**припадна**	[pri'padna]
bruise (hématome)	**синина** (f)	[sini'na]
bump (lump)	**подутина** (f)	[pɔduti'na]
to bruise oneself	**ударя се**	[u'darʲa sɛ]
bruise (contusion)	**натъртване** (n)	[na'tɪrtvanɛ]
to get bruised	**ударя се**	[u'darʲa sɛ]
to limp (vi)	**куцам**	['kutsam]
dislocation	**изкълчване** (n)	[is'kɪltʃvanɛ]
to dislocate (vt)	**навехна**	[na'vɛhna]
fracture	**фрактура** (f)	[frak'tura]
to have a fracture	**счупя**	['stʃupʲa]
cut (e.g., paper ~)	**порязване** (n)	[pɔ'rʲazvanɛ]
to cut oneself	**порежа се**	[pɔ'rɛʒa sɛ]
bleeding	**кръвотечение** (n)	[krɪvɔtɛ'tʃəniɛ]
burn (injury)	**изгаряне** (n)	[iz'garʲanɛ]
to scald oneself	**опаря се**	[ɔ'parʲa se]
to prick (vt)	**бодна**	['bɔdna]
to prick oneself	**убода се**	[ubɔ'da sɛ]
to injure (vt)	**нараня**	[nara'ɲa]
injury	**рана** (f)	['rana]
wound	**рана** (f)	['rana]
trauma	**травма** (f)	['travma]
to be delirious	**бълнувам**	[bɪl'nuvam]
to stutter (vi)	**заеквам**	[za'ɛkvam]
sunstroke	**слънчев удар** (m)	['slɪntʃəv 'udar]

73. Symptoms. Treatments. Part 2

pain	**болка** (f)	['bɔlka]
splinter (in foot, etc.)	**трънче** (m)	['trɪntʃə]
sweat (perspiration)	**пот** (f)	[pɔt]
to sweat (perspire)	**потя се**	[pɔ'tʲa sɛ]
vomiting	**повръщане** (n)	[pɔv'rɪʃtanɛ]

convulsions	**гърчове** (m pl)	['gırʧɔvɛ]
pregnant (adj)	**бременна**	['brɛmɛna]
to be born	**родя се**	[rɔ'dʲa sɛ]
delivery, labor	**раждане** (n)	['raʒdanɛ]
to deliver (~ a baby)	**раждам**	['raʒdam]
abortion	**аборт** (m)	[a'bɔrt]
breathing, respiration	**дишане** (n)	['diʃʌnɛ]
inhalation	**вдишване** (n)	['vdiʃvanɛ]
exhalation	**издишване** (n)	[iz'diʃvanɛ]
to exhale (vi)	**издишам**	[iz'diʃʌm]
to inhale (vi)	**направя вдишване**	[nap'ravʲa 'vdiʃvanɛ]
disabled person	**инвалид** (m)	[inva'lid]
cripple	**сакат човек** (m)	[sa'kat ʧɔ'vɛk]
drug addict	**наркоман** (m)	[narkɔ'man]
deaf (adj)	**глух**	[gluh]
dumb, mute	**ням**	[ɲam]
deaf-and-dumb (adj)	**глухоням**	[gluhɔ'ɲam]
mad, insane (adj)	**луд**	[lut]
madman	**луд** (m)	[lut]
madwoman	**луда** (f)	['luda]
to go insane	**полудея**	[pɔlu'dɛja]
gene	**ген** (m)	[gɛn]
immunity	**имунитет** (m)	[imuni'tɛt]
hereditary (adj)	**наследствен**	[nas'lɛdstvɛn]
congenital (adj)	**вроден**	[vrɔ'dɛn]
virus	**вирус** (m)	['virus]
microbe	**микроб** (m)	[mik'rɔb]
bacterium	**бактерия** (f)	[bak'tɛrija]
infection	**инфекция** (f)	[in'fɛktsija]

74. Symptoms. Treatments. Part 3

hospital	**болница** (f)	['bɔlnitsa]
patient	**пациент** (m)	[patsi'ɛnt]
diagnosis	**диагноза** (f)	[diag'nɔza]
cure	**лекуване** (n)	[lɛ'kuvanɛ]
medical treatment	**лекуване** (n)	[lɛ'kuvanɛ]
to get treatment	**лекувам се**	[lɛ'kuvam sɛ]
to treat (vt)	**лекувам**	[lɛ'kuvam]
to nurse (look after)	**грижа се**	['griʒa sɛ]
care (nursing ~)	**грижа** (f)	['griʒa]
operation, surgery	**операция** (f)	[ɔpɛ'ratsija]
to bandage (head, limb)	**превържа**	[prɛ'vırʒa]

bandaging	**превързване** (n)	[prɛ'vɪrzvane]
vaccination	**ваксиниране** (n)	[vaksi'niranɛ]
to vaccinate (vt)	**ваксинирам**	[vaksi'niram]
injection, shot	**инжекция** (f)	[in'ʒɛktsija]
to give an injection	**инжектирам**	[inʒɛk'tiram]
amputation	**ампутация** (f)	[ampu'tatsija]
to amputate (vt)	**ампутирам**	[ampu'tiram]
coma	**кома** (f)	['kɔma]
to be in a coma	**намирам се в кома**	[na'miram sɛ v 'kɔma]
intensive care	**реанимация** (f)	[rɛani'matsija]
to recover (~ from flu)	**оздравявам**	[ɔzdra'vʲavam]
state (patient's ~)	**състояние** (n)	[sɪstɔ'janiɛ]
consciousness	**съзнание** (n)	[sɪz'naniɛ]
memory (faculty)	**памет** (f)	['pamɛt]
to extract (tooth)	**вадя**	['vadʲa]
filling	**пломба** (f)	['plɔmba]
to fill (a tooth)	**пломбирам**	[plɔm'biram]
hypnosis	**хипноза** (f)	[hip'nɔza]
to hypnotize (vt)	**хипнотизирам**	[hipnɔti'ziram]

75. Doctors

doctor	**лекар** (m)	['lɛkar]
nurse	**медицинска сестра** (f)	[mɛdi'tsinska sɛst'ra]
private physician	**личен лекар** (m)	['litʃən 'lɛkar]
dentist	**зъболекар** (m)	[zɪbɔ'lɛkar]
ophthalmologist	**очен лекар** (m)	['ɔtʃən 'lɛkar]
internist	**терапевт** (m)	[tɛra'pɛvt]
surgeon	**хирург** (m)	[hi'rurg]
psychiatrist	**психиатър** (m)	[psihi'atɪr]
pediatrician	**педиатър** (m)	[pɛdi'atɪr]
psychologist	**психолог** (m)	[psihɔ'lɔg]
gynecologist	**гинеколог** (m)	[ginɛkɔ'lɔg]
cardiologist	**кардиолог** (m)	[kardiɔ'lɔg]

76. Medicine. Drugs. Accessories

medicine, drug	**лекарство** (n)	[lɛ'karstvɔ]
remedy	**средство** (n)	['srɛtstvɔ]
to prescribe (vt)	**предпиша**	[prɛt'piʃʌ]
prescription	**рецепта** (f)	[rɛ'tsəpta]
tablet, pill	**таблетка** (f)	[tab'lɛtka]

ointment	**мехлем** (m)	[mɛh'lɛm]
ampule	**ампула** (f)	[am'pula]
mixture	**микстура** (f)	[miks'tura]
syrup	**сироп** (m)	[si'rɔp]
pill	**хапче** (n)	['haptʃə]
powder	**прах** (m)	[prah]
bandage	**бинт** (m)	[bint]
cotton wool	**памук** (m)	[pa'muk]
iodine	**йод** (m)	[jod]
Band-Aid	**пластир** (m)	[plas'tir]
eyedropper	**капкомер** (m)	[kapkɔ'mɛr]
thermometer	**термометър** (m)	[tɛrmɔ'mɛtɪr]
syringe	**спринцовка** (f)	[sprin'tsɔfka]
wheelchair	**инвалидна количка** (f)	[inva'lidna kɔ'litʃka]
crutches	**патерици** (f pl)	['patɛritsi]
painkiller	**обезболяващо средство** (n)	[ɔbɛzbɔ'ʎavaʃtɔ s'rɛtstvɔ]
laxative	**очистително** (n)	[ɔtʃis'titɛlnɔ]
spirit (ethanol)	**спирт** (m)	[spirt]
medicinal herbs	**билка** (f)	['bilka]
herbal (~ tea)	**билков**	['bilkɔv]

77. Smoking. Tobacco products

tobacco	**тютюн** (m)	[ty'tyn]
cigarette	**цигара** (f)	[tsi'gara]
cigar	**пура** (f)	['pura]
pipe	**лула** (f)	[lu'la]
pack (of cigarettes)	**кутия** (f)	[ku'tija]
matches	**кибрит** (m)	[kib'rit]
matchbox	**кибритена кутийка** (f)	[kib'ritɛna ku'tijka]
lighter	**запалка** (f)	[za'palka]
ashtray	**пепелник** (m)	[pɛpɛl'nik]
cigarette case	**табакера** (f)	[taba'kɛra]
cigarette holder	**мундщук** (m)	[mundʃ'tuk]
filter (cigarette tip)	**филтър** (m)	['filtɪr]
to smoke (vi, vt)	**пуша**	['puʃʌ]
to light a cigarette	**запаля**	[za'paʎa]
smoking	**пушене** (n)	['puʃɛnɛ]
smoker	**пушач** (m)	[pu'ʃʌtʃ]
stub, butt (of cigarette)	**фас** (m)	[fas]
smoke, fumes	**пушек** (m)	['puʃɛk]
ash	**пепел** (f)	['pɛpɛl]

HUMAN HABITAT

City

78. City. Life in the city

city, town	**град** (m)	[grad]
capital city	**столица** (f)	['stɔlitsa]
village	**село** (n)	['sɛlɔ]
city map	**план** (m) **на града**	[plan na gra'da]
downtown	**център** (m) **на града**	['tsəntır na gra'da]
suburb	**предградие** (n)	[prɛdg'radiɛ]
suburban (adj)	**крайградски**	[krajg'radski]
outskirts	**покрайнина** (f)	[pɔkrajni'na]
environs (suburbs)	**околности** (pl)	[ɔ'kɔlnɔsti]
city block	**квартал** (m)	[kvar'tal]
residential block	**жилищен квартал** (m)	['ʒiliʃtɛn kvar'tal]
traffic	**движение** (n)	[dvi'ʒɛniɛ]
traffic lights	**светофар** (m)	[svɛtɔ'far]
public transportation	**градски транспорт** (m)	['gratski trans'pɔrt]
intersection	**кръстовище** (n)	[krıs'tɔviʃtɛ]
crosswalk	**зебра** (f)	['zɛbra]
pedestrian underpass	**подлез** (m)	['pɔdlɛz]
to cross (vt)	**пресичам**	[prɛ'sitʃam]
pedestrian	**пешеходец** (m)	[pɛʃɛ'hɔdɛts]
sidewalk	**тротоар** (m)	[trɔtɔ'ar]
bridge	**мост** (m)	[mɔst]
bank (riverbank)	**кей** (m)	[kɛj]
fountain	**фонтан** (m)	[fɔn'tan]
allée	**алея** (f)	[a'lɛja]
park	**парк** (m)	[park]
boulevard	**булевард** (m)	[bulɛ'vard]
square	**площад** (m)	[plɔʃ'tad]
avenue (wide street)	**голяма широка улица** (f)	[gɔ'ʎama ʃi'rɔka 'ulitsa]
street	**улица** (f)	['ulitsa]
side street	**пресечка** (f)	[prɛ'sɛtʃka]
dead end	**задънена улица** (f)	[za'dınɛna 'ulitsa]
house	**къща** (f)	['kıʃta]
building	**сграда** (f)	['zgrada]

skyscraper	**небостъргач** (m)	[nɛbɔstɪr'gatʃ]
facade	**фасада** (f)	[fa'sada]
roof	**покрив** (m)	['pɔkriv]
window	**прозорец** (m)	[prɔ'zɔrɛts]
arch	**арка** (f)	['arka]
column	**колона** (f)	[kɔ'lɔna]
corner	**ъгъл** (m)	['ɪgɪl]
store window	**витрина** (f)	[vit'rina]
store sign	**табела** (f)	[ta'bɛla]
poster	**афиш** (m)	[a'fiʃ]
advertising poster	**постер** (m)	['pɔstɛr]
billboard	**билборд** (m)	[bil'bɔrd]
garbage, trash	**боклук** (m)	[bɔk'luk]
garbage can	**кошче** (n)	['kɔʃtʃə]
to litter (vi)	**правя боклук**	['pravʲa bɔk'luk]
garbage dump	**сметище** (n)	['smɛtiʃtɛ]
phone booth	**телефонна будка** (f)	[tɛlɛ'fɔŋa 'butka]
lamppost	**стълб** (m) **с фенер**	[stɪlp s fɛ'nɛr]
bench (park ~)	**пейка** (f)	['pɛjka]
police officer	**полицай** (m)	[pɔli'tsaj]
police	**полиция** (f)	[pɔ'litsija]
beggar	**сиромах** (m)	[sirɔ'mah]
homeless, bum	**бездомник** (m)	[bɛz'dɔmnik]

79. Urban institutions

store	**магазин** (m)	[maga'zin]
drugstore, pharmacy	**аптека** (f)	[ap'tɛka]
optical store	**оптика** (f)	['ɔptika]
shopping mall	**търговски център** (m)	[tɪr'gɔvski 'tsəntɪr]
supermarket	**супермаркет** (m)	[supɛr'markɛt]
bakery	**хлебарница** (f)	[hlɛ'barnitsa]
baker	**фурнаджия** (f)	[furna'dʒija]
candy store	**сладкарница** (f)	[slad'karnitsa]
grocery store	**бакалия** (f)	[baka'lija]
butcher shop	**месарница** (f)	[mɛ'sarnitsa]
produce store	**магазинче** (n) **за плодове и зеленчуци**	[maga'zintʃə za plɔdɔ'vɛ i zɛlɛn'tʃutsi]
market	**пазар** (m)	[pa'zar]
coffee house	**кафене** (n)	[kafɛ'nɛ]
restaurant	**ресторант** (m)	[rɛstɔ'rant]
pub	**бирария** (f)	[bi'rarija]
pizzeria	**пицария** (f)	[pitsa'rija]

hair salon	**фризьорски салон** (m)	[fri'zзrski sa'lɔn]
post office	**поща** (f)	['pɔʃta]
dry cleaners	**химическо чистене** (n)	[hi'mitʃəskɔ 'tʃistɛnɛ]
photo studio	**фотостудио** (n)	[fɔtɔs'tudiɔ]
shoe store	**магазин** (m) **за обувки**	[maga'zin za ɔ'bufki]
bookstore	**книжарница** (f)	[kni'ʒarnitsa]
sporting goods store	**магазин** (m) **за спортни стоки**	[maga'zin za 'spɔrtni 'stɔki]
clothes repair	**поправка** (f) **на дрехи**	[pɔp'rafka na 'drɛhi]
formal wear rental	**дрехи** (f pl) **под наем**	['drɛhi pɔd 'naɛm]
movie rental store	**филми** (m pl) **под наем**	['filmi pɔd 'naɛm]
circus	**цирк** (m)	[tsirk]
zoo	**зоологическа градина** (f)	[zɔ:lɔ'gitʃəska gra'dina]
movie theater	**кино** (n)	['kinɔ]
museum	**музей** (m)	[mu'zɛj]
library	**библиотека** (f)	[bibliɔ'tɛka]
theater	**театър** (m)	[tɛ'atır]
opera	**опера** (f)	['ɔpɛra]
nightclub	**нощен клуб** (m)	['nɔʃtɛn klub]
casino	**казино** (n)	[ka'zinɔ]
mosque	**джамия** (f)	[dʒa'mija]
synagogue	**синагога** (f)	[sina'gɔga]
cathedral	**катедрала** (f)	[katɛd'rala]
temple	**храм** (m)	[hram]
church	**църква** (f)	['tsırkva]
college	**институт** (m)	[insti'tut]
university	**университет** (m)	[univɛrsi'tɛt]
school	**училище** (n)	[u'tʃiliʃtɛ]
prefecture	**префектура** (f)	[prɛfɛk'tura]
city hall	**кметство** (n)	['kmɛtstvɔ]
hotel	**хотел** (m)	[hɔ'tɛl]
bank	**банка** (f)	['baŋka]
embassy	**посолство** (n)	[pɔ'sɔlstvɔ]
travel agency	**туристическа агенция** (f)	[turis'titʃəska a'gɛntsija]
information office	**справки** (m pl)	['spravki]
money exchange	**обменно бюро** (n)	[ɔb'mɛŋɔ 'byrɔ]
subway	**метро** (n)	[mɛt'rɔ]
hospital	**болница** (f)	['bɔlnitsa]
gas station	**бензиностанция** (f)	[bɛnzinɔs'tantsija]
parking lot	**паркинг** (m)	['parkiŋg]

80. Signs

store sign	**табела** (f)	[ta'bɛla]
notice (written text)	**надпис** (m)	['nadpis]
poster	**постер** (m)	['pɔstɛr]
direction sign	**указател** (m)	[uka'zatɛl]
arrow (sign)	**стрелка** (f)	[strɛl'ka]
caution	**предпазване** (n)	[prɛd'pazvanɛ]
warning sign	**предупреждение** (n)	[prɛduprɛʒ'dɛniɛ]
to warn (vt)	**предупредя**	[prɛduprɛ'dʲa]
day off	**почивен ден** (m)	[pɔ'ʧivɛn 'dɛn]
timetable (schedule)	**разписание** (n)	[raspi'saniɛ]
opening hours	**работно време** (n)	[ra'bɔtnɔ 'vrɛmɛ]
WELCOME!	**ДОБРЕ ДОШЛИ!**	[dɔb'rɛ dɔʃ'li]
ENTRANCE	**ВХОД**	[vhɔt]
EXIT	**ИЗХОД**	['ishɔt]
PUSH	**БУТНИ**	[but'ni]
PULL	**ДРЪПНИ**	[drɪp'ni]
OPEN	**ОТВОРЕНО**	[ɔt'vɔrɛnɔ]
CLOSED	**ЗАТВОРЕНО**	[zat'vɔrɛnɔ]
WOMEN	**ЖЕНИ**	[ʒɛ'ni]
MEN	**МЪЖЕ**	[mɪ'ʒɛ]
DISCOUNTS	**НАМАЛЕНИЕ**	[nama'lɛniɛ]
SALE	**РАЗПРОДАЖБА**	[resprɔ'daʒba]
NEW!	**НОВА СТОКА**	['nɔva 'stɔka]
FREE	**БЕЗПЛАТНО**	[bɛsp'latnɔ]
ATTENTION!	**ВНИМАНИЕ!**	[vni'maniɛ]
NO VACANCIES	**НЯМА СВОБОДНИ МЕСТА**	['ɲama svɔ'bɔdni mɛs'ta]
RESERVED	**РЕЗЕРВИРАНО**	[rɛzɛr'viranɔ]
ADMINISTRATION	**АДМИНИСТРАЦИЯ**	[administ'raʦija]
STAFF ONLY	**ЗАБРАНЕНО ЗА ВЪНШНИ ЛИЦА**	[zab'ranenɔ za vɛnʃni 'liʦa]
BEWARE OF THE DOG!	**ЗЛО КУЧЕ**	[zlɔ 'kuʧə]
NO SMOKING	**ПУШЕНЕТО ЗАБРАНЕНО!**	[puʃɛ'netɔ zab'ranenɔ]
DO NOT TOUCH!	**НЕ ПИПАЙ!**	[nɛ 'pipaj]
DANGEROUS	**ОПАСНО**	[ɔ'pasnɔ]
DANGER	**ОПАСНОСТ**	[ɔ'pasnɔst]
HIGH TENSION	**ВИСОКО НАПРЕЖЕНИЕ**	[vi'sɔkɔ naprɛ'ʒɛniɛ]
NO SWIMMING!	**КЪПАНЕТО ЗАБРАНЕНО**	['kɪpanɛtɔ zabra'nɛnɔ]

OUT OF ORDER	**НЕ РАБОТИ**	[nɛ ra'bɔti]
FLAMMABLE	**ОГНЕОПАСНО**	[ɔgnɛɔ'pasnɔ]
FORBIDDEN	**ЗАБРАНЕНО**	[zabra'nɛnɔ]
NO TRESPASSING!	**МИНАВАНЕТО ЗАБРАНЕНО**	[mi'navanɛtɔ zabra'nɛnɔ]
WET PAINT	**ПАЗИ СЕ ОТ БОЯТА**	[pazi se ɔt bɔ'jɑta]

81. Urban transportation

bus	**автобус** (m)	[avtɔ'bus]
streetcar	**трамвай** (m)	[tram'vaj]
trolley	**тролей** (m)	[trɔ'lɛj]
route (of bus)	**маршрут** (m)	[marʃ'rut]
number (e.g., bus ~)	**номер** (m)	['nɔmɛr]
to go by ...	**пътувам с ...**	[pı'tuvam s]
to get on (~ the bus)	**качвам се в ...**	['katʃvam sɛ v]
to get off ...	**сляза от ...**	['sʎaza ɔt]
stop (e.g., bus ~)	**спирка** (f)	['spirka]
next stop	**следваща спирка** (f)	['slɛdvaʃta 'spirka]
terminus	**последна спирка** (f)	[pɔs'lɛdna 'spirka]
schedule	**разписание** (n)	[raspi'saniɛ]
to wait (vt)	**чакам**	['tʃakam]
ticket	**билет** (m)	[bi'lɛt]
fare	**цена** (f) **на билета**	[tsə'na na bi'lɛta]
cashier (ticket seller)	**касиер** (m)	[kasi'ɛr]
ticket inspection	**контрола** (f)	[kɔnt'rɔla]
conductor	**контрольор** (m)	[kɔntrɔ'lɜr]
to be late (for ...)	**закъснявам**	[zakıs'ɲavam]
to miss (~ the train, etc.)	**закъснея за ...**	[zakıs'nɛjɑ za]
to be in a hurry	**бързам**	['bırzam]
taxi, cab	**такси** (n)	[tak'si]
taxi driver	**таксиметров шофьор** (m)	[taksi'mɛtrɔf ʃɔfɜr]
by taxi	**с такси**	[s tak'si]
taxi stand	**пиаца** (f) **на такси**	[pi'atsa na tak'si]
to call a taxi	**извикам такси**	[iz'vikam tak'si]
to take a taxi	**взема такси**	['vzɛma tak'si]
traffic	**улично движение** (n)	['ulitʃnɔ dvi'ʒɛniɛ]
traffic jam	**задръстване** (n)	[zad'rıstvanɛ]
rush hour	**час пик** (m)	[tʃas 'pik]
to park (vi)	**паркирам се**	[par'kiram sɛ]
to park (vt)	**паркирам**	['parkiram]
parking lot	**паркинг** (m)	['parkiŋ]

subway	**метро** (n)	[mɛt'rɔ]
station	**станция** (f)	['stantsija]
to take the subway	**пътувам с метро**	[pı'tuvam s mɛt'rɔ]
train	**влак** (m)	[vlak]
train station	**гара** (f)	['gara]

82. Sightseeing

monument	**паметник** (m)	['pamɛtnik]
fortress	**крепост** (f)	['krɛpɔst]
palace	**дворец** (m)	[dvɔ'rɛts]
castle	**замък** (m)	['zamık]
tower	**кула** (f)	['kula]
mausoleum	**мавзолей** (m)	[mavzɔ'lɛj]
architecture	**архитектура** (f)	[arhitɛk'tura]
medieval (adj)	**средновековен**	[srɛdnɔvɛ'kɔvɛn]
ancient (adj)	**старинен**	[sta'rinɛn]
national (adj)	**национален**	[natsiɔ'nalɛn]
well-known (adj)	**известен**	[iz'vɛstɛn]
tourist	**турист** (m)	[tu'rist]
guide (person)	**гид** (m)	[gid]
excursion, guided tour	**екскурзия** (f)	[ɛks'kurzija]
to show (vt)	**показвам**	[pɔ'kazvam]
to tell (vt)	**разказвам**	[ras'kazvam]
to find (vt)	**намеря**	[na'mɛrʲa]
to get lost (lose one's way)	**загубя се**	[za'gubʲa sɛ]
map (e.g., subway ~)	**схема** (f)	['shɛma]
map (e.g., city ~)	**план** (m)	[plan]
souvenir, gift	**сувенир** (m)	[suvɛ'nir]
gift shop	**сувенирен магазин** (m)	[suvɛ'nirɛn maga'zin]
to take pictures	**снимам**	['snimam]
to be photographed	**снимам се**	['snimam sɛ]

83. Shopping

to buy (purchase)	**купувам**	[ku'puvam]
purchase	**покупка** (f)	[pɔ'kupka]
to go shopping	**пазарувам**	[paza'ruvam]
to be open (ab. store)	**магазинът работи**	[maga'zina ra'bɔti]
to be closed	**затваря се**	[zat'varʲa sɛ]
footwear	**обувки** (f pl)	[ɔ'bufki]
clothes, clothing	**облекло** (n)	[ɔblɛk'lɔ]

cosmetics	**козметика** (f)	[kɔz'mɛtika]
food products	**продукти** (m pl)	[prɔ'dukti]
gift, present	**подарък** (m)	[pɔ'darɪk]
salesman	**продавач** (m)	[prɔda'vatʃ]
saleswoman	**продавачка** (f)	[prɔda'vatʃka]
check out, cash desk	**каса** (f)	['kasa]
mirror	**огледало** (n)	[ɔglɛ'dalɔ]
counter (in shop)	**щанд** (m)	[ʃtand]
fitting room	**пробна** (f)	['prɔbna]
to try on	**пробвам**	['prɔbvam]
to fit (ab. dress, etc.)	**подхождам**	[pɔd'hɔʒdam]
to like (I like ...)	**харесвам**	[ha'rɛsvam]
price	**цена** (f)	[ʦə'na]
price tag	**етикет** (m)	[ɛti'kɛt]
to cost (vt)	**струвам**	['struvam]
How much?	**Колко?**	['kɔlkɔ]
discount	**намаление** (n)	[nama'lɛniɛ]
inexpensive (adj)	**нескъп**	[nɛs'kɪp]
cheap (adj)	**евтин**	['ɛftin]
expensive (adj)	**скъп**	[skɪp]
It's expensive	**Това е скъпо**	[tɔ'va ɛ 'skɪpɔ]
rental (n)	**под наем** (m)	[pɔd 'naɛm]
to rent (~ a tuxedo)	**взимам под наем**	['vzimam pɔd 'naɛm]
credit	**кредит** (m)	['krɛdit]
on credit (adv)	**на кредит**	[na 'krɛdit]

84. Money

money	**пари** (pl)	[pa'ri]
currency exchange	**обмяна** (f)	[ɔb'mʲana]
exchange rate	**курс** (m)	[kurs]
ATM	**банкомат** (m)	[baŋkɔ'mat]
coin	**монета** (f)	[mɔ'nɛta]
dollar	**долар** (m)	['dɔlar]
euro	**евро** (n)	['ɛvrɔ]
lira	**лира** (f)	['lira]
Deutschmark	**марка** (f)	['marka]
franc	**франк** (m)	[fraŋk]
pound sterling	**британска лира** (f)	[bri'tanska 'lira]
yen	**йена** (f)	['jəna]
debt	**дълг** (m)	[dɪlg]
debtor	**длъжник** (m)	[dlɪʒ'nik]

to lend (money)	**давам на заем**	['davam na 'zaɛm]
to borrow (vi, vt)	**взема на заем**	['vzɛma na 'zaɛm]
bank	**банка** (f)	['baŋka]
account	**сметка** (f)	['smɛtka]
to deposit into the account	**внеса в сметка**	[vnɛ'sa v 'smɛtka]
credit card	**кредитна карта** (f)	['krɛditna 'karta]
cash	**налични пари** (pl)	[na'litʃni pa'ri]
check	**чек** (m)	[tʃek]
to write a check	**подпиша чек**	[pɔt'piʃʌ tʃək]
checkbook	**чекова книжка** (f)	['tʃəkɔva 'kniʃka]
wallet	**портфейл** (m)	[pɔrt'fɛjl]
change purse	**портмоне** (n)	[pɔrtmɔ'nɛ]
safe	**сейф** (m)	[sɛjf]
heir	**наследник** (m)	[nas'lɛdnik]
inheritance	**наследство** (n)	[nas'lɛdstvɔ]
fortune (wealth)	**състояние** (n)	[sɪstɔ'janiɛ]
lease, rent	**наем** (m)	['naɛm]
rent money	**наем** (m)	['naɛm]
to rent (sth from sb)	**наемам**	[na'ɛmam]
price	**цена** (f)	[tsə'na]
cost	**стойност** (f)	['stɔjnɔst]
sum	**сума** (f)	['suma]
to spend (vt)	**харча**	['hartʃa]
expenses	**разходи** (m pl)	['rashɔdi]
to economize (vi, vt)	**пестя**	[pɛs'tʲa]
economical	**пестелив**	[pɛstɛ'lif]
to pay (vi, vt)	**плащам**	['plaʃtam]
payment	**плащане** (n)	['plaʃtanɛ]
change (give the ~)	**ресто** (n)	['rɛstɔ]
tax	**данък** (m)	['danɪk]
fine	**глоба** (f)	['glɔba]
to fine (vt)	**глобявам**	[glɔ'bʲavam]

85. Post. Postal service

post office	**поща** (f)	['pɔʃta]
mail (letters, etc.)	**поща** (f)	['pɔʃta]
mailman	**пощальон** (m)	[pɔʃta'lɜn]
opening hours	**работно време** (n)	[ra'bɔtnɔ 'vrɛmɛ]
letter	**писмо** (n)	[pis'mɔ]
registered letter	**препоръчано писмо** (n)	[prɛpɔ'rɪtʃanɔ pis'mɔ]

postcard	**картичка** (f)	['kartitʃka]
telegram	**телеграма** (f)	[tɛlɛg'rama]
parcel	**колет** (m)	[kɔ'lɛt]
money transfer	**паричен превод** (m)	[pa'ritʃən 'prɛvɔd]
to receive (vt)	**получа**	[pɔ'lutʃa]
to send (vt)	**изпратя**	[isp'ratʲa]
sending	**изпращане** (n)	[isp'raʃtanɛ]
address	**адрес** (m)	[ad'rɛs]
ZIP code	**пощенски код** (m)	['pɔʃtɛnski kɔd]
sender	**подател** (m)	[pɔ'datɛl]
receiver, addressee	**получател** (m)	[pɔlu'tʃatɛl]
name	**име** (n)	['imɛ]
family name	**фамилия** (f)	[fa'milijɑ]
rate (of postage)	**тарифа** (f)	[ta'rifa]
standard (adj)	**обикновен**	[ɔbiknɔ'vɛn]
economical (adj)	**икономичен**	[ikɔnɔ'mitʃən]
weight	**тегло** (n)	[tɛg'lɔ]
to weigh up (vt)	**претеглям**	[prɛ'tɛgʎam]
envelope	**плик** (m)	[plik]
postage stamp	**марка** (f)	['marka]

Dwelling. House. Home

86. House. Dwelling

house	**къща** (f)	['kɪʃta]
at home (adv)	**вкъщи**	['vkɪʃti]
courtyard	**двор** (m)	[dvɔr]
fence	**ограда** (f)	[ɔg'rada]
brick (n)	**тухла** (f)	['tuhla]
brick (as adj)	**тухлен**	['tuhlɛn]
stone (n)	**камък** (m)	['kamɪk]
stone (as adj)	**каменен**	['kamɛnɛn]
concrete (n)	**бетон** (m)	[bɛ'tɔn]
concrete (as adj)	**бетонен**	[bɛ'tɔnɛn]
new (new-built)	**нов**	[nɔv]
old (adj)	**стар**	[star]
decrepit (house)	**вехт**	[vɛht]
modern (adj)	**съвременен**	[sɪv'rɛmɛnɛn]
multistory (adj)	**многоетажен**	[mnɔgɔɛ'taʒɛn]
high (adj)	**висок**	[vi'sɔk]
floor, story	**етаж** (m)	[ɛ'taʒ]
single-story (adj)	**едноетажен**	[ɛdnɔɛ'taʒɛn]
ground floor	**долен етаж** (m)	['dɔlɛn ɛ'taʒ]
top floor	**горен етаж** (m)	['gɔrɛn ɛ'taʒ]
roof	**покрив** (m)	['pɔkriv]
chimney (stack)	**тръба** (f)	[trɪ'ba]
roof tiles	**керемида** (f)	[kɛrɛ'mida]
tiled (adj)	**керемиден**	[kɛrɛ'midɛn]
loft (attic)	**таван** (m)	[ta'van]
window	**прозорец** (m)	[prɔ'zɔrɛʦ]
glass	**стъкло** (n)	[stɪk'lɔ]
window ledge	**перваз** (m) **за прозорец**	[pɛr'vas za prɔ'zɔrɛʦ]
shutters	**капаци** (m pl)	[ka'paʦi]
wall	**стена** (f)	[stɛ'na]
balcony	**балкон** (m)	[bal'kɔn]
downspout	**улук** (m)	[u'luk]
upstairs (to be ~)	**горе**	['gɔrɛ]
to go upstairs	**качвам се**	['kaʧvam sɛ]
to come down	**слизам**	['slizam]
to move (to new premises)	**премествам се**	[prɛ'mɛstvam sɛ]

87. House. Entrance. Lift

entrance	**вход** (m)	[vhɔd]
stairs (stairway)	**стълба** (f)	['stɪlba]
steps	**стъпала** (n pl)	[stɪpa'la]
banisters	**парапет** (m)	[para'pɛt]
lobby (hotel ~)	**хол** (m)	[hɔl]
mailbox	**пощенска кутия** (f)	['pɔʃtɛnska ku'tijɑ]
trash container	**контейнер** (m) **за отпадъци**	[kɔn'tɛjnɛr za ɔt'padɪtsi]
trash chute	**шахта** (f) **за боклук**	['ʃʌhta za bɔk'luk]
elevator	**асансьор** (m)	[asan'sɜr]
freight elevator	**товарен асансьор** (m)	[tɔ'varɛn asan'sɜr]
elevator cage	**кабина** (f)	[ka'bina]
to take the elevator	**возя се в асансьора**	['vɔzʲa sɛ v asan'sɜra]
apartment	**апартамент** (m)	[aparta'mɛnt]
residents, inhabitants	**живущи** (m pl)	[ʒi'vuʃti]
neighbor (masc.)	**съсед** (m)	[sɪ'sɛd]
neighbor (fem.)	**съседка** (f)	[sɪ'sɛdka]
neighbors	**съседи** (m pl)	[sɪ'sɛdi]

88. House. Electricity

electricity	**електричество** (n)	[ɛlɛkt'ritʃəstvɔ]
light bulb	**крушка** (f)	['kruʃka]
switch	**изключвател** (m)	[izklytʃ'vatɛl]
fuse	**бушон** (m)	[bu'ʃɔn]
cable, wire (electric ~)	**кабел** (m)	['kabɛl]
wiring	**инсталация** (f)	[insta'latsijɑ]
electricity meter	**електромер** (m)	[ɛlektrɔ'mer]
readings	**показание** (n)	[pɔka'zaniɛ]

89. House. Doors. Locks

door	**врата** (f)	[vra'ta]
vehicle gate	**порта** (f)	['pɔrta]
handle, doorknob	**дръжка** (f)	['drɪʃka]
to unlock (unbolt)	**отключа**	[ɔtk'lytʃa]
to open (vt)	**отварям**	[ɔt'varʲam]
to close (vt)	**затварям**	[zat'varʲam]
key	**ключ** (m)	[klytʃ]
bunch (of keys)	**връзка** (f)	['vrɪska]

to creak (door hinge)	**скърцам**	['skırtsam]
creak	**скърцане** (n)	['skırtsanɛ]
hinge (of door)	**панта** (f)	['panta]
doormat	**килимче** (n)	[ki'limtʃə]
door lock	**брава** (f)	['brava]
keyhole	**ключалка** (f)	[kly'tʃalka]
bolt (sliding bar)	**резе** (n)	[rɛ'zɛ]
door latch	**резе** (n)	[rɛ'zɛ]
padlock	**катинар** (m)	[kati'nar]
to ring (~ the door bell)	**звъня**	[zvı'ɲa]
ringing (sound)	**звънец** (m)	[zvı'nets]
doorbell	**звънец** (m)	[zvı'nets]
doorbell button	**бутон** (m)	[bu'tɔn]
knock (at the door)	**чукане** (n)	['tʃukanɛ]
to knock (vi)	**чукам**	['tʃukam]
code	**код** (m)	[kɔd]
code lock	**брава** (f) **с код**	['brava s kɔd]
door phone	**домофон** (m)	[dɔmɔ'fɔn]
number (on the door)	**номер** (m)	['nɔmɛr]
doorplate	**табелка** (f)	[ta'bɛlka]
peephole	**шпионка** (f)	[ʃpi'ɔŋka]

90. Country house

village	**село** (n)	['sɛlɔ]
vegetable garden	**зеленчукова градина** (f)	[zɛlɛn'tʃukɔva gra'dina]
fence	**ограда** (f)	[ɔg'rada]
picket fence	**плет** (m)	[plɛt]
wicket gate	**вратичка** (f) **на ограда**	[vra'titʃka na ɔg'rada]
granary	**хамбар** (m)	[ham'bar]
cellar	**мазе** (n)	[ma'zɛ]
shed (in garden)	**плевня** (f)	['plɛvɲa]
well (water)	**кладенец** (m)	['kladɛnɛts]
stove (wood-fired ~)	**печка** (f)	['pɛtʃka]
to stoke the stove	**паля**	['paʎa]
firewood	**дърва** (pl)	[dır'va]
log (firewood)	**цепеница** (f)	['tsəpɛnitsa]
veranda, stoop	**веранда** (f)	[vɛ'randa]
terrace (patio)	**тераса** (f)	[tɛ'rasa]
swing (hanging seat)	**люлка** (f)	['lylka]

91. Villa. Mansion

country house	**извънградска къща** (f)	[izvɪŋ'ratska 'kɪʃta]
villa (by sea)	**вила** (f)	['vila]
wing (of building)	**крило** (n)	[kri'lɔ]
garden	**градина** (f)	[gra'dina]
park	**парк** (m)	[park]
tropical greenhouse	**оранжерия** (f)	[ɔran'ʒɛrijɑ]
to look after (garden, etc.)	**грижа се**	['griʒa sɛ]
swimming pool	**басейн** (m)	[ba'sɛjn]
gym	**спортна зала** (f)	['spɔrtna 'zala]
tennis court	**тенис корт** (m)	['tɛnis kɔrt]
home theater room	**кинотеатър** (m)	['kinɔtɛ'atɪr]
garage	**гараж** (m)	[ga'raʒ]
private property	**частна собственост** (f)	['ʧasna 'sɔpstvɛnɔst]
private land	**частни владения** (n pl)	['ʧasni vla'dɛnijɑ]
warning (caution)	**предупреждение** (n)	[prɛduprɛʒ'dɛniɛ]
warning sign	**предупредителен надпис** (m)	[prɛduprɛ'ditɛlɛn 'natpis]
security	**охрана** (f)	[ɔh'rana]
security guard	**охранител** (m)	[ɔhra'nitɛl]
burglar alarm	**сигнализация** (f)	[signali'zaʦijɑ]

92. Castle. Palace

castle	**замък** (m)	['zamɪk]
palace	**дворец** (m)	[dvɔ'rɛʦ]
fortress	**крепост** (f)	['krɛpɔst]
wall (round castle)	**стена** (f)	[stɛ'na]
tower	**кула** (f)	['kula]
keep, donjon	**главна кула** (f)	['glavna 'kula]
portcullis	**подемна врата** (f)	[pɔ'dɛmna vra'ta]
underground passage	**подземен проход** (m)	[pɔ'ʣɛmɛn 'prɔhɔt]
moat	**ров** (m)	[rɔv]
chain	**верига** (f)	[vɛ'riga]
arrow loop	**бойница** (f)	[bɔj'niʦa]
magnificent (adj)	**великолепен**	[vɛlikɔ'lɛpɛn]
majestic (adj)	**величествен**	[vɛ'liʧəstvɛn]
impregnable (adj)	**непристъпен**	[nɛpris'tɪpɛn]
medieval (adj)	**средновековен**	[srɛdnɔvɛ'kɔvɛn]

93. Apartment

apartment	**апартамент** (m)	[aparta'mɛnt]
room	**стая** (f)	['staja]
bedroom	**спалня** (f)	['spalɲa]
dining room	**столова** (f)	[stɔlɔ'va]
living room	**гостна** (f)	['gɔstna]
study (home office)	**кабинет** (m)	[kabi'nɛt]
entry room	**антре** (n)	[ant'rɛ]
bathroom	**баня** (f)	['baɲa]
half bath	**тоалетна** (f)	[tɔa'lɛtna]
ceiling	**таван** (m)	[ta'van]
floor	**под** (m)	[pɔd]
corner	**ъгъл** (m)	['ɪgɪl]

94. Apartment. Cleaning

to clean (vi, vt)	**подреждам**	[pɔd'rɛʒdam]
dust	**прах** (f)	[prah]
dusty (adj)	**прашен**	['praʃɛn]
to dust (vt)	**изтривам прах**	[ist'rivam prah]
vacuum cleaner	**прахосмукачка** (f)	[prahɔsmu'katʃka]
to vacuum (vt)	**почиствам с прахосмукачка**	[pɔ'tʃistvam s prahɔsmu'katʃka]
to sweep (vi, vt)	**мета**	[mɛ'ta]
sweepings	**боклук** (m)	[bɔk'luk]
order	**ред** (m)	[rɛd]
disorder, mess	**безпорядък** (m)	[bɛzpɔ'rʲadɪk]
mop	**четка** (f) **за под**	['tʃətka za pɔd]
dust cloth	**парцал** (m)	[par'tsal]
broom	**метла** (f)	[mɛt'la]
dustpan	**лопатка** (f) **за боклук**	[lɔ'patka za bɔk'luk]

95. Furniture. Interior

furniture	**мебели** (pl)	['mɛbɛli]
table	**маса** (f)	['masa]
chair	**стол** (m)	[stɔl]
bed	**легло** (n)	[lɛg'lɔ]
couch, sofa	**диван** (m)	[di'van]
armchair	**фотьойл** (m)	[fɔ'tʲɔjl]
bookcase	**книжен шкаф** (m)	['kniʒɛn ʃkaf]
shelf	**рафт** (m)	[raft]

set of shelves	**етажерка** (f)	[ɛta'ʒɛrka]
wardrobe	**гардероб** (m)	[gardɛ'rɔb]
coat rack	**закачалка** (f)	[zaka'ʧalka]
coat stand	**закачалка** (f)	[zaka'ʧalka]
dresser	**скрин** (m)	[skrin]
coffee table	**малка масичка** (f)	['malka 'masiʧka]
mirror	**огледало** (n)	[ɔglɛ'dalɔ]
carpet	**килим** (m)	[ki'lim]
rug, small carpet	**килимче** (n)	[ki'limʧə]
fireplace	**камина** (f)	[ka'mina]
candle	**свещ** (m)	[svɛʃt]
candlestick	**свещник** (m)	['svɛʃtnik]
drapes	**пердета** (n pl)	[pɛr'dɛta]
wallpaper	**тапети** (m pl)	[ta'pɛti]
blinds (jalousie)	**щора** (f)	['ʃtɔra]
table lamp	**лампа** (f) **за маса**	['lampa za 'masa]
wall lamp (sconce)	**светилник** (m)	[svɛ'tilnik]
floor lamp	**лампион** (m)	[lampi'ɔn]
chandelier	**полилей** (m)	[pɔli'lɛj]
leg (of chair, table)	**крак** (f)	[krak]
armrest	**подлакътник** (m)	[pɔd'lakıtnik]
back (backrest)	**облегалка** (f)	[ɔblɛ'galka]
drawer	**чекмедже** (n)	[ʧəkmɛ'ʤɛ]

96. Bedding

bedclothes	**спално бельо** (n)	['spalnɔ bɛ'lɜ]
pillow	**възглавница** (f)	[vızg'lavniʦa]
pillowcase	**калъфка** (f)	[ka'lıfka]
blanket (comforter)	**одеяло** (n)	[ɔdɛ'jalɔ]
sheet	**чаршаф** (m)	[ʧar'ʃʌf]
bedspread	**завивка** (f)	[za'vivka]

97. Kitchen

kitchen	**кухня** (f)	['kuhɲa]
gas	**газ** (m)	[gas]
gas cooker	**газова печка** (f)	['gazɔva 'pɛʧka]
electric cooker	**електрическа печка** (f)	[ɛlɛkt'riʧəska 'pɛʧka]
oven	**фурна** (f)	['furna]
microwave oven	**микровълнова печка** (f)	[mikrɔ'vılnɔva 'pɛʧka]
refrigerator	**хладилник** (m)	[hla'dilnik]

freezer	**фризер** (m)	[ˈfrizɛr]
dishwasher	**съдомиялна машина** (f)	[sɪdɔmiˈjɑlna maˈʃina]
meat grinder	**месомелачка** (f)	[mɛsɔmɛˈlatʃka]
juicer	**сокоизстисквачка** (f)	[sɔkɔizstiskˈvatʃka]
toaster	**тостер** (m)	[ˈtɔstɛr]
mixer	**миксер** (m)	[ˈmiksɛr]
coffee maker	**кафеварка** (f)	[kafɛˈvarka]
coffee pot	**кафеник** (m)	[kafɛˈnik]
coffee grinder	**кафемелачка** (f)	[kafɛmɛˈlatʃka]
kettle	**чайник** (m)	[ˈtʃajnik]
teapot	**чайник** (m)	[ˈtʃajnik]
lid	**капачка** (f)	[kaˈpatʃka]
tea strainer	**цедка** (f)	[ˈtsətka]
spoon	**лъжица** (f)	[lɪˈʒitsa]
teaspoon	**чаена лъжица** (f)	[ˈtʃaɛna lɪˈʒitsa]
tablespoon	**супена лъжица** (f)	[ˈsupɛna lɪˈʒitsa]
fork	**вилица** (f)	[ˈvilitsa]
knife	**нож** (m)	[nɔʒ]
tableware (dishes)	**съдове** (m pl)	[ˈsɪdɔvɛ]
plate (dinner ~)	**чиния** (f)	[tʃiˈnijɑ]
saucer	**малка чинийка** (f)	[ˈmalka tʃiˈnijka]
shot glass	**чашка** (f)	[ˈtʃaʃka]
glass (~ of water)	**чаша** (f)	[ˈtʃaʃʌ]
cup	**чаша** (f)	[ˈtʃaʃʌ]
sugar bowl	**захарница** (f)	[zaharˈnitsa]
salt shaker	**солница** (f)	[sɔlˈnitsa]
pepper shaker	**пиперница** (f)	[piˈpɛrnitsa]
butter dish	**съд** (m) **за краве масло**	[sɪt za ˈkravɛ masˈlɔ]
saucepan	**тенджера** (f)	[ˈtɛndʒɛra]
frying pan	**тиган** (m)	[tiˈgan]
ladle	**черпак** (m)	[tʃərˈpak]
colander	**гевгир** (m)	[gɛvˈgir]
tray	**табла** (f)	[ˈtabla]
bottle	**бутилка** (f)	[buˈtilka]
jar (glass)	**буркан** (m)	[burˈkan]
can	**тенекия** (f)	[tɛnɛˈkijɑ]
bottle opener	**отварачка** (f)	[ɔtvaˈratʃka]
can opener	**отварачка** (f)	[ɔtvaˈratʃka]
corkscrew	**тирбушон** (m)	[tirbuˈʃɔn]
filter	**филтър** (m)	[ˈfiltɪr]
to filter (vt)	**филтрирам**	[filtˈriram]
trash	**боклук** (m)	[bɔkˈluk]
trash can	**кофа** (f) **за боклук**	[ˈkɔfa za bɔkˈluk]

98. Bathroom

bathroom	**баня** (f)	['baɲa]
water	**вода** (f)	[vɔ'da]
tap, faucet	**смесител** (m)	[smɛ'sitɛl]
hot water	**топла вода** (f)	['tɔpla vɔ'da]
cold water	**студена вода** (f)	[stu'dɛna vɔ'da]
toothpaste	**паста** (f) **за зъби**	['pasta za 'zɪbi]
to brush one's teeth	**мия си зъбите**	['mijɑ si 'zɪbitɛ]
to shave (vi)	**бръсна се**	['brɪsna sɛ]
shaving foam	**пяна** (f) **за бръснене**	['pʲana za 'brɪsnɛnɛ]
razor	**бръснач** (m)	[brɪs'natʃ]
to wash (one's hands, etc.)	**мия**	['mijɑ]
to take a bath	**мия се**	['mijɑ sɛ]
shower	**душ** (m)	[duʃ]
to take a shower	**вземам душ**	['vzɛmam duʃ]
bathtub	**вана** (f)	['vana]
toilet (toilet bowl)	**тоалетна чиния** (f)	[tɔa'lɛtna tʃi'nijɑ]
sink (washbasin)	**мивка** (f)	['mivka]
soap	**сапун** (m)	[sa'pun]
soap dish	**сапуниерка** (f)	[sapuni'ɛrka]
sponge	**гъба** (f)	['gɪba]
shampoo	**шампоан** (m)	[ʃʌmpɔ'an]
towel	**кърпа** (f)	['kɪrpa]
bathrobe	**хавлиен халат** (m)	[hav'lien ha'lat]
laundry (process)	**пране** (n)	[pra'nɛ]
washing machine	**перална машина** (f)	[pɛ'ralna ma'ʃina]
to do the laundry	**пера**	[pɛ'ra]
laundry detergent	**прах** (m) **за пране**	[prah za pra'nɛ]

99. Household appliances

TV set	**телевизор** (m)	[tɛlɛ'vizɔr]
tape recorder	**касетофон** (m)	[kasɛtɔ'fɔn]
video, VCR	**видео** (n)	['vidɛɔ]
radio	**радиоприемник** (m)	[radiɔpri'ɛmnik]
player (CD, MP3, etc.)	**плейър** (m)	['plɛɪr]
video projector	**прожекционен апарат** (m)	[prɔʒɛktsi'ɔnɛn apa'rat]
home movie theater	**домашно кино** (n)	[dɔ'maʃnɔ 'kinɔ]
DVD player	**DVD плейър** (m)	[divi'di 'plɛɪr]

amplifier	**усилвател** (m)	[usil'vatɛl]
video game console	**игрова приставка** (f)	[igrɔ'va pris'tafka]
video camera	**видеокамера** (f)	[vidɛɔ'kamɛra]
camera (photo)	**фотоапарат** (m)	[fɔtɔapa'rat]
digital camera	**цифров фотоапарат** (m)	['ʦifrɔv fɔtɔapa'rat]
vacuum cleaner	**прахосмукачка** (f)	[prahɔsmu'katʧka]
iron (e.g., steam ~)	**ютия** (f)	[ju'tijɑ]
ironing board	**дъска** (f) **за гладене**	[dɪs'ka za 'gladɛnɛ]
telephone	**телефон** (m)	[tɛlɛ'fɔn]
mobile phone	**мобилен телефон** (m)	[mɔ'bilɛn tɛlɛ'fɔn]
typewriter	**пишеща машинка** (f)	['piʃɛʃta ma'ʃiŋka]
sewing machine	**шевна машина** (f)	['ʃɛvna ma'ʃina]
microphone	**микрофон** (m)	[mikrɔ'fɔn]
headphones	**слушалки** (f pl)	[slu'ʃʌlki]
remote control (TV)	**пулт** (m)	[pult]
CD, compact disc	**CD диск** (m)	[si'di disk]
cassette	**касета** (f)	[ka'sɛta]
vinyl record	**плоча** (f)	['plɔʧa]

100. Repairs. Renovation

renovations	**ремонт** (m)	[rɛ'mɔnt]
to renovate (vt)	**правя ремонт**	['prav'a rɛ'mɔnt]
to repair (vt)	**ремонтирам**	[rɛmɔn'tiram]
to put in order	**подреждам**	[pɔd'rɛʒdam]
to redo (do again)	**преправям**	[prɛp'rav'am]
paint	**боя** (f)	[bɔ'jɑ]
to paint (~ a wall)	**боядисвам**	[bɔjɑ'disvam]
house painter	**бояджия** (m)	[bɔjɑ'ʤijɑ]
paintbrush	**четка** (f)	['ʧetka]
whitewash	**вар** (f)	[var]
to whitewash (vt)	**варосвам**	[va'rɔsvam]
wallpaper	**тапети** (m pl)	[ta'pɛti]
to wallpaper (vt)	**слагам тапети**	['slagam ta'pɛti]
varnish	**лак** (m)	[lak]
to varnish (vt)	**лакирам**	[la'kiram]

101. Plumbing

water	**вода** (f)	[vɔ'da]
hot water	**топла вода** (f)	['tɔpla vɔ'da]

cold water	**студена вода** (f)	[stu'dɛna vɔ'da]
tap, faucet	**смесител** (m)	[smɛ'sitɛl]
drop (of water)	**капка** (f)	['kapka]
to drip (vi)	**капя**	['kapʲa]
to leak (ab. pipe)	**тека**	[tɛ'ka]
leak (pipe ~)	**теч** (f)	[tɛʧ]
puddle	**локва** (f)	['lɔkva]
pipe	**тръба** (f)	[trı'ba]
stop valve	**вентил** (m)	['vɛntil]
to be clogged up	**запуша се**	[za'puʃʌ sɛ]
tools	**инструменти** (m pl)	[instru'mɛnti]
adjustable wrench	**раздвижен ключ** (m)	[razd'viʒen klyʧ]
to unscrew, untwist (vt)	**отвъртам**	[ɔt'vırtam]
to screw (tighten)	**завъртам**	[za'vırtam]
to unclog (vt)	**отпушвам**	[ɔt'puʃvam]
plumber	**водопроводчик** (m)	[vɔdɔprɔ'vɔdʧik]
basement	**мазе** (n)	[ma'zɛ]
sewerage (system)	**канализация** (f)	[kanali'zaʦija]

102. Fire. Conflagration

fire (to catch ~)	**огън** (m)	['ɔgın]
flame	**пламък** (m)	['plamık]
spark	**искра** (f)	[isk'ra]
smoke (from fire)	**пушек** (m)	['puʃɛk]
torch (flaming stick)	**факел** (m)	['fakɛl]
campfire	**клада** (f)	['klada]
gas, gasoline	**бензин** (m)	[bɛn'zin]
kerosene (for aircraft)	**газ** (f)	[gaz]
flammable (adj)	**горивен**	[gɔ'riven]
explosive (adj)	**взривоопасен**	[vzrivɔ:'pasɛn]
NO SMOKING	**ПУШЕНЕТО ЗАБРАНЕНО!**	[puʃɛ'netɔ zab'ranenɔ]
safety	**безопасност** (f)	[bɛzɔ'pasnɔst]
danger	**опасност** (f)	[ɔ'pasnɔst]
dangerous (adj)	**опасен**	[ɔ'pasɛn]
to catch fire	**запаля се**	[za'paʎa sɛ]
explosion	**експлозия** (f)	[ɛksp'lɔzija]
to set fire	**подпаля**	[pɔd'paʎa]
incendiary (arsonist)	**подпалвач** (m)	[pɔdpal'vaʧ]
arson	**подпалване** (n)	[pɔd'palvanɛ]
to blaze (vi)	**пламтя**	[plam'tʲa]
to burn (be on fire)	**горя**	[gɔ'rʲa]

to burn down	**изгоря**	[izgɔ'rʲa]
fireman	**пожарникар** (m)	[pɔʒarni'kar]
fire truck	**пожарна кола** (f)	[pɔ'ʒarna kɔ'la]
fire department	**пожарен екип** (f)	[pɔ'ʒarɛn ɛ'kip]
fire truck ladder	**пожарна стълба** (f)	[pɔ'ʒarna 'stɪlba]
fire hose	**маркуч** (m)	[mar'kuʧ]
fire extinguisher	**пожарогасител** (m)	[pɔʒarɔga'sitɛl]
helmet	**каска** (f)	['kaska]
siren	**сирена** (f)	[si'rɛna]
to call out	**викам**	['vikam]
to call for help	**викам за помощ**	['vikam za 'pɔmɔʃt]
rescuer	**спасител** (m)	[spa'sitɛl]
to rescue (vt)	**спасявам**	[spa'sʲavam]
to arrive (vi)	**пристигна**	[pris'tigna]
to extinguish (vt)	**загасявам**	[zaga'sʲavam]
water	**вода** (f)	[vɔ'da]
sand	**пясък** (m)	['pʲasɪk]
ruins (destruction)	**руини** (pl)	[rui'ni]
to collapse (building, etc.)	**рухна**	['ruhna]
to fall down (vi)	**срутя се**	['srutʲa sɛ]
to cave in (ceiling, floor)	**съборя се**	[sɪ'bɔrʲa sɛ]
piece of wreckage	**отломка** (f)	[ɔt'lɔmka]
ash	**пепел** (f)	['pɛpɛl]
to suffocate (die)	**задуша се**	[zadu'ʃʌ sɛ]
to be killed (perish)	**загина**	[za'gina]

HUMAN ACTIVITIES

Job. Business. Part 1

103. Office. Working in the office

office (of firm)	**офис** (m)	['ɔfis]
office (of director, etc.)	**кабинет** (m)	[kabi'nɛt]
front desk	**рецепция** (f)	[rɛ'tsəptsija]
secretary	**секретар** (m)	[sɛkrɛ'tar]
director	**директор** (m)	[di'rɛktɔr]
manager	**мениджър** (m)	['mɛnidʒır]
accountant	**счетоводител** (m)	[stʃətɔvɔ'ditɛl]
employee	**сътрудник** (m)	[sıt'rudnik]
furniture	**мебели** (pl)	['mɛbɛli]
desk	**маса** (f)	['masa]
desk chair	**фотьойл** (m)	[fɔ'tɜjl]
chest of drawers	**шкафче** (n)	['ʃkaftʃə]
coat stand	**закачалка** (f)	[zaka'tʃalka]
computer	**компютър** (m)	[kɔm'pytır]
printer	**принтер** (m)	['printɛr]
fax machine	**факс** (m)	[faks]
photocopier	**ксерокс** (m)	['ksɛrɔks]
paper	**хартия** (f)	[har'tija]
office supplies	**канцеларски принадлежности** (f pl)	[kantsə'larski prinad'lɛʒnɔsti]
mouse pad	**подложка** (f) **за мишка**	[pɔd'lɔʃka za 'miʃka]
sheet (of paper)	**лист** (m)	[list]
catalog	**каталог** (m)	[kata'lɔg]
phone book (directory)	**справочник** (m)	[spra'vɔtʃnik]
documentation	**документация** (f)	[dɔkumɛn'tatsija]
brochure (e.g., 12 pages ~)	**брошура** (f)	[brɔ'ʃura]
leaflet	**листовка** (f)	[lis'tɔfka]
sample	**образец** (m)	[ɔbra'zɛts]
training meeting	**тренинг** (m)	['trɛniŋg]
meeting (of managers)	**съвещание** (n)	[sıvɛʃ'taniɛ]
lunch time	**обедна почивка** (f)	['ɔbɛdna pɔ'tʃivka]
to make a copy	**ксерокопирам**	[ksɛrɔkɔ'piram]

to make copies	**размножа**	[razmnɔ'ʒa]
to receive a fax	**получавам факс**	[pɔlu'ʧavam faks]
to send a fax	**изпращам факс**	[izp'raʃtam faks]
to call (by phone)	**обаждам се**	[ɔ'baʒdam sɛ]
to answer (vt)	**отговоря**	[ɔtgɔ'vɔrʲa]
to put through	**свържа**	['svɪrʒa]
to arrange, to set up	**назначавам**	[nazna'ʧavam]
to demonstrate (vt)	**демонстрирам**	[dɛmɔnst'riram]
to be absent	**отсъствам**	[ɔ'ʦɪstvam]
absence	**отсъствие** (n)	[ɔ'ʦɪstviɛ]

104. Business processes. Part 1

business	**дело** (n), **бизнес** (m)	['dɛlɔ], ['biznɛs]
firm	**фирма** (f)	['firma]
company	**компания** (f)	[kɔm'panija]
corporation	**корпорация** (f)	[kɔrpɔ'raʦija]
enterprise	**предприятие** (n)	[prɛdpri'jatiɛ]
agency	**агенция** (f)	[a'gɛnʦija]
agreement (contract)	**договор** (m)	['dɔgɔvɔr]
contract	**контракт** (m)	[kɔnt'rakt]
deal	**сделка** (f)	['sdɛlka]
order (to place an ~)	**поръчка** (f)	[pɔ'rɪʧka]
term (of contract)	**условие** (n)	[us'lɔviɛ]
wholesale (adv)	**на едро**	[na 'ɛdrɔ]
wholesale (adj)	**на едро**	[na 'ɛdrɔ]
wholesale (n)	**продажба** (f) **на едро**	[prɔ'daʒba na 'ɛdrɔ]
retail (adj)	**на дребно**	[na 'drɛbnɔ]
retail (n)	**продажба** (f) **на дребно**	[prɔ'daʒba na 'drɛbnɔ]
competitor	**конкурент** (m)	[kɔŋku'rɛnt]
competition	**конкуренция** (f)	[kɔŋku'rɛnʦija]
to compete (vi)	**конкурирам**	[kɔŋku'riram]
partner (associate)	**партньор** (m)	[part'nɜr]
partnership	**партньорство** (n)	[part'nɜrstvɔ]
crisis	**криза** (f)	['kriza]
bankruptcy	**фалит** (m)	[fa'lit]
to go bankrupt	**фалирам**	[fa'liram]
difficulty	**трудност** (f)	['trudnɔst]
problem	**проблем** (m)	[prɔb'lɛm]
catastrophe	**катастрофа** (f)	[katast'rɔfa]
economy	**икономика** (f)	[ikɔ'nɔmika]
economic (~ growth)	**икономически**	[ikɔnɔ'miʧəski]

economic recession	**икономически спад** (m)	[ikonɔ'mitʃəski spat]
goal (aim)	**цел** (f)	[tsəl]
task	**задача** (f)	[za'datʃa]
to trade (vi)	**търгувам**	[tır'guvam]
network (distribution ~)	**мрежа** (f)	['mreʒa]
inventory (stock)	**склад** (m)	[sklad]
assortment	**асортимент** (m)	[asɔrti'mɛnt]
leader (leading company)	**лидер** (m)	['lidɛr]
large (~ company)	**голям**	[gɔ'ʎam]
monopoly	**монопол** (m)	[mɔnɔ'pɔl]
theory	**теория** (f)	[tɛ'ɔrija]
practice	**практика** (f)	['praktika]
experience (in my ~)	**опит** (m)	['ɔpit]
trend (tendency)	**тенденция** (f)	[tɛn'dɛntsija]
development	**развитие** (n)	[raz'vitiɛ]

105. Business processes. Part 2

benefit, profit	**изгода** (f)	[iz'gɔda]
profitable (adj)	**изгоден**	[iz'gɔdɛn]
delegation (group)	**делегация** (f)	[dɛlɛ'gatsija]
salary	**работна заплата** (f)	[ra'bɔtna zap'lata]
to correct (an error)	**поправям**	[pɔp'ravʲam]
business trip	**командировка** (f)	[kɔmandi'rɔvka]
commission	**комисия** (f)	[kɔ'misija]
to control (vt)	**контролирам**	[kɔntrɔ'liram]
conference	**конференция** (f)	[kɔnfɛ'rɛntsija]
license	**лиценз** (m)	[li'tsənz]
reliable (~ partner)	**надежден**	[na'dɛʒdɛn]
initiative (undertaking)	**начинание** (n)	[natʃi'naniɛ]
norm (standard)	**норма** (f)	['nɔrma]
circumstance	**обстоятелство** (n)	[ɔbstɔ'jatɛlstvɔ]
duty (of employee)	**задължение** (n)	[zadı'ʒɛniɛ]
organization (company)	**организация** (f)	[ɔrgani'zatsija]
organization (process)	**организиране** (n)	[ɔrgani'ziranɛ]
organized (adj)	**организиран**	[ɔrgani'ziran]
cancellation	**отмяна** (f)	[ɔt'mʲana]
to cancel (call off)	**отменя**	[ɔtmɛ'ɲa]
report (official ~)	**отчет** (m)	[ɔ'tʃɛt]
patent	**патент** (m)	[pa'tɛnt]
to patent (obtain patent)	**патентовам**	[patɛn'tɔvam]
to plan (vt)	**планирам**	[pla'niram]

bonus (money)	**премия** (f)	['prɛmija]
professional (adj)	**професионален**	[prɔfɛsiɔ'nalɛn]
procedure	**процедура** (f)	[prɔtsə'dura]
to examine (contract, etc.)	**разгледам**	[razg'lɛdam]
calculation	**изчисляване** (n)	[istʃis'ʎavanɛ]
reputation	**репутация** (f)	[rɛpu'tatsija]
risk	**риск** (m)	[risk]
to manage, to run	**ръководя**	[rıkɔ'vɔdʲa]
information	**сведения** (n pl)	['svɛdɛnija]
property	**собственост** (f)	['sɔbstvɛnɔst]
union	**съюз** (m)	[sı'juz]
life insurance	**застраховка** (f) **живот**	[zastra'hɔfka ʒi'vɔt]
to insure (vt)	**застраховам**	[zastra'hɔvam]
insurance	**застраховка** (f)	[zastra'hɔfka]
auction (~ sale)	**търгове** (n)	['tırgɔvɛ]
to notify (inform)	**уведомявам**	[uvɛdɔ'mʲavam]
management (process)	**управление** (n)	[uprav'lɛniɛ]
service (~ industry)	**услуга** (f)	[us'luga]
forum	**форум** (m)	['fɔrum]
to function (vi)	**функционирам**	[fuŋktsiɔ'niram]
stage (phase)	**етап** (m)	[ɛ'tap]
legal (~ services)	**юридически**	[juri'ditʃəski]
lawyer (legal expert)	**юрист** (m)	[ju'rist]

106. Production. Works

plant	**завод** (m)	[za'vɔd]
factory	**фабрика** (f)	['fabrika]
workshop	**цех** (m)	[tsəh]
works, production site	**производство** (n)	[prɔiz'vɔtstvɔ]
industry	**промишленост** (f)	[prɔ'miʃlɛnɔst]
industrial (adj)	**промишлен**	[prɔ'miʃlɛn]
heavy industry	**тежка промишленост** (f)	['tɛʃka prɔ'miʃlɛnɔst]
light industry	**лека промишленост** (f)	['lɛka prɔ'miʃlɛnɔst]
products	**продукция** (f)	[prɔ'duktsija]
to produce (vt)	**произвеждам**	[prɔiz'vɛʒdam]
raw materials	**суровини** (f pl)	[surɔvi'ni]
foreman	**бригадир** (m)	[briga'dir]
workers team	**бригада** (f)	[bri'gada]
worker	**работник** (m)	[ra'bɔtnik]
working day	**работен ден** (m)	[ra'bɔtɛn dɛn]
pause	**почивка** (f)	[pɔ'tʃifka]

meeting	**събрание** (n)	[sıb'raniɛ]
to discuss (vt)	**обсъждам**	[ɔb'sıʒdam]
plan	**план** (m)	[plan]
to fulfill the plan	**изпълнявам план**	[izpıl'ɲavam plan]
rate of output	**норма** (f)	['nɔrma]
quality	**качество** (n)	['katʃəstvɔ]
checking (control)	**контрола** (f)	[kɔnt'rɔla]
quality control	**контрол** (m) **за качество**	[kɔnt'rɔl za 'katʃəstvɔ]
work safety	**безопасност** (f) **на труда**	[bɛzɔ'pasnɔst na tru'da]
discipline	**дисциплина** (f)	[distsip'lina]
violation (of safety rules, etc.)	**нарушение** (n)	[naru'ʃɛniɛ]
to violate (rules)	**нарушавам**	[naru'ʃʌvam]
strike	**стачка** (f)	['statʃka]
striker	**стачник** (m)	['statʃnik]
to be on strike	**стачкувам**	[statʃ'kuvam]
labor union	**профсъюз** (m)	[prɔfsı'juz]
to invent (machine, etc.)	**изобретявам**	[izɔbrɛ'tʲavam]
invention	**изобретение** (n)	[izɔbrɛ'tɛniɛ]
research	**изследване** (n)	[iss'lɛdvanɛ]
to improve (make better)	**подобрявам**	[pɔdɔb'rʲavam]
technology	**технология** (f)	[tɛhnɔ'lɔgija]
technical drawing	**чертеж** (m)	[tʃər'tɛʒ]
load, cargo	**товар** (m)	[tɔ'var]
loader (person)	**хамалин** (m)	[ha'malin]
to load (vehicle, etc.)	**натоварвам**	[natɔ'varvam]
loading (process)	**товарене** (n)	[tɔ'varɛnɛ]
to unload (vi, vt)	**разтоварвам**	[raztɔ'varvam]
unloading	**разтоварване** (n)	[raztɔ'varvanɛ]
transportation	**транспорт** (m)	[trans'pɔrt]
transportation company	**транспортна компания** (f)	[trans'pɔrtna kɔm'panija]
to transport (vt)	**транспортирам**	[transpɔr'tiram]
freight car	**вагон** (m)	[va'gɔn]
cistern	**цистерна** (f)	[tsis'tɛrna]
truck	**камион** (m)	[kami'ɔn]
machine tool	**машина** (f)	[ma'ʃina]
mechanism	**механизъм** (m)	[mɛha'nizım]
industrial waste	**отпадъци** (pl)	[ɔt'padıtsi]
packing (process)	**опаковане** (f)	[ɔpa'kɔvanɛ]
to pack (vt)	**опаковам**	[ɔpa'kɔvam]

107. Contract. Agreement

contract	**контракт** (m)	[kɔnt'rakt]
agreement	**съглашение** (n)	[sɪgla'ʃɛniɛ]
addendum	**приложение** (n)	[prilɔ'ʒɛniɛ]
to sign a contract	**сключа договор**	['sklyʧa 'dɔgɔvɔr]
signature	**подпис** (m)	['pɔtpis]
to sign (vt)	**подпиша**	[pɔt'piʃʌ]
stamp (seal)	**печат** (m)	[pɛ'ʧat]
subject of contract	**предмет** (m) **на договор**	[prɛd'mɛt na 'dɔgɔvɔr]
clause	**точка** (f)	['tɔʧka]
parties (in contract)	**страни** (f pl)	[stra'ni]
legal address	**юридически адрес** (m)	[juri'diʧəski ad'rɛs]
to break the contract	**наруша договор**	[naru'ʃʌ 'dɔgɔvɔr]
commitment	**задължение** (n)	[zadɪ'ʒɛniɛ]
responsibility	**отговорност** (n)	[ɔtgɔ'vɔrnɔst]
force majeure	**форсмажор** (m)	[fɔrs ma'ʒɔr]
dispute	**спор** (m)	[spɔr]
penalties	**глоба** (f)	['glɔba]

108. Import & Export

import	**внос** (m)	[vnɔs]
importer	**вносител** (m)	[vnɔ'sitɛl]
to import (vt)	**внасям**	['vnasʲam]
import (e.g., ~ goods)	**вносен**	['vnɔsɛn]
exporter	**износител** (m)	[iznɔ'sitɛl]
to export (vi, vt)	**изнасям**	[iz'nasʲam]
goods	**стока** (f)	['stɔka]
consignment, lot	**партида** (f)	[par'tida]
weight	**тегло** (n)	[tɛg'lɔ]
volume	**обем** (m)	[ɔ'bɛm]
cubic meter	**кубически метър** (m)	[ku'biʧəski 'mɛtɪr]
manufacturer	**производител** (m)	[prɔizvɔ'ditɛl]
transportation company	**транспортна компания** (f)	[trans'pɔrtna kɔm'panijɑ]
container	**контейнер** (m)	[kɔn'tɛjnɛr]
border	**граница** (f)	['granitsa]
customs	**митница** (f)	['mitnitsa]
customs duty	**мито** (n)	[mi'tɔ]
customs officer	**митничар** (m)	[mitni'ʧar]

smuggling	**контрабанда** (f)	[kɔntra'banda]
contraband (goods)	**контрабанда** (f)	[kɔntra'banda]

109. Finances

stock (share)	**акция** (f)	['aktsija]
bond (certificate)	**облигация** (f)	[ɔbli'gatsija]
bill of exchange	**полица** (f)	['pɔlitsa]
stock exchange	**борса** (f)	['bɔrsa]
stock price	**курс** (m) **на акции**	[kurs na 'aktsi:]
to go down	**поевтинея**	[pɔεfti'nεja]
to go up	**поскъпнея**	[pɔskɪp'nεja]
shareholding	**дял** (m)	[dʲal]
controlling interest	**контролен пакет** (m)	[kɔnt'rɔlεn pa'kεt]
investment	**инвестиции** (f pl)	[invεs'titsi:]
to invest (vt)	**инвестирам**	[invεs'tiram]
percent	**лихвен процент** (m)	['lihvεn prɔ'tsənt]
interest (on investment)	**проценти** (m pl)	[prɔ'tsənti]
profit	**печалба** (f)	[pε'tʃalba]
profitable (adj)	**печеливш**	[pεtʃə'livʃ]
tax	**данък** (m)	['danɪk]
currency (foreign ~)	**валута** (f)	[va'luta]
national (adj)	**национален**	[natsiɔ'nalεn]
exchange (currency ~)	**обмяна** (f)	[ɔb'mʲana]
accountant	**счетоводител** (m)	[stʃətɔvɔ'ditεl]
accounting	**счетоводство** (n)	[stʃətɔ'vɔdstvɔ]
bankruptcy	**фалит** (m)	[fa'lit]
collapse, crash	**фалит** (m)	[fa'lit]
ruin	**фалиране** (n)	[fa'liranε]
to be ruined	**фалирам**	[fa'liram]
inflation	**инфлация** (f)	[inf'latsija]
devaluation	**девалвация** (f)	[dεval'vatsija]
capital	**капитал** (m)	[kapi'tal]
income	**доход** (m)	['dɔhɔd]
turnover	**оборот** (m)	[ɔbɔ'rɔt]
resources	**ресурси** (pl)	[rε'sursi]
monetary resources	**парични средства** (n pl)	[pa'ritʃni 'srεtstva]

110. Marketing

marketing	**маркетинг** (m)	[mar'kɛtiŋg]
market	**пазар** (m)	[pa'zar]
market segment	**пазарен сегмент** (m)	[pa'zarɛn sɛg'mɛnt]
product	**продукт** (m)	[prɔ'dukt]
goods	**стока** (f)	['stɔka]
trademark	**търговска марка** (f)	[tɪr'gɔfska 'marka]
logotype	**фирмена марка** (f)	['firmɛna 'marka]
logo	**лого** (n)	['lɔgɔ]
demand	**търсене** (n)	['tɪrsɛnɛ]
supply	**предложение** (n)	[prɛdlɔ'ʒɛniɛ]
need	**нужда** (f)	['nuʒda]
consumer	**потребител** (m)	[pɔtrɛ'bitɛl]
analysis	**анализ** (m)	[a'naliz]
to analyze (vt)	**анализирам**	[anali'ziram]
positioning	**позициониране** (n)	[pɔzitsiɔ'niranɛ]
to position (vt)	**позиционирам**	[pɔzitsiɔ'niram]
price	**цена** (f)	[tsə'na]
pricing policy	**ценова политика** (f)	[tsənɔ'va pɔli'tika]
formation of price	**ценообразуване** (n)	[tsənɔ:bra'zuvanɛ]

111. Advertising

advertising	**реклама** (f)	[rɛk'lama]
to advertise (vt)	**рекламирам**	[rɛkla'miram]
budget	**бюджет** (m)	[by'dʒɛt]
ad, advertisement	**реклама** (f)	[rɛk'lama]
TV advertising	**телевизионна реклама** (f)	[tɛlɛvizi'ɔŋa rek'lama]
radio advertising	**радио реклама** (f)	['radiɔ rɛk'lama]
outdoor advertising	**външна реклама** (f)	['vɪnʃna rɛk'lama]
mass media	**средства** (n pl) **за масова информация**	['srɛtstva za 'masɔva infɔr'matsija]
periodical (n)	**периодично издание** (n)	[pɛriɔ'ditʃnɔ iz'daniɛ]
image (public appearance)	**имидж** (m)	['imidʒ]
slogan	**лозунг** (m)	['lɔzuŋg]
motto (maxim)	**девиз** (m)	[dɛ'viz]
campaign	**кампания** (f)	[kam'panija]
advertising campaign	**рекламна кампания** (f)	[rɛk'lamna kam'panija]
target group	**целева аудитория** (f)	[tsəlɛ'va audi'tɔrija]

business card	**визитка** (f)	[vi'zitka]
leaflet	**листовка** (f)	[lis'tɔfka]
brochure (e.g., 12 pages ~)	**брошура** (f)	[brɔ'ʃura]
pamphlet	**диплянка** (f)	[dip'ʎaŋka]
newsletter	**бюлетин** (n)	[bylɛ'tin]
store sign	**табела** (f)	[ta'bɛla]
poster	**постер** (m)	['pɔstɛr]
billboard	**билборд** (m)	[bil'bɔrd]

112. Banking

bank	**банка** (f)	['baŋka]
branch (of bank, etc.)	**клон** (m)	[klɔn]
bank clerk, consultant	**консултант** (m)	[kɔnsul'tant]
manager (director)	**управител** (m)	[up'ravitɛl]
banking account	**сметка** (f)	['smɛtka]
account number	**номер** (m) **на сметка**	['nɔmɛr na 'smɛtka]
checking account	**текуща сметка** (f)	[tɛ'kuʃta 'smɛtka]
savings account	**спестовна сметка** (f)	[spɛs'tɔvna 'smɛtka]
to open an account	**откривам сметка**	[ɔtk'rivam 'smɛtka]
to close the account	**закривам сметка**	[zak'rivam 'smɛtka]
deposit	**влог** (m)	[vlɔg]
to make a deposit	**направя влог**	[nap'ravʲa vlɔk]
wire transfer	**превод** (m)	['prɛvɔd]
to wire, to transfer	**направя превод**	[nap'ravʲa 'prɛvɔd]
sum	**сума** (f)	['suma]
How much?	**Колко?**	['kɔlkɔ]
signature	**подпис** (m)	['pɔtpis]
to sign (vt)	**подпиша**	[pɔt'piʃʌ]
credit card	**кредитна карта** (f)	['krɛditna 'karta]
code	**код** (m)	[kɔd]
credit card number	**номер** (m) **на кредитна карта**	['nɔmɛr na 'krɛditna 'karta]
ATM	**банкомат** (m)	[baŋkɔ'mat]
check	**чек** (m)	[ʧek]
to write a check	**подпиша чек**	[pɔt'piʃʌ ʧək]
checkbook	**чекова книжка** (f)	['ʧəkɔva 'kniʃka]
loan (bank ~)	**кредит** (m)	['krɛdit]
to apply for a loan	**кандидатствам за кредит**	[kandi'daʦtvam za 'krɛdit]

to get a loan	**взимам кредит**	['vzimam 'krɛdit]
to give a loan	**предоставям кредит**	[prɛdɔs'tavʲam 'krɛdit]
guarantee	**гаранция** (f)	[ga'rantsija]

113. Telephone. Phone conversation

telephone	**телефон** (m)	[tɛlɛ'fɔn]
mobile phone	**мобилен телефон** (m)	[mɔ'bilɛn tɛlɛ'fɔn]
answering machine	**телефонен секретар** (m)	[tɛlɛ'fɔnɛn sɛkrɛ'tar]
to call (telephone)	**обаждам се**	[ɔ'baʒdam sɛ]
phone call	**обаждане** (n)	[ɔ'baʒdane]
to dial a number	**набирам номер**	[na'biram 'nɔmɛr]
Hello!	**Ало!**	['alɔ]
to ask (vt)	**питам**	['pitam]
to answer (vi, vt)	**отговарям**	[ɔtgɔ'varʲam]
to hear (vt)	**чувам**	['ʧuvam]
well (adv)	**добре**	[dɔb'rɛ]
not well (adv)	**лошо**	['lɔʃɔ]
noises (interference)	**шумове** (m pl)	['ʃumɔvɛ]
receiver	**слушалка** (f)	[slu'ʃʌlka]
to pick up (~ the phone)	**вдигам слушалката**	['vdigam slu'ʃʌlkata]
to hang up (~ the phone)	**затварям телефона**	[zat'varʲam tɛlɛ'fɔna]
busy (adj)	**заета**	[za'ɛta]
to ring (ab. phone)	**звъня**	[zvɪ'ɲa]
telephone book	**телефонен справочник** (m)	[tɛlɛ'fɔnɛn spra'vɔʧnik]
local (adj)	**местен**	['mɛstɛn]
long distance (~ call)	**междуградски**	[mɛʒdug'radski]
international (adj)	**международен**	[mɛʒduna'rɔdɛn]

114. Mobile telephone

mobile phone	**мобилен телефон** (m)	[mɔ'bilɛn tɛlɛ'fɔn]
display	**дисплей** (m)	[disp'lɛj]
button	**бутон** (m)	[bu'tɔn]
SIM card	**SIM-карта** (f)	[sim 'karta]
battery	**батерия** (f)	[ba'tɛrija]
to be dead (battery)	**изтощавам**	[iztɔʃ'tavam]
charger	**зареждащо устройство** (n)	[za'rɛʒdaʃtɔ ust'rɔjstvɔ]
menu	**меню** (n)	[mɛ'ny]

settings	**настройки** (f pl)	[nast'rɔjki]
tune (melody)	**мелодия** (f)	[mɛ'lɔdijɑ]
to select (vt)	**избера**	[izbɛ'ra]
calculator	**калкулатор** (m)	[kalku'latɔr]
voice mail	**телефонен секретар** (m)	[tɛlɛ'fɔnɛn sɛkrɛ'tar]
alarm clock	**будилник** (m)	[bu'dilnik]
contacts	**телефонен справочник** (m)	[tɛlɛ'fɔnɛn spra'vɔtʃnik]
SMS (text message)	**SMS съобщение** (n)	[ɛsɛ'mɛs sɪɔbʃ'tɛniɛ]
subscriber	**абонат** (m)	[abɔ'nat]

115. Stationery

ballpoint pen	**химикалка** (f)	[himi'kalka]
fountain pen	**перодръжка** (f)	[perɔd'rɪʒka]
pencil	**молив** (m)	['mɔliv]
highlighter	**маркер** (m)	['markɛr]
felt-tip pen	**флумастер** (m)	[flu'mastɛr]
notepad	**тефтер** (m)	[tɛf'tɛr]
agenda (diary)	**ежедневник** (m)	[ɛʒɛd'nɛvnik]
ruler	**линийка** (f)	['linijka]
calculator	**калкулатор** (m)	[kalku'latɔr]
eraser	**гума** (f)	['guma]
thumbtack	**кабърче** (n)	['kabɪrtʃə]
paper clip	**кламер** (m)	['klamɛr]
glue	**лепило** (n)	[lɛ'pilɔ]
stapler	**телбод** (m)	[tɛl'bɔt]
hole punch	**перфоратор** (m)	[pɛrfɔ'ratɔr]
pencil sharpener	**острилка** (f)	[ɔst'rilka]

116. Various kinds of documents

account (report)	**отчет** (m)	[ɔ'tʃɛt]
agreement	**съглашение** (n)	[sɪgla'ʃɛniɛ]
application form	**заявка** (f)	[za'jɑvka]
authentic (adj)	**оригинален**	[ɔrigi'nalɛn]
badge (identity tag)	**бадж** (m)	[badʒ]
business card	**визитка** (f)	[vi'zitka]
certificate (~ of quality)	**сертификат** (m)	[sɛrtifi'kat]
check (e.g., draw a ~)	**чек** (m)	[tʃek]
check (in restaurant)	**сметка** (f)	['smɛtka]

constitution	**конституция** (f)	[konsti'tutsija]
contract	**договор** (m)	['dɔgɔvɔr]
copy	**копие** (n)	['kɔpiɛ]
copy (of contract, etc.)	**екземпляр** (m)	[ɛkzɛmp'ʎar]
customs declaration	**декларация** (f)	[dɛkla'ratsija]
document	**документ** (m)	[dɔku'mɛnt]
driver's license	**шофьорска книжка** (f)	[ʃɔ'fʲɔrska 'kniʃka]
addendum	**приложение** (n)	[prilɔ'ʒɛniɛ]
form	**анкета** (f)	[a'ŋkɛta]
identity card, ID	**удостоверение** (n)	[udɔstɔvɛ'rɛniɛ]
inquiry (request)	**запитване** (n)	[za'pitvanɛ]
invitation card	**покана** (f)	[pɔ'kana]
invoice	**сметка** (f)	['smɛtka]
law	**закон** (m)	[za'kɔn]
letter (mail)	**писмо** (n)	[pis'mɔ]
letterhead	**бланка** (f)	['blaŋka]
list (of names, etc.)	**списък** (m)	['spisɪk]
manuscript	**ръкопис** (m)	[rɪkɔ'pis]
newsletter	**бюлетина** (f)	[bylɛ'tina]
note (short message)	**записка** (f)	['zapiska]
pass (for worker, visitor)	**пропуск** (m)	['prɔpusk]
passport	**паспорт** (m)	[pas'pɔrt]
permit	**разрешение** (n)	[razrɛ'ʃɛniɛ]
résumé	**резюме** (n)	[rɛzy'mɛ]
debt note, IOU	**разписка** (f)	['raspiska]
receipt (for purchase)	**квитанция** (f)	[kvi'tantsija]
sales slip, receipt	**бележка** (f)	[be'lɛʃka]
report	**рапорт** (m)	['rapɔrt]
to show (ID, etc.)	**предявявам**	[prɛdʲa'vʲavam]
to sign (vt)	**подпиша**	[pɔt'piʃʌ]
signature	**подпис** (m)	['pɔtpis]
stamp (seal)	**печат** (m)	[pɛ'tʃat]
text	**текст** (m)	[tɛkst]
ticket (for entry)	**билет** (m)	[bi'lɛt]
to cross out	**задраскам**	[zad'raskam]
to fill out (~ a form)	**попълня**	[pɔ'pɪlɲa]
waybill	**фактура** (f)	[fak'tura]
will (testament)	**завещание** (n)	[zavɛʃ'taniɛ]

117. Kinds of business

accounting services	**счетоводни услуги** (f pl)	[stʃətɔ'vɔdni us'lugi]
advertising	**реклама** (f)	[rɛk'lama]

advertising agency	**рекламна агенция** (f)	[rɛk'lamna a'gɛntsija]
air-conditioners	**климатици** (m pl)	[klima'titsi]
airline	**авиокомпания** (f)	[aviɔkɔm'panija]
alcoholic drinks	**алкохолни напитки** (f pl)	[alkɔ'hɔlni na'pitki]
antiquities	**антиквариат** (m)	[antikvari'at]
art gallery	**галерия** (f)	[ga'lɛrija]
audit services	**одиторски услуги** (f pl)	[ɔ'ditɔrski us'lugi]
banks	**банков бизнес** (m)	['baŋkɔv 'biznɛs]
bar	**бар** (m)	[bar]
beauty parlor	**козметичен салон** (m)	[kɔzmɛ'titʃən sa'lɔn]
bookstore	**книжарница** (f)	[kni'ʒarnitsa]
brewery	**пивоварна** (f)	[pivɔ'varna]
business center	**бизнес-център** (m)	['biznɛs 'tsəntɪr]
business school	**бизнес-училище** (n)	['biznɛs u'tʃiliʃtɛ]
casino	**казино** (n)	[ka'zinɔ]
construction	**строителство** (n)	[strɔ'itɛlstvɔ]
consulting	**консултиране** (n)	[kɔnsul'tiranɛ]
dental clinic	**стоматология** (f)	[stɔmatɔ'lɔgija]
design	**дизайн** (m)	[di'zajn]
drugstore, pharmacy	**аптека** (f)	[ap'tɛka]
dry cleaners	**химическо чистене** (n)	[hi'mitʃəskɔ 'tʃistɛnɛ]
employment agency	**агенция** (f) **за подбор на персонал**	[a'gɛntsija za pɔd'bɔr na pɛrsɔ'nal]
financial services	**финансови услуги** (f pl)	[fi'nansɔvi us'lugi]
food products	**хранителни стоки** (f pl)	[hra'nitɛlni 'stɔki]
funeral home	**погребални услуги** (pl)	[pɔgrɛ'balni us'lugi]
furniture (e.g., house ~)	**мебели** (pl)	['mɛbɛli]
garment	**облекло** (n)	[ɔblɛk'lɔ]
hotel	**хотел** (m)	[hɔ'tɛl]
ice-cream	**сладолед** (m)	[sladɔ'lɛd]
industry	**промишленост** (f)	[prɔ'miʃlɛnɔst]
insurance	**застраховане** (n)	[zastra'hɔvanɛ]
Internet	**интернет** (m)	[intɛr'nɛt]
investment	**инвестиции** (f pl)	[invɛs'titsi:]
jeweler	**златар** (m)	[zla'tar]
jewelry	**златарски изделия** (n pl)	[zla'tarski iz'dɛlija]
laundry (shop)	**пералня** (f)	[pɛ'ralɲa]
legal advisor	**юридически услуги** (f pl)	[juri'ditʃəski us'lugi]
light industry	**лека промишленост** (f)	['lɛka prɔ'miʃlɛnɔst]
magazine	**списание** (n)	[spi'saniɛ]
mail-order selling	**каталожна търговия** (f)	[kata'lɔʒna tɪrgɔ'vija]
medicine	**медицина** (f)	[mɛdi'tsina]
movie theater	**кинотеатър** (m)	['kinɔtɛ'atɪr]
museum	**музей** (m)	[mu'zɛj]

news agency	**информационна агенция** (f)	[informatsi'ɔŋa a'gɛntsija]
newspaper	**вестник** (m)	['vɛsnik]
nightclub	**нощен клуб** (m)	['nɔʃtɛn klub]
oil (petroleum)	**нефт** (m)	[nɛft]
parcels service	**куриерска служба** (f)	[kuri'ɛrska 'sluʒba]
pharmaceuticals	**фармацевтика** (f)	[farma'tsəftika]
printing (industry)	**полиграфия** (f)	[pɔligra'fija]
publishing house	**издателство** (n)	[iz'datɛlstvɔ]
radio (~ station)	**радио** (n)	['radiɔ]
real estate	**недвижими имоти** (pl)	[nɛd'viʒimi i'mɔti]
restaurant	**ресторант** (m)	[rɛstɔ'rant]
security agency	**охранителна агенция** (f)	[ɔhra'nitɛlna a'gɛntsija]
sports	**спорт** (m)	[spɔrt]
stock exchange	**борса** (f)	['bɔrsa]
store	**магазин** (m)	[maga'zin]
supermarket	**супермаркет** (m)	[supɛr'markɛt]
swimming pool	**басейн** (m)	[ba'sɛjn]
tailors	**ателие** (n)	[atɛli'ɛ]
television	**телевизия** (f)	[tɛlɛ'vizija]
theater	**театър** (m)	[tɛ'atır]
trade	**търговия** (f)	[tırgɔ'vija]
transportation	**превоз** (m)	['prɛvɔs]
travel	**туризъм** (m)	[tu'rizım]
veterinarian	**ветеринар** (m)	[vɛtɛri'nar]
warehouse	**склад** (m)	[sklad]
waste collection	**извозване** (n) **на боклук**	[iz'vɔzvanɛ na bɔk'luk]

Job. Business. Part 2

118. Show. Exhibition

exhibition, show	**изложба** (f)	[iz'lɔʒba]
trade show	**търговска изложба** (f)	[tɪr'gɔfska iz'lɔʒba]
participation	**участие** (n)	[u'ʧastiɛ]
to participate (vi)	**участвам**	[u'ʧastvam]
participant (exhibitor)	**участник** (m)	[u'ʧasnik]
director	**директор** (m)	[di'rɛktɔr]
organizer's office	**дирекция** (f)	[di'rɛktsija]
organizer	**организатор** (m)	[ɔrgani'zatɔr]
to organize (vt)	**организирам**	[ɔrgani'ziram]
participation form	**заявка** (f) **за участие**	[za'jafka za u'ʧastiɛ]
to fill out (vt)	**попълня**	[pɔ'pɪlɲa]
details	**детайли** (m pl)	[dɛ'tajli]
information	**информация** (f)	[infɔr'matsija]
price	**цена** (f)	[tsə'na]
including	**включително**	[vkly'ʧitɛlnɔ]
to include (vt)	**включвам**	['vklyʧvam]
to pay (vi, vt)	**плащам**	['plaʃtam]
registration fee	**регистрационна такса** (f)	[rɛgistratsi'ɔɲa 'taksa]
entrance	**вход** (m)	[vhɔd]
pavilion, hall	**павилион** (m)	[pavili'ɔn]
to register (vt)	**регистрирам**	[rɛgist'riram]
badge (identity tag)	**бадж** (m)	[badʒ]
booth, stand	**щанд** (m)	[ʃtand]
to reserve, to book	**резервирам**	[rɛzɛr'viram]
display case	**витрина** (f)	[vit'rina]
spotlight	**светилник** (m)	[svɛ'tilnik]
design	**дизайн** (m)	[di'zajn]
to place (put, set)	**нареждам**	[na'rɛʒdam]
distributor	**дистрибутор** (m)	[distri'butɔr]
supplier	**доставчик** (m)	[dɔs'tavʧik]
country	**страна** (f)	[stra'na]
foreign (adj)	**чуждестранен**	[ʧuʒdɛst'ranɛn]
product	**продукт** (m)	[prɔ'dukt]

association	**асоциация** (f)	[asɔʦi'aʦija]
conference hall	**конферентна зала** (f)	[kɔnfɛ'rɛntna 'zala]
congress	**конгрес** (m)	[kɔŋg'rɛs]
contest (competition)	**конкурс** (m)	[kɔ'ŋkurs]
visitor	**посетител** (m)	[pɔsɛ'titɛl]
to visit (attend)	**посещавам**	[pɔsɛʃ'tavam]
customer	**клиент** (m)	[kli'ɛnt]

119. Mass Media

newspaper	**вестник** (m)	['vɛsnik]
magazine	**списание** (n)	[spi'saniɛ]
press (printed media)	**преса** (f)	['prɛsa]
radio	**радио** (n)	['radiɔ]
radio station	**радиостанция** (f)	[radiɔs'tanʦija]
television	**телевизия** (f)	[tɛlɛ'vizija]
presenter, host	**водещ** (m)	['vɔdɛʃt]
newscaster	**диктор** (m)	['diktɔr]
commentator	**коментатор** (m)	[kɔmɛn'tatɔr]
journalist	**журналист** (m)	[ʒurna'list]
correspondent (reporter)	**кореспондент** (m)	[kɔrɛspɔn'dɛnt]
press photographer	**фотокореспондент** (m)	[fɔtɔkɔrɛspɔn'dɛnt]
reporter	**репортер** (m)	[repɔr'tɛr]
editor	**редактор** (m)	[rɛ'daktɔr]
editor-in-chief	**главен редактор** (m)	['glavɛn rɛ'daktɔr]
to subscribe (to ...)	**абонирам се**	[abɔ'niram sɛ]
subscription	**абониране** (n)	[abɔ'niranɛ]
subscriber	**абонат** (m)	[abɔ'nat]
to read (vi, vt)	**чета**	[ʧə'tɪ]
reader	**читател** (m)	[ʧi'tatɛl]
circulation (of newspaper)	**тираж** (m)	[ti'raʒ]
monthly (adj)	**месечен**	['mɛsɛʧən]
weekly (adj)	**седмичен**	['sɛdmiʧən]
issue (edition)	**брой** (m)	[brɔj]
new (~ issue)	**последен**	[pɔs'lɛdɛn]
headline	**заглавие** (n)	[zag'laviɛ]
short article	**кратка статия** (f)	['kratka 'statija]
column (regular article)	**рубрика** (f)	['rubrika]
article	**статия** (f)	['statija]
page	**страница** (f)	['straniʦa]
reportage, report	**репортаж** (m)	[rɛpɔr'taʒ]
event (happening)	**събитие** (n)	[sɪ'bitiɛ]

sensation (news)	**сензация** (f)	[sɛn'zatsija]
scandal	**скандал** (m)	[skan'dal]
scandalous (adj)	**скандален**	[skan'dalɛn]
great (~ scandal)	**голям (скандал)**	[gɔ'ʎam skan'dal]
program	**предаване** (n)	[prɛ'davanɛ]
interview	**интервю** (n)	[intɛr'vy]
live broadcast	**пряко предаване** (n)	['prʲakɔ prɛ'davanɛ]
channel	**канал** (m)	[ka'nal]

120. Agriculture

agriculture	**селско стопанство** (n)	['sɛlskɔ stɔ'panstvɔ]
peasant (masc.)	**селянин** (m)	['sɛʎanin]
peasant (fem.)	**селянка** (f)	['sɛʎaŋka]
farmer	**фермер** (m)	['fɛrmɛr]
tractor	**трактор** (m)	['traktɔr]
combine, harvester	**комбайн** (m)	[kɔm'bajn]
plow	**плуг** (m)	[plug]
to plow (vi, vt)	**ора**	[ɔ'ra]
plowland	**разорана нива** (f)	[razɔ'rana 'niva]
furrow (in field)	**бразда** (f)	[braz'da]
to sow (vi, vt)	**сея**	['sɛja]
seeder	**сеялка** (f)	[sɛ'jalka]
sowing (process)	**сеитба** (f)	[sɛ'idba]
scythe	**коса** (f)	[kɔ'sa]
to mow, to scythe	**кося**	[kɔ'sʲa]
spade (tool)	**лопата** (f)	[lɔ'pata]
to dig (to till)	**копая**	[kɔ'paja]
hoe	**мотика** (f)	[mɔ'tika]
to hoe, to weed	**плевя**	[plɛ'vʲa]
weed (plant)	**плевел** (m)	['plɛvɛl]
watering can	**лейка** (f)	['lɛjka]
to water (plants)	**поливам**	[pɔ'livam]
watering (act)	**поливане** (n)	[pɔ'livanɛ]
pitchfork	**вила** (f)	['vila]
rake	**гребло** (n)	[grɛb'lɔ]
fertilizer	**тор** (m)	[tɔr]
to fertilize (vt)	**наторявам**	[natɔ'rʲavam]
manure (fertilizer)	**оборски тор** (m)	[ɔ'bɔrski tɔr]
field	**поле** (n)	[pɔ'lɛ]

meadow	**ливада** (f)	[li'vada]
vegetable garden	**зеленчукова градина** (f)	[zɛlɛn'ʧukɔva gra'dina]
orchard (e.g., apple ~)	**градина** (f)	[gra'dina]
to pasture (vt)	**паса**	[pa'sa]
herdsman	**пастир** (m)	[pas'tir]
pastureland	**пасище** (n)	['pasiʃtɛ]
cattle breeding	**животновъдство** (n)	[ʒivɔtnɔ'vɪdstvɔ]
sheep farming	**овцевъдство** (n)	[ɔvʦə'vɪdstvɔ]
plantation	**плантация** (f)	[plan'taʦija]
row (garden bed ~s)	**леха** (f)	[lɛ'ha]
hothouse	**парник** (m)	['parnik]
drought (lack of rain)	**суша** (f)	['suʃʌ]
dry (~ summer)	**сушав**	['suʃʌv]
cereal crops	**зърнени култури** (pl)	['zɪrnɛni kul'turi]
to harvest, to gather	**събирам**	[sɪ'biram]
miller (person)	**воденичар** (n)	[vɔdɛni'ʧar]
mill (e.g., gristmill)	**воденица** (f)	[vɔdɛ'niʦa]
to grind (grain)	**меля зърно**	['mɛʎa 'zɪrnɔ]
flour	**брашно** (n)	[braʃ'nɔ]
straw	**слама** (f)	['slama]

121. Building. Building process

construction site	**строеж** (m)	[strɔ'ɛʃ]
to build (vt)	**строя**	[strɔ'ja]
construction worker	**строител** (m)	[strɔ'itɛl]
project	**проект** (m)	[prɔ'ɛkt]
architect	**архитект** (m)	[arhi'tɛkt]
worker	**работник** (m)	[ra'bɔtnik]
foundation (of building)	**фундамент** (m)	[funda'mɛnt]
roof	**покрив** (m)	['pɔkriv]
foundation pile	**пилот** (m)	[pi'lɔt]
wall	**стена** (f)	[stɛ'na]
reinforcing bars	**арматура** (f)	[arma'tura]
scaffolding	**скеле** (n)	['skɛlɛ]
concrete	**бетон** (m)	[bɛ'tɔn]
granite	**гранит** (m)	[gra'nit]
stone	**камък** (m)	['kamɪk]
brick	**тухла** (f)	['tuhla]
sand	**пясък** (m)	['pʲasɪk]

cement	**цимент** (m)	[ʦi'mɛnt]
plaster (for walls)	**мазилка** (f)	[ma'zilka]
to plaster (vt)	**слагам мазилка**	['slagam ma'zilka]
paint	**боя** (f)	[bɔ'jɑ]
to paint (~ a wall)	**боядисвам**	[bɔjɑ'disvam]
barrel	**бъчва** (f)	['bɪʧva]
crane	**кран** (m)	[kran]
to lift (vt)	**вдигам**	['vdigam]
to lower (vt)	**спускам**	['spuskam]
bulldozer	**булдозер** (m)	[bul'dɔzɛr]
excavator	**екскаватор** (m)	[ɛkska'vatɔr]
scoop, bucket	**кофа** (f)	['kɔfa]
to dig (excavate)	**копая**	[kɔ'pajɑ]
hard hat	**каска** (f)	['kaska]

122. Science. Research. Scientists

science	**наука** (f)	[na'uka]
scientific (adj)	**научен**	[na'uʧən]
scientist	**учен** (m)	['uʧən]
theory	**теория** (f)	[tɛ'ɔrijɑ]
axiom	**аксиома** (f)	[aksi'ɔma]
analysis	**анализ** (m)	[a'naliz]
to analyze (vt)	**анализирам**	[anali'ziram]
argument (strong ~)	**аргумент** (m)	[argu'mɛnt]
substance (matter)	**вещество** (n)	[vɛʃtɛst'vɔ]
hypothesis	**хипотеза** (f)	[hipɔ'tɛza]
dilemma	**дилема** (f)	[di'lɛma]
dissertation	**дисертация** (f)	[disɛr'taʦijɑ]
dogma	**догма** (f)	['dɔgma]
doctrine	**доктрина** (f)	[dɔkt'rina]
research	**изследване** (n)	[iss'lɛdvanɛ]
to do research	**изследвам**	[iss'lɛdvam]
testing	**контрола** (f)	[kɔnt'rɔla]
laboratory	**лаборатория** (f)	[labɔra'tɔrijɑ]
method	**метод** (m)	['mɛtɔd]
molecule	**молекула** (f)	[mɔlɛ'kula]
monitoring	**мониторинг** (m)	[mɔni'tɔriŋg]
discovery (act, event)	**откритие** (n)	[ɔtk'ritiɛ]
postulate	**постулат** (m)	[pɔstu'lat]
principle	**принцип** (m)	['prinʦip]
forecast	**прогноза** (f)	[prɔg'nɔza]
prognosticate (vt)	**прогнозирам**	[prɔgnɔ'ziram]

synthesis	**синтеза** (f)	[sin'tɛza]
trend (tendency)	**тенденция** (f)	[tɛn'dɛnʦija]
theorem	**теорема** (f)	[tɛɔ'rɛma]
teachings	**учение** (n)	[u'ʧəniɛ]
fact	**факт** (m)	[fakt]
expedition	**експедиция** (f)	[ɛkspɛ'diʦija]
experiment	**експеримент** (m)	[ɛkspɛri'mɛnt]
academician	**академик** (m)	[akadɛ'mik]
bachelor (e.g., ~ of Arts)	**бакалавър** (m)	[baka'lavır]
doctor (PhD)	**доктор** (m)	['dɔktɔr]
Associate Professor	**доцент** (m)	[dɔ'ʦənt]
Master (e.g., ~ of Arts)	**магистър** (m)	[ma'gistır]
professor	**професор** (m)	[prɔ'fɛsɔr]

Professions and occupations

123. Job search. Dismissal

job	**работа** (f)	['rabɔta]
staff (work force)	**щат** (m)	[ʃtat]
career	**кариера** (f)	[kari'ɛra]
prospects	**перспектива** (f)	[pɛrspɛk'tiva]
skills (mastery)	**майсторство** (n)	['majstɔrstvɔ]
selection (screening)	**подбиране** (n)	[pɔd'biranɛ]
employment agency	**агенция** (f) **за подбор на персонал**	[a'gɛntsija za pɔd'bɔr na pɛrsɔ'nal]
résumé	**резюме** (n)	[rɛzy'mɛ]
interview (for job)	**интервю** (n)	[intɛr'vy]
vacancy, opening	**вакантно място** (n)	[va'kantnɔ 'mʲastɔ]
salary, pay	**работна заплата** (f)	[ra'bɔtna zap'lata]
pay, compensation	**плащане** (n)	['plaʃtanɛ]
position (job)	**длъжност** (f)	['dlɪʒnɔst]
duty (of employee)	**задължение** (n)	[zadɪ'ʒɛniɛ]
range of duties	**кръг** (m)	[krɪg]
busy (I'm ~)	**зает**	[za'ɛt]
to fire (dismiss)	**уволня**	[uvɔl'ɲa]
dismissal	**уволнение** (n)	[uvɔl'nɛniɛ]
unemployment	**безработица** (f)	[bɛzra'bɔtitsa]
unemployed (n)	**безработен човек** (m)	[bɛzra'bɔtɛn tʃɔ'vɛk]
retirement	**пенсия** (f)	['pɛnsija]
to retire (from job)	**пенсионирам се**	[pɛnsiɔ'niram sɛ]

124. Business people

director	**директор** (m)	[di'rɛktɔr]
manager (director)	**управител** (m)	[up'ravitɛl]
boss	**ръководител** (m)	[rɪkɔvɔ'ditɛl]
superior	**началник** (m)	[na'tʃalnik]
superiors	**началство** (n)	[na'tʃalstvɔ]
president	**президент** (m)	[prɛzi'dɛnt]
chairman	**председател** (m)	[prɛdsɛ'datɛl]

deputy (substitute)	**заместник** (m)	[za'mɛsnik]
assistant	**помощник** (m)	[pɔ'mɔʃtnik]
secretary	**секретар** (m)	[sɛkrɛ'tar]
personal assistant	**личен секретар** (m)	['litʃən sɛkrɛ'tar]
businessman	**бизнесмен** (m)	[biznɛs'mɛn]
entrepreneur	**предприемач** (m)	[prɛdpriɛ'matʃ]
founder	**основател** (m)	[ɔsnɔ'vatɛl]
to found (vt)	**основа**	[ɔsnɔ'va]
incorporator	**учредител** (m)	[utʃrɛ'ditɛl]
partner	**партньор** (m)	[part'nɜr]
stockholder	**акционер** (m)	[aktsiɔ'nɛr]
millionaire	**милионер** (m)	[miliɔ'nɛr]
billionaire	**милиардер** (m)	[miliar'dɛr]
owner, proprietor	**собственик** (m)	['sɔbstvɛnik]
landowner	**земевладелец** (m)	[zɛmɛvla'dɛlɛts]
client	**клиент** (m)	[kli'ɛnt]
regular client	**постоянен клиент** (m)	[pɔstɔ'janɛn kli'ɛnt]
buyer (customer)	**купувач** (m)	[kupu'vatʃ]
visitor	**посетител** (m)	[pɔsɛ'titɛl]
professional (n)	**професионалист** (m)	[prɔfɛsiɔna'list]
expert	**експерт** (m)	[ɛks'pɛrt]
specialist	**специалист** (m)	[spɛtsia'list]
banker	**банкер** (m)	[ba'ŋkɛr]
broker	**брокер** (m)	['brɔkɛr]
cashier, teller	**касиер** (m)	[kasi'ɛr]
accountant	**счетоводител** (m)	[stʃətɔvɔ'ditɛl]
security guard	**охранител** (m)	[ɔhra'nitɛl]
investor	**инвеститор** (m)	[invɛs'titɔr]
debtor	**длъжник** (m)	[dlɪʒ'nik]
creditor	**кредитор** (m)	[krɛ'ditɔr]
borrower	**заемател** (m)	[zaɛ'matɛl]
importer	**вносител** (m)	[vnɔ'sitɛl]
exporter	**износител** (m)	[iznɔ'sitɛl]
manufacturer	**производител** (m)	[prɔizvɔ'ditɛl]
distributor	**дистрибутор** (m)	[distri'butɔr]
middleman	**посредник** (m)	[pɔs'rɛdnik]
consultant	**консултант** (m)	[kɔnsul'tant]
sales representative	**представител** (m)	[prɛds'tavitɛl]
agent	**агент** (m)	[a'gɛnt]
insurance agent	**застрахователен агент** (m)	[zastrahɔ'vatelen agent]

125. Service professions

cook	**готвач** (m)	[gɔt'vatʃ]
chef (kitchen chef)	**главен готвач** (m)	['glavɛn gɔt'vatʃ]
baker	**фурнаджия** (f)	[furna'dʒija]
bartender	**барман** (m)	['barman]
waiter	**сервитьор** (m)	[sɛrvi'tɜr]
waitress	**сервитьорка** (f)	[sɛrvi'tɜrka]
lawyer, attorney	**адвокат** (m)	[advɔ'kat]
lawyer (legal expert)	**юрист** (m)	[ju'rist]
notary	**нотариус** (m)	[nɔ'tarius]
electrician	**монтьор** (m)	[mɔn'tɜr]
plumber	**водопроводчик** (m)	[vɔdɔprɔ'vɔdtʃik]
carpenter	**дърводелец** (m)	[dɪrvɔ'dɛlɛts]
masseur	**масажист** (m)	[masa'ʒist]
masseuse	**масажистка** (f)	[masa'ʒistka]
doctor	**лекар** (m)	['lɛkar]
taxi driver	**таксиметров шофьор** (m)	[taksi'mɛtrɔf ʃɔf3r]
driver	**шофьор** (m)	[ʃɔ'f3r]
delivery man	**куриер** (m)	[kuri'ɛr]
chambermaid	**камериерка** (f)	[kamɛri'ɛrka]
security guard	**охранител** (m)	[ɔhra'nitɛl]
flight attendant	**стюардеса** (f)	[styar'dɛsa]
teacher (in primary school)	**учител** (m)	[u'tʃitɛl]
librarian	**библиотекар** (m)	[bibliɔtɛ'kar]
translator	**преводач** (m)	[prɛvɔ'datʃ]
interpreter	**преводач** (m)	[prɛvɔ'datʃ]
guide	**гид** (m)	[gid]
hairdresser	**фризьор** (m)	[fri'zʲɔr]
mailman	**пощальон** (m)	[pɔʃta'l3n]
salesman (store staff)	**продавач** (m)	[prɔda'vatʃ]
gardener	**градинар** (m)	[gradi'nar]
domestic servant	**слуга** (m)	[slu'ga]
maid	**слугиня** (f)	[slu'giɲa]
cleaner (cleaning lady)	**чистачка** (f)	[tʃis'tatʃka]

126. Military professions and ranks

private	**редник** (m)	['rɛdnik]
sergeant	**сержант** (m)	[sɛr'ʒant]

lieutenant	**лейтенант** (m)	[lɛjtɛ'nant]
captain	**капитан** (m)	[kapi'tan]
major	**майор** (m)	[ma'jor]
colonel	**полковник** (m)	[pɔl'kɔvnik]
general	**генерал** (m)	[gɛnɛ'ral]
marshal	**маршал** (m)	['marʃʌl]
admiral	**адмирал** (m)	[admi'ral]
military man	**военен** (m)	[vɔ'ɛnɛn]
soldier	**войник** (m)	[vɔj'nik]
officer	**офицер** (m)	[ɔfi'ʦər]
commander	**командир** (m)	[kɔman'dir]
border guard	**митничар** (m)	[mitni'ʧar]
radio operator	**радист** (m)	[ra'dist]
scout (searcher)	**разузнавач** (m)	[razuzna'vaʧ]
pioneer (sapper)	**сапьор** (m)	[sa'pɜr]
marksman	**стрелец** (m)	[strɛ'lɛʦ]
navigator	**щурман** (m)	['ʃturman]

127. Officials. Priests

king	**крал** (m)	[kral]
queen	**кралица** (f)	[kra'liʦa]
prince	**принц** (m)	[prinʦ]
princess	**принцеса** (f)	[prin'ʦəsa]
tsar, czar	**цар** (m)	[ʦar]
czarina	**царица** (f)	[ʦa'riʦa]
president	**президент** (m)	[prɛzi'dɛnt]
Secretary (~ of State)	**министър** (m)	[mi'nistır]
prime minister	**министър-председател**	[mi'nistır prɛdsɛ'datɛl]
senator	**сенатор** (m)	[sɛ'natɔr]
diplomat	**дипломат** (m)	[diplɔ'mat]
consul	**консул** (m)	['kɔnsul]
ambassador	**посланик** (m)	[pɔs'lanik]
advisor (military ~)	**съветник** (m)	[sı'vɛtnik]
official (civil servant)	**чиновник** (m)	[ʧi'nɔvnik]
prefect	**префект** (m)	[prɛ'fɛkt]
mayor	**кмет** (m)	[kmɛt]
judge	**съдия** (m)	[sıdi'ja]
district attorney (prosecutor)	**прокурор** (m)	[prɔku'rɔr]
missionary	**мисионер** (m)	[misiɔ'nɛr]

monk	**монах** (m)	[mɔ'nah]
abbot	**абат** (m)	[a'bat]
rabbi	**равин** (m)	[ra'vin]
vizier	**везир** (m)	[vɛ'zir]
shah	**шах** (m)	[ʃʌh]
sheikh	**шейх** (m)	[ʃɛjh]

128. Agricultural professions

beekeeper	**пчеловъд** (m)	[ptʃəlɔ'vɪd]
herder, shepherd	**пастир** (m)	[pas'tir]
agronomist	**агроном** (m)	[agrɔ'nɔm]
cattle breeder	**животновъд** (m)	[ʒivɔtnɔ'vɪd]
veterinarian	**ветеринар** (m)	[vɛtɛri'nar]
farmer	**фермер** (m)	['fɛrmɛr]
winemaker	**винар** (m)	[vi'nar]
zoologist	**зоолог** (m)	[zɔ:'lɔg]
cowboy	**каубой** (m)	['kaubɔj]

129. Art professions

actor	**актьор** (m)	[ak'tɜr]
actress	**актриса** (f)	[akt'risa]
singer (masc.)	**певец** (m)	[pɛ'vɛʦ]
singer (fem.)	**певица** (f)	[pɛ'viʦa]
dancer (masc.)	**танцьор** (m)	[tan'ʦɜr]
dancer (fem.)	**танцьорка** (f)	[tan'ʦɜrka]
performing artist (masc.)	**артист** (m)	[ar'tist]
performing artist (fem.)	**артистка** (f)	[ar'tistka]
musician	**музикант** (m)	[muzi'kant]
pianist	**пианист** (m)	[pia'nist]
guitar player	**китарист** (m)	[kita'rist]
conductor (orchestra ~)	**диригент** (m)	[diri'gɛnt]
composer	**композитор** (m)	[kɔmpɔ'zitɔr]
impresario	**импресарио** (m)	[imprɛ'sariɔ]
movie director	**режисьор** (m)	[rɛʒi'sɜr]
producer	**продуцент** (m)	[prɔdu'ʦənt]
scriptwriter	**сценарист** (m)	[sʦəna'rist]
critic	**критик** (m)	[kri'tik]
writer	**писател** (m)	[pi'satɛl]

poet	**поет** (m)	[pɔ'ɛt]
sculptor	**скулптор** (m)	['skulptɔr]
artist (painter)	**художник** (m)	[hu'dɔʒnik]
juggler	**жонгльор** (m)	[ʒɔŋg'lɜr]
clown	**клоун** (m)	['klɔun]
acrobat	**акробат** (m)	[akrɔ'bat]
magician	**фокусник** (m)	['fɔkusnik]

130. Various professions

doctor	**лекар** (m)	['lɛkar]
nurse	**медицинска сестра** (f)	[mɛdi'ʦinska sɛst'ra]
psychiatrist	**психиатър** (m)	[psihi'atɪr]
dentist	**стоматолог** (m)	[stɔmatɔ'lɔg]
surgeon	**хирург** (m)	[hi'rurg]
astronaut	**астронавт** (m)	[astrɔ'naft]
astronomer	**астроном** (m)	[astrɔ'nɔm]
driver (of taxi, etc.)	**шофьор** (m)	[ʃɔ'fɜr]
engineer (train driver)	**машинист** (m)	[maʃi'nist]
mechanic	**механик** (m)	[mɛ'hanik]
miner	**миньор** (m)	[mi'nɜr]
worker	**работник** (m)	[ra'bɔtnik]
metalworker	**шлосер** (m)	['ʃlɔsɛr]
joiner (carpenter)	**дърводелец** (m)	[dɪrvɔ'dɛlɛʦ]
turner	**стругар** (m)	[stru'gar]
construction worker	**строител** (m)	[strɔ'itɛl]
welder	**заварчик** (m)	[za'varʧik]
professor (title)	**професор** (m)	[prɔ'fɛsɔr]
architect	**архитект** (m)	[arhi'tɛkt]
historian	**историк** (m)	[istɔ'rik]
scientist	**учен** (m)	['uʧən]
physicist	**физик** (m)	[fi'zik]
chemist (scientist)	**химик** (m)	[hi'mik]
archeologist	**археолог** (m)	[arhɛɔ'lɔg]
geologist	**геолог** (m)	[gɛɔ'lɔg]
researcher	**изследовател** (m)	[izslɛdɔ'vatɛl]
babysitter	**детегледачка** (f)	[dɛtɛglɛ'daʧka]
teacher, educator	**учител, педагог** (m)	[u'ʧitɛl], [pɛda'gɔg]
editor	**редактор** (m)	[rɛ'daktɔr]
editor-in-chief	**главен редактор** (m)	['glavɛn rɛ'daktɔr]
correspondent	**кореспондент** (m)	[kɔrɛspɔn'dɛnt]
typist (fem.)	**машинописка** (f)	[maʃinɔ'piska]

designer	**дизайнер** (m)	[di'zajnɛr]
computer expert	**компютърен специалист** (m)	[kɔm'pytırɛn spɛtsia'list]
programmer	**програмист** (m)	[prɔgra'mist]
engineer (designer)	**инженер** (m)	[inʒɛ'nɛr]
sailor	**моряк** (m)	[mɔ'rʲak]
seaman	**матрос** (m)	[mat'rɔs]
rescuer	**спасител** (m)	[spa'sitɛl]
fireman	**пожарникар** (m)	[pɔʒarni'kar]
policeman	**полицай** (m)	[pɔli'tsaj]
watchman	**пазач** (m)	[pa'zatʃ]
detective	**детектив** (m)	[dɛtɛk'tif]
customs officer	**митничар** (m)	[mitni'tʃar]
bodyguard	**телохранител** (n)	[tɛlɔhra'nitel]
prison guard	**надзирател** (m)	[nadzi'ratɛl]
inspector	**инспектор** (m)	[ins'pɛktɔr]
sportsman	**спортист** (m)	[spɔr'tist]
trainer, coach	**треньор** (m)	[trɛ'nɜr]
butcher	**месар** (m)	[mɛ'sar]
cobbler	**обущар** (m)	[ɔbuʃ'tar]
merchant	**търговец** (m)	[tır'gɔvɛts]
loader (person)	**хамалин** (m)	[ha'malin]
fashion designer	**моделиер** (m)	[mɔdɛli'ɛr]
model (fem.)	**модел** (m)	[mɔ'dɛl]

131. Occupations. Social status

schoolboy	**ученик** (m)	[utʃə'nik]
student (college ~)	**студент** (m)	[stu'dɛnt]
philosopher	**философ** (m)	[filɔ'sɔf]
economist	**икономист** (m)	[ikɔnɔ'mist]
inventor	**изобретател** (m)	[izɔbrɛ'tatɛl]
unemployed (n)	**безработен човек** (m)	[bɛzra'bɔtɛn tʃɔ'vɛk]
retiree	**пенсионер** (m)	[pɛnsiɔ'nɛr]
spy, secret agent	**шпионин** (m)	[ʃpi'ɔnin]
prisoner	**затворник** (m)	[zat'vɔrnik]
striker	**стачник** (m)	['statʃnik]
bureaucrat	**бюрократ** (m)	[byrɔk'rat]
traveler	**пътешественик** (m)	[pıtɛ'ʃɛstvɛnik]
homosexual	**хомосексуалист** (m)	[hɔmɔsɛksua'list]
hacker	**хакер** (m)	['hakɛr]

hippie	**хипи** (m)	['hipi]
bandit	**бандит** (m)	[ban'dit]
hit man, killer	**наемен убиец** (m)	[na'ɛmɛn u'biɛʦ]
drug addict	**наркоман** (m)	[narkɔ'man]
drug dealer	**наркотрафикант** (m)	[narkɔtrafi'kant]
prostitute (fem.)	**проститутка** (f)	[prɔsti'tutka]
pimp	**сутеньор** (m)	[sutɛ'nɜr]
sorcerer	**магьосник** (m)	[ma'gʲɔsnik]
sorceress	**магьосница** (f)	[ma'gʲɔsniʦa]
pirate	**пират** (m)	[pi'rat]
slave	**роб** (m)	[rɔb]
samurai	**самурай** (m)	[samu'raj]
savage (primitive)	**дивак** (m)	[di'vak]

Sports

132. Kinds of sports. Sportspersons

sportsman	**спортист** (m)	[spɔr'tist]
kind of sports	**вид** (m) **спорт**	[vid spɔrt]
basketball	**баскетбол** (m)	['baskɛtbɔl]
basketball player	**баскетболист** (m)	[baskɛtbɔ'list]
baseball	**бейзбол** (m)	[bɛjz'bɔl]
baseball player	**бейзболист** (m)	[bɛjzbɔ'list]
soccer	**футбол** (m)	['fudbɔl]
soccer player	**футболист** (m)	[fudbɔ'list]
goalkeeper	**вратар** (m)	[vra'tar]
hockey	**хокей** (m)	['hɔkɛj]
hockey player	**хокеист** (m)	[hɔkɛ'ist]
volleyball	**волейбол** (m)	['vɔlɛjbɔl]
volleyball player	**волейболист** (m)	[vɔlɛjbɔ'list]
boxing	**бокс** (m)	[bɔks]
boxer	**боксьор** (m)	[bɔk'sɜr]
wrestling	**борба** (f)	[bɔr'ba]
wrestler	**борец** (m)	[bɔ'rɛʦ]
karate	**карате** (n)	[ka'ratɛ]
karate fighter	**каратист** (m)	[kara'tist]
judo	**джудо** (n)	['ʤudɔ]
judo athlete	**джудист** (m)	[ʤu'dist]
tennis	**тенис** (m)	['tɛnis]
tennis player	**тенисист** (m)	[tɛni'sist]
swimming	**плуване** (n)	['pluvanɛ]
swimmer	**плувец** (m)	[plu'vɛʦ]
fencing	**фехтовка** (f)	[fɛh'tɔfka]
fencer	**фехтувач** (m)	[fɛhtu'vaʧ]
chess	**шахмат** (m)	['ʃʌh'mat]
chess player	**шахматист** (m)	[ʃʌhma'tist]

alpinism	**алпинизъм** (m)	[alpi'nizım]
alpinist	**алпинист** (m)	[alpi'nist]
running	**бягане** (n)	['bʲaganɛ]
runner	**бегач** (m)	[bɛ'gatʃ]
athletics	**лека атлетика** (f)	['lɛka at'lɛtika]
athlete	**атлет** (m)	[at'lɛt]
horseback riding	**конен спорт** (m)	['kɔnɛn spɔrt]
horse rider	**ездач** (m)	[ɛz'datʃ]
figure skating	**фигурно пързаляне** (n)	['figurnɔ pır'zaʎanɛ]
figure skater (masc.)	**фигурист** (m)	[figu'rist]
figure skater (fem.)	**фигуристка** (f)	[figu'ristka]
weightlifting	**тежка атлетика** (f)	['tɛʃka at'lɛtika]
car racing	**автомобилни състезания** (n pl)	[avtɔmɔ'bilni sıstɛ'zanija]
racing driver	**автомобилен състезател** (m)	[avtɔmɔ'bilɛn sıstɛ'zatɛl]
cycling	**колоездене** (n)	[kɔlɔ'ɛzdɛnɛ]
cyclist	**колоездач** (m)	[kɔlɔɛz'datʃ]
broad jump	**скокове** (m pl) **на дължина**	['skɔkɔvɛ na dıʒi'na]
pole vault	**овчарски скок** (m)	[ɔf'tʃarski skɔk]
jumper	**скачач** (m)	[ska'tʃatʃ]

133. Kinds of sports. Miscellaneous

football	**американски футбол** (m)	[amɛri'kanski 'fudbɔl]
badminton	**бадминтон** (m)	['badmintɔn]
biathlon	**биатлон** (m)	[biat'lɔn]
billiards	**билярд** (m)	[bi'ʎard]
bobsled	**бобслей** (m)	[bɔbs'lɛj]
bodybuilding	**културизъм** (m)	[kultu'rizım]
water polo	**водна топка** (f)	['vɔdna 'tɔpka]
handball	**хандбал** (m)	['handbal]
golf	**голф** (m)	[gɔlf]
rowing	**гребане** (n)	['grɛbanɛ]
scuba diving	**дайвинг** (m)	['dajviŋg]
cross-country skiing	**ски бягане** (n pl)	[ski 'bʲaganɛ]
ping-pong	**тенис** (m) **на маса**	['tɛnis na 'masa]
sailing	**спорт** (m) **с платноходки**	[spɔrt s platnɔ'hɔtki]
rally racing	**рали** (n)	['rali]

rugby	**ръгби** (n)	['rɪgbi]
snowboarding	**сноуборд** (m)	['snɔubɔrt]

134. Gym

barbell	**щанга** (f)	['ʃtaŋga]
dumbbells	**гири** (f pl)	['giri]
training machine	**тренажор** (m)	[trɛna'ʒɔr]
bicycle trainer	**велоергометър** (m)	[vɛlɔɛrgɔ'mɛtɪr]
treadmill	**писта за бягане** (f)	['pista za 'bʲaganɛ]
horizontal bar	**лост** (m)	[lɔst]
parallel bars	**успоредка** (f)	['uspɔrɛtka]
vaulting horse	**кон** (m)	[kɔn]
mat (in gym)	**дюшек** (m)	[dy'ʃɛk]
aerobics	**аеробика** (f)	[aə'rɔbika]
yoga	**йога** (f)	['joga]

135. Hockey

hockey	**хокей** (m)	['hɔkɛj]
hockey player	**хокеист** (m)	[hɔkɛ'ist]
to play hockey	**играя хокей**	[ig'rajɑ 'hɔkɛj]
ice	**лед** (m)	[lɛd]
puck	**шайба** (f)	['ʃʌjba]
hockey stick	**стик** (m)	[stik]
ice skates	**кънки** (pl)	['kɪŋki]
board	**мантинела** (f)	[manti'nɛla]
shot	**удар** (m)	['udar]
goaltender	**вратар** (m)	[vra'tar]
goal (score)	**гол** (m)	[gɔl]
to score a goal	**вкарам гол**	['fkaram gɔl]
period	**третина** (f)	[trɛ'tina]
substitutes bench	**резервна скамейка** (f)	[rɛ'zɛrvna ska'mɛjka]

136. Football

soccer	**футбол** (m)	['fudbɔl]
soccer player	**футболист** (m)	[fudbɔ'list]
to play soccer	**играя футбол**	[ig'rajɑ 'fudbɔl]

major league	**висша лига** (f)	['visʃʌ 'liga]
soccer club	**футболен клуб** (m)	['fudbɔlɛn klub]
coach	**треньор** (m)	[trɛ'nɜr]
owner, proprietor	**собственик** (m)	['sɔbstvɛnik]
team	**отбор** (m)	[ɔt'bɔr]
team captain	**капитан** (m) **на отбора**	[kapi'tan na ɔd'bɔra]
player	**играч** (m)	[ig'ratʃ]
substitute	**резервен играч** (m)	[rɛ'zɛrvɛn ig'ratʃ]
forward	**нападател** (m)	[napa'datɛl]
center forward	**централен нападател** (m)	[tsənt'ralɛn napa'datɛl]
striker, scorer	**голмайстор** (m)	[gɔl'majstɔr]
defender, back	**защитник** (m)	[zaʃ'titnik]
halfback	**полузащитник** (m)	[pɔluzaʃ'titnik]
match	**мач** (m)	[matʃ]
to meet (vi, vt)	**срещам се**	['srɛʃtam sɛ]
final	**финал** (m)	[fi'nal]
semi-final	**полуфинал** (m)	[pɔlufi'nal]
championship	**шампионат** (m)	[ʃʌmpiɔ'nat]
period, half	**полувреме** (n)	[pɔluv'rɛmɛ]
first period	**първо полувреме** (n)	['pɪrvɔ pɔluv'rɛmɛ]
half-time	**почивка** (f)	[pɔ'tʃifka]
goal	**врата** (f)	[vra'ta]
goalkeeper	**вратар** (m)	[vra'tar]
goalpost	**странична греда** (f)	[stra'nitʃna grɛ'da]
crossbar	**напречната греда** (f)	[naprɛtʃnata grɛ'da]
net	**мрежа** (f)	['mreʒa]
to concede a goal	**пропусна топка**	[prɔ'pusna 'tɔpka]
ball	**топка** (f)	['tɔpka]
pass	**пас** (m)	[pas]
kick	**удар** (m)	['udar]
to kick (~ the ball)	**бия**	['bijɑ]
free kick	**наказателен удар** (m)	[naka'zatɛlɛn 'udar]
corner kick	**ъглов удар** (m)	['ɪglɔv 'udar]
attack	**атака** (f)	[a'taka]
counterattack	**контраатака** (f)	['kɔntra:'taka]
combination	**комбинация** (f)	[kɔmbi'natsijɑ]
referee	**арбитър** (m)	[ar'bitɪr]
to whistle (vi)	**свиря**	['svirʲa]
whistle (sound)	**свирка** (f)	['svirka]
foul, misconduct	**нарушение** (n)	[naru'ʃɛniɛ]
to commit a foul	**наруша**	[naru'ʃʌ]
to send off	**отстраня**	[ɔtstra'ɲa]
yellow card	**жълт картон** (m)	[ʒɪlt kar'tɔn]

red card	**червен картон** (m)	[ʧər'vɛn kar'tɔn]
disqualification	**дисквалификация** (f)	[diskvalifi'kaʦija]
to disqualify (vt)	**дисквалифицирам**	[diskvalifi'ʦiram]
penalty kick	**дузпа** (f)	['duspa]
wall	**стена** (f)	[stɛ'na]
to score (vi, vt)	**вкарам**	['fkaram]
goal (score)	**гол** (m)	[gɔl]
to score a goal	**вкарам гол**	['fkaram gɔl]
substitution	**смяна** (f)	['smʲana]
to replace (vt)	**сменя**	[smɛ'ɲa]
rules	**правила** (n pl)	[pravi'la]
tactics	**тактика** (f)	['taktika]
stadium	**стадион** (m)	[stadi'ɔn]
stand (bleachers)	**трибуна** (f)	[tri'buna]
fan, supporter	**запалянко** (m)	[zapa'ʎaŋkɔ]
to shout (vi)	**викам**	['vikam]
scoreboard	**табло** (n)	[tab'lɔ]
score	**резултат** (m)	[rɛzul'tat]
defeat	**поражение** (n)	[pɔra'ʒɛniɛ]
to lose (not win)	**загубя**	[za'gubʲa]
draw	**наравно**	[na'ravnɔ]
to draw (vi)	**завърша наравно**	[za'vırʃʌ na'ravnɔ]
victory	**победа** (f)	[pɔ'bɛda]
to win (vi, vt)	**победя**	[pɔbɛ'dʲa]
champion	**шампион** (m)	[ʃʌm'piɔn]
best (adj)	**най-добър**	[naj dɔ'bır]
to congratulate (vt)	**поздравявам**	[pɔzdra'vʲavam]
commentator	**коментатор** (m)	[kɔmɛn'tatɔr]
to commentate (vt)	**коментирам**	[kɔmɛn'tiram]
broadcast	**предаване** (n)	[prɛ'davanɛ]

137. Alpine skiing

skis	**ски** (pl)	[ski]
to ski (vi)	**карам ски**	['karam ski]
mountain-ski resort	**планински курорт** (m)	[pla'ninski ku'rɔrt]
ski lift	**лифт** (m)	[lift]
ski poles	**щеки** (f pl)	['ʃtɛki]
slope	**склон** (m)	[sklɔn]
slalom	**слалом** (m)	['slalɔm]

138. Tennis. Golf

golf	**голф** (m)	[gɔlf]
golf club	**голф клуб** (m)	[gɔlf 'klub]
golfer	**играч** (m) **на голф**	[ig'ratʃ na gɔlf]
hole	**дупка** (f)	['dupka]
club	**стик** (m)	[stik]
golf trolley	**количка** (f) **за голф**	[kɔ'litʃka za gɔlf]
tennis	**тенис** (m)	['tɛnis]
tennis court	**корт** (m)	[kɔrt]
serve	**сервис** (m)	['sɛrvis]
to serve (vt)	**сервирам**	[sɛr'viram]
racket	**ракета** (f)	[ra'keta]
net	**мрежа** (f)	['mreʒa]
ball	**топка** (f)	['tɔpka]

139. Chess

chess	**шахмат** (m)	['ʃʌh'mat]
chessmen	**шахматни фигури** (f pl)	['ʃʌh'matni 'figuri]
chess player	**шахматист** (m)	[ʃʌhma'tist]
chessboard	**шахматна дъска** (f)	['ʃʌhmatna dıs'ka]
chessman	**фигура** (f)	['figura]
White (white pieces)	**бели** (pl)	['bɛli]
Black (black pieces)	**черни** (pl)	['tʃərni]
pawn	**пионка** (f)	[pi'ɔŋka]
bishop	**офицер** (m)	[ɔfi'tsər]
knight	**кон** (m)	[kɔn]
rook (castle)	**топ** (m)	[tɔp]
queen	**царица** (f)	[tsa'ritsa]
king	**цар** (m)	[tsar]
move	**ход** (m)	[hɔd]
to move (vi, vt)	**предвижвам**	[prɛd'viʒvam]
to sacrifice (vt)	**жертвам**	['ʒɛrtvam]
castling	**рокада** (f)	[rɔ'kada]
check	**шах** (m)	[ʃʌh]
checkmate	**мат** (m)	[mat]
chess tournament	**шахматен турнир** (m)	['ʃʌhmatɛn tur'nir]
Grand Master	**гросмайстор** (m)	[grɔs'majstɔr]
combination	**комбинация** (f)	[kɔmbi'natsija]
game (in chess)	**партия** (f)	['partija]
checkers	**шашки** (pl)	['ʃʌʃki]

140. Boxing

boxing	**бокс** (m)	[bɔks]
fight (bout)	**бой** (m)	[bɔj]
boxing match	**двубой** (m)	[dvu'bɔj]
round (in boxing)	**рунд** (m)	[rund]
ring	**ринг** (m)	[riŋg]
gong	**гонг** (m)	[gɔŋg]
punch	**удар** (m)	['udar]
knock-down	**нокдаун** (m)	[nɔk'daun]
knockout	**нокаут** (m)	[nɔ'kaut]
to knock out	**нокаутирам**	[nɔkau'tiram]
boxing glove	**боксьорска ръкавица** (f)	[bɔk'sʲɔrska rɪka'vitsa]
referee	**рефер** (m)	['rɛfɛr]
lightweight	**лека категория** (f)	['lɛka katɛ'gɔrijɑ]
middleweight	**средна категория** (f)	['srɛdna katɛ'gɔrijɑ]
heavyweight	**тежка категория** (f)	['tɛʃka katɛ'gɔrijɑ]

141. Sports. Miscellaneous

Olympic Games	**олимпийски игри** (f pl)	[ɔlim'pijski ig'ri]
winner	**победител** (m)	[pɔbɛ'ditɛl]
to be winning	**побеждавам**	[pɔbɛʒ'davam]
to win (vi)	**спечеля**	[spɛ'ʧəʎa]
leader	**водач** (m)	[vɔ'daʧ]
to lead (vi)	**водя**	['vɔdʲa]
first place	**първо място** (n)	['pɪrvɔ 'mʲastɔ]
second place	**второ място** (n)	['ftɔrɔ 'mʲastɔ]
third place	**трето място** (n)	['trɛtɔ 'mʲastɔ]
medal	**медал** (m)	[mɛ'dal]
trophy	**трофей** (m)	[trɔ'fɛj]
prize cup (trophy)	**купа** (f)	[ku'pa]
prize (in game)	**награда** (f)	[nag'rada]
main prize	**първа награда** (f)	['pɪrva nag'rada]
record	**рекорд** (m)	[rɛ'kɔrd]
to set a record	**поставям рекорд**	[pɔs'tavʲam rɛ'kɔrd]
final	**финал** (m)	[fi'nal]
final (adj)	**финален**	[fi'nalɛn]
champion	**шампион** (m)	[ʃʌm'piɔn]
championship	**шампионат** (m)	[ʃʌmpiɔ'nat]

stadium	**стадион** (m)	[stadi'ɔn]
stand (bleachers)	**трибуна** (f)	[tri'buna]
fan, supporter	**запалянко** (m)	[zapa'ʎaŋkɔ]
opponent, rival	**съперник** (m)	[sı'pɛrnik]
start	**старт** (m)	[start]
finish line	**финиш** (m)	['finiʃ]
defeat	**загуба** (f)	['zaguba]
to lose (not win)	**загубя**	[za'gubʲa]
referee	**съдия** (m)	[sıdi'jɑ]
jury	**жури** (n)	['ʒuri]
score	**резултат** (m)	[rɛzul'tat]
draw	**наравно** (n)	[na'ravnɔ]
to draw (vi)	**завърша наравно**	[za'vırʃʌ na'ravnɔ]
point	**точка** (f)	['tɔʧka]
result (final score)	**резултат** (m)	[rɛzul'tat]
half-time	**почивка** (f)	[pɔ'ʧifka]
doping	**допинг** (m)	['dɔpiŋg]
to penalize (vt)	**наказвам**	[na'kazvam]
to disqualify (vt)	**дисквалифицирам**	[diskvalifi'ʦiram]
apparatus	**уред** (m)	['urɛd]
javelin	**копие** (n)	['kɔpie]
shot put ball	**гюлле** (n)	[gy'lɛ]
ball (snooker, etc.)	**топка** (f)	['tɔpka]
aim (target)	**цел** (f)	[ʦəl]
target	**мишена** (f)	[mi'ʃɛna]
to shoot (vi)	**стрелям**	['strɛʎam]
precise (~ shot)	**точен**	['tɔʧən]
trainer, coach	**треньор** (m)	[trɛ'nɜr]
to train (sb)	**тренирам**	[trɛ'niram]
to train (vi)	**тренирам се**	[trɛ'niram sɛ]
training	**тренировка** (f)	[trɛni'rɔfka]
gym	**спортна зала** (f)	['spɔrtna 'zala]
exercise (physical)	**упражнение** (n)	[upraʒ'nɛniɛ]
warm-up (of athlete)	**загряване** (n)	[zag'rʲavane]

Education

142. School

school	**училище** (n)	[u'ʧiliʃtɛ]
headmaster	**директор** (m) **на училище**	[di'rɛktɔr na u'ʧiliʃtɛ]
pupil (boy)	**ученик** (m)	[uʧə'nik]
pupil (girl)	**ученичка** (f)	[uʧə'niʧka]
schoolboy	**ученик** (m)	[uʧə'nik]
schoolgirl	**ученичка** (f)	[uʧə'niʧka]
to teach (sb)	**уча**	['uʧa]
to learn (language, etc.)	**уча**	['uʧa]
to learn by heart	**уча наизуст**	['uʧa nai'zust]
to study (work to learn)	**уча се**	['uʧa sɛ]
to be in school	**уча**	['uʧa]
to go to school	**отивам на училище**	[ɔ'tivam na u'ʧiliʃtɛ]
alphabet	**алфавит** (m)	[alfa'vit]
subject (at school)	**предмет** (m)	[prɛd'mɛt]
classroom	**клас** (m)	[klas]
lesson	**час** (m)	[ʧas]
recess	**междучасие** (n)	[meʒdu'ʧasie]
school bell	**звънец** (m)	[zvɪ'neʦ]
school desk	**чин** (m)	[ʧin]
chalkboard	**дъска** (f)	[dɪs'ka]
grade	**бележка** (f)	[be'lɛʃka]
good grade	**добра оценка** (f)	[dɔb'ra ɔ'ʦəŋka]
bad grade	**лоша оценка** (f)	['lɔʃʌ ɔ'ʦəŋka]
to give a grade	**пиша оценка** (f)	['piʃʌ ɔ'ʦəŋka]
mistake, error	**грешка** (f)	['grɛʃka]
to make mistakes	**правя грешки**	['pravʲa 'grɛʃki]
to correct (an error)	**поправям**	[pɔp'ravʲam]
cheat sheet	**пищов** (m)	[piʃ'tɔv]
homework	**домашно** (n)	[dɔ'maʃnɔ]
exercise (in education)	**упражнение** (n)	[upraʒ'nɛniɛ]
to be present	**присъствам**	[pri'sɪstvam]
to be absent	**отсъствам**	[ɔ'ʦɪstvam]

to punish (vt)	**наказвам**	[na'kazvam]
punishment	**наказание** (n)	[naka'zaniɛ]
conduct (behavior)	**поведение** (n)	[pɔvɛ'dɛniɛ]
report card	**дневник** (m)	['dnɛvnik]
pencil	**молив** (m)	['mɔliv]
eraser	**гума** (f)	['guma]
chalk	**тебешир** (m)	[tɛbɛ'ʃir]
pencil case	**несесер** (m)	[nɛsɛ'sɛr]
schoolbag	**раница** (f)	['ranitsa]
pen	**химикалка** (f)	[himi'kalka]
school notebook	**тетрадка** (f)	[tɛt'radka]
textbook	**учебник** (m)	[u'tʃəbnik]
compasses	**пергел** (m)	[pɛr'gɛl]
to draw (a blueprint, etc.)	**чертая**	[tʃər'taja]
technical drawing	**чертеж** (m)	[tʃər'tɛʒ]
poem	**стихотворение** (n)	[stihɔtvɔ'rɛniɛ]
by heart (adv)	**наизуст**	[nai'zust]
to learn by heart	**уча наизуст**	['utʃa nai'zust]
school vacation	**ваканция** (f)	[va'kantsija]
to be on vacation	**във ваканция съм**	[vɪf va'kantsija sɪm]
to spend one's vacation	**прекарвам ваканция**	[prɛ'karvam va'kantsija]
test (written math ~)	**контролна работа** (f)	[kɔnt'rɔlna 'rabɔta]
essay (composition)	**съчинение** (n)	[sɪtʃi'nɛniɛ]
dictation	**диктовка** (f)	[dik'tɔfka]
exam	**изпит** (m)	['ispit]
to take an exam	**полагам изпити**	[pɔ'lagam 'ispiti]
experiment (chemical ~)	**опит** (m)	['ɔpit]

143. College. University

academy	**академия** (f)	[aka'dɛmija]
university	**университет** (m)	[univɛrsi'tɛt]
faculty (section)	**факултет** (m)	[fakul'tɛt]
student (masc.)	**студент** (m)	[stu'dɛnt]
student (fem.)	**студентка** (f)	[stu'dɛntka]
lecturer (teacher)	**преподавател** (m)	[prɛpɔda'vatɛl]
lecture hall, room	**аудитория** (f)	[audi'tɔrija]
graduate	**абсолвент** (m)	[absɔl'vɛnt]
diploma	**диплома** (f)	['diplɔma]
dissertation	**дисертация** (f)	[disɛr'tatsija]
study (report)	**изследване** (n)	[iss'lɛdvanɛ]
laboratory	**лаборатория** (f)	[labɔra'tɔrija]

lecture	**лекция** (f)	['lɛkʦija]
course mate	**състудент** (m)	[sɪstu'dɛnt]
scholarship	**стипендия** (f)	[sti'pɛndija]
academic degree	**научна степен** (f)	[na'uʧna 'stɛpɛn]

144. Sciences. Disciplines

mathematics	**математика** (f)	[matɛ'matika]
algebra	**алгебра** (f)	['algɛbra]
geometry	**геометрия** (f)	[gɛɔ'mɛtrija]
astronomy	**астрономия** (f)	[astrɔ'nɔmija]
biology	**биология** (f)	[biɔ'lɔgija]
geography	**география** (f)	[gɛɔg'rafija]
geology	**геология** (f)	[gɛɔ'lɔgija]
history	**история** (f)	[is'tɔrija]
medicine	**медицина** (f)	[mɛdi'ʦina]
pedagogy	**педагогика** (f)	[pɛda'gɔgika]
law	**право** (n)	['pravɔ]
physics	**физика** (f)	['fizika]
chemistry	**химия** (f)	['himija]
philosophy	**философия** (f)	[filɔ'sɔfija]
psychology	**психология** (f)	[psihɔ'lɔgija]

145. Writing system. Orthography

grammar	**граматика** (f)	[gra'matika]
vocabulary	**лексика** (f)	['lɛksika]
phonetics	**фонетика** (f)	[fɔ'nɛtika]
noun	**съществително име** (n)	[sɪʃtɛst'vitɛlnɔ 'imɛ]
adjective	**прилагателно име** (n)	[prila'gatɛlnɔ 'imɛ]
verb	**глагол** (m)	[gla'gɔl]
adverb	**наречие** (n)	[na'rɛʧiɛ]
pronoun	**местоимение** (n)	[mɛstɔi'mɛniɛ]
interjection	**междуметие** (n)	[mɛʒdu'mɛtiɛ]
preposition	**предлог** (m)	[prɛd'lɔg]
root	**корен** (m) **на думата**	['kɔrɛn na 'dumata]
ending	**окончание** (n)	[ɔkɔn'ʧaniɛ]
prefix	**представка** (f)	[prɛʦ'tafka]
syllable	**сричка** (f)	['sriʧka]
suffix	**наставка** (f)	[nas'tafka]
stress mark	**ударение** (n)	[uda'rɛniɛ]

apostrophe	**апостроф** (m)	[apɔst'rɔf]
period, dot	**точка** (f)	['tɔʧka]
comma	**запетая** (f)	[zapɛ'tajɑ]
semicolon	**точка** (f) **и запетая**	['tɔʧka i zapɛ'tajɑ]
colon	**двоеточие** (n)	[dvɔɛ'tɔʧiɛ]
ellipsis	**многоточие** (n)	[mnɔgɔ'tɔʧiɛ]
question mark	**въпросителен знак** (m)	[vɪprɔ'sitelen 'znak]
exclamation point	**удивителна** (f)	[udi'vitɛlna]
quotation marks	**кавички** (pl)	[ka'viʧki]
in quotation marks	**в кавички**	[v ka'viʧki]
parenthesis	**скоби** (f pl)	['skɔbi]
in parenthesis	**в скоби**	[v 'skɔbi]
hyphen	**дефис** (m)	[dɛ'fis]
dash	**тире** (n)	[ti'rɛ]
space (between words)	**бяло поле** (n)	['bʲalɔ pɔ'lɛ]
letter	**буква** (f)	['bukva]
capital letter	**главна буква** (f)	['glavna 'bukva]
vowel (n)	**гласен звук** (m)	['glasɛn zvuk]
consonant (n)	**съгласен звук** (m)	[sɪg'lasɛn zvuk]
sentence	**изречение** (n)	[izrɛ'ʧəniɛ]
subject	**подлог** (m)	['pɔdlɔg]
predicate	**сказуемо** (n)	[ska'zuɛmɔ]
line	**ред** (m)	[rɛd]
on a new line	**от нов ред**	[ɔt 'nɔv rɛt]
paragraph	**абзац** (m)	[ab'zaʦ]
word	**дума** (f)	['duma]
group of words	**словосъчетание** (n)	[slɔvɔsɪʧə'taniɛ]
expression	**израз** (m)	['izraz]
synonym	**синоним** (m)	[sinɔ'nim]
antonym	**антоним** (m)	[antɔ'nim]
rule	**правило** (n)	['pravilɔ]
exception	**изключение** (n)	[izkly'ʧəniɛ]
correct (adj)	**верен**	['vɛrɛn]
conjugation	**спрежение** (n)	[sprɛ'ʒɛniɛ]
declension	**склонение** (n)	[sklɔ'nɛniɛ]
nominal case	**падеж** (m)	[pa'dɛʒ]
question	**въпрос** (m)	[vɪp'rɔs]
to underline (vt)	**подчертая**	[pɔdʧər'tajɑ]
dotted line	**пунктир** (m)	[puŋk'tir]

146. Foreign languages

language	**език** (m)	[ɛ'zik]
foreign language	**чужд език** (m)	[ʧuʒd ɛ'zik]
to study (vt)	**изучавам**	[izu'ʧavam]
to learn (language, etc.)	**уча**	['uʧa]
to read (vi, vt)	**чета**	[ʧə'tı]
to speak (vi, vt)	**говоря**	[gɔ'vɔrʲa]
to understand (vt)	**разбирам**	[raz'biram]
to write (vt)	**пиша**	['piʃʌ]
fast (adv)	**бързо**	['bırzɔ]
slowly (adv)	**бавно**	['bavnɔ]
fluently (adv)	**свободно**	[svɔ'bɔdnɔ]
rules	**правила** (n pl)	[pravi'la]
grammar	**граматика** (f)	[gra'matika]
vocabulary	**лексика** (f)	['lɛksika]
phonetics	**фонетика** (f)	[fɔ'nɛtika]
textbook	**учебник** (m)	[u'ʧəbnik]
dictionary	**речник** (m)	['rɛʧnik]
teach-yourself book	**самоучител** (m)	[samɔu'ʧitɛl]
phrasebook	**разговорник** (m)	[razgɔ'vɔrnik]
cassette	**касета** (f)	[ka'sɛta]
videotape	**видеокасета** (f)	[vidɛɔka'sɛta]
CD, compact disc	**CD диск** (m)	[si'di disk]
DVD	**DVD** (m)	[divi'di]
alphabet	**алфавит** (m)	[alfa'vit]
to spell (vt)	**спелувам**	[spɛ'luvam]
pronunciation	**произношение** (n)	[prɔiznɔ'ʃɛniɛ]
accent	**акцент** (m)	[ak'ʦənt]
with an accent	**с акцент**	[s ak'ʦənt]
without an accent	**без акцент**	[bɛz ak'ʦənt]
word	**дума** (f)	['duma]
meaning	**смисъл** (m)	['smisıl]
course (e.g., a French ~)	**курсове** (m pl)	['kursɔvɛ]
to sign up	**запиша се**	[za'piʃʌ sɛ]
teacher	**преподавател** (m)	[prɛpɔda'vatɛl]
translation (process)	**превод** (m)	['prɛvɔd]
translation (text, etc.)	**превод** (m)	['prɛvɔd]
translator	**преводач** (m)	[prɛvɔ'daʧ]
interpreter	**преводач** (m)	[prɛvɔ'daʧ]
polyglot	**полиглот** (m)	[pɔlig'lɔt]
memory	**памет** (f)	['pamɛt]

147. Fairy tale characters

Santa Claus	**Дядо Коледа**	['dʲadɔ 'kɔleda]
mermaid	**русалка** (f)	[ru'salka]
magician, wizard	**вълшебник** (m)	[vɪl'ʃɛbnik]
fairy	**вълшебница** (f)	[vɪl'ʃɛbnitsa]
magic (adj)	**вълшебен**	[vɪl'ʃɛbɛn]
magic wand	**вълшебна пръчица** (f)	[vɪl'ʃɛbna 'prɪtʃitsa]
fairy tale	**приказка** (f)	['prikaska]
miracle	**чудо** (n)	['tʃudɔ]
dwarf	**джудже** (n)	[dʒu'dʒɛ]
to turn into ...	**превърна се в ...**	[prɛ'vɪrna sɛ v]
ghost	**привидение** (n)	[privi'dɛniɛ]
phantom	**призрак** (m)	['prizrak]
monster	**чудовище** (n)	[tʃu'dɔviʃtɛ]
dragon	**ламя** (f)	[la'mʲa]
giant	**великан** (m)	[vɛli'kan]

148. Zodiac Signs

Aries	**Овен** (m)	[ɔ'vɛn]
Taurus	**Телец** (m)	[tɛ'lɛts]
Gemini	**Близнаци** (m pl)	[bliz'natsi]
Cancer	**Рак** (m)	[rak]
Leo	**Лъв** (m)	[lɪv]
Virgo	**Дева** (f)	['dɛva]
Libra	**Везни** (f pl)	[vɛz'ni]
Scorpio	**Скорпион** (m)	[skɔrpi'ɔn]
Sagittarius	**Стрелец** (m)	[strɛ'lɛts]
Capricorn	**Козирог** (m)	['kɔzirɔg]
Aquarius	**Водолей** (m)	[vɔdɔ'lɛj]
Pisces	**Риби** (f pl)	['ribi]
character	**характер** (m)	[ha'raktɛr]
features of character	**черти** (f pl) **на характера**	[tʃər'ti na ha'raktɛra]
behavior	**поведение** (n)	[pɔvɛ'dɛniɛ]
to tell fortunes	**гледам**	['glɛdam]
fortune-teller	**гледачка** (f)	[glɛ'datʃka]
horoscope	**хороскоп** (m)	[hɔrɔs'kɔp]

Arts

149. Theater

theater	**театър** (m)	[tɛ'atır]
opera	**опера** (f)	['ɔpɛra]
operetta	**оперета** (f)	[ɔpɛ'rɛta]
ballet	**балет** (m)	[ba'lɛt]
theater poster	**афиш** (m)	[a'fiʃ]
theatrical company	**трупа** (f)	['trupa]
tour	**гастроли** (m pl)	[gast'rɔli]
to be on tour	**гастролирам**	[gastrɔ'liram]
to rehearse (vi, vt)	**репетирам**	[rɛpɛ'tiram]
rehearsal	**репетиция** (f)	[rɛpɛ'tiʦija]
repertoire	**репертоар** (m)	[rɛpɛrtu'ar]
performance	**представление** (n)	[prɛdstav'lɛniɛ]
theatrical show	**спектакъл** (m)	[spɛk'takıl]
play	**пиеса** (f)	[pi'ɛsa]
ticket	**билет** (m)	[bi'lɛt]
Box office	**билетна каса** (f)	[bi'lɛtna 'kasa]
lobby, foyer	**хол** (m)	[hɔl]
coat check	**гардероб** (m)	[gardɛ'rɔb]
coat check tag	**номерче** (n)	['nɔmerʧe]
binoculars	**бинокъл** (m)	[bi'nɔkıl]
usher	**контрольор** (m)	[kɔntrɔ'lɜr]
orchestra seats	**партер** (m)	['partɛr]
balcony	**балкон** (m)	[bal'kɔn]
dress circle	**първи балкон** (m)	['pırvi bal'kɔn]
box	**ложа** (f)	['lɔʒa]
row	**ред** (m)	[rɛd]
seat	**място** (n)	['mʲastɔ]
audience	**публика** (f)	['publika]
spectator	**зрител** (m)	['zritɛl]
to clap (vi, vt)	**аплодирам**	[aplɔ'diram]
applause	**аплодисменти** (m pl)	[aplɔdis'mɛnti]
ovation	**овации** (f pl)	[ɔ'vaʦi:]
stage	**сцена** (f)	['sʦəna]
curtain	**завеса** (f)	[za'vɛsa]
scenery	**декорация** (f)	[dɛkɔ'raʦija]
backstage	**кулиси** (f pl)	[ku'lisi]

scene (e.g., the last ~)	**сцена** (f)	['stsəna]
act	**действие** (n)	['dɛjstviɛ]
intermission	**антракт** (m)	[ant'rakt]

150. Cinema

actor	**актьор** (m)	[ak'tɜr]
actress	**актриса** (f)	[akt'risa]
movies (industry)	**кино** (n)	['kinɔ]
movie	**филм** (m)	[film]
episode	**серия** (f)	['sɛrijɑ]
detective	**детективски филм** (m)	[dɛtɛk'tifski film]
action movie	**екшън филм** (m)	['ɛkʃɪn film]
adventure movie	**приключенски филм** (m)	[prikly'ʧənski film]
science fiction movie	**фантастичен филм** (f)	[fantas'tiʧən film]
horror movie	**филм** (m) **на ужаси**	[film na 'uʒasi]
comedy movie	**кинокомедия** (f)	[kinɔkɔ'mɛdijɑ]
melodrama	**мелодрама** (f)	[mɛlɔd'rama]
drama	**драма** (f)	['drama]
fictional movie	**игрален филм** (m)	[ig'ralɛn film]
documentary	**документален филм** (m)	[dɔkumɛn'talɛn film]
cartoon	**анимационен филм** (m)	[animatsi'ɔnɛn film]
silent movies	**нямо кино** (n)	['ɲamɔ 'kinɔ]
role (part)	**роля** (f)	['rɔʎa]
leading role	**главна роля** (f)	['glavna 'rɔʎa]
to play (vi, vt)	**играя**	[ig'rajɑ]
movie star	**кинозвезда** (f)	[kinɔzvɛz'da]
well-known (adj)	**известен**	[iz'vɛstɛn]
famous (adj)	**прочут**	[prɔ'ʧut]
popular (adj)	**популярен**	[pɔpu'ʎarɛn]
script (screenplay)	**сценарий** (m)	[stsə'narij]
scriptwriter	**сценарист** (m)	[stsəna'rist]
movie director	**режисьор** (m)	[rɛʒi'sɜr]
producer	**продуцент** (m)	[prɔdu'tsənt]
assistant	**асистент** (m)	[asis'tɛnt]
cameraman	**оператор** (m)	[ɔpɛ'ratɔr]
stuntman	**каскадьор** (m)	[kaska'dɜr]
to shoot a movie	**снимам филм**	['snimam film]
audition, screen test	**проби** (f pl)	['prɔbi]
shooting	**снимане** (n)	['snimanɛ]
movie crew	**снимачен екип** (m)	[sni'maʧən ɛ'kip]
movie set	**снимачна площадка** (f)	[sni'maʧna plɔʃ'tatka]

camera	**кинокамера** (f)	[kinɔ'kamɛra]
movie theater	**кинотеатър** (m)	['kinɔtɛ'atır]
screen (e.g., big ~)	**екран** (m)	[ɛk'ran]
to show a movie	**прожектирам филм**	[prɔʒɛk'tiram film]
soundtrack	**звукова пътека** (f)	['zvukɔva pı'tɛka]
special effects	**специални ефекти** (m pl)	[spɛtsi'alni ɛ'fɛkti]
subtitles	**субтитри** (pl)	[sup'titri]
credits	**титри** (pl)	['titri]
translation	**превод** (m)	['prɛvɔd]

151. Painting

art	**изкуство** (n)	[iz'kustvɔ]
fine arts	**изящни изкуства** (n pl)	[i'zʲaʃtni is'kustva]
art gallery	**галерия** (f)	[ga'lɛrija]
art exhibition	**изложба** (f) **на картини**	[iz'lɔʒba na kar'tini]
painting (art)	**живопис** (m)	[ʒivɔ'pis]
graphic art	**графика** (f)	['grafika]
abstract art	**абстракционизъм** (m)	[abstraktsiɔ'nizım]
impressionism	**импресионизъм** (m)	[imprɛsiɔ'nizım]
picture (painting)	**картина** (f)	[kar'tina]
drawing	**рисунка** (f)	[ri'suŋka]
poster	**постер** (m)	['pɔstɛr]
illustration (picture)	**илюстрация** (f)	[ilyst'ratsija]
miniature	**миниатюра** (f)	[minia'tyra]
copy (of painting, etc.)	**копие** (n)	['kɔpiɛ]
reproduction	**репродукция** (f)	[rɛprɔ'duktsija]
mosaic	**мозайка** (f)	[mɔ'zajka]
stained glass	**стъклопис** (m)	[stıklɔ'pis]
fresco	**фреска** (f)	['frɛska]
engraving	**гравюра** (f)	[gra'vyra]
bust (sculpture)	**бюст** (m)	[byst]
sculpture	**скулптура** (f)	[skulp'tura]
statue	**статуя** (f)	['statuja]
plaster of Paris	**гипс** (m)	[gips]
plaster (as adj)	**от гипс**	[ɔt gips]
portrait	**портрет** (m)	[pɔrt'rɛt]
self-portrait	**автопортрет** (m)	[avtɔpɔrt'rɛt]
landscape painting	**пейзаж** (m)	[pɛj'zaʒ]
still life	**натюрморт** (m)	[natyr'mɔrt]
caricature	**карикатура** (f)	[karika'tura]
sketch	**скица** (f)	['skitsa]
paint	**боя** (f)	[bɔ'ja]

watercolor	**акварел** (m)	[akva'rɛl]
oil (paint)	**маслени бои** (f pl)	['maslɛni bɔ'i]
pencil	**молив** (m)	['mɔliv]
Indian ink	**туш** (m)	[tuʃ]
charcoal	**въглен** (m)	['vɪglɛn]
to draw (vi, vt)	**рисувам**	[ri'suvam]
to paint (vi, vt)	**рисувам**	[ri'suvam]
to pose (vi)	**позирам**	[pɔ'ziram]
artist's model (masc.)	**модел** (m)	[mɔ'dɛl]
artist's model (fem.)	**модел** (m)	[mɔ'dɛl]
artist (painter)	**художник** (m)	[hu'dɔʒnik]
work of art	**произведение** (n)	[prɔizvɛ'dɛniɛ]
masterpiece	**шедьовър** (m)	[ʃɛ'dʒvɪr]
artist's workshop	**ателие** (n)	[atɛli'ɛ]
canvas (cloth)	**платно** (n)	[plat'nɔ]
easel	**статив** (m)	[sta'tif]
palette	**палитра** (f)	[pa'litra]
frame (of picture, etc.)	**рамка** (f)	['ramka]
restoration	**реставрация** (f)	[rɛstav'ratsija]
to restore (vt)	**реставрирам**	[rɛstav'riram]

152. Literature & Poetry

literature	**литература** (f)	[litɛra'tura]
author (writer)	**автор** (m)	['aftɔr]
pseudonym	**псевдоним** (m)	[psɛvdɔ'nim]
book	**книга** (f)	['kniga]
volume	**том** (m)	[tɔm]
table of contents	**съдържание** (n)	[sɪdɪr'ʒaniɛ]
page	**страница** (f)	['stranitsa]
main character	**главен герой** (m)	['glavɛn gɛ'rɔj]
autograph	**автограф** (m)	[aftɔg'raf]
short story	**разказ** (m)	['razkaz]
story (novella)	**повест** (f)	['pɔvɛst]
novel	**роман** (m)	[rɔ'man]
work (writing)	**съчинение** (n)	[sɪtʃi'nɛniɛ]
fable	**басня** (f)	['basɲa]
detective novel	**детективски роман** (m)	[dɛtɛk'tifski rɔ'man]
poem (verse)	**стихотворение** (n)	[stihɔtvɔ'rɛniɛ]
poetry	**поезия** (f)	[pɔ'ɛzija]
poem (epic, ballad)	**поема** (f)	[pɔ'ɛma]
poet	**поет** (m)	[pɔ'ɛt]

fiction	**белетристика** (f)	[bɛlɛt'ristika]
science fiction	**научна фантастика** (f)	[na'utʃna fan'tastika]
adventures	**приключения** (n pl)	[prikly'tʃɘnijɑ]
educational literature	**учебна литература** (f)	[u'tʃəbna litɛra'tura]
children's literature	**детска литература** (f)	['dɛtska litɛra'tura]

153. Circus

circus	**цирк** (m)	[tsirk]
program	**програма** (f)	[prɔg'rama]
performance	**представление** (n)	[prɛdstav'lɛniɛ]
act (circus ~)	**номер** (m)	['nɔmɛr]
circus ring	**арена** (f)	[a'rɛna]
pantomime (act)	**пантомима** (f)	[pantɔ'mima]
clown	**клоун** (m)	['klɔun]
acrobat	**акробат** (m)	[akrɔ'bat]
acrobatics	**акробатика** (f)	[akrɔ'batika]
gymnast	**гимнастик** (m)	[gimnas'tik]
gymnastics	**гимнастика** (f)	[gim'nastika]
somersault	**салто** (n)	['saltɔ]
athlete (strongman)	**атлет** (m)	[at'lɛt]
animal-tamer	**укротител** (m)	[ukrɔ'titɛl]
equestrian	**ездач** (m)	[ɛz'datʃ]
assistant	**асистент** (m)	[asis'tɛnt]
stunt	**трик** (m)	[trik]
magic trick	**фокус** (m)	['fɔkus]
conjurer, magician	**фокусник** (m)	['fɔkusnik]
juggler	**жонгльор** (m)	[ʒɔŋg'lɜr]
to juggle (vi, vt)	**жонглирам**	[ʒɔŋg'liram]
animal trainer	**дресьор** (m)	[drɛ'sɜr]
animal training	**дресиране** (n)	[drɛ'siranɛ]
to train (animals)	**дресирам**	[drɛ'siram]

154. Music. Pop music

music	**музика** (f)	['muzika]
musician	**музикант** (m)	[muzi'kant]
musical instrument	**музикален инструмент** (m)	[muzi'kalɛn instru'mɛnt]
to play ...	**свиря на ...**	['sviʲa na]
guitar	**китара** (f)	[ki'tara]
violin	**цигулка** (f)	[tsi'gulka]

cello	**чело** (n)	['ʧɛlɔ]
double bass	**контрабас** (m)	[kɔntra'bas]
harp	**арфа** (f)	['arfa]
piano	**пиано** (n)	[pi'anɔ]
grand piano	**роял** (m)	[rɔ'jɑl]
organ	**орган** (m)	[ɔr'gan]
wind instruments	**духови инструменти** (m pl)	['duhɔvi instru'mɛnti]
oboe	**обой** (m)	[ɔ'bɔj]
saxophone	**саксофон** (m)	[saksɔ'fɔn]
clarinet	**кларнет** (m)	[klar'nɛt]
flute	**флейта** (f)	['flɛjta]
trumpet	**тръба** (f)	[trɪ'ba]
accordion	**акордеон** (m)	[akɔrdɛ'ɔn]
drum	**барабан** (m)	[bara'ban]
duo	**дует** (m)	[du'ɛt]
trio	**трио** (n)	['triɔ]
quartet	**квартет** (m)	[kvar'tɛt]
choir	**хор** (m)	[hɔr]
orchestra	**оркестър** (m)	[ɔr'kɛstɪr]
pop music	**поп музика** (f)	[pɔp 'muzika]
rock music	**рок музика** (f)	[rɔk 'muzika]
rock group	**рок-група** (f)	[rɔk 'grupa]
jazz	**джаз** (m)	[ʤaz]
idol	**кумир** (m)	[ku'mir]
admirer, fan	**почитател** (m)	[pɔʧi'tatɛl]
concert	**концерт** (m)	[kɔn'ʦɛrt]
symphony	**симфония** (f)	[sim'fɔnijɑ]
composition	**съчинение** (n)	[sɪʧi'nɛniɛ]
to compose (write)	**съчинявам**	[sɪʧi'ɲavam]
singing	**пеене** (n)	['pɛ:nɛ]
song	**песен** (f)	['pɛsɛn]
tune (melody)	**мелодия** (f)	[mɛ'lɔdijɑ]
rhythm	**ритъм** (m)	['ritɪm]
blues	**блус** (m)	[blus]
sheet music	**ноти** (f pl)	['nɔti]
baton	**диригентска палка** (f)	[diri'gɛnska 'palka]
bow	**лък** (m)	[lɪk]
string	**струна** (f)	['struna]
case (e.g., guitar ~)	**калъф** (m)	[ka'lɪf]

Rest. Entertainment. Travel

155. Trip. Travel

tourism	**туризъм** (m)	[tu'rizɪm]
tourist	**турист** (m)	[tu'rist]
trip, voyage	**пътешествие** (n)	[pɪtɛ'ʃɛstviɛ]
adventure	**приключение** (n)	[prikly'ʧəniɛ]
trip, journey	**пътуване** (n)	[pɪ'tuvanɛ]
vacation	**отпуска** (f)	['ɔtpuska]
to be on vacation	**бъда в отпуска**	['bɪda v 'ɔtpuska]
rest	**почивка** (f)	[pɔ'ʧifka]
train	**влак** (m)	[vlak]
by train	**с влак**	[s vlak]
airplane	**самолет** (m)	[samɔ'lɛt]
by airplane	**със самолет**	[sɪs samɔ'lɛt]
by car	**с кола**	[s kɔ'la]
by ship	**с кораб**	[s 'kɔrap]
luggage	**багаж** (m)	[ba'gaʃ]
suitcase, luggage	**куфар** (m)	['kufar]
luggage cart	**количка** (f) **за багаж**	[kɔ'liʧka za ba'gaʃ]
passport	**паспорт** (m)	[pas'pɔrt]
visa	**виза** (f)	['viza]
ticket	**билет** (m)	[bi'lɛt]
air ticket	**самолетен билет** (m)	[samɔ'lɛtɛn bi'lɛt]
guidebook	**пътеводител** (m)	[pɪtɛvɔ'ditɛl]
map	**карта** (f)	['karta]
area (rural ~)	**местност** (f)	['mɛstnɔst]
place, site	**място** (n)	['mʲastɔ]
exotic (n)	**екзотика** (f)	[ɛk'zɔtika]
exotic (adj)	**екзотичен**	[ɛkzɔ'tiʧən]
amazing (adj)	**удивителен**	[udi'vitɛlɛn]
group	**група** (f)	['grupa]
excursion	**екскурзия** (f)	[ɛks'kurzija]
guide (person)	**гид** (m)	[gid]

156. Hotel

hotel	**хотел** (m)	[hɔ'tɛl]
motel	**мотел** (m)	[mɔ'tɛl]
three-star	**три звезди**	[tri zvɛz'di]
five-star	**пет звезди**	[pɛt zvɛz'di]
to stay (in hotel, etc.)	**отсядам (в хотел)**	[ɔ'tsʲadam f hɔ'tɛl]
room	**стая** (f) **в хотел**	['staja f hɔ'tel]
single room	**еднинична стая** (f)	[ɛdi'nitʃna 'staja]
double room	**двойна стая** (f)	['dvɔjna 'staja]
to book a room	**резервирам стая**	[rɛzɛr'viram 'staja]
half board	**полупансион** (m)	[pɔlupansi'ɔn]
full board	**пълен пансион** (m)	['pılɛn pansi'ɔn]
with bath	**с баня**	[s 'baɲa]
with shower	**с душ**	[s duʃ]
satellite television	**сателитна телевизия** (f)	[satɛ'litna tɛlɛ'vizija]
air-conditioner	**климатик** (m)	[klima'tik]
towel	**кърпа** (f)	['kırpa]
key	**ключ** (m)	[klytʃ]
administrator	**администратор** (m)	[administ'ratɔr]
chambermaid	**камериерка** (f)	[kamɛri'ɛrka]
porter, bellboy	**носач** (m)	[nɔ'satʃ]
doorman	**портиер** (m)	[pɔrti'ɛr]
restaurant	**ресторант** (m)	[rɛstɔ'rant]
pub, bar	**бар** (m)	[bar]
breakfast	**закуска** (f)	[za'kuska]
dinner	**вечеря** (f)	[vɛ'tʃərʲa]
buffet	**шведска маса** (f)	['ʃvɛtska 'masa]
lobby	**вестибюл** (m)	[vɛsti'byl]
elevator	**асансьор** (m)	[asan'sɜr]
DO NOT DISTURB	**НЕ МЕ БЕЗПОКОЙТЕ!**	[nɛ mɛ bɛspɔ'kɔjtɛ]
NO SMOKING	**ПУШЕНЕТО ЗАБРАНЕНО!**	[puʃɛ'netɔ zab'ranenɔ]

157. Books. Reading

book	**книга** (f)	['kniga]
author	**автор** (m)	['aftɔr]
writer	**писател** (m)	[pi'satɛl]
to write (~ a book)	**напиша**	[na'piʃʌ]
reader	**читател** (m)	[tʃi'tatɛl]

to read (vi, vt)	**чета**	[ʧə'tɪ]
reading (activity)	**четене** (n)	['ʧətɛnɛ]
silently (to oneself)	**на ум**	[na 'um]
aloud (adv)	**на глас**	[na 'glas]
to publish (vt)	**издавам**	[iz'davam]
publishing (process)	**издание** (n)	[iz'daniɛ]
publisher	**издател** (m)	[iz'datɛl]
publishing house	**издателство** (n)	[iz'datɛlstvɔ]
to come out (be released)	**излизам**	[iz'lizam]
release (of a book)	**излизане** (n)	[iz'lizanɛ]
print run	**тираж** (m)	[ti'raʒ]
bookstore	**книжарница** (f)	[kni'ʒarniʦa]
library	**библиотека** (f)	[bibliɔ'tɛka]
story (novella)	**повест** (f)	['pɔvɛst]
short story	**разказ** (m)	['razkaz]
novel	**роман** (m)	[rɔ'man]
detective novel	**детективски роман** (m)	[dɛtɛk'tifski rɔ'man]
memoirs	**мемоари** (pl)	[mɛmɔ'ari]
legend	**легенда** (f)	[lɛ'gɛnda]
myth	**мит** (m)	[mit]
poetry, poems	**стихове** (m pl)	[stihɔ'vɛ]
autobiography	**автобиография** (f)	[aftɔbiɔg'rafijɑ]
selected works	**избрани съчинения**	[izb'rani sɪʧi'nɛnijɑ]
science fiction	**фантастика** (f)	[fan'tastika]
title	**название** (n)	[naz'vaniɛ]
introduction	**въведение** (n)	[vɪvɛ'dɛniɛ]
title page	**заглавна страница** (f)	[zag'lavna 'straniʦa]
chapter	**глава** (f)	[gla'va]
extract	**откъс** (m)	['ɔtkɪs]
episode	**епизод** (m)	[ɛpi'zɔd]
plot (storyline)	**сюжет** (m)	[sy'ʒɛt]
contents	**съдържание** (n)	[sɪdɪr'ʒaniɛ]
main character	**главен герой** (m)	['glavɛn gɛ'rɔj]
volume	**том** (m)	[tɔm]
cover	**корица** (f)	[kɔ'riʦa]
binding	**подвързия** (f)	[pɔdvɪr'zijɑ]
bookmark	**marker** (m)	['marker]
page	**страница** (f)	['straniʦa]
to flick through	**прелиствам**	[prɛ'listvam]
margins	**полета** (n pl)	[pɔ'lɛta]

annotation	**бележка** (f)	[be'lɛʃka]
footnote	**забележка** (f)	[zabɛ'lɛʃka]
text	**текст** (m)	[tɛkst]
type, font	**шрифт** (m)	[ʃrift]
misprint, typo	**печатна грешка** (f)	[pɛ'ʧatna 'grɛʃka]
translation	**превод** (m)	['prɛvɔd]
to translate (vt)	**превеждам**	[prɛ'vɛʒdam]
original (n)	**оригинал** (m)	[ɔrigi'nal]
famous (adj)	**прочут**	[prɔ'ʧut]
unknown (adj)	**неизвестен**	[nɛiz'vɛstɛn]
interesting (adj)	**интересен**	[intɛ'rɛsɛn]
bestseller	**бестселър** (m)	[bɛs'ʦɛlɪr]
dictionary	**речник** (m)	['rɛʧnik]
textbook	**учебник** (m)	[u'ʧəbnik]
encyclopedia	**енциклопедия** (f)	[ɛnʦiklɔ'pɛdija]

158. Hunting. Fishing

hunting	**лов** (m)	[lɔv]
to hunt (vi, vt)	**ловувам**	[lɔ'vuvam]
hunter	**ловец** (m)	[lɔ'vɛʦ]
to shoot (vi)	**стрелям**	['strɛʎam]
rifle	**пушка** (f)	['puʃka]
bullet (shell)	**патрон** (m)	[pat'rɔn]
shot (lead balls)	**сачма** (f)	[saʧ'ma]
trap (e.g., bear ~)	**капан** (m)	[ka'pan]
snare (for birds, etc.)	**примка** (f)	['primka]
to lay a trap	**залагам капан**	[za'lagam ka'pan]
poacher	**бракониер** (m)	[brakɔni'ɛr]
game (in hunting)	**дивеч** (f)	['divɛʧ]
hound dog	**ловно куче** (n)	['lɔvnɔ 'kuʧə]
safari	**сафари** (n)	[sa'fari]
mounted animal	**препарирано животно** (n)	[prɛpa'riranɔ ʒi'vɔtnɔ]
fisherman	**рибар** (m)	[ri'bar]
fishing	**риболов** (m)	[ribɔ'lɔv]
to fish (vi)	**ловя риба**	[lɔ'vʲa 'riba]
fishing rod	**въдица** (f)	['vɪdiʦa]
fishing line	**месина** (f)	[mɛ'sina]
hook	**кука** (f)	['kuka]
float	**плувка** (f)	['plufka]

bait	**стръв** (f)	[strıv]
to cast a line	**хвърлям въдица**	['hvırʎam 'vıdiʦa]
to bite (ab. fish)	**кълва**	[kıl'va]
catch (of fish)	**улов** (m)	['ulɔf]
ice-hole	**дупка** (f) **в леда**	['dupka v lɛ'da]
fishing net	**мрежа** (f)	['mreʒa]
boat	**лодка** (f)	['lɔtka]
to net (catch with net)	**ловя с мрежа**	[lɔ'vʲa s 'mrɛʒa]
to cast the net	**хвърлям мрежа**	['hvırʎam 'mrɛʒa]
to haul in the net	**изваждам мрежа**	[iz'vaʒdam 'mrɛʒa]
whaler (person)	**китоловец** (m)	[kitɔ'lɔvɛʦ]
whaleboat	**китоловен кораб** (m)	[kitɔ'lɔvɛn 'kɔrap]
harpoon	**харпун** (m)	[har'pun]

159. Games. Billiards

billiards	**билярд** (m)	[bi'ʎard]
billiard room, hall	**билярдна зала** (f)	[bi'ʎardna 'zala]
ball	**билярдна топка** (f)	[bi'ʎardna 'tɔpka]
to pocket a ball	**вкарам топка**	['fkaram 'tɔpka]
cue	**щека** (f)	['ʃtɛka]
pocket	**дупка** (f)	['dupka]

160. Games. Playing cards

diamonds	**каро** (n)	[ka'rɔ]
spades	**пики** (f pl)	['piki]
hearts	**купи** (f pl)	['kupi]
clubs	**спатии** (f pl)	[spa'ti:]
ace	**асо** (n)	[a'sɔ]
king	**поп** (m)	[pɔp]
queen	**дама** (f)	['dama]
jack, knave	**вале** (m)	[va'lɛ]
playing card	**карта** (f)	['karta]
cards	**карти** (f pl)	['karti]
trump	**коз** (m)	[kɔs]
deck of cards	**тесте** (n)	[tɛs'tɛ]
to deal (vi, vt)	**раздавам**	[raz'davam]
to shuffle (cards)	**размесвам**	[raz'mɛsvam]
lead, turn (n)	**ход** (m)	[hɔd]
cardsharp	**шмекер** (m)	['ʃmɛkɛr]

161. Casino. Roulette

casino	**казино** (n)	[ka'zinɔ]
roulette (game)	**рулетка** (f)	[ru'lɛtka]
bet, stake	**залагане** (n)	[za'laganɛ]
to place bets	**залагам**	[za'lagam]
red	**червено** (n)	[ʧər'vɛnɔ]
black	**черно** (n)	['ʧərnɔ]
to bet on red	**залагам на червено**	[za'lagam na ʧər'vɛnɔ]
to bet on black	**залагам на черно**	[za'lagam na 'ʧərnɔ]
croupier (dealer)	**крупие** (n)	[krupi'ɛ]
to turn the wheel	**въртя барабан**	[vɪr'tʲa bara'ban]
rules (of game)	**правила** (n pl) **на игра**	[pravi'la na ig'ra]
chip	**пул** (m)	[pul]
to win (vi, vt)	**спечеля**	[spɛ'ʧəʎa]
winnings	**печалба** (f)	[pɛ'ʧalba]
to lose (~ 100 dollars)	**загубя**	[za'gubʲa]
loss	**загуба** (f)	['zaguba]
player	**играч** (m)	[ig'raʧ]
blackjack (card game)	**блекджек** (m)	[blɛk'ʤɛk]
craps (dice game)	**игра** (f) **на зарове**	[ig'ra na 'zarɔve]
slot machine	**игрален автомат** (m)	[ig'ralɛn aftɔ'mat]

162. Rest. Games. Miscellaneous

to walk, to stroll (vi)	**разхождам се**	[ras'hɔʒdam sɛ]
walk, stroll	**разходка** (f)	[ras'hɔtka]
road trip	**пътуване** (n)	[pɪ'tuvanɛ]
adventure	**приключение** (n)	[prikly'ʧəniɛ]
picnic	**пикник** (m)	['piknik]
game (chess, etc.)	**игра** (f)	[ig'ra]
player	**играч** (m)	[ig'raʧ]
game (one ~ of chess)	**партия** (f)	['partijɑ]
collector (e.g., philatelist)	**колекционер** (m)	[kɔlɛkʦiɔ'nɛr]
to collect (vt)	**колекционирам**	[kɔlɛkʦiɔ'niram]
collection	**колекция** (f)	[kɔ'lɛkʦijɑ]
crossword puzzle	**кръстословица** (f)	[krɪstɔs'lɔviʦa]
racetrack (hippodrome)	**хиподрум** (m)	[hipɔd'rum]
discotheque	**дискотека** (f)	[diskɔ'tɛka]
sauna	**сауна** (f)	['sauna]
lottery	**лотария** (f)	[lɔ'tarijɑ]

camping trip	**поход** (m)	['pɔhɔt]
camp	**лагер** (m)	['lagɛr]
tent (for camping)	**палатка** (f)	[pa'latka]
compass	**компас** (m)	[kɔm'pas]
camper	**турист** (m)	[tu'rist]
to watch (movie, etc.)	**гледам**	['glɛdam]
viewer	**телезрител** (m)	[tɛlɛz'ritɛl]
TV show	**телевизионно предаване** (n)	[tɛlɛvizi'ɔŋɔ prɛ'davanɛ]

163. Photography

camera (photo)	**фотоапарат** (m)	[fɔtɔapa'rat]
photo, picture	**снимка** (f)	['snimka]
photographer	**фотограф** (m)	[fɔtɔg'raf]
photo studio	**фотостудио** (n)	[fɔtɔs'tudiɔ]
photo album	**фотоалбум** (m)	[fɔtɔal'bum]
camera lens	**обектив** (m)	[ɔbɛk'tiv]
telephoto lens	**телеобектив** (m)	[tɛlɛɔbɛk'tif]
filter	**филтър** (m)	['filtır]
lens	**леща** (f)	['lɛʃta]
optics (high-quality ~)	**оптика** (f)	['ɔptika]
diaphragm (aperture)	**диафрагма** (f)	[diaf'ragma]
exposure time	**експозиция** (f)	[ɛkspɔ'zitsija]
viewfinder	**визьор** (m)	[vi'zʲɔr]
digital camera	**цифрова камера** (f)	['tsifrɔva 'kamɛra]
tripod	**статив** (m)	[sta'tif]
flash	**светкавица** (f)	[svɛt'kavitsa]
to photograph (vt)	**снимам**	['snimam]
to take pictures	**снимам**	['snimam]
to be photographed	**снимам се**	['snimam sɛ]
focus	**рязкост** (f)	['rʲaskɔst]
to adjust the focus	**нагласявам рязкост**	[nagla'sʲavam 'rʲaskɔst]
sharp, in focus (adj)	**рязък**	['rʲazık]
sharpness	**рязкост** (f)	['rʲaskɔst]
contrast	**контраст** (m)	[kɔnt'rast]
contrasty (adj)	**контрастен**	[kɔnt'rastɛn]
picture (photo)	**снимка** (f)	['snimka]
negative (n)	**негатив** (m)	[nɛga'tif]
film (a roll of ~)	**фотолента** (f)	['fɔtɔ'lɛnta]
frame (still)	**кадър** (m)	['kadır]
to print (photos)	**печатам**	[pɛ'tʃatam]

164. Beach. Swimming

beach	**плаж** (m)	[plaʒ]
sand	**пясък** (m)	['pʲasık]
deserted (beach)	**пустинен**	[pus'tinɛn]
suntan	**тен** (m)	[tɛn]
to get a tan	**пека се**	[pɛ'ka sɛ]
tan (adj)	**почернял**	[pɔʧər'ɲal]
sunscreen	**крем** (m) **за тен**	[krɛm za tɛn]
bikini	**бикини** (pl)	[bi'kini]
bathing suit	**бански костюм** (m)	['banski kɔs'tym]
swim briefs	**плувки** (pl)	['pluvki]
swimming pool	**басейн** (m)	[ba'sɛjn]
to swim (vi)	**плувам**	['pluvam]
shower	**душ** (m)	[duʃ]
to change (one's clothes)	**преобличам се**	[prɛɔb'liʧam sɛ]
towel	**кърпа** (f)	['kırpa]
boat	**лодка** (f)	['lɔtka]
motorboat	**катер** (m)	['katɛr]
water ski	**водни ски** (pl)	['vɔdni ski]
paddle boat	**водно колело** (n)	['vɔdnɔ kɔlɛ'lɔ]
surfing	**сърфинг** (m)	['sırfiŋg]
surfer	**сърфист** (m)	[sır'fist]
scuba set	**акваланг** (m)	[akva'laŋg]
flippers (swimfins)	**плавници** (f pl)	['plavniʦi]
mask	**маска** (f)	['maska]
diver	**гмуркач** (m)	[gmur'kaʧ]
to dive (vi)	**гмуркам се**	['gmurkam sɛ]
underwater (adv)	**под вода**	[pɔd vɔ'da]
beach umbrella	**чадър** (m)	[ʧa'dır]
beach chair	**шезлонг** (m)	[ʃɛz'lɔŋg]
sunglasses	**очила** (pl)	[ɔʧi'la]
air mattress	**плажен дюшек** (m)	[pla'ʒɛn dy'ʃɛk]
to play (amuse oneself)	**играя**	[ig'rajɑ]
to go for a swim	**къпя се**	['kıpʲa sɛ]
beach ball	**топка** (f)	['tɔpka]
to inflate (vt)	**надувам**	[na'duvam]
inflatable, air- (adj)	**надуваем**	[nadu'vaɛm]
wave	**вълна** (f)	[vıl'na]
buoy	**шамандура** (f)	[ʃʌman'dura]
to drown (ab. person)	**давя се**	['davʲa sɛ]

to save, to rescue	**спасявам**	[spa'sʲavam]
life vest	**спасителна жилетка** (f)	[spa'sitɛlna ʒi'lɛtka]
to observe, to watch	**наблюдавам**	[nably'davam]
lifeguard	**спасител** (m)	[spa'sitɛl]

TECHNICAL EQUIPMENT. TRANSPORTATION

Technical equipment

165. Computer

computer	**компютър** (m)	[kɔm'pytır]
notebook, laptop	**лаптоп** (m)	[lap'tɔp]
to turn on	**включа**	['vklytʃa]
to turn off	**изключа**	[isk'lytʃa]
keyboard	**клавиатура** (f)	[klavia'tura]
key	**клавиш** (m)	[kla'viʃ]
mouse	**мишка** (f)	['miʃka]
mouse pad	**подложка** (f) **за мишка**	[pɔd'lɔʃka za 'miʃka]
button	**бутон** (m)	[bu'tɔn]
cursor	**курсор** (m)	[kur'sɔr]
monitor	**монитор** (m)	[mɔ'nitɔr]
screen	**екран** (m)	[ɛk'ran]
hard disk	**твърд диск** (m)	['tvırd 'disk]
hard disk volume	**капацитет** (m) **на твърдия диск**	[kapatsi'tɛt na 'tvırdijɑ disk]
memory	**памет** (f)	['pamɛt]
random access memory	**операционна памет** (f)	[ɔpɛratsi'ɔŋa 'pamɛt]
file	**файл** (m)	[fajl]
folder	**папка** (f)	['papka]
to open (vt)	**отворя**	[ɔt'vɔrʲa]
to close (vt)	**затворя**	[zat'vɔrʲa]
to save (vt)	**съхраня**	[sıhra'ɲa]
to delete (vt)	**изтрия**	[ist'rijɑ]
to copy (vt)	**копирам**	[kɔ'piram]
to sort (vt)	**сортирам**	[sɔr'tiram]
to transfer (copy)	**копира**	[kɔ'pira]
program	**програма** (f)	[prɔg'rama]
software	**софтуер** (m)	[sɔftu'ɛr]
programmer	**програмист** (m)	[prɔgra'mist]
to program (vt)	**програмирам**	[prɔgra'miram]
hacker	**хакер** (m)	['hakɛr]

password	**парола** (f)	[pa'rɔla]
virus	**вирус** (m)	['virus]
to find, to detect	**намеря**	[na'mɛrʲa]
byte	**байт** (m)	[bajt]
megabyte	**мегабайт** (m)	[mɛga'bajt]
data	**данни** (pl)	['daɲi]
database	**база** (f) **данни**	['baza 'daɲi]
cable (USB, etc.)	**кабел** (m)	['kabɛl]
to disconnect (vt)	**разединя**	[razɛdi'ɲa]
to connect (sth to sth)	**съединя**	[sɪɛdi'ɲa]

166. Internet. E-mail

Internet	**интернет** (m)	[intɛr'nɛt]
browser	**браузър** (m)	['brauzɪr]
search engine	**търсачка** (f)	[tɪr'satʃka]
provider	**интернет доставчик** (m)	['intɛrnɛt dɔs'taftʃik]
web master	**уеб майстор** (m)	[u'əb 'majstɔr]
website	**уеб сайт** (m)	[u'əb sajt]
web page	**уеб страница** (f)	[uəb 'stranitsa]
address	**адрес** (m)	[ad'rɛs]
address book	**адресна книга** (f)	[ad'rɛsna 'kniga]
mailbox	**пощенска кутия** (f)	['pɔʃtɛnska ku'tija]
mail	**поща** (f)	['pɔʃta]
message	**съобщение** (n)	[sɪɔbʃ'tɛniɛ]
sender	**подател** (m)	[pɔ'datɛl]
to send (vt)	**изпратя**	[isp'ratʲa]
sending (of mail)	**изпращане** (n)	[isp'raʃtanɛ]
receiver	**получател** (m)	[pɔlu'tʃatɛl]
to receive (vt)	**получа**	[pɔ'lutʃa]
correspondence	**кореспонденция** (f)	[kɔrɛspɔn'dɛntsija]
to correspond (vi)	**кореспондирам**	[kɔrɛspɔn'diram]
file	**файл** (m)	[fajl]
to download (vt)	**свалям**	['svaʎam]
to create (vt)	**създам**	[sɪz'dam]
to delete (vt)	**изтрия**	[ist'rija]
deleted (adj)	**изтрит**	[ist'rit]
connection (ADSL, etc.)	**връзка** (f)	['vrɪska]
speed	**скорост** (f)	['skɔrɔst]

modem	**модем** (m)	[mɔ'dɛm]
access	**достъп** (m)	['dɔstɪp]
port (e.g., input ~)	**порт** (m)	[pɔrt]
connection (make a ~)	**връзка** (f)	['vrɪska]
to connect to ... (vi)	**се свържа с ...**	[sɛ 'svɪrʒa s]
to select (vt)	**избера**	[izbɛ'ra]
to search (for ...)	**търся**	['tɪrsʲa]

167. Electricity

electricity	**електричество** (n)	[ɛlɛkt'riʧəstvɔ]
electrical (adj)	**електрически**	[ɛlɛkt'riʧəski]
electric power station	**електроцентрала** (f)	[ɛlɛktrɔʦənt'rala]
energy	**енергия** (f)	[ɛ'nɛrgijɑ]
electric power	**електроенергия** (f)	[ɛlɛktrɔɛ'nɛrgijɑ]
light bulb	**крушка** (f)	['kruʃka]
flashlight	**фенер** (m)	[fɛ'nɛr]
street light	**фенер** (m)	[fɛ'nɛr]
light	**електричество** (n)	[ɛlɛkt'riʧəstvɔ]
to turn on	**включвам**	['vklyʧvam]
to turn off	**изключвам**	[isk'lyʧvam]
to turn off the light	**изключвам ток**	[isk'lyʧvam tɔk]
to burn out (vi)	**прегоря**	[prɛgɔ'rʲa]
short circuit	**късо съединение** (n)	['kɪsɔ sɪɛdi'nɛniɛ]
broken wire	**прекъсване** (n)	[prɛ'kɪsvanɛ]
contact	**контакт** (m)	[kɔn'takt]
light switch	**изключвател** (m)	[izklyʧ'vatɛl]
wall socket	**контакт** (m)	[kɔn'takt]
plug	**щепсел** (m)	['ʃtɛpsel]
extension cord	**удължител** (m)	[udɪ'ʒitɛl]
fuse	**предпазител** (m)	[prɛd'pazitɛl]
cable, wire	**кабел** (m)	['kabɛl]
wiring	**инсталация** (f)	[insta'laʦijɑ]
ampere	**ампер** (m)	[am'pɛr]
amperage	**сила** (f) **на тока**	['sila na 'tɔka]
volt	**волт** (m)	[vɔlt]
voltage	**напрежение** (n)	[naprɛ'ʒɛniɛ]
electrical device	**електроуред** (m)	[ɛlɛktrɔ'urɛd]
indicator	**индикатор** (m)	[indi'katɔr]
electrician	**електротехник** (m)	[ɛlɛktrɔtɛh'nik]
to solder (vt)	**запоявам**	[zapɔ'jɑvam]

soldering iron	**поялник** (m)	[pɔ'jalnik]
electric current	**ток** (m)	[tɔk]

168. Tools

tool, instrument	**инструмент** (m)	[instru'mɛnt]
tools	**инструменти** (m pl)	[instru'mɛnti]
equipment (factory ~)	**оборудване** (n)	[ɔbɔ'rudvanɛ]
hammer	**чук** (m)	[ʧuk]
screwdriver	**отвертка** (f)	[ɔt'vɛrtka]
ax	**брадва** (f)	['bradva]
saw	**трион** (m)	[tri'ɔn]
to saw (vt)	**режа с трион**	['rɛʒa s tri'ɔn]
plane (tool)	**ренде** (n)	[rɛn'dɛ]
to plane (vt)	**рендосвам**	[rɛn'dɔsvam]
soldering iron	**поялник** (m)	[pɔ'jalnik]
to solder (vt)	**запоявам**	[zapɔ'javam]
file (for metal)	**пила** (f)	[pi'la]
carpenter pincers	**клещи** (pl)	['klɛʃti]
lineman's pliers	**плоски клещи** (pl)	['plɔski 'klɛʃti]
chisel	**длето** (n)	[dlɛ'tɔ]
drill bit	**свредел** (n)	[svrɛ'dɛl]
electric drill	**дрелка** (f)	['drɛlka]
to drill (vi, vt)	**пробивам (с дрелка)**	[prɔ'bivam s 'drɛlka]
knife	**нож** (m)	[nɔʒ]
pocket knife	**джобен нож** (m)	['ʤɔbɛn nɔʒ]
folding (~ knife)	**сгъваем**	[sgɪ'vaɛm]
blade	**острие** (n)	[ɔstri'ɛ]
sharp (blade, etc.)	**остър**	['ɔstɪr]
blunt (adj)	**тъп**	[tɪp]
to become blunt	**затъпявам се**	[zatɪ'pʲavam sɛ]
to sharpen (vt)	**точа**	['tɔʧa]
bolt	**болт** (m)	[bɔlt]
nut	**гайка** (f)	['gajka]
thread (of a screw)	**резба** (f)	[rɛz'ba]
wood screw	**винт** (m)	[vint]
nail	**пирон** (m)	[pi'rɔn]
nailhead	**глава** (f)	[gla'va]
ruler (for measuring)	**линийка** (f)	['linijka]
tape measure	**рулетка** (f)	[ru'lɛtka]
spirit level	**нивелир** (n)	[nivɛ'lir]

magnifying glass	**лупа** (f)	['lupa]
measuring instrument	**измервателен уред** (m)	[izmɛr'vatɛlɛn 'urɛd]
to measure (vt)	**измервам**	[iz'mɛrvam]
scale (of thermometer, etc.)	**скала** (f)	['skala]
readings	**показание** (n)	[pɔka'zaniɛ]
compressor	**компресор** (m)	[kɔmp'rɛsɔr]
microscope	**микроскоп** (m)	[mikrɔs'kɔp]
pump (e.g., water ~)	**помпа** (f)	['pɔmpa]
robot	**робот** (m)	[rɔ'bɔt]
laser	**лазер** (m)	['lazɛr]
wrench	**гаечен ключ** (m)	['gaɛʧən klyʧ]
adhesive tape	**тиксо** (n)	['tiksɔ]
glue	**лепило** (n)	[lɛ'pilɔ]
emery paper	**шмиргелова хартия** (f)	['ʃmirgɛlɔva har'tijɑ]
spring	**пружина** (f)	[pru'ʒina]
magnet	**магнит** (m)	[mag'nit]
gloves	**ръкавици** (f pl)	[rɪka'viʦi]
rope	**въже** (n)	[vɪ'ʒɛ]
cord	**шнур** (m)	[ʃnur]
wire (e.g., telephone ~)	**кабел** (m)	['kabɛl]
cable	**кабел** (m)	['kabɛl]
sledgehammer	**боен чук** (m)	['bɔɛn ʧuk]
crowbar	**лом** (m)	[lɔm]
ladder	**стълба** (f)	['stɪlba]
stepladder	**подвижна стълба** (f)	[pɔd'viʒna 'stɪlba]
to screw (tighten)	**завъртам**	[za'vɪrtam]
to unscrew, untwist (vt)	**отвъртам**	[ɔt'vɪrtam]
to tighten (vt)	**притискам**	[pri'tiskam]
to glue, to stick	**залепвам**	[za'lɛpvam]
to cut (vt)	**режа**	['rɛʒa]
malfunction (fault)	**неизправност** (f)	[nɛisp'ravnɔst]
repair (mending)	**поправка** (f)	[pɔp'rafka]
to repair, to mend (vt)	**ремонтирам**	[rɛmɔn'tiram]
to adjust (machine, etc.)	**регулирам**	[rɛgu'liram]
to check (to examine)	**проверявам**	[prɔvɛ'rʲavam]
checking	**проверка** (f)	[prɔ'vɛrka]
readings	**показание** (n)	[pɔka'zaniɛ]
reliable (machine)	**сигурен**	['sigurɛn]
complicated (adj)	**сложен**	['slɔʒɛn]
to rust (get rusted)	**ръждясвам**	[rɪʒ'dʲasvam]
rusty, rusted (adj)	**ръждясал**	[rɪʒ'dʲasal]
rust	**ръжда** (f)	[rɪʒ'da]

Transportation

169. Airplane

airplane	**самолет** (m)	[samɔ'lɛt]
air ticket	**самолетен билет** (m)	[samɔ'lɛtɛn bi'lɛt]
airline	**авиокомпания** (f)	[aviɔkɔm'panija]
airport	**летище** (n)	[lɛ'tiʃtɛ]
supersonic (adj)	**свръхзвуков**	[svrɪhz'vukɔv]
captain	**командир на самолет** (m)	[kɔman'dir na samɔ'lɛt]
crew	**екипаж** (m)	[ɛki'paʒ]
pilot	**пилот** (m)	[pi'lɔt]
flight attendant	**стюардеса** (f)	[styar'dɛsa]
navigator	**щурман** (m)	['ʃturman]
wings	**крила** (pl)	[kri'la]
tail	**опашка** (f)	[ɔ'paʃka]
cockpit	**кабина** (f)	[ka'bina]
engine	**двигател** (m)	[dvi'gatɛl]
undercarriage	**шаси** (pl)	[ʃʌ'si]
turbine	**турбина** (f)	[tur'bina]
propeller	**перка** (f)	['pɛrka]
black box	**черна кутия** (f)	['ʧərna ku'tija]
control column	**кормило** (n)	[kɔr'milɔ]
fuel	**гориво** (n)	[gɔ'rivɔ]
safety card	**инструкция** (f)	[inst'ruktsija]
oxygen mask	**кислородна маска** (f)	[kislɔ'rɔdna 'maska]
uniform	**униформа** (f)	[uni'fɔrma]
life vest	**спасителна жилетка** (f)	[spa'sitɛlna ʒi'lɛtka]
parachute	**парашут** (m)	[para'ʃut]
takeoff	**излитане** (n)	[iz'litanɛ]
to take off (vi)	**излитам**	[iz'litam]
runway	**писта** (f) **за излитане**	['pista za iz'litanɛ]
visibility	**видимост** (f)	['vidimɔst]
flight (act of flying)	**полет** (m)	['pɔlɛt]
altitude	**височина** (f)	[visɔʧi'na]
air pocket	**въздушна яма** (f)	[vɪz'duʃna 'jama]
seat	**място** (n)	['mʲastɔ]
headphones	**слушалки** (f pl)	[slu'ʃʌlki]

folding tray	**прибираща се масичка** (f)	[pri'biraçə sɛ 'masitʃka]
airplane window	**илюминатор** (m)	[ilymi'natɔr]
aisle	**проход** (m)	['prɔhɔd]

170. Train

train	**влак** (m)	[vlak]
suburban train	**електрически влак** (m)	[ɛlɛkt'ritʃəski vlak]
express train	**бърз влак** (m)	['bɪrz vlak]
diesel locomotive	**дизелов локомотив** (m)	['dizɛlɔf lɔkɔmɔ'tif]
steam engine	**парен локомотив** (m)	['parɛn lɔkɔmɔ'tiv]
passenger car	**вагон** (m)	[va'gɔn]
dining car	**вагон-ресторант** (m)	[va'gɔn rɛstɔ'rant]
rails	**релси** (f pl)	['rɛlsi]
railroad	**железница** (f)	[ʒɛ'lɛznitsa]
railway tie	**траверса** (f)	[tra'vɛrsa]
platform (railway ~)	**платформа** (f)	[plat'fɔrma]
track (~ 1, 2, etc.)	**коловоз** (m)	[kɔlɔ'vɔs]
semaphore	**семафор** (m)	[sɛma'fɔr]
station	**гара** (f)	['gara]
engineer	**машинист** (m)	[maʃi'nist]
porter (of luggage)	**носач** (m)	[nɔ'satʃ]
train steward	**стюард** (m) **във влак**	[sty'ard vʰf vlak]
passenger	**пътник** (m)	['pɪtnik]
conductor	**контрольор** (m)	[kɔntrɔ'lɜr]
corridor (in train)	**коридор** (m)	[kɔri'dɔr]
emergency break	**аварийна спирачка** (f)	[ava'rijna spi'ratʃka]
compartment	**купе** (n)	[ku'pɛ]
berth	**легло** (n)	[lɛg'lɔ]
upper berth	**горно легло** (n)	['gɔrnɔ lɛg'lɔ]
lower berth	**долно легло** (n)	['dɔlnɔ lɛg'lɔ]
bed linen	**спално бельо** (n)	['spalnɔ bɛ'lɜ]
ticket	**билет** (m)	[bi'lɛt]
schedule	**разписание** (n)	[raspi'saniɛ]
information display	**табло** (n)	[tab'lɔ]
to leave, to depart	**заминавам**	[zami'navam]
departure (of train)	**заминаване** (n)	[zami'navanɛ]
to arrive (ab. train)	**пристигам**	[pris'tigam]
arrival	**пристигане** (n)	[pris'tiganɛ]
to arrive by train	**пристигна с влак**	[pris'tigna s vlak]
to get on the train	**качвам се във влак**	['katʃvam sɛ vɪf vlak]

to get off the train	**слизам от влак**	['slizam ɔt vlak]
steam engine	**парен локомотив** (m)	['parɛn lɔkɔmɔ'tiv]
stoker, fireman	**огняр** (m)	[ɔg'ɲar]
firebox	**пещ** (m) **на локомотив**	[pɛʃt na lɔkɔmɔ'tif]
coal	**въглища** (f)	['vɪgliʃta]

171. Ship

ship	**кораб** (m)	['kɔrab]
vessel	**плавателен съд** (m)	[pla'vatɛlɛn sɪd]
steamship	**параход** (m)	[para'hɔd]
riverboat	**моторен кораб** (m)	[mɔ'tɔrɛn 'kɔrab]
ocean liner	**рейсов кораб** (m)	['rɛjsɔv 'kɔrab]
cruiser	**крайцер** (m)	['krajʦər]
yacht	**яхта** (f)	['jɑhta]
tugboat	**влекач** (m)	[vlɛ'katʃ]
barge	**шлеп** (m)	[ʃlɛp]
ferry	**сал** (m)	[sal]
sailing ship	**платноходка** (f)	[platnɔ'hɔdka]
brigantine	**бригантина** (f)	[brigan'tina]
ice breaker	**ледоразбивач** (m)	[lɛdɔrazbi'vatʃ]
submarine	**подводница** (f)	[pɔd'vɔdniʦa]
boat (flat-bottomed ~)	**лодка** (f)	['lɔtka]
dinghy	**лодка** (f)	['lɔtka]
lifeboat	**спасителна лодка** (f)	[spa'sitɛlna 'lɔtka]
motorboat	**катер** (m)	['katɛr]
captain	**капитан** (m)	[kapi'tan]
seaman	**матрос** (m)	[mat'rɔs]
sailor	**моряк** (m)	[mɔ'rʲak]
crew	**екипаж** (m)	[ɛki'paʒ]
boatswain	**боцман** (m)	['bɔʦman]
ship's boy	**юнга** (m)	['juŋga]
cook	**корабен готвач** (m)	['kɔrabɛn gɔt'vatʃ]
ship's doctor	**корабен лекар** (m)	['kɔrabɛn 'lɛkar]
deck	**палуба** (f)	['paluba]
mast	**мачта** (f)	['matʃta]
sail	**корабно платно** (n)	['kɔrabnɔ plat'nɔ]
hold	**трюм** (m)	[trym]
bow (prow)	**нос** (m)	[nɔs]
stern	**кърма** (f)	[kɪr'ma]
oar	**гребло** (n)	[grɛb'lɔ]

screw propeller	**витло** (n)	[vit'lɔ]
cabin	**каюта** (f)	[ka'juta]
wardroom	**каюткомпания** (f)	[kajutkɔm'panijɑ]
engine room	**машинно отделение** (n)	[ma'ʃiŋɔ ɔtdɛ'lɛniɛ]
bridge	**капитански мостик** (m)	[kapi'tanski 'mɔstik]
radio room	**радиобудка** (f)	['radiɔ'butka]
wave (radio)	**вълна** (f)	[vɪl'na]
logbook	**корабен дневник** (m)	['kɔrabɛn 'dnɛvnik]
spyglass	**далекоглед** (m)	[dalɛkɔg'lɛd]
bell	**камбана** (f)	[kam'bana]
flag	**знаме** (n)	['znamɛ]
rope (mooring ~)	**дебело въже** (n)	[dɛ'bɛlɔ vɪ'ʒɛ]
knot (bowline, etc.)	**възел** (m)	['vɪzel]
deckrail	**дръжка** (f)	['drɪʃka]
gangway	**трап** (m)	[trap]
anchor	**котва** (f)	['kɔtva]
to weigh anchor	**вдигна котва**	['vdigna 'kɔtva]
to drop anchor	**хвърля котва**	['hvɪrʎa 'kɔtva]
anchor chain	**котвена верига** (f)	['kɔtvɛna vɛ'riga]
port (harbor)	**пристанище** (n)	[pris'taniʃtɛ]
berth, wharf	**кей** (m)	[kɛj]
to berth (moor)	**акостирам**	[akɔs'tiram]
to cast off	**отплувам**	[ɔtp'luvam]
trip, voyage	**пътешествие** (n)	[pɪtɛ'ʃɛstviɛ]
cruise (sea trip)	**морско пътешествие** (n)	['mɔrskɔ pɪtɛ'ʃɛstviɛ]
course (route)	**курс** (m)	[kurs]
route (itinerary)	**маршрут** (m)	[marʃ'rut]
fairway	**фарватер** (m)	[far'vatɛr]
shallows (shoal)	**плитчина** (f)	[pliʧi'na]
to run aground	**заседна на плитчина**	[za'sɛdna na pliʧi'na]
storm	**буря** (f)	['burʲa]
signal	**сигнал** (m)	[sig'nal]
to sink (vi)	**потъвам**	[pɔ'tɪvam]
SOS	**SOS**	[sɔs]
ring buoy	**спасителен пояс** (m)	[spa'sitilɛn 'pɔjɑs]

172. Airport

airport	**летище** (n)	[lɛ'tiʃtɛ]
airplane	**самолет** (m)	[samɔ'lɛt]
airline	**авиокомпания** (f)	[aviɔkɔm'panijɑ]
air-traffic controller	**авиодиспечер** (m)	[aviɔdis'pɛʧər]

departure	**излитане** (n)	[iz'litanɛ]
arrival	**кацане** (n)	['katsanɛ]
to arrive (by plane)	**кацна**	['katsna]
departure time	**време** (n) **на излитане**	['vrɛmɛ na iz'litanɛ]
arrival time	**време** (n) **на кацане**	['vrɛmɛ na 'katsanɛ]
to be delayed	**закъснявам**	[zakɪs'ɲavam]
flight delay	**закъснение** (n) **на излитане**	[zakɪs'nɛniɛ na iz'litanɛ]
information board	**информационно табло** (n)	[infɔrmatsi'ɔɲɔ tab'lɔ]
information	**информация** (f)	[infɔr'matsija]
to announce (vt)	**обявявам**	[ɔbʲa'vʲavam]
flight (e.g., next ~)	**рейс** (m)	[rɛjs]
customs	**митница** (f)	['mitnitsa]
customs officer	**митничар** (m)	[mitni'ʧar]
customs declaration	**декларация** (f)	[dɛkla'ratsija]
to fill out the declaration	**попълня декларация**	[pɔ'pɪlɲa dɛkla'ratsija]
passport control	**паспортен контрол** (m)	[pas'pɔrtɛn kɔnt'rɔl]
luggage	**багаж** (m)	[ba'gaʃ]
hand luggage	**ръчен багаж** (m)	['rɪʧən ba'gaʃ]
Lost Luggage Desk	**търсене** (n) **на багаж**	['tɪrsɛnɛ na ba'gaʃ]
luggage cart	**количка** (f)	[kɔ'liʧka]
landing	**кацане** (n)	['katsanɛ]
landing strip	**писта** (f) **за кацане**	['pista za 'katsanɛ]
to land (vi)	**кацам**	['katsam]
airstairs	**стълба** (f)	['stɪlba]
check-in	**регистрация** (f)	[rɛgist'ratsija]
check-in desk	**гише** (n) **за регистрация**	[gi'ʃɛ za rɛgist'ratsija]
to check-in (vi)	**регистрирам се**	[rɛgist'riram sɛ]
boarding pass	**бордна карта** (f)	['bɔrdna 'karta]
departure gate	**излизане** (n)	[iz'lizanɛ]
transit	**транзит** (m)	[tran'zit]
to wait (vt)	**чакам**	['ʧakam]
departure lounge	**чакалня** (f)	[ʧa'kalɲa]
to see off	**изпращам**	[isp'raʃtam]
to say goodbye	**сбогувам се**	[sbɔ'guvam sɛ]

173. Bicycle. Motorcycle

bicycle	**колело** (n)	[kɔlɛ'lɔ]
scooter	**моторолер** (m)	['mɔtɔ'rɔler]

motorcycle, bike	**мотоциклет** (m)	[mɔtɔtsik'lɛt]
to go by bicycle	**карам колело**	['karam kɔlɛ'lɔ]
handlebars	**волан** (m)	[vɔ'lan]
pedal	**педал** (m)	[pɛ'dal]
brakes	**спирачки** (f pl)	[spi'ratʃki]
bicycle seat	**седло** (n)	[sɛd'lɔ]
pump	**помпа** (f)	['pɔmpa]
luggage rack	**багажник** (m)	[ba'gaʒnik]
front lamp	**фенер** (m)	[fɛ'nɛr]
helmet	**шлем** (m)	[ʃlɛm]
wheel	**колело** (n)	[kɔlɛ'lɔ]
fender	**калник** (n)	['kalnik]
rim	**джанта** (f)	['dʒanta]
spoke	**спица** (f)	['spitsa]

Cars

174. Types of cars

automobile, car	**автомобил** (m)	[avtɔmɔ'bil]
sports car	**спортен автомобил** (m)	['spɔrtɛn avtɔmɔ'bil]
limousine	**лимузина** (f)	[limu'zina]
off-road vehicle	**джип** (m)	[ʤip]
convertible	**кабриолет** (m)	[kabriɔ'lɛt]
minibus	**микробус** (m)	[mikrɔ'bus]
ambulance	**бърза помощ** (f)	['bırza 'pɔmɔʃt]
snowplow	**снегорин** (m)	[snɛgɔ'rin]
truck	**камион** (m)	[kami'ɔn]
tank truck	**автоцистерна** (f)	[avtɔʦis'tɛrna]
van (small truck)	**фургон** (m)	[fur'gɔn]
tractor (big rig)	**влекач** (m)	[vlɛ'kaʧ]
trailer	**ремарке** (n)	[rɛmar'kɛ]
comfortable (adj)	**комфортен**	[kɔm'fɔrtɛn]
second hand (adj)	**употребяван**	[upɔtrɛ'bʲavan]

175. Cars. Bodywork

hood	**капак** (m)	[ka'pak]
fender	**калник** (m)	['kalnik]
roof	**покрив** (m)	['pɔkriv]
windshield	**предно стъкло** (n)	['prɛdnɔ stık'lɔ]
rear-view mirror	**огледало** (n) **за задно виждане**	[ɔglɛ'dalɔ za 'zadnɔ 'viʒdanɛ]
windshield washer	**стъкломиячка** (f)	[stʰklɔmi'jaʧka]
windshield wipers	**чистачки** (f pl)	[ʧis'taʧki]
side window	**странично стъкло** (n)	[stra'niʧnɔ stık'lɔ]
window lift	**стъклоповдигач** (m)	[stıklɔpɔvdi'gaʧ]
antenna	**антена** (f)	[an'tɛna]
sun roof	**шибидах** (m)	[ʃibi'dah]
bumper	**броня** (f)	['brɔɲa]
trunk	**багажник** (m)	[ba'gaʒnik]
door	**врата** (f)	[vra'ta]

door handle	**дръжка** (f)	['drıʃka]
door lock	**ключалка** (f)	[kly'ʧalka]
license plate	**номер** (m)	['nɔmɛr]
muffler	**гърне** (n)	[gır'nɛ]
gas tank	**резервоар** (m) **за бензин**	[rɛzɛrvɔ'ar za bɛn'zin]
tail pipe	**ауспух** (m)	['auspuh]
gas, accelerator	**газ** (m)	[gas]
pedal	**педал** (m)	[pɛ'dal]
gas pedal	**газ** (m)	[gas]
brake	**спирачки** (f pl)	[spi'raʧki]
brake pedal	**спирачка** (f)	[spi'raʧka]
to slow down (to brake)	**удрям спирачка**	['udrʲam spi'raʧka]
parking brake	**ръчна спирачка** (f)	['rıʧna spi'raʧka]
clutch	**съединител** (m)	[sıɛdi'nitɛl]
clutch pedal	**педал** (m) **на съединител**	[pɛ'dal na sıɛdi'nitɛl]
clutch plate	**диск** (m) **на съединител**	[disk na sıɛdi'nitɛl]
shock absorber	**амортизатор** (m)	[amɔrti'zatɔr]
wheel	**колело** (n)	[kɔlɛ'lɔ]
spare tire	**резервна гума** (f)	[rɛ'zɛrvna 'guma]
tire	**гума** (f)	['guma]
hubcap	**капак** (m)	[ka'pak]
driving wheels	**водещи колела** (pl)	['vɔdɛʃti kɔlɛ'la]
front-wheel drive (as adj)	**с предно задвижване**	[s 'prɛdnɔ zad'viʒvanɛ]
rear-wheel drive (as adj)	**със задно задвижване**	[sıs 'zadnɔ zad'viʒvanɛ]
all-wheel drive (as adj)	**с пълно задвижване**	[s 'pılnɔ zad'viʒvanɛ]
gearbox	**скоростна кутия** (f)	['skɔrɔstna ku'tija]
automatic (adj)	**автоматичен**	[aftɔma'tiʧən]
mechanical (adj)	**механически**	[mɛha'niʧəski]
gear shift	**лост** (m) **на скоростна кутия**	[lɔst na 'skɔrɔstna kutija]
headlight	**фар** (m)	[far]
headlights	**фарове** (m pl)	['farɔvɛ]
low beam	**къси светлини** (f pl)	['kısi svɛtli'ni]
high beam	**дълги светлини** (f pl)	['dılgi svɛtli'ni]
brake light	**сигнал** (m) **стоп**	[sig'nal stɔp]
parking lights	**габаритни светлини** (f pl)	[gaba'ritni svɛtli'ni]
hazard lights	**аварийни светлини** (f pl)	[ava'rijni svɛtli'ni]
fog lights	**фарове** (m pl) **за мъгла**	['farɔvɛ za mıg'la]
turn signal	**мигач** (m)	[mi'gaʧ]
back-up light	**заден ход** (m)	['zadɛn hɔd]

176. Cars. Passenger compartment

car inside	**салон** (m)	[sa'lɔn]
leather (as adj)	**кожен**	['kɔʒɛn]
velour (as adj)	**велурен**	[vɛ'lurɛn]
upholstery	**тапицерия** (f)	[tapi'ʦərija]
instrument (gage)	**уред** (m)	['urɛd]
dashboard	**бордово табло** (n)	['bɔrdɔvɔ tab'lɔ]
speedometer	**скоростомер** (m)	[skɔrɔstɔ'mɛr]
needle (pointer)	**стрелка** (f)	[strɛl'ka]
odometer	**километраж** (m)	[kilɔmɛt'raʃ]
indicator (sensor)	**датчик** (m)	['datʧik]
level	**ниво** (n)	[ni'vɔ]
warning light	**крушка** (f)	['kruʃka]
steering wheel	**волан** (m)	[vɔ'lan]
horn	**сигнал** (m)	[sig'nal]
button	**бутон** (m)	[bu'tɔn]
switch	**превключвател** (m)	[prɛvklyʧ'vatɛl]
seat	**седалка** (f)	[sɛ'dalka]
backrest	**облегалка** (f)	[ɔblɛ'galka]
headrest	**възглавница** (f)	[vɪzg'lavniʦa]
seat belt	**предпазен колан** (m)	[prɛd'pazɛn kɔ'lan]
to fasten the belt	**слагам колан**	['slagam kɔ'lan]
adjustment (of seats)	**регулиране** (n)	[rɛgu'liranɛ]
airbag	**въздушна възглавница** (f)	[vɪz'duʃna vɪzg'lavniʦa]
air-conditioner	**климатик** (m)	[klima'tik]
radio	**радио** (n)	['radiɔ]
CD player	**CD плейър** (m)	[si'di 'plɛɪr]
to turn on	**включа**	['vklyʧa]
antenna	**антена** (f)	[an'tɛna]
glove box	**жабка** (f)	['ʒabka]
ashtray	**пепелник** (m)	[pɛpɛl'nik]

177. Cars. Engine

engine	**двигател** (m)	[dvi'gatɛl]
motor	**мотор** (m)	[mɔ'tɔr]
diesel (as adj)	**дизелов**	['dizɛlɔv]
gasoline (as adj)	**бензинов**	[bɛn'zinɔv]
engine volume	**обем** (m) **на двигателя**	[ɔ'bɛm na dvi'gatɛʎa]
power	**мощност** (f)	['mɔʃtnɔst]

horsepower	**конска сила** (f)	['kɔnska 'sila]
piston	**бутало** (n)	[bu'talɔ]
cylinder	**цилиндър** (m)	[ʦi'lindır]
valve	**клапа** (f)	['klapa]
injector	**инжектор** (m)	[in'ʒɛktɔr]
generator	**генератор** (m)	[gɛnɛ'ratɔr]
carburetor	**карбуратор** (m)	[karbu'ratɔr]
engine oil	**моторно масло** (n)	[mɔ'tɔrnɔ mas'lɔ]
radiator	**радиатор** (m)	[radi'atɔr]
coolant	**охлаждаща течност** (f)	[ɔh'laʒdaʃta 'tɛʧnɔst]
cooling fan	**вентилатор** (m)	[vɛnti'latɔr]
battery (accumulator)	**акумулатор** (m)	[akumu'latɔr]
starter	**стартер** (m)	['startɛr]
ignition	**запалване** (n)	[za'palvanɛ]
spark plug	**запалителна свещ** (f)	[zapa'litɛlna svɛʃt]
terminal (of battery)	**клема** (f)	['klɛma]
positive terminal	**плюс** (m)	[plys]
negative terminal	**минус** (m)	['minus]
fuse	**предпазител** (m)	[prɛd'pazitɛl]
air filter	**въздушен филтър** (m)	[vız'duʃɛn 'filtır]
oil filter	**маслен филтър** (m)	['maslɛn 'filtır]
fuel filter	**филтър** (m) **за гориво**	['filtır za gɔ'rivɔ]

178. Cars. Crash. Repair

car accident	**катастрофа** (f)	[katast'rɔfa]
road accident	**пътно-транспортно произшествие** (n)	['pıtnɔ trans'pɔrtnɔ prɔiz'ʃɛstviɛ]
to run into ...	**блъсна се в ...**	['blısna sɛ v]
to have an accident	**катастрофирам**	[katastrɔ'firam]
damage	**повреда** (f)	[pɔv'rɛda]
intact (adj)	**цял**	[ʦʲal]
to break down (vi)	**счупя се**	['sʧupʲa sɛ]
towrope	**автомобилно въже** (n)	[avtɔmɔ'bilnɔ vı'ʒɛ]
puncture	**спукване** (n)	['spukvanɛ]
to be flat	**спусна**	['spusna]
to pump up	**напомпвам**	[na'pɔmpvam]
pressure	**налягане** (n)	[na'ʎaganɛ]
to check (to examine)	**проверя**	[prɔvɛ'rʲa]
repair	**ремонт** (m)	[rɛ'mɔnt]
auto repair shop	**автосервиз** (m)	[avtɔsɛr'vis]
spare part	**резервна част** (f)	[rɛ'zɛrvna ʧast]

part	**детайл** (m)	[dɛ'tajl]
bolt (with nut)	**болт** (m)	[bɔlt]
screw bolt (without nut)	**винт** (m)	[vint]
nut	**гайка** (f)	['gajka]
washer	**шайба** (f)	['ʃʌjba]
bearing	**лагер** (m)	['lagɛr]
tube	**тръба** (f)	[trı'ba]
gasket (head ~)	**уплътнение** (n)	[uplıt'nɛniɛ]
cable, wire	**кабел** (m)	['kabɛl]
jack	**крик** (m)	[krik]
wrench	**гаечен ключ** (m)	['gaɛʧən klyʧ]
hammer	**чук** (m)	[ʧuk]
pump	**помпа** (f)	['pɔmpa]
screwdriver	**отвертка** (f)	[ɔt'vɛrtka]
fire extinguisher	**пожарогасител** (m)	[pɔʒarɔga'sitɛl]
warning triangle	**авариен триъгълник** (m)	[ava'riɛn tri'ıgılnik]
to stall (vi)	**заглъхвам**	[zag'lıhvam]
stalling	**спиране** (n)	['spiranɛ]
to be broken	**счупен съм**	['sʧupen sım]
to overheat (vi)	**прегря се**	[prɛg'rʲa sɛ]
to be clogged up	**запуша се**	[za'puʃʌ sɛ]
to freeze up (pipes, etc.)	**замръзна**	[zam'rızna]
to burst (vi, ab. tube)	**спука се**	['spuka sɛ]
pressure	**налягане** (n)	[na'ʎaganɛ]
level	**ниво** (n)	[ni'vɔ]
slack (~ belt)	**слаб**	[slap]
dent	**вдлъбнатина** (f)	[vdlıbnati'na]
abnormal noise (motor)	**тракане** (n)	['trakanɛ]
crack	**пукнатина** (f)	[puknati'na]
scratch	**драскотина** (f)	[draskɔ'tina]

179. Cars. Road

road	**път** (m)	[pıt]
highway	**автомагистрала** (f)	[avtɔmagist'rala]
freeway	**шосе** (n)	[ʃɔ'sɛ]
direction (way)	**посока** (f)	[pɔ'sɔka]
distance	**разстояние** (n)	[rastɔ'jɑniɛ]
bridge	**мост** (m)	[mɔst]
parking lot	**паркинг** (m)	['parkiŋg]
square	**площад** (m)	[plɔʃ'tad]
interchange	**кръстовище** (n)	[krıs'tɔviʃtɛ]

tunnel	**тунел** (m)	[tu'nɛl]
gas station	**бензиностанция** (f)	[bɛnzinɔs'tantsija]
parking lot	**паркинг** (m)	['parkiŋg]
gas pump	**бензиностанция** (f)	[bɛnzinɔs'tantsija]
auto repair shop	**автосервиз** (m)	[avtɔsɛr'vis]
to get gas	**заредя**	[zarɛ'dʲa]
fuel	**гориво** (n)	[gɔ'rivɔ]
jerrycan	**туба** (f)	['tuba]
asphalt	**асфалт** (m)	[as'falt]
road markings	**маркировка** (f)	[marki'rɔfka]
curb	**бордюр** (m)	[bɔr'dyr]
guardrail	**мантинела** (f)	[manti'nɛla]
ditch	**канавка** (f)	[ka'nafka]
roadside (shoulder)	**банкет** (m)	[ba'ŋkɛt]
lamppost	**стълб** (m)	[stɪlb]
to drive (a car)	**карам**	['karam]
to turn (~ to the left)	**завивам**	[za'vivam]
to make a U-turn	**обръщам се**	[ɔb'rɪʃtam sɛ]
reverse (~ gear)	**заден ход** (m)	['zadɛn hɔd]
to honk (vi)	**сигнализирам**	[signali'ziram]
honk (sound)	**звуков сигнал** (m)	['zvukɔf sig'nal]
to get stuck	**заседна**	[za'sɛdna]
to spin (in mud)	**буксувам**	[buk'suvam]
to cut, to turn off	**гася**	[ga'sʲa]
speed	**скорост** (f)	['skɔrɔst]
to exceed the speed limit	**превиша скорост**	[prɛvi'ʃʌ 'skɔrɔst]
to give a ticket	**глобявам**	[glɔ'bʲavam]
traffic lights	**светофар** (m)	[svɛtɔ'far]
driver's license	**шофьорска книжка** (f)	[ʃɔ'fʲɔrska 'kniʃka]
grade crossing	**прелез** (m)	['prɛlɛz]
intersection	**кръстовище** (n)	[krɪs'tɔviʃtɛ]
crosswalk	**пешеходна пътека** (f)	[pɛʃɛ'hɔdna pɪ'tɛka]
bend, curve	**завой** (m)	[za'vɔj]
pedestrian zone	**пешеходна зона** (f)	[pɛʃɛ'hɔdna 'zɔna]

180. Traffic signs

rules of the road	**правила** (n pl) **за улично движение**	[pravi'la za 'ulitʃnɔ dvi'ʒɛniɛ]
traffic sign	**пътен знак** (m)	['pɪtɛn znak]
passing (overtaking)	**изпреварване** (n)	[isprɛ'varvanɛ]
curve	**завой** (m)	[za'vɔj]
U-turn	**обръщане** (n)	[ɔb'rɪʃtanɛ]
traffic circle	**кръгово движение** (n)	['krɪgɔvɔ dvi'ʒɛniɛ]
No entry	**влизането забранено**	['vlizanɛtɔ zabra'nɛnɔ]

No vehicles allowed	**движението забранено**	[dvi'ʒɛniɛtɔ zabra'nɛnɔ]
No passing	**изпреварването забранено**	[izprɛ'varvanɛtɔ zabra'nɛnɔ]
No parking	**паркирането забранено**	[par'kiranɛtɔ zabra'nɛnɔ]
No stopping	**спирането забранено**	['spiranɛtɔ zabra'nɛnɔ]
dangerous turn	**остър завой** (m)	['ɔstır za'vɔj]
steep descent	**стръмно спускане** (n)	['strımnɔ 'spuskanɛ]
one-way traffic	**еднопосочно движение** (n)	[ɛdnɔpɔ'sɔtʃnɔ dvi'ʒɛniɛ]
crosswalk	**пешеходна пътека** (f)	[pɛʃɛ'hɔdna pı'tɛka]
slippery road	**хлъзгав път** (m)	['hlızgaf pıt]
YIELD	**дай път**	[daj pıt]

PEOPLE. LIFE EVENTS

Life events

181. Holidays. Event

celebration, holiday	**празник** (m)	['praznik]
national day	**национален празник** (m)	[natsiɔ'nalɛn 'praznik]
public holiday	**празничен ден** (m)	['praznitʃən dɛn]
to commemorate (vt)	**празнувам**	[praz'nuvam]
event (happening)	**събитие** (n)	[sı'bitiɛ]
event (organized activity)	**мероприятие** (n)	[mɛrɔpri'jatiɛ]
banquet (party)	**банкет** (m)	[ba'ŋkɛt]
reception (formal party)	**прием** (m)	['priɛm]
feast	**пир** (m)	[pir]
anniversary	**годишнина** (f)	[gɔ'diʃnina]
jubilee	**юбилей** (m)	[jubi'lɛj]
to celebrate (vt)	**отбележа**	[ɔtbɛ'lɛʒa]
New Year	**Нова година** (f)	['nɔva gɔ'dina]
Happy New Year!	**Честита нова година!**	[tʃəs'tita 'nɔva gɔ'dina]
Christmas	**Коледа**	['kɔlɛda]
Merry Christmas!	**Весела Коледа!**	['vɛsɛla 'kɔlɛda]
Christmas tree	**коледна елха** (f)	['kɔlɛdna ɛl'ha]
fireworks	**заря** (f)	[za'rʲa]
wedding	**сватба** (f)	['svatba]
groom	**годеник** (m)	[gɔdɛ'nik]
bride	**годеница** (f)	[gɔdɛ'nitsa]
to invite (vt)	**каня**	['kaɲa]
invitation card	**покана** (f)	[pɔ'kana]
guest	**гост** (m)	[gɔst]
to visit (~ your parents, etc.)	**отивам на гости**	[ɔ'tivam na 'gɔsti]
to greet the guests	**посрещам гости**	[pɔs'rɛʃtam 'gɔsti]
gift, present	**подарък** (m)	[pɔ'darık]
to give (sth as present)	**подарявам**	[pɔda'rʲavam]
to receive gifts	**получавам подаръци**	[pɔlu'tʃavam pɔ'darıtsi]
bouquet (of flowers)	**букет** (m)	[bu'kɛt]

congratulations	**поздравление** (n)	[pɔzdrav'lɛniɛ]
to congratulate (vt)	**поздравявам**	[pɔzdra'vʲavam]
greeting card	**поздравителна картичка** (f)	[pɔzdra'vitɛlna 'kartiʧka]
to send a postcard	**изпратя картичка**	[isp'ratʲa 'kartiʧka]
to get a postcard	**получа картичка**	[pɔ'luʧa 'kartiʧka]
toast	**тост** (m)	[tɔst]
to offer (a drink, etc.)	**черпя**	['ʧərpʲa]
champagne	**шампанско** (n)	[ʃʌm'panskɔ]
to have fun	**веселя се**	[vɛsɛ'ʎa sɛ]
fun, merriment	**веселба** (f)	[vɛsɛl'ba]
joy (emotion)	**радост** (f)	['radɔst]
dance	**танц** (m)	[tanʦ]
to dance (vi, vt)	**танцувам**	[tan'ʦuvam]
waltz	**валс** (m)	[vals]
tango	**танго** (n)	[ta'ŋgɔ]

182. Funerals. Burial

cemetery	**гробища** (pl)	['grɔbiʃta]
grave, tomb	**гроб** (m)	[grɔp]
gravestone	**надгробен паметник** (m)	[nadg'rɔbɛn 'pamɛtnik]
fence	**ограда** (f)	[ɔg'rada]
chapel	**параклис** (m)	[pa'raklis]
death	**смърт** (f)	[smɪrt]
to die (vi)	**умра**	[um'ra]
the deceased	**покойник** (m)	[pɔ'kɔjnik]
mourning	**траур** (m)	['traur]
to bury (vt)	**погребвам**	[pɔg'rɛbvam]
funeral home	**погребални услуги** (pl)	[pɔgrɛ'balni us'lugi]
funeral	**погребение** (n)	[pɔgrɛ'bɛniɛ]
wreath	**венец** (m)	[vɛ'nɛʦ]
casket	**ковчег** (m)	[kɔf'ʧəg]
hearse	**катафалка** (f)	[kata'falka]
shroud	**саван** (m)	[sa'van]
cremation urn	**урна** (f)	['urna]
crematory	**крематориум** (m)	[krɛma'tɔrium]
obituary	**некролог** (m)	[nɛkrɔ'lɔg]
to cry (weep)	**плача**	['plaʧa]
to sob (vi)	**ридая**	[ri'dajɑ]

183. War. Soldiers

platoon	**взвод** (m)	[vzvɔd]
company	**рота** (f)	['rɔta]
regiment	**полк** (m)	[pɔlk]
army	**армия** (f)	['armija]
division	**дивизия** (f)	[di'vizija]
section, squad	**отряд** (m)	[ɔt'rʲat]
host (army)	**войска** (f)	[vɔjs'ka]
soldier	**войник** (m)	[vɔj'nik]
officer	**офицер** (m)	[ɔfi'ʦər]
private	**редник** (m)	['rɛdnik]
sergeant	**сержант** (m)	[sɛr'ʒant]
lieutenant	**лейтенант** (m)	[lɛjtɛ'nant]
captain	**капитан** (m)	[kapi'tan]
major	**майор** (m)	[ma'jor]
colonel	**полковник** (m)	[pɔl'kɔvnik]
general	**генерал** (m)	[gɛnɛ'ral]
sailor	**моряк** (m)	[mɔ'rʲak]
captain	**капитан** (m)	[kapi'tan]
boatswain	**боцман** (m)	['bɔʦman]
artilleryman	**артилерист** (m)	[artilɛ'rist]
paratrooper	**десантчик** (m)	[dɛ'santʧik]
pilot	**летец** (m)	[lɛ'tɛʦ]
navigator	**щурман** (m)	['ʃturman]
mechanic	**механик** (m)	[mɛ'hanik]
pioneer (sapper)	**сапьор** (m)	[sa'pɜr]
parachutist	**парашутист** (m)	[paraʃu'tist]
reconnaissance scout	**разузнавач** (m)	[razuzna'vaʧ]
sniper	**снайперист** (m)	[snajpɛ'rist]
patrol (group)	**патрул** (m)	[pat'rul]
to patrol (vt)	**патрулирам**	[patru'liram]
sentry, guard	**часови** (m)	[ʧasɔ'vi]
warrior	**войник** (m)	[vɔj'nik]
hero	**герой** (m)	[gɛ'rɔj]
heroine	**героиня** (f)	[gɛrɔ'iɲa]
patriot	**патриот** (m)	[patri'ɔt]
traitor	**предател** (m)	[prɛ'datɛl]
to betray (vt)	**предавам**	[prɛ'davam]
deserter	**дезертьор** (m)	[dɛzɛr'tʲɔr]
to desert (vi)	**дезертирам**	[dɛzɛr'tiram]

mercenary	**наемник** (m)	[na'ɛmnik]
recruit	**новобранец** (m)	[nɔvɔb'ranɛʦ]
volunteer	**доброволец** (m)	[dɔbrɔ'vɔlɛʦ]
dead (n)	**убит** (m)	[u'bit]
wounded (n)	**ранен** (m)	[ra'nɛn]
prisoner of war	**пленник** (m)	['plɛŋik]

184. War. Military actions. Part 1

war	**война** (f)	[vɔj'na]
to be at war	**воювам**	[vɔ'juvam]
civil war	**гражданска война** (f)	['graʒdanska vɔj'na]
treacherously (adv)	**вероломно**	[vɛrɔ'lɔmnɔ]
declaration of war	**обявяване** (n)	[ɔbʲa'vʲavanɛ]
to declare (~ war)	**обявя**	[ɔbʲa'vʲa]
aggression	**агресия** (f)	[ag'rɛsija]
to attack (invade)	**нападам**	[na'padam]
to invade (vt)	**завземам**	[zav'zɛmam]
invader	**окупатор** (m)	[ɔku'patɔr]
conqueror	**завоевател** (m)	[zavɔɛ'vatɛl]
defense	**отбрана** (f)	[ɔtb'rana]
to defend (a country, etc.)	**отбранявам**	[ɔtbra'ɲavam]
to defend oneself	**отбранявам се**	[ɔtbra'ɲavam sɛ]
enemy	**враг** (m)	[vrag]
foe, adversary	**противник** (m)	[prɔ'tivnik]
enemy (as adj)	**вражески**	['vraʒɛski]
strategy	**стратегия** (f)	[stra'tɛgija]
tactics	**тактика** (f)	['taktika]
order	**заповед** (f)	['zapɔvɛd]
command (order)	**команда** (f)	[kɔ'manda]
to order (vt)	**заповядвам**	[zapɔ'vʲadvam]
mission	**задача** (f)	[za'daʧa]
secret (adj)	**секретен**	[sɛk'rɛtɛn]
battle	**сражение** (n)	[sra'ʒɛniɛ]
combat	**бой** (m)	[bɔj]
attack	**атака** (f)	[a'taka]
storming (assault)	**щурм** (m)	[ʃturm]
to storm (vt)	**щурмувам**	[ʃtur'muvam]
siege (to be under ~)	**обсада** (f)	[ɔb'sada]
offensive (n)	**настъпление** (n)	[nastɪp'lɛniɛ]
to go on the offensive	**настъпвам**	[nas'tɪpvam]

retreat	**отстъпление** (n)	[ɔtstɪp'lɛniɛ]
to retreat (vi)	**отстъпвам**	[ɔts'tɪpvam]
encirclement	**обкръжение** (n)	[ɔpkrɪ'ʒɛniɛ]
to encircle (vt)	**обкръжавам**	[ɔpkrɪ'ʒavam]
bombing (by aircraft)	**бомбардиране** (n)	[bɔmbar'diranɛ]
to drop a bomb	**хвърлям бомба**	['hvɪrʎam 'bɔmba]
to bomb (vt)	**бомбардирам**	[bɔmbar'diram]
explosion	**експлозия** (f)	[ɛksp'lɔzijɑ]
shot	**изстрел** (m)	['isstrɛl]
to fire a shot	**изстрелям**	[isst'rɛʎam]
firing (burst of ~)	**стрелба** (f)	[strɛl'ba]
to take aim (at ...)	**целя се в ...**	['tsəʎa sɛ v]
to point (a gun)	**насоча**	[na'sɔtʃa]
to hit (the target)	**улуча**	[u'lutʃa]
to sink (~ a ship)	**потопя**	[pɔtɔ'pʲa]
hole (in a ship)	**дупка** (f)	['dupka]
to founder, to sink (vi)	**потъвам**	[pɔ'tɪvam]
front (war ~)	**фронт** (m)	[frɔnt]
rear (homefront)	**тил** (m)	[til]
evacuation	**евакуация** (f)	[ɛvaku'atsijɑ]
to evacuate (vt)	**евакуирам**	[ɛvaku'iram]
barbwire	**бодлив тел** (m)	[bɔd'liv tɛl]
barrier (anti tank ~)	**заграждение** (n)	[zagraʒ'dɛnie]
watchtower	**кула** (f)	['kula]
hospital	**военна болница** (f)	[vɔ'ɛŋa 'bɔlnitsa]
to wound (vt)	**раня**	[ra'ɲa]
wound	**рана** (f)	['rana]
wounded (n)	**ранен** (m)	[ra'nɛn]
to be wounded	**получа нараняване**	[pɔ'lutʃa nara'ɲavanɛ]
serious (wound)	**тежък**	['tɛʒɪk]

185. War. Military actions. Part 2

captivity	**плен** (m)	[plɛn]
to take captive	**пленявам**	[plɛ'ɲavam]
to be in captivity	**намирам се в плен**	[na'miram sɛ v plɛn]
to be taken prisoner	**попадна в плен**	[pɔ'padna v plɛn]
concentration camp	**концлагер** (m)	['kɔnts'lagɛr]
prisoner of war	**пленник** (m)	['plɛŋik]
to escape (vi)	**бягам**	['bʲagam]
to betray (vt)	**предам**	[prɛ'dam]

betrayer	**предател** (m)	[prɛ'datɛl]
betrayal	**предателство** (n)	[prɛ'datɛlstvɔ]
to execute (shoot)	**разстрелям**	[rasst'rɛʎam]
execution (by firing squad)	**разстрелване** (n)	[rasst'rɛlvanɛ]
equipment (military gear)	**военна униформа** (f)	[vɔ'ɛŋa uni'fɔrma]
shoulder board	**пагон** (m)	[pa'gɔn]
gas mask	**противогаз** (m)	[prɔtivɔ'gas]
radio transmitter	**радиостанция** (f)	[radiɔs'tanʦijɑ]
cipher, code	**шифър** (m)	['ʃifır]
secrecy	**конспирация** (f)	[kɔnspi'raʦijɑ]
password	**парола** (f)	[pa'rɔla]
land mine	**мина** (f)	['mina]
to mine (road, etc.)	**минирам**	[mi'niram]
minefield	**минно поле** (n)	['miŋɔ pɔ'lɛ]
air-raid warning	**въздушна тревога** (f)	[vız'duʃna trɛ'vɔga]
alarm (warning)	**тревога** (f)	[trɛ'vɔga]
signal	**сигнал** (m)	[sig'nal]
signal flare	**сигнална ракета** (f)	[sig'nalna ra'kɛta]
headquarters	**щаб** (m)	[ʃtab]
reconnaissance	**разузнаване** (n)	[razuz'navanɛ]
situation	**обстановка** (f)	[ɔpsta'nɔfka]
report	**рапорт** (m)	['rapɔrt]
ambush	**засада** (f)	[za'sada]
reinforcement (of army)	**подкрепа** (f)	[pɔtk'rɛpa]
target	**мишена** (f)	[mi'ʃɛna]
proving ground	**полигон** (m)	[pɔli'gɔn]
military exercise	**маневри** (m pl)	[ma'nɛvri]
panic	**паника** (f)	['panika]
devastation	**разруха** (f)	[raz'ruha]
destruction, ruins	**разрушения** (n pl)	[razru'ʃɛnijɑ]
to destroy (vt)	**разрушавам**	[razru'ʃʌvam]
to survive (vi, vt)	**оцелея**	[ɔʦə'lɛjɑ]
to disarm (vt)	**обезоръжа**	[ɔbɛzɔrı'ʒa]
to handle (~ a gun)	**служа си**	['sluʒa si]
Attention!	**Мирно!**	['mirnɔ]
At ease!	**Свободно!**	[svɔ'bɔdnɔ]
feat (of courage)	**подвиг** (m)	['pɔdvig]
oath (vow)	**клетва** (f)	['klɛtva]
to swear (an oath)	**заклевам се**	[zak'lɛvam sɛ]
decoration (medal, etc.)	**награда** (f)	[nag'rada]
to award (give medal to)	**награждавам**	[nagraʒ'davam]

medal	**медал** (m)	[mɛ'dal]
order (e.g., ~ of Merit)	**орден** (m)	['ɔrdɛn]
victory	**победа** (f)	[pɔ'bɛda]
defeat	**поражение** (n)	[pɔra'ʒɛniɛ]
armistice	**примирие** (n)	[pri'miriɛ]
banner (standard)	**знаме** (n)	['znamɛ]
glory (honor, fame)	**слава** (f)	['slava]
parade	**парад** (m)	[pa'rat]
to march (on parade)	**марширувам**	[marʃi'ruvam]

186. Weapons

weapons	**оръжие** (n)	[ɔ'rɪʒiɛ]
firearm	**огнестрелно оръжие** (n)	[ɔgnɛst'rɛlnɔ ɔ'rɪʒiɛ]
cold weapons (knives, etc.)	**хладно оръжие** (n)	['hladnɔ ɔ'rɪʒiɛ]
chemical weapons	**химическо оръжие** (n)	[hi'mitʃəskɔ ɔ'rɪʒiɛ]
nuclear (adj)	**ядрен**	['jadrɛn]
nuclear weapons	**ядрено оръжие** (n)	['jadrɛnɔ ɔ'rɪʒiɛ]
bomb	**бомба** (f)	['bɔmba]
atomic bomb	**атомна бомба** (f)	['atɔmna 'bɔmba]
pistol (gun)	**пистолет** (m)	[pistɔ'lɛt]
rifle	**пушка** (f)	['puʃka]
submachine gun	**автомат** (m)	[aftɔ'mat]
machine gun	**картечница** (f)	[kar'tɛtʃnitsa]
muzzle	**дуло** (n)	['dulɔ]
barrel	**цев** (m)	[tsəv]
caliber	**калибър** (m)	[ka'libɪr]
trigger	**спусък** (m)	['spusɪk]
sight (aiming device)	**мерник** (m)	['mɛrnik]
magazine	**магазин** (m)	[maga'zin]
butt (of rifle)	**приклад** (m)	[prik'lad]
hand grenade	**граната** (f)	[gra'nata]
explosive	**експлозив** (n)	[ɛksplɔ'zif]
bullet	**куршум** (m)	[kur'ʃum]
cartridge	**патрон** (m)	[pat'rɔn]
charge	**заряд** (m)	[za'rʲad]
ammunition	**боеприпаси** (pl)	[bɔɛp'ripasi]
bomber (aircraft)	**бомбардировач** (m)	[bɔmbardirɔ'vatʃ]
fighter	**изтребител** (m)	[istrɛ'bitɛl]

helicopter	**хеликоптер** (m)	[hɛli'kɔptɛr]
anti-aircraft gun	**зенитно оръдие** (n)	[zɛ'nitnɔ ɔ'rɪdiɛ]
tank	**танк** (m)	[taŋk]
tank gun	**оръдие** (n)	[ɔ'rɪdiɛ]
artillery	**артилерия** (f)	[arti'lɛrija]
to lay (a gun)	**насоча**	[na'sɔʧa]
shell (projectile)	**снаряд** (m)	[sna'rʲad]
mortar bomb	**мина** (f)	['mina]
mortar	**миномет** (m)	[minɔ'mɛt]
splinter (shell fragment)	**парче** (n)	[par'ʧə]
submarine	**подводница** (f)	[pɔd'vɔdnitsa]
torpedo	**торпедо** (n)	[tɔr'pɛdɔ]
missile	**ракета** (f)	[ra'keta]
to load (gun)	**зареждам**	[za'rɛʒdam]
to shoot (vi)	**стрелям**	['strɛʎam]
to point at (the cannon)	**целя се (в ...)**	['tsəʎa sɛ v]
bayonet	**щик** (m)	[ʃtik]
epee	**шпага** (f)	['ʃpaga]
saber (e.g., cavalry ~)	**сабя** (f)	['sabʲa]
spear (weapon)	**копие** (n)	['kɔpie]
bow	**лък** (m)	[lɪk]
arrow	**стрела** (f)	[strɛ'la]
musket	**мускет** (m)	[mus'kɛt]
crossbow	**арбалет** (m)	[arba'lɛt]

187. Ancient people

primitive (prehistoric)	**първобитен**	[pɪrvɔ'bitɛn]
prehistoric (adj)	**доисторически**	[dɔistɔ'riʧəski]
ancient (~ civilization)	**древен**	['drɛvɛn]
Stone Age	**Каменен век** (m)	['kamɛnɛn vɛk]
Bronze Age	**бронзова епоха** (f)	['brɔnzɔva ɛ'pɔha]
Ice Age	**ледникова епоха** (f)	['lɛdnikɔva ɛ'pɔha]
tribe	**племе** (n)	['plɛmɛ]
cannibal	**човекоядец** (m)	[ʧɔvɛkɔ'jadɛts]
hunter	**ловец** (m)	[lɔ'vɛts]
to hunt (vi, vt)	**ловувам**	[lɔ'vuvam]
mammoth	**мамут** (m)	[ma'mut]
cave	**пещера** (f)	[pɛʃtɛ'ra]
fire	**огън** (m)	['ɔgɪn]
campfire	**клада** (f)	['klada]
rock painting	**скална рисунка** (f)	['skalna ri'suŋka]

tool (e.g., stone ax)	**оръдие** (n) **на труда**	[ɔ'rɪdiɛ na tru'da]
spear	**копие** (n)	['kɔpie]
stone ax	**каменна брадва** (f)	['kamɛŋa 'bradva]
to be at war	**воювам**	[vɔ'juvam]
to domesticate (vt)	**опитомявам**	[ɔpitɔ'mʲavam]
idol	**идол** (m)	['idɔl]
to worship (vt)	**покланям се**	[pɔk'laɲam sɛ]
superstition	**суеверие** (n)	[suɛ'vɛriɛ]
evolution	**еволюция** (f)	[ɛvɔ'lyʦija]
development	**развитие** (n)	[raz'vitiɛ]
disappearance (extinction)	**изчезване** (n)	[iz'ʧəzvanɛ]
to adapt oneself	**приспособявам се**	[prispɔsɔ'bʲavam sɛ]
archeology	**археология** (f)	[arhɛɔ'lɔgija]
archeologist	**археолог** (m)	[arhɛɔ'lɔg]
archeological (adj)	**археологически**	[arhɛɔlɔ'giʧəski]
excavation site	**разкопки** (pl)	[ras'kɔpki]
excavations	**разкопки** (pl)	[ras'kɔpki]
find (object)	**находка** (f)	[na'hɔtka]
fragment	**фрагмент** (m)	[frag'mɛnt]

188. Middle Ages

people (ethnic group)	**народ** (m)	[na'rɔd]
peoples	**народи** (m pl)	[na'rɔdi]
tribe	**племе** (n)	['plɛmɛ]
tribes	**племена** (n pl)	[plɛmɛ'na]
barbarians	**варвари** (m pl)	['varvari]
Gauls	**гали** (m pl)	['gali]
Goths	**готи** (m pl)	['gɔti]
Slavs	**славяни** (m pl)	[sla'vʲani]
Vikings	**викинги** (m pl)	['vikiŋgi]
Romans	**римляни** (m pl)	['rimʎani]
Roman (adj)	**римски**	['rimski]
Byzantines	**византийци** (m pl)	[vizan'tijʦi]
Byzantium	**Византия** (f)	[vi'zantija]
Byzantine (adj)	**византийски**	[vizan'tijski]
emperor	**император** (m)	[impɛ'ratɔr]
leader, chief	**вожд** (m)	[vɔʒd]
powerful (~ king)	**могъщ**	[mɔ'gɪʃt]
king	**крал** (m)	[kral]
ruler (sovereign)	**владетел** (m)	[vla'dɛtɛl]
knight	**рицар** (m)	['riʦar]

feudal lord	**феодал** (m)	[fɛɔ'dal]
feudal (adj)	**феодален**	[fɛɔ'dalɛn]
vassal	**васал** (m)	[va'sal]
duke	**херцог** (m)	[hɛr'tsɔg]
earl	**граф** (m)	[graf]
baron	**барон** (m)	[ba'rɔn]
bishop	**епископ** (m)	[ɛpis'kɔp]
armor	**доспехи** (pl)	[dɔs'pɛhi]
shield	**щит** (m)	[ʃtit]
sword	**меч** (m)	[mɛtʃ]
visor	**забрало** (n)	[zab'ralɔ]
chainmail	**ризница** (f)	['riznitsa]
crusade	**кръстоносен поход** (m)	[krɪstɔ'nɔsɛn 'pɔhɔd]
crusader	**кръстоносец** (m)	[krɪstɔ'nɔsɛts]
territory	**територия** (f)	[tɛri'tɔrija]
to attack (invade)	**нападам**	[na'padam]
to conquer (vt)	**завоювам**	[zavɔ'juvam]
to occupy (invade)	**завзема**	[zav'zɛma]
siege (to be under ~)	**обсада** (f)	[ɔb'sada]
besieged (adj)	**обсаден**	[ɔpsa'dɛn]
to besiege (vt)	**обсаждам**	[ɔp'saʒdam]
inquisition	**инквизиция** (f)	[iŋkvi'zitsija]
inquisitor	**инквизитор** (m)	[iŋkvi'zitɔr]
torture	**измъчване** (n)	[iz'mɪtʃvanɛ]
cruel (adj)	**жесток**	[ʒɛs'tɔk]
heretic	**еретик** (m)	[ɛrɛ'tik]
heresy	**ерес** (f)	['ɛrɛs]
seafaring	**мореплаване** (n)	[mɔrɛp'lavanɛ]
pirate	**пират** (m)	[pi'rat]
piracy	**пиратство** (n)	[pi'ratstvɔ]
boarding (attack)	**абордаж** (m)	[abɔr'daʒ]
loot, booty	**плячка** (f)	['pʎatʃka]
treasures	**съкровища** (n pl)	[sɪk'rɔviʃta]
discovery	**откритие** (n)	[ɔtk'ritiɛ]
to discover (new land, etc.)	**откривам**	[ɔtk'rivam]
expedition	**експедиция** (f)	[ɛkspɛ'ditsija]
musketeer	**мускетар** (m)	[muskɛ'tar]
cardinal	**кардинал** (m)	[kardi'nal]
heraldry	**хералдика** (f)	[hɛ'raldika]
heraldic (adj)	**хералдически**	[hɛral'ditʃəski]

189. Leader. Chief. Authorities

king	**крал** (m)	[kral]
queen	**кралица** (f)	[kra'lit͡sa]
royal (adj)	**кралски**	['kralski]
kingdom	**кралство** (n)	['kralstvɔ]
prince	**принц** (m)	[print͡s]
princess	**принцеса** (f)	[prin't͡sәsa]
president	**президент** (m)	[prɛzi'dɛnt]
vice-president	**вицепрезидент** (m)	['vit͡sәprɛzi'dɛnt]
senator	**сенатор** (m)	[sɛ'natɔr]
monarch	**монарх** (m)	[mɔ'narh]
ruler (sovereign)	**владетел** (m)	[vla'dɛtɛl]
dictator	**диктатор** (m)	[dik'tatɔr]
tyrant	**тиранин** (m)	[ti'ranin]
magnate	**магнат** (m)	[mag'nat]
director	**директор** (m)	[di'rɛktɔr]
chief	**шеф** (m)	[ʃɛf]
manager (director)	**управител** (m)	[up'ravitɛl]
boss	**бос** (m)	[bɔs]
owner	**собственик** (m)	['sɔbstvɛnik]
head (~ of delegation)	**глава** (f)	[gla'va]
authorities	**власти** (f pl)	['vlasti]
superiors	**началство** (n)	[na't͡ʃalstvɔ]
governor	**губернатор** (m)	[gubɛr'natɔr]
consul	**консул** (m)	['kɔnsul]
diplomat	**дипломат** (m)	[diplɔ'mat]
mayor	**кмет** (m)	[kmɛt]
sheriff	**шериф** (m)	[ʃɛ'rif]
emperor	**император** (m)	[impɛ'ratɔr]
tsar, czar	**цар** (m)	[t͡sar]
pharaoh	**фараон** (m)	[fara'ɔn]
khan	**хан** (m)	[han]

190. Road. Way. Directions

road	**път** (m)	[pɪt]
way (direction)	**път** (m)	[pɪt]
freeway	**шосе** (n)	[ʃɔ'sɛ]
highway	**автомагистрала** (f)	[avtɔmagist'rala]
interstate	**първостепенен път** (m)	[pɪrvɔs'tɛpɛnɛn pɪt]

main road	**главен път** (m)	['glavɛn pıt]
dirt road	**междуселски път** (m)	[mɛʒdu'sɛlski pıt]
pathway	**пътека** (f)	[pı'tɛka]
footpath (troddenpath)	**пътечка** (f)	[pı'tɛʧka]
Where?	**Къде?**	[kı'dɛ]
Where (to)?	**Къде?**	[kı'dɛ]
Where … from?	**Откъде?**	[ɔtkı'dɛ]
direction (way)	**посока** (f)	[pɔ'sɔka]
to point (~ the way)	**посочвам**	[pɔ'sɔʧvam]
to the left	**наляво**	[na'ʎavɔ]
to the right	**вдясно**	['vdʲasnɔ]
straight ahead (adv)	**направо**	[nap'ravɔ]
back (e.g., to turn ~)	**назад**	[na'zad]
bend, curve	**завой** (m)	[za'vɔj]
to turn (~ to the left)	**завивам**	[za'vivam]
to make a U-turn	**обръщам се**	[ɔb'rıʃtam sɛ]
to be visible	**виждам се**	['viʒdam sɛ]
to appear (come into view)	**покажа се**	[pɔ'kaʒa sɛ]
stop, halt (in journey)	**спиране** (n)	['spiranɛ]
to rest, to halt (vi)	**почивам си**	[pɔ'ʧivam si]
rest (pause)	**почивка** (f)	[pɔ'ʧifka]
to lose one's way	**загубя се**	[za'gubʲa sɛ]
to lead to … (ab. road)	**водя към …**	['vɔdʲa kım]
to arrive at …	**изляза на …**	[iz'ʎaza na]
stretch (of road)	**отрязък** (m)	[ɔt'rʲazık]
asphalt	**асфалт** (m)	[as'falt]
curb	**бордюр** (m)	[bɔr'dyr]
ditch	**канавка** (f)	[ka'nafka]
manhole	**капак** (m)	[ka'pak]
roadside (shoulder)	**банкет** (m)	[ba'ŋkɛt]
pit, pothole	**дупка** (f)	['dupka]
to go (on foot)	**вървя**	[vır'vʲa]
to pass (overtake)	**изпреваря**	[izprɛ'varʲa]
step (footstep)	**крачка** (f)	['kraʧka]
on foot (adv)	**пеш**	[pɛʃ]
to block (road)	**преградя**	[prɛgra'dʲa]
boom barrier	**бариера** (f)	[bari'ɛra]
dead end	**задънена улица** (f)	[za'dınɛna 'ulitsa]

191. Breaking the law. Criminals. Part 1

bandit **бандит** (m) [ban'dit]
crime **престъпление** (n) [prɛstɪp'lɛniɛ]
criminal (person) **престъпник** (m) [prɛs'tɪpnik]

thief **крадец** (m) [kra'dɛʦ]
to steal (vi, vt) **крада** [kra'da]
stealing, theft **кражба** (f) ['kraʒba]

to kidnap (vt) **отвлека** [ɔtvlɛ'ka]
kidnapping **отвличане** (n) [ɔtv'liʧanɛ]
kidnapper **похитител** (m) [pɔhi'titɛl]

ransom **откуп** (m) ['ɔtkup]
to demand ransom **искам откуп** ['iskam 'ɔtkup]

to rob (vt) **грабя** ['grabʲa]
robber **грабител** (m) [gra'bitɛl]

to extort (vt) **изнудвам** [iz'nudvam]
extortionist **изнудвач** (m) [iznud'vaʧ]
extortion **изнудване** (n) [iz'nudvanɛ]

to murder, to kill **убия** [u'bijɑ]
murder **убийство** (n) [u'bijstvɔ]
murderer **убиец** (m) [u'biɛʦ]

gunshot **изстрел** (m) ['isstrɛl]
to fire a shot **изстрелям** [isst'rɛʎam]
to shoot to death **застрелям** [zast'rɛʎam]
to shoot (vi) **стрелям** ['strɛʎam]
shooting **стрелба** (f) [strɛl'ba]

incident (fight, etc.) **произшествие** (n) [prɔis'ʃɛstviɛ]
fight, brawl **сбиване** (n) ['zbivanɛ]
victim **жертва** (f) ['ʒɛrtva]

to damage (vt) **повредя** [pɔvrɛ'dʲa]
damage **щета** (f) [ʃtɛ'ta]
dead body **труп** (m) [trup]
grave (~ crime) **тежък** ['tɛʒɪk]

to attack (vt) **нападна** [na'padna]
to beat (dog, person) **бия** ['bijɑ]
to beat up **набия** [na'bijɑ]
to take (rob of sth) **отнема** [ɔt'nɛma]
to stab to death **заколя** [za'kɔʎa]
to maim (vt) **осакатя** [ɔsaka'tʲa]
to wound (vt) **раня** [ra'ɲa]
blackmail **шантаж** (m) [ʃʌn'taʒ]

to blackmail (vt)	**шантажирам**	[ʃʌnta'ʒiram]
blackmailer	**шантажист** (m)	[ʃʌnta'ʒist]
protection racket	**рекет** (m)	['rɛkɛt]
racketeer	**рекетьор** (m)	[rɛkɛ'tʲɔr]
gangster	**гангстер** (m)	['gaŋgstɛr]
mafia, Mob	**мафия** (f)	['mafijɑ]
pickpocket	**джебчия** (m)	[ʤɛb'ʧijɑ]
burglar	**разбивач** (m) **на врати**	[razbi'vaʧ na vra'ti]
smuggling	**контрабанда** (f)	[kɔntra'banda]
smuggler	**контрабандист** (m)	[kɔntraban'dist]
forgery	**фалшификат** (m)	[falʃifi'kat]
to forge (counterfeit)	**фалшифицирам**	[falʃifi'ʦiram]
fake (forged)	**фалшив**	[fal'ʃiv]

192. Breaking the law. Criminals. Part 2

rape	**изнасилване** (n)	[izna'silvanɛ]
to rape (vt)	**изнасиля**	[izna'siʎa]
rapist	**насилник** (m)	[na'silnik]
maniac	**маниак** (m)	[mani'ak]
prostitute (fem.)	**проститутка** (f)	[prɔsti'tutka]
prostitution	**проституция** (f)	[prɔsti'tuʦijɑ]
pimp	**сутеньор** (m)	[sutɛ'nɜr]
drug addict	**наркоман** (m)	[narkɔ'man]
drug dealer	**наркотрафикант** (m)	[narkɔtrafi'kant]
to blow up (bomb)	**взривя**	[vzri'vʲa]
explosion	**експлозия** (f)	[ɛksp'lɔzijɑ]
to set fire	**подпаля**	[pɔd'paʎa]
incendiary (arsonist)	**подпалвач** (m)	[pɔdpal'vaʧ]
terrorism	**тероризъм** (m)	[tɛrɔ'rizɪm]
terrorist	**терорист** (m)	[tɛrɔ'rist]
hostage	**заложник** (m)	[za'lɔʒnik]
to swindle (vt)	**измамя**	[iz'mamʲa]
swindle	**измама** (f)	[iz'mama]
swindler	**мошеник** (m)	[mɔ'ʃɛnik]
to bribe (vt)	**подкупя**	[pɔd'kupʲa]
bribery	**подкуп** (m)	['pɔtkup]
bribe	**рушвет** (m)	[ruʃ'vɛt]
poison	**отрова** (f)	[ɔt'rɔva]
to poison (vt)	**отровя**	[ɔt'rɔvʲa]

to poison oneself	**отровя се**	[ɔt'rɔvʲa sɛ]
suicide (act)	**самоубийство** (n)	[samɔu'bijstvɔ]
suicide (person)	**самоубиец** (m)	[samɔu'biɛʦ]
to threaten (vt)	**заплашвам**	[zap'laʃvam]
threat	**заплаха** (f)	[zap'laha]
to make an attempt	**покушавам се**	[pɔku'ʃʌvam sɛ]
attempt (attack)	**покушение** (n)	[pɔku'ʃɛniɛ]
to steal (a car)	**открадна**	[ɔtk'radna]
to hijack (a plane)	**отвлека**	[ɔtvlɛ'ka]
revenge	**отмъщение** (n)	[ɔtmɪʃ'tɛniɛ]
to revenge (vt)	**отмъщавам**	[ɔtmɪʃ'tavam]
to torture (vt)	**изтезавам**	[istɛ'zavam]
torture	**измъчване** (n)	[iz'mɪʧvanɛ]
to torment (vt)	**измъчвам**	[iz'mɪʧvam]
pirate	**пират** (m)	[pi'rat]
hooligan	**хулиган** (m)	[huli'gan]
armed (adj)	**въоръжен**	[vɪɔrɪ'ʒɛn]
violence	**насилие** (n)	[na'siliɛ]
spying (n)	**шпионаж** (m)	[ʃpiɔ'naʒ]
to spy (vi)	**шпионирам**	[ʃpiɔ'niram]

193. Police. Law. Part 1

justice	**правосъдие** (n)	[pravɔ'sɪdiɛ]
court (court room)	**съд** (m)	[sɪt]
judge	**съдия** (m)	[sɪdi'jɑ]
jurors	**съдебни заседатели** (m pl)	[sɪ'dɛbni zasɛ'datɛli]
jury trial	**съд** (m) **със съдебни заседатели**	[sɪt sɪs sɪ'dɛbni zasɛ'datɛli]
to judge (vt)	**съдя**	['sɪdʲa]
lawyer, attorney	**адвокат** (m)	[advɔ'kat]
accused	**подсъдим** (m)	[pɔdsɪ'dim]
dock	**подсъдима скамейка** (f)	[pɔdsɪ'dima ska'mɛjka]
charge	**обвинение** (n)	[ɔbvi'nɛniɛ]
accused	**обвиняем** (m)	[ɔbvi'ɲaɛm]
sentence	**присъда** (f)	[pri'sɪda]
to sentence (vt)	**осъдя**	[ɔ'sɪdʲa]
guilty (culprit)	**виновник** (m)	[vi'nɔvnik]
to punish (vt)	**накажа**	[na'kaʒa]

punishment	**наказание** (n)	[naka'zaniɛ]
fine (penalty)	**глоба** (f)	['glɔba]
life imprisonment	**доживотен затвор** (m)	[dɔʒi'vɔtɛn zat'vɔr]
death penalty	**смъртно наказание** (n)	['smɪrtnɔ naka'zaniɛ]
electric chair	**електрически стол** (m)	[ɛlɛkt'riʧəski stɔl]
gallows	**бесилка** (f)	[bɛ'silka]
to execute (vt)	**екзекутирам**	[ɛkzɛku'tiram]
execution	**екзекуция** (f)	[ɛkzɛ'kuʦija]
prison, jail	**затвор** (m)	[zat'vɔr]
cell	**килия** (f)	[ki'lija]
escort	**караул** (m)	[kara'ul]
prison guard	**надзирател** (m)	[naʣi'ratɛl]
prisoner	**затворник** (m)	[zat'vɔrnik]
handcuffs	**белезници** (pl)	[bɛlɛz'niʦi]
to handcuff (vt)	**сложа белезници**	['slɔʒa bɛlɛz'niʦi]
prison break	**бягство** (n)	['bʲakstvɔ]
to break out (vi)	**избягам**	[iz'bʲagam]
to disappear (vi)	**изчезна**	[iz'ʧəzna]
to release (from prison)	**освободя**	[ɔsvɔbɔ'dʲa]
amnesty	**амнистия** (f)	[am'nistija]
police	**полиция** (f)	[pɔ'liʦija]
police officer	**полицай** (m)	[pɔli'ʦaj]
police station	**полицейско управление** (n)	[pɔli'ʦəjskɔ uprav'lɛniɛ]
billy club	**палка** (f)	['palka]
bullhorn	**рупор** (m)	['rupɔr]
patrol car	**патрулка** (f)	[pat'rulka]
siren	**сирена** (f)	[si'rɛna]
to turn on the siren	**включа сирена**	['vklyʧa si'rɛna]
siren call	**звук** (m) **на сирена**	[zvuk na si'rɛna]
crime scene	**място** (n) **на произшествието**	['mʲastɔ na prɔis'ʃɛstviɛtɔ]
witness	**свидетел** (m)	[svi'dɛtɛl]
freedom	**свобода** (f)	[svɔbɔ'da]
accomplice	**съучастник** (m)	[sɪu'ʧasnik]
to flee (vi)	**скрия се**	['skrija 'sɛ]
trace (to leave a ~)	**следа** (f)	[slɛ'da]

194. Police. Law. Part 2

search (investigation)	**издирване** (n)	[iz'dirvanɛ]
to look for ...	**издирвам**	[iz'dirvam]

suspicion	**подозрение** (n)	[pɔdɔz'rɛniɛ]
suspicious (suspect)	**подозрителен**	[pɔdɔz'ritɛlɛn]
to stop (cause to halt)	**спра**	[spra]
to detain (keep in custody)	**задържа**	[zadır'ʒa]
case (lawsuit)	**дело** (n)	['dɛlɔ]
investigation	**следствие** (n)	['slɛdstviɛ]
detective	**детектив** (m)	[dɛtɛk'tif]
investigator	**следовател** (m)	[slɛdɔ'vatɛl]
hypothesis	**версия** (f)	['vɛrsiјɑ]
motive	**мотив** (m)	[mɔ'tiv]
interrogation	**разпит** (m)	['raspit]
to interrogate (vt)	**разпитвам**	[ras'pitvam]
to question (vt)	**разпитвам**	[ras'pitvam]
check (identity ~)	**проверка** (f)	[prɔ'vɛrka]
round-up	**хайка** (f)	['hajka]
search (~ warrant)	**обиск** (m)	['ɔbisk]
chase (pursuit)	**преследване** (n)	[prɛs'lɛdvanɛ]
to pursue, to chase	**преследвам**	[prɛs'lɛdvam]
to track (a criminal)	**следя**	[slɛ'dʲa]
arrest	**арест** (m)	['arɛst]
to arrest (sb)	**арестувам**	[arɛs'tuvam]
to catch (thief, etc.)	**заловя**	[zalɔ'vʲa]
capture	**залавяне** (n)	[za'lavʲanɛ]
document	**документ** (m)	[dɔku'mɛnt]
proof (evidence)	**доказателство** (n)	[dɔka'zatɛlstvɔ]
to prove (vt)	**доказвам**	[dɔ'kazvam]
footprint	**следа** (f)	[slɛ'da]
fingerprints	**отпечатъци** (m pl) **на пръстите**	[ɔtpɛ'ʧatıʦi na 'prıstitɛ]
piece of evidence	**улика** (f)	['ulika]
alibi	**алиби** (n)	[a'libi]
innocent (not guilty)	**невиновен**	[nɛvi'nɔvɛn]
injustice	**несправедливост** (f)	[nɛspravɛd'livɔst]
unjust, unfair (adj)	**несправедлив**	[nɛspravɛd'liv]
criminal (adj)	**криминален**	[krimi'nalɛn]
to confiscate (vt)	**конфискувам**	[kɔnfis'kuvam]
drug (illegal substance)	**наркотик** (m)	[narkɔ'tik]
weapon, gun	**оръжие** (n)	[ɔ'rıʒiɛ]
to disarm (vt)	**обезоръжа**	[ɔbɛzɔrı'ʒa]
to order (command)	**заповядвам**	[zapɔ'vʲadvam]
to disappear (vi)	**изчезна**	[iz'ʧəzna]
law	**закон** (m)	[za'kɔn]
legal, lawful (adj)	**законен**	[za'kɔnɛn]
illegal, illicit (adj)	**незаконен**	[nɛza'kɔnɛn]

responsibility (blame)	**отговорност** (f)	[ɔtgɔ'vɔrnɔst]
responsible (adj)	**отговорен**	[ɔtgɔ'vɔrɛn]

NATURE

The Earth. Part 1

195. Outer space

cosmos	**космос** (m)	['kɔsmɔs]
space (as adj)	**космически**	[kɔs'mitʃəski]
outer space	**космическо пространство** (n)	[kɔs'mitʃəskɔ prɔst'ranstvɔ]
world	**свят** (m)	[svʲat]
universe	**вселена** (f)	[vsɛ'lɛna]
galaxy	**галактика** (f)	[ga'laktika]
star	**звезда** (f)	[zvɛz'da]
constellation	**съзвездие** (n)	[sɪz'vɛzdiɛ]
planet	**планета** (f)	[pla'nɛta]
satellite	**спътник** (m)	['spɪtnik]
meteorite	**метеорит** (m)	[mɛtɛɔ'rit]
comet	**комета** (f)	[kɔ'mɛta]
asteroid	**астероид** (m)	[astɛrɔ'id]
orbit	**орбита** (f)	['ɔrbita]
to revolve (~ around the Earth)	**въртя се**	[vɪr'tʲa sɛ]
atmosphere	**атмосфера** (f)	[atmɔs'fɛra]
the Sun	**Слънце**	['slɪntsə]
solar system	**Слънчева система** (f)	['slɪntʃəva sis'tɛma]
solar eclipse	**слънчево затъмнение** (n)	['slɪntʃəvɔ zatɪmnɛniɛ]
the Earth	**Земя**	[zɛ'mʲa]
the Moon	**Луна**	[lu'na]
Mars	**Марс**	[mars]
Venus	**Венера**	[vɛ'nɛra]
Jupiter	**Юпитер**	['jupitɛr]
Saturn	**Сатурн**	[sa'turn]
Mercury	**Меркурий**	[mɛr'kurij]
Uranus	**Уран**	[u'ran]
Neptune	**Нептун**	[nɛp'tun]
Pluto	**Плутон**	[plu'tɔn]

Milky Way	**Млечен Път**	['mlɛtʃən pɪt]
Great Bear	**Голяма Мечка**	[gɔ'ʎama 'mɛtʃka]
North Star	**Полярна Звезда**	[pɔ'ʎarna zvɛz'da]
Martian	**марсианец** (m)	[marsi'anɛts]
extraterrestrial (n)	**извънземен** (m)	[izvɪn'zɛmɛn]
alien	**пришелец** (m)	[priʃɛ'lɛts]
flying saucer	**летяща чиния** (f)	[lɛ'tʲaʃta tʃi'nija]
spaceship	**космически кораб** (m)	[kɔs'mitʃəski 'kɔrab]
space station	**орбитална станция** (f)	[ɔrbi'talna 'stantsija]
blast-off	**старт** (m)	[start]
engine	**двигател** (m)	[dvi'gatɛl]
nozzle	**дюза** (f)	['dyza]
fuel	**гориво** (n)	[gɔ'rivɔ]
cockpit, flight deck	**кабина** (f)	[ka'bina]
antenna	**антена** (f)	[an'tɛna]
porthole	**илюминатор** (m)	[ilymi'natɔr]
solar battery	**слънчева батерия** (f)	['slɪntʃəva ba'tɛrija]
spacesuit	**скафандър** (m)	[ska'fandɪr]
weightlessness	**безтегловност** (f)	[bɛstɛg'lɔvnɔst]
oxygen	**кислород** (m)	[kislɔ'rɔd]
docking (in space)	**свързване** (n)	['svɪrzvanɛ]
to dock (vi, vt)	**свързвам се**	['svɪrzvam sɛ]
observatory	**обсерватория** (f)	[ɔpsɛrva'tɔrija]
telescope	**телескоп** (m)	[tɛlɛs'kɔp]
to observe (vt)	**наблюдавам**	[nably'davam]
to explore (vt)	**изследвам**	[iss'lɛdvam]

196. The Earth

the Earth	**Земя**	[zɛ'mʲa]
globe (the Earth)	**земно кълбо** (n)	['zɛmnɔ kɪl'bɔ]
planet	**планета** (f)	[pla'nɛta]
atmosphere	**атмосфера** (f)	[atmɔs'fɛra]
geography	**география** (f)	[gɛɔg'rafija]
nature	**природа** (f)	[pri'rɔda]
globe (table ~)	**глобус** (m)	['glɔbus]
map	**карта** (f)	['karta]
atlas	**атлас** (m)	[at'las]
Europe	**Европа**	[ɛv'rɔpa]
Asia	**Азия**	['azija]

Africa	**Африка**	['afrika]
Australia	**Австралия**	[afst'ralijɑ]
America	**Америка**	[a'mɛrika]
North America	**Северна Америка**	['sɛvɛrna a'mɛrika]
South America	**Южна Америка**	['juʒna a'mɛrika]
Antarctica	**Антарктида**	[antark'tida]
the Arctic	**Арктика**	['arktika]

197. Cardinal directions

north	**север** (m)	['sɛvɛr]
to the north	**на север**	[na 'sɛvɛr]
in the north	**на север**	[na 'sɛvɛr]
northern (adj)	**северен**	['sɛvɛrɛn]
south	**юг** (m)	[jug]
to the south	**на юг**	[na jug]
in the south	**на юг**	[na jug]
southern (adj)	**южен**	['juʒɛn]
west	**запад** (m)	['zapad]
to the west	**на запад**	[na 'zapat]
in the west	**на запад**	[na 'zapat]
western (adj)	**западен**	['zapadɛn]
east	**изток** (m)	['istɔk]
to the east	**на изток**	[na 'istɔk]
in the east	**на изток**	[na 'istɔk]
eastern (adj)	**източен**	['istɔʧən]

198. Sea. Ocean

sea	**море** (n)	[mɔ'rɛ]
ocean	**океан** (m)	[ɔkɛ'an]
gulf (bay)	**залив** (m)	['zalif]
straits	**пролив** (m)	['prɔliv]
continent (mainland)	**материк** (m)	[matɛ'rik]
island	**остров** (m)	['ɔstrɔv]
peninsula	**полуостров** (m)	[pɔlu'ɔstrɔv]
archipelago	**архипелаг** (m)	[arhipɛ'lag]
bay, cove	**залив** (m)	['zalif]
harbor	**залив** (m)	['zalif]
lagoon	**лагуна** (f)	[la'guna]
cape	**нос** (m)	[nɔs]

atoll	**атол** (m)	[a'tɔl]
reef	**риф** (m)	[rif]
coral	**корал** (m)	[kɔ'ral]
coral reef	**коралов риф** (m)	[kɔ'ralɔv rif]
deep (adj)	**дълбок**	[dɪl'bɔk]
depth (deep water)	**дълбочина** (f)	[dɪlbɔʧi'na]
abyss	**бездна** (f)	['bɛzna]
trench (e.g., Mariana ~)	**падина** (f)	[padi'na]
current, stream	**течение** (n)	[tɛ'ʧəniɛ]
to surround (bathe)	**мия**	['mijɑ]
shore	**бряг** (m)	[brʲag]
coast	**крайбрежие** (n)	[krajb'rɛʒiɛ]
high tide	**прилив** (m)	['priliv]
low tide	**отлив** (m)	['ɔtliv]
sandbank	**плитчина** (f)	[pliʧi'na]
bottom	**дъно** (n)	['dɪnɔ]
wave	**вълна** (f)	[vɪl'na]
crest (~ of a wave)	**гребен** (m) **на вълна**	['grɛbɛn na vɪl'na]
froth (foam)	**пяна** (f)	['pʲana]
storm	**буря** (f)	['burʲa]
hurricane	**ураган** (m)	[ura'gan]
tsunami	**цунами** (n)	[ʦu'nami]
calm (dead ~)	**безветрие** (n)	[bɛz'vɛtriɛ]
quiet, calm (adj)	**спокоен**	[spɔ'kɔɛn]
pole	**полюс** (m)	['pɔlys]
polar (adj)	**полярен**	[pɔ'ʎarɛn]
latitude	**ширина** (f)	[ʃiri'na]
longitude	**дължина** (f)	[dɪʒi'na]
parallel	**паралел** (f)	[para'lɛl]
equator	**екватор** (m)	[ɛk'vatɔr]
sky	**небе** (n)	[nɛ'bɛ]
horizon	**хоризонт** (m)	[hɔri'zɔnt]
air	**въздух** (m)	['vɪzduh]
lighthouse	**фар** (m)	[far]
to dive (vi)	**гмуркам се**	['gmurkam sɛ]
to sink (ab. boat)	**потъна**	[pɔ'tɪna]
treasures	**съкровища** (n pl)	[sɪk'rɔviʃta]

199. Seas' and Oceans' names

Atlantic Ocean	**Атлантически океан**	[atlan'tiʧəski ɔkɛ'an]
Indian Ocean	**Индийски океан**	[in'dijski ɔkɛ'an]

Pacific Ocean	**Тихи океан**	['tihi ɔkɛ'an]
Arctic Ocean	**Северен Ледовит океан**	['sɛvɛrɛn lɛdɔ'vit ɔkɛ'an]
Black Sea	**Черно море**	['ʧərnɔ mɔ'rɛ]
Red Sea	**Червено море**	[ʧər'vɛnɔ mɔ'rɛ]
Yellow Sea	**Жълто море**	['ʒıltɔ mɔ'rɛ]
White Sea	**Бяло море**	['bʲalɔ mɔ'rɛ]
Caspian Sea	**Каспийско море**	['kaspijskɔ mɔ'rɛ]
Dead Sea	**Мъртво море**	['mırtvɔ mɔ'rɛ]
Mediterranean Sea	**Средиземно море**	[srɛdi'zɛmnɔ mɔ'rɛ]
Aegean Sea	**Егейско море**	[ɛ'gɛjskɔ mɔ'rɛ]
Adriatic Sea	**Адриатическо море**	[adria'tiʧəskɔ mɔ'rɛ]
Arabian Sea	**Арабско море**	[a'rapskɔ mɔ'rɛ]
Sea of Japan	**Японско море**	[jɑ'pɔnskɔ mɔ'rɛ]
Bering Sea	**Берингово море**	[bɛ'riŋgɔvɔ mɔ'rɛ]
South China Sea	**Южнокитайско море**	[juʒnɔki'tajskɔ mɔ'rɛ]
Coral Sea	**Коралово море**	[kɔ'ralɔvɔ mɔ'rɛ]
Tasman Sea	**Тасманово море**	[tas'manɔvɔ mɔ'rɛ]
Caribbean Sea	**Карибско море**	[ka'ribskɔ mɔ'rɛ]
Barents Sea	**Баренцово море**	[ba'rɛntsɔvɔ mɔ'rɛ]
Kara Sea	**Карско море**	['karskɔ mɔ'rɛ]
North Sea	**Северно море**	['sɛvɛrnɔ mɔ'rɛ]
Baltic Sea	**Балтийско море**	[bal'tijskɔ mɔ'rɛ]
Norwegian Sea	**Норвежко море**	[nɔr'vɛʃkɔ mɔ'rɛ]

200. Mountains

mountain	**планина** (f)	[plani'na]
mountain range	**планинска верига** (f)	[pla'ninska vɛ'riga]
mountain ridge	**планински хребет** (m)	[pla'ninski hrɛ'bɛt]
summit, top	**връх** (m)	[vrıh]
peak	**връх** (m)	[vrıh]
foot (of mountain)	**подножие** (n)	[pɔd'nɔʒiɛ]
slope (mountainside)	**склон** (m)	[sklɔn]
volcano	**вулкан** (m)	[vul'kan]
active volcano	**действащ вулкан** (m)	['dɛjstvaʃt vul'kan]
dormant volcano	**изгаснал вулкан** (m)	[iz'gasnal vul'kan]
eruption	**изригване** (n)	[iz'rigvanɛ]
crater	**кратер** (m)	['kratɛr]
magma	**магма** (f)	['magma]
lava	**лава** (f)	['lava]

molten (~ lava)	**нажежен**	[naʒɛ'ʒɛn]
canyon	**каньон** (m)	[ka'ɲʲɔn]
gorge	**дефиле** (n)	[dɛfi'lɛ]
crevice	**тясна клисура** (f)	['tʲasna kli'sura]
abyss (chasm)	**пропаст** (f)	['prɔpast]
pass, col	**превал** (m)	[prɛ'val]
plateau	**плато** (n)	['platɔ]
cliff	**скала** (f)	[ska'la]
hill	**хълм** (m)	[hɪlm]
glacier	**ледник** (m)	['lɛdnik]
waterfall	**водопад** (m)	[vɔdɔ'pad]
geyser	**гейзер** (m)	['gɛjzɛr]
lake	**езеро** (n)	['ɛzɛrɔ]
plain	**равнина** (f)	[ravni'na]
landscape	**пейзаж** (m)	[pɛj'zaʒ]
echo	**ехо** (n)	['ɛhɔ]
alpinist	**алпинист** (m)	[alpi'nist]
rock climber	**катерач** (m)	[katɛ'ratʃ]
to conquer (in climbing)	**покорявам**	[pɔkɔ'rʲavam]
climb (an easy ~)	**възкачване** (n)	[vɪs'katʃvanɛ]

201. Mountains names

Alps	**Алпи**	['alpi]
Mont Blanc	**Мон Блан**	[mɔn blan]
Pyrenees	**Пиринеи**	[piri'nɛi]
Carpathians	**Карпати**	[kar'pati]
Ural Mountains	**Урал**	[u'ral]
Caucasus	**Кавказ**	[kaf'kaz]
Elbrus	**Елбрус**	[ɛlb'rus]
Altai	**Алтай**	[al'taj]
Pamir Mountains	**Памир**	[pa'mir]
Himalayas	**Хималаи**	[hima'lai]
Everest	**Еверест**	[ɛvɛ'rɛst]
Andes	**Анди**	['andi]
Kilimanjaro	**Килиманджаро**	[kiliman'dʒarɔ]

202. Rivers

river	**река** (f)	[rɛ'ka]
spring (natural source)	**извор** (m)	['izvɔr]

riverbed	**корито** (n)	[kɔ'ritɔ]
basin	**басейн** (m)	[ba'sɛjn]
to flow into ...	**вливам се**	['vlivam sɛ]
tributary	**приток** (m)	['pritɔk]
bank (of river)	**бряг** (m)	[brʲag]
current, stream	**течение** (n)	[tɛ'ʧəniɛ]
downstream (adv)	**надолу по течението**	[na'dɔlu pɔ tɛ'ʧəniɛtɔ]
upstream (adv)	**нагоре по течението**	[na'gɔrɛ pɔ tɛ'ʧəniɛtɔ]
inundation	**наводнение** (n)	[navɔd'nɛniɛ]
flooding	**пролетно пълноводие** (n)	[prɔ'lɛtnɔ pılnɔ'vɔdiɛ]
to overflow (vi)	**разливам се**	[raz'livam sɛ]
to flood (vt)	**потопявам**	[pɔtɔ'pʲavam]
shallows (shoal)	**плитчина** (f)	[pliʧi'na]
rapids	**праг** (m)	[prag]
dam	**яз** (m)	[jɑz]
canal	**канал** (m)	[ka'nal]
artificial lake	**водохранилище** (n)	[vɔdɔhra'niliʃtɛ]
sluice, lock	**шлюз** (m)	[ʃlyz]
water body (pond, etc.)	**водоем** (m)	[vɔdɔ'ɛm]
swamp, bog	**блато** (n)	['blatɔ]
marsh	**тресавище** (n)	[trɛ'saviʃtɛ]
whirlpool	**водовъртеж** (m)	[vɔdɔvır'tɛʒ]
stream (brook)	**ручей** (m)	['ruʧəj]
drinking (ab. water)	**питеен**	[pi'tɛ:n]
fresh (~ water)	**сладководен**	[slatkɔ'vɔdɛn]
ice	**лед** (m)	[lɛd]
to freeze (ab. river, etc.)	**замръзна**	[zam'rızna]

203. Rivers' names

Seine	**Сена**	['sɛna]
Loire	**Лоара**	[lɔ'ara]
Thames	**Темза**	['tɛmza]
Rhine	**Рейн**	[rɛjn]
Danube	**Дунав**	['dunav]
Volga	**Волга**	['vɔlga]
Don	**Дон**	[dɔn]
Lena	**Лена**	['lɛna]
Yellow River	**Хуанхъ**	[huan 'hı]

Yangtze	**Яндзъ**	[jan'dzɪ]
Mekong	**Меконг**	[mɛ'kɔŋg]
Ganges	**Ганг**	[gaŋg]
Nile River	**Нил**	[nil]
Congo	**Конго**	['kɔŋgɔ]
Okavango	**Окаванго**	[ɔka'vaŋgɔ]
Zambezi	**Замбези**	[zam'bɛzi]
Limpopo	**Лимпопо**	[limpɔ'pɔ]

204. Forest

forest	**гора** (f)	[gɔ'ra]
forest (as adj)	**горски**	['gɔrski]
thick forest	**гъсталак** (m)	[gɪsta'lak]
grove	**горичка** (f)	[gɔ'riʧka]
forest clearing	**поляна** (f)	[pɔ'ʎana]
thicket	**храсталак** (m)	[hrasta'lak]
scrubland	**храсталак** (m)	[hrasta'lak]
footpath (troddenpath)	**пътечка** (f)	[pɪ'tɛʧka]
gully	**овраг** (m)	[ɔv'rag]
tree	**дърво** (n)	[dɪr'vɔ]
leaf	**лист** (m)	[list]
leaves	**шума** (f)	['ʃuma]
fall of leaves	**листопад** (m)	[listɔ'pad]
to fall (ab. leaves)	**опадвам**	[ɔ'padvam]
top (of the tree)	**връх** (m)	[vrɪh]
branch	**клонка** (m)	['klɔŋka]
bough	**дебел клон** (m)	[dɛ'bɛl klɔn]
bud (on shrub, tree)	**пъпка** (f)	['pɪpka]
needle (of pine tree)	**игла** (f)	[ig'la]
pine cone	**шишарка** (f)	[ʃi'ʃʌrka]
hollow (in a tree)	**хралупа** (f)	[hra'lupa]
nest	**гнездо** (n)	[gnɛz'dɔ]
burrow (animal hole)	**дупка** (f)	['dupka]
trunk	**стъбло** (n)	[stɪb'lɔ]
root	**корен** (m)	['kɔrɛn]
bark	**кора** (f)	[kɔ'ra]
moss	**мъх** (m)	[mɪh]
to uproot (vt)	**изкоренявам**	[izkɔrɛ'ɲavam]
to chop down	**сека**	[sɛ'ka]

to deforest (vt)	**изсичам**	[is'sitʃam]
tree stump	**пън** (m)	[pɪn]
campfire	**клада** (f)	['klada]
forest fire	**пожар** (m)	[pɔ'ʒar]
to extinguish (vt)	**загасявам**	[zaga'sʲavam]
forest ranger	**горски пазач** (m)	['gɔrski pa'zatʃ]
protection	**опазване** (n)	[ɔ'pazvanɛ]
to protect (~ nature)	**опазвам**	[ɔ'pazvam]
poacher	**бракониер** (m)	[brakɔni'ɛr]
trap (e.g., bear ~)	**капан** (m)	[ka'pan]
to gather, to pick (vt)	**събирам**	[sɪ'biram]
to lose one's way	**загубя се**	[za'gubʲa sɛ]

205. Natural resources

natural resources	**природни ресурси** (m pl)	[pri'rɔdni rɛ'sursi]
minerals	**полезни изкопаеми** (n pl)	[pɔ'lɛzni iskɔ'paɛmi]
deposits	**залежи** (pl)	[za'lɛʒi]
field (e.g., oilfield)	**находище** (n)	[na'hɔdiʃtɛ]
to mine (extract)	**добивам**	[dɔ'bivam]
mining (extraction)	**добиване** (n)	[dɔ'bivanɛ]
ore	**руда** (f)	[ru'da]
mine (e.g., for coal)	**рудник** (m)	['rudnik]
mine shaft, pit	**шахта** (f)	['ʃʌhta]
miner	**миньор** (m)	[mi'nɜr]
gas	**газ** (m)	[gas]
gas pipeline	**газопровод** (m)	[gazɔprɔ'vɔd]
oil (petroleum)	**нефт** (m)	[nɛft]
oil pipeline	**нефтопровод** (m)	[nɛftɔprɔ'vɔd]
oil well	**нефтена кула** (f)	['nɛftɛna 'kula]
derrick	**сондажна кула** (f)	[sɔn'daʒna 'kula]
tanker	**танкер** (m)	['taŋkɛr]
sand	**пясък** (m)	['pʲasɪk]
limestone	**варовик** (m)	[va'rɔvik]
gravel	**дребен чакъл** (m)	['drɛbɛn tʃa'kɪl]
peat	**торф** (m)	[tɔrf]
clay	**глина** (f)	['glina]
coal	**въглища** (pl)	['vɪgliʃta]
iron	**желязо** (n)	[ʒɛ'ʎazɔ]
gold	**злато** (n)	['zlatɔ]
silver	**сребро** (n)	[srɛb'rɔ]

nickel	**никел** (m)	['nikɛl]
copper	**мед** (f)	[mɛd]
zinc	**цинк** (m)	[ʦiŋk]
manganese	**манган** (m)	[ma'ŋgan]
mercury	**живак** (m)	[ʒi'vak]
lead	**олово** (n)	[ɔ'lɔvɔ]
mineral	**минерал** (m)	[minɛ'ral]
crystal	**кристал** (m)	[kris'tal]
marble	**мрамор** (m)	['mramɔr]
uranium	**уран** (m)	[u'ran]

The Earth. Part 2

206. Weather

weather	**време** (n)	['vrɛmɛ]
weather forecast	**прогноза** (f) **за времето**	[prɔg'nɔza za 'vrɛmɛtɔ]
temperature	**температура** (f)	[tɛmpɛra'tura]
thermometer	**термометър** (m)	[tɛrmɔ'mɛtɪr]
barometer	**барометър** (m)	[barɔ'mɛtɪr]
humidity	**влажност** (f)	['vlaʒnɔst]
heat (extreme ~)	**пек** (m)	[pɛk]
hot (torrid)	**горещ**	[gɔ'rɛʃt]
it's hot	**горещо**	[gɔ'rɛʃtɔ]
it's warm	**топло**	['tɔplɔ]
warm (moderately hot)	**топъл**	['tɔpɪl]
it's cold	**студено**	[stu'dɛnɔ]
cold (adj)	**студен**	[stu'dɛn]
sun	**слънце** (n)	['slɪntsə]
to shine (vi)	**грея**	['grɛja]
sunny (day)	**слънчев**	['slɪntʃəv]
to come up (vi)	**изгрея**	[izg'rɛja]
to set (vi)	**заляза**	[za'ʎaza]
cloud	**облак** (m)	['ɔblak]
cloudy (adj)	**облачен**	['ɔblatʃən]
rain cloud	**голям облак** (m)	[gɔ'ʎam 'ɔblak]
somber (gloomy)	**навъсен**	[na'vɪsɛn]
rain	**дъжд** (m)	[dɪʒd]
it's raining	**вали дъжд**	[va'li dɪʒt]
rainy (day)	**дъждовен**	[dɪʒ'dɔvɛn]
to drizzle (vi)	**ръмя**	[rɪ'mʲa]
pouring rain	**пороен дъжд** (m)	[pɔ'rɔɛn dɪʒd]
downpour	**порой** (m)	[pɔ'rɔj]
heavy (e.g., ~ rain)	**силен**	['silɛn]
puddle	**локва** (f)	['lɔkva]
to get wet (in rain)	**намокря се**	[na'mɔkrʲa sɛ]
fog (mist)	**мъгла** (f)	[mɪg'la]
foggy	**мъглив**	[mɪg'lif]
snow	**сняг** (m)	[sɲag]
it's snowing	**вали сняг**	[va'li sɲag]

207. Severe weather. Natural disasters

thunderstorm	**гръмотевична буря** (f)	[grɪmɔ'tɛvitʃna 'burʲa]
lightning (~ strike)	**мълния** (f)	['mɪlnija]
to flash (vi)	**блясвам**	['bʎasvam]
thunder	**гръм** (m)	[grɪm]
to thunder (vi)	**гърмя**	[gɪr'mʲa]
it's thundering	**гърми**	[gɪr'mi]
hail	**градушка** (f)	[gra'duʃka]
it's hailing	**пада градушка**	['pada gra'duʃka]
to flood (vt)	**потопя**	[pɔtɔ'pʲa]
flood, inundation	**наводнение** (n)	[navɔd'nɛniɛ]
earthquake	**земетресение** (n)	[zɛmɛtrɛ'sɛniɛ]
tremor, quake	**трус** (m)	[trus]
epicenter	**епицентър** (m)	[ɛpi'tsəntɪr]
eruption	**изригване** (n)	[iz'rigvanɛ]
lava	**лава** (f)	['lava]
twister, tornado	**торнадо** (n)	[tɔr'nadɔ]
typhoon	**тайфун** (m)	[taj'fun]
hurricane	**ураган** (m)	[ura'gan]
storm	**буря** (f)	['burʲa]
tsunami	**цунами** (n)	[tsu'nami]
cyclone	**циклон** (m)	[tsik'lɔn]
bad weather	**лошо време** (n)	['lɔʃɔ 'vrɛmɛ]
fire (accident)	**пожар** (m)	[pɔ'ʒar]
disaster	**катастрофа** (f)	[katast'rɔfa]
meteorite	**метеорит** (m)	[mɛtɛɔ'rit]
avalanche	**лавина** (f)	[la'vina]
snowslide	**лавина** (f)	[la'vina]
blizzard	**виелица** (f)	[vi'ɛlitsa]
snowstorm	**снежна буря** (f)	['snɛʒna 'burʲa]

208. Noises. Sounds

silence (quiet)	**тишина** (f)	[tiʃi'na]
sound	**звук** (m)	[zvuk]
noise	**шум** (m)	[ʃum]
to make noise	**шумя**	[ʃu'mʲa]
noisy (adj)	**шумен**	['ʃumɛn]
loudly (to speak, etc.)	**силно**	['silnɔ]

loud (voice, etc.)	**силен**	['silɛn]
constant (continuous)	**постоянен**	[pɔstɔ'janɛn]
shout (n)	**вик** (m)	[vik]
to shout (vi)	**викам**	['vikam]
whisper	**шепот** (m)	['ʃɛpɔt]
to whisper (vi, vt)	**шептя**	[ʃɛp'tʲa]
barking (of dog)	**лай** (m)	[laj]
to bark (vi)	**лая**	['laja]
groan (of pain)	**стон** (m)	[stɔn]
to groan (vi)	**стена**	['stɛna]
cough	**кашлица** (f)	['kaʃliʦa]
to cough (vi)	**кашлям**	['kaʃʎam]
whistle	**свирене** (n)	['svirɛnɛ]
to whistle (vi)	**свиря**	['svirʲa]
knock (at the door)	**тракане** (n)	['trakanɛ]
to knock (at the door)	**чукам**	['ʧukam]
to crack (vi)	**пращя**	[praʃ'tʲa]
crack (plank, etc.)	**трясък** (m)	['trʲasık]
siren	**сирена** (f)	[si'rɛna]
whistle (factory ~)	**сирена** (f)	[si'rɛna]
to whistle (ship, train)	**буча**	[bu'ʧa]
honk (signal)	**клаксон** (m)	['klaksɔn]
to honk (vi)	**сигнализирам**	[signali'ziram]

209. Winter

winter (n)	**зима** (f)	['zima]
winter (as adj)	**зимен**	['zimɛn]
in winter	**през зимата**	[prɛz 'zimata]
snow	**сняг** (m)	[sɲag]
it's snowing	**вали сняг**	[va'li sɲag]
snowfall	**снеговалеж** (m)	[snɛgɔva'lɛʒ]
snowdrift	**преспа** (f)	['prɛspa]
snowflake	**снежинка** (f)	[snɛ'ʒiŋka]
snowball	**снежна топка** (f)	['snɛʒna 'tɔpka]
snowman	**снежен човек** (m)	['snɛʒɛn ʧɔ'vɛk]
icicle	**ледена висулка** (f)	['lɛdɛna vi'sulka]
December	**декември** (m)	[dɛ'kɛmvri]
January	**януари** (m)	[janu'ari]
February	**февруари** (m)	[fɛvru'ari]
severe frost	**мраз** (m)	[mraz]

frosty (weather, air)	**мразовит**	[mrazɔ'vit]
below zero (adv)	**под нулата**	[pɔt 'nulata]
first frost	**леко застудяване** (n)	['lɛkɔ zastu'dʲavanɛ]
hoarfrost	**скреж** (m)	[skrɛʒ]
cold (cold weather)	**студ** (m)	[stut]
it's cold	**студено**	[stu'dɛnɔ]
fur coat	**кожено палто** (n)	['kɔʒɛnɔ pal'tɔ]
mittens	**ръкавици с един пръст** (f pl)	[rɪka'vitsi s ɛ'din prɪst]
to get sick	**разболявам**	[razbɔ'ʎavam]
cold (illness)	**настинка** (f)	[nas'tiŋka]
to catch a cold	**настина**	[nas'tina]
ice	**лед** (m)	[lɛd]
black ice	**поледица** (f)	[pɔ'lɛditsa]
to freeze (ab. river, etc.)	**замръзна**	[zam'rɪzna]
ice floe	**леден блок** (m)	['lɛdɛn blɔk]
skis	**ски** (pl)	[ski]
skier	**скиор** (m)	[ski'ɔr]
to ski (vi)	**карам ски**	['karam ski]
to skate (vi)	**пързалям се с кънки**	[pɪr'zaʎam sɛ s 'kɪŋki]

Fauna

210. Mammals. Predators

predator	**хищник** (m)	['hiʃtnik]
tiger	**тигър** (m)	['tigɪr]
lion	**лъв** (m)	[lɪv]
wolf	**вълк** (m)	[vɪlk]
fox	**лисица** (f)	[li'sitsa]
jaguar	**ягуар** (m)	[jagu'ar]
leopard	**леопард** (m)	[lɛɔ'pard]
cheetah	**гепард** (m)	[gɛ'pard]
black panther	**пантера** (f)	[pan'tɛra]
puma	**пума** (f)	['puma]
snow leopard	**снежен барс** (m)	['snɛʒɛn bars]
lynx	**рис** (f)	[ris]
coyote	**койот** (m)	[kɔ'jot]
jackal	**чакал** (m)	[ʧa'kal]
hyena	**хиена** (f)	[hi'ɛna]

211. Wild animals

animal	**животно** (n)	[ʒi'vɔtnɔ]
beast (animal)	**звяр** (m)	[zvʲar]
squirrel	**катерица** (f)	['katɛritsa]
hedgehog	**таралеж** (m)	[tara'lɛʒ]
hare	**заек** (m)	['zaɛk]
rabbit	**питомен заек** (m)	['pitɔmɛn 'zaɛk]
badger	**язовец** (m)	['jazɔvɛts]
raccoon	**енот** (m)	[ɛ'nɔt]
hamster	**хамстер** (m)	['hamstɛr]
marmot	**мармот** (m)	[mar'mɔt]
mole	**къртица** (f)	[kɪr'titsa]
mouse	**мишка** (f)	['miʃka]
rat	**плъх** (m)	[plɪh]
bat	**прилеп** (m)	['prilɛp]
ermine	**хермелин** (m)	[hɛrmɛ'lin]
sable	**самур** (m)	[sa'mur]

marten	**бялка** (f)	['bʲalka]
weasel	**невестулка** (f)	[nɛvɛs'tulka]
mink	**норка** (f)	['nɔrka]
beaver	**бобър** (m)	['bɔbır]
otter	**видра** (f)	['vidra]
horse	**кон** (m)	[kɔn]
moose	**лос** (m)	[lɔs]
deer	**елен** (m)	[ɛ'lɛn]
camel	**камила** (f)	[ka'mila]
bison	**бизон** (m)	[bi'zɔn]
aurochs	**зубър** (m)	['zubır]
buffalo	**бивол** (m)	['bivɔl]
zebra	**зебра** (f)	['zɛbra]
antelope	**антилопа** (f)	[anti'lɔpa]
roe deer	**сърна** (f)	[sır'na]
fallow deer	**лопатар** (m)	[lɔpa'tar]
chamois	**сърна** (f)	[sır'na]
wild boar	**глиган** (m)	[gli'gan]
whale	**кит** (m)	[kit]
seal	**тюлен** (m)	[ty'lɛn]
walrus	**морж** (m)	[mɔrʒ]
fur seal	**морска котка** (f)	['mɔrska 'kɔtka]
dolphin	**делфин** (m)	[dɛl'fin]
bear	**мечка** (f)	['mɛʧka]
polar bear	**бяла мечка** (f)	['bʲala 'mɛʧka]
panda	**панда** (f)	['panda]
monkey	**маймуна** (f)	[maj'muna]
chimpanzee	**шимпанзе** (n)	[ʃimpan'zɛ]
orangutan	**орангутан** (m)	[ɔraŋgu'tan]
gorilla	**горила** (f)	[gɔ'rila]
macaque	**макак** (m)	[ma'kak]
gibbon	**гибон** (m)	[gi'bɔn]
elephant	**слон** (m)	[slɔn]
rhinoceros	**носорог** (m)	[nɔsɔ'rɔg]
giraffe	**жираф** (m)	[ʒi'raf]
hippopotamus	**хипопотам** (m)	[hipɔpɔ'tam]
kangaroo	**кенгуру** (n)	['kɛŋguru]
koala (bear)	**коала** (f)	[kɔ'ala]
mongoose	**мангуста** (f)	[ma'ŋgusta]
chinchilla	**чинчила** (f)	[ʧin'ʧila]
skunk	**скунс** (m)	[skuns]
porcupine	**бодливец** (m)	[bɔd'livɛʦ]

212. Domestic animals

cat	**котка** (f)	['kɔtka]
tomcat	**котарак** (m)	[kɔta'rak]
horse	**кон** (m)	[kɔn]
stallion	**жребец** (m)	[ʒrɛ'bɛʦ]
mare	**кобила** (f)	[kɔ'bila]
cow	**крава** (f)	['krava]
bull	**бик** (m)	[bik]
ox	**вол** (m)	[vɔl]
sheep	**овца** (f)	[ɔv'ʦa]
ram	**овен** (m)	[ɔ'vɛn]
goat	**коза** (f)	[kɔ'za]
billy goat, he-goat	**козел** (m)	[kɔ'zɛl]
donkey	**магаре** (n)	[ma'garɛ]
mule	**муле** (n)	['mulɛ]
pig	**свиня** (f)	[svi'ɲa]
piglet	**прасе** (n)	[pra'sɛ]
rabbit	**питомен заек** (m)	['pitɔmɛn 'zaɛk]
hen (chicken)	**кокошка** (f)	[kɔ'kɔʃka]
rooster	**петел** (m)	[pɛ'tɛl]
duck	**патица** (f)	['patiʦa]
drake	**паток** (m)	[pa'tɔk]
goose	**гъсок** (m)	[gɪ'sɔk]
tom turkey	**пуяк** (m)	['pujɑk]
turkey (hen)	**пуйка** (f)	['pujka]
domestic animals	**домашни животни** (n pl)	[dɔ'maʃni ʒi'vɔtni]
tame (e.g., ~ hamster)	**питомен**	['pitɔmɛn]
to tame (vt)	**опитомявам**	[ɔpitɔ'mʲavam]
to breed (vt)	**отглеждам**	[ɔtg'lɛʒdam]
farm	**ферма** (f)	['fɛrma]
poultry	**домашна птица** (f)	[dɔ'maʃna 'ptiʦa]
cattle	**добитък** (m)	[dɔ'bitɪk]
herd (cattle)	**стадо** (n)	['stadɔ]
stable	**обор** (m)	[ɔ'bɔr]
pigsty	**кочина** (f)	['kɔʧina]
cowshed	**краварник** (m)	[kra'varnik]
rabbit hutch	**зайчарник** (m)	[zaj'ʧarnik]
hen house	**курник** (m)	['kurnik]

213. Dogs. Dog breeds

dog	**куче** (n)	['kutʃə]
sheepdog	**овчарско куче** (n)	[ɔf'tʃarskɔ 'kutʃə]
poodle	**пудел** (m)	['pudɛl]
dachshund	**дакел** (m)	['dakɛl]
bulldog	**булдог** (m)	[bul'dɔg]
boxer	**боксер** (m)	[bɔk'sɛr]
mastiff	**мастиф** (m)	[mas'tif]
rottweiler	**ротвайлер** (m)	[rɔt'vajlɛr]
Doberman	**доберман** (m)	['dɔbɛrman]
basset	**басет** (m)	['basɛt]
bobtail	**бобтейл** (m)	['bɔbtɛjl]
Dalmatian	**далматинец** (m)	[dalmati'nɛts]
cocker spaniel	**кокер шпаньол** (m)	['kɔkɛr ʃpa'nɜl]
Newfoundland	**нюфаундленд** (m)	[ny'faundlɛnd]
Saint Bernard	**санбернар** (m)	[sanbɛr'nar]
husky	**сибирско хъски** (n)	[si'birskɔ 'hɪski]
Chow Chow	**чау-чау** (n)	['tʃau 'tʃau]
spitz	**шпиц** (m)	[ʃpits]
pug	**мопс** (m)	[mɔps]

214. Sounds made by animals

barking (n)	**лай** (m)	[laj]
to bark (vi)	**лая**	['lajɑ]
to meow (vi)	**мяукам**	[mʲa'ukam]
to purr (vi)	**мъркам**	['mɪrkam]
to moo (vi)	**муча**	[mu'tʃa]
to bellow (bull)	**рева**	[rɛ'va]
to growl (vi)	**ръмжа**	[rɪm'ʒa]
howl (n)	**вой** (m)	[vɔj]
to howl (vi)	**вия**	['vijɑ]
to whine (vi)	**скимтя**	[skim'tʲa]
to bleat (sheep)	**блея**	['blɛjɑ]
to oink, to grunt (pig)	**грухтя**	[gruh'tʲa]
to squeal (vi)	**врещя**	[vrɛʃ'tʲa]
to croak (vi)	**крякам**	['krʲakam]
to buzz (insect)	**бръмча**	[brɪm'tʃa]
to stridulate (vi)	**цвърча**	[tsvɪr'tʃa]

215. Young animals

cub	**малкото** (n) **на животно**	['malkɔtɔ na ʒi'vɔtnɔ]
kitten	**котенце** (n)	['kɔtɛntsə]
baby mouse	**мишле** (n)	[miʃ'lɛ]
pup, puppy	**кученце** (n)	['kutʃəntsə]
leveret	**зайче** (n)	['zajtʃə]
baby rabbit	**зайче** (n)	['zajtʃə]
wolf cub	**вълче** (n)	[vɪl'tʃə]
fox cub	**лисиче** (n)	[li'sitʃə]
bear cub	**мече** (n)	[mɛ'tʃə]
lion cub	**лъвче** (n)	['lɪftʃə]
tiger cub	**тигърче** (n)	['tigɪrtʃə]
elephant calf	**слонче** (n)	['slɔntʃə]
piglet	**прасе** (n)	[pra'sɛ]
calf (young cow, bull)	**теле** (n)	['tɛlɛ]
kid (young goat)	**яре** (n)	['jarɛ]
lamb	**агне** (n)	['agnɛ]
fawn (young deer)	**еленче** (n)	[ɛ'lɛntʃə]
young camel	**камилче** (n)	[ka'miltʃə]
baby snake	**змийче** (n)	[zmij'tʃə]
baby frog	**жабче** (n)	['ʒaptʃə]
nestling	**пиле** (n)	['pilɛ]
chick (of chicken)	**пиле** (n)	['pilɛ]
duckling	**пате** (n)	['patɛ]

216. Birds

bird	**птица** (f)	['ptitsa]
pigeon	**гълъб** (m)	['gɪlɪb]
sparrow	**врабче** (n)	[vrab'tʃə]
tit	**синигер** (m)	[sini'gɛr]
magpie	**сврака** (f)	['svraka]
raven	**гарван** (m)	['garvan]
crow	**врана** (f)	['vrana]
jackdaw	**гарга** (f)	['garga]
rook	**полски гарван** (m)	['pɔlski 'garvan]
duck	**патица** (f)	['patitsa]
goose	**гъсок** (m)	[gɪ'sɔk]
pheasant	**фазан** (m)	[fa'zan]
eagle	**орел** (m)	[ɔ'rɛl]
hawk	**ястреб** (m)	['jastrɛb]

falcon	**сокол** (m)	[sɔ'kɔl]
vulture	**гриф** (m)	[grif]
condor (Andean ~)	**кондор** (m)	[kɔn'dɔr]
swan	**лебед** (m)	['lɛbɛd]
crane	**жерав** (m)	['ʒɛrav]
stork	**щъркел** (m)	['ʃtɪrkɛl]
parrot	**папагал** (m)	[papa'gal]
hummingbird	**колибри** (m)	[kɔ'libri]
peacock	**паун** (m)	[pa'un]
ostrich	**щраус** (m)	['ʃtraus]
heron	**чапла** (f)	['ʧapla]
flamingo	**фламинго** (n)	[fla'miŋgɔ]
pelican	**пеликан** (m)	[pɛli'kan]
nightingale	**славей** (m)	['slavɛj]
swallow	**лястовица** (f)	['ʎastɔviʦa]
thrush	**кос** (m)	[kɔs]
song thrush	**кос** (m)	[kɔs]
blackbird	**черен кос** (m)	['ʧərɛn kɔs]
swift	**бързолет** (m)	[bɪrzɔ'lɛt]
lark	**чучулига** (f)	[ʧuʧu'liga]
quail	**пъдпъдък** (m)	[pɪdpɪ'dɪk]
woodpecker	**кълвач** (m)	[kɪl'vaʧ]
cuckoo	**кукувица** (f)	['kukuviʦa]
owl	**сова** (f)	['sɔva]
eagle owl	**бухал** (m)	['buhal]
wood grouse	**глухар** (m)	[glu'har]
black grouse	**тетрев** (m)	['tɛtrɛv]
partridge	**яребица** (f)	['jarɛbiʦa]
starling	**скорец** (m)	[skɔ'rɛʦ]
canary	**канарче** (n)	[ka'narʧə]
hazel grouse	**лещарка** (f)	[le'ɕarka]
chaffinch	**чинка** (f)	['ʧiŋka]
bullfinch	**червенушка** (f)	[ʧərvɛ'nuʃka]
seagull	**чайка** (f)	['ʧajka]
albatross	**албатрос** (m)	[albat'rɔs]
penguin	**пингвин** (m)	[piŋg'vin]

217. Birds. Singing and sounds

to sing (vi)	**пея**	['pɛja]
to call (animal, bird)	**кряскам**	['krʲaskam]

to crow (rooster)	**кукуригам**	[kuku'rigam]
cock-a-doodle-doo	**кукуригу**	[kuku'rigu]
to cluck (hen)	**кудкудякам**	[kudku'dʲakam]
to caw (vi)	**грача**	['gratʃa]
to quack (duck)	**крякам**	['krʲakam]
to cheep (vi)	**пищя**	[piʃ'tʲa]
to chirp, to twitter	**чуруликам**	[tʃuru'likam]

218. Fish. Marine animals

bream	**платика** (f)	[pla'tika]
carp	**шаран** (m)	[ʃʌ'ran]
perch	**костур** (m)	[kɔs'tur]
catfish	**сом** (m)	[sɔm]
pike	**щука** (f)	['ʃtuka]
salmon	**сьомга** (f)	['sɜmga]
sturgeon	**есетра** (f)	[ɛ'sɛtra]
herring	**селда** (f)	['sɛlda]
Atlantic salmon	**сьомга** (f)	['sɜmga]
mackerel	**скумрия** (f)	[skum'rijɑ]
flatfish	**калкан** (m)	[kal'kan]
zander, pike perch	**бяла риба** (f)	['bʲala 'riba]
cod	**треска** (f)	['trɛska]
tuna	**риба тон** (m)	['riba tɔn]
trout	**пъстърва** (f)	[pɪs'tɪrva]
eel	**змиорка** (f)	[zmi'ɔrka]
electric ray	**електрически скат** (m)	[ɛlɛkt'ritʃəski skat]
moray eel	**мурена** (f)	[mu'rɛna]
piranha	**пираня** (f)	[pi'raɲa]
shark	**акула** (f)	[a'kula]
dolphin	**делфин** (m)	[dɛl'fin]
whale	**кит** (m)	[kit]
crab	**морски рак** (m)	['mɔrski rak]
jellyfish	**медуза** (f)	[mɛ'duza]
octopus	**октопод** (m)	[ɔktɔ'pɔd]
starfish	**морска звезда** (f)	['mɔrska zvɛz'da]
sea urchin	**морски таралеж** (m)	['mɔrski tara'lɛʒ]
seahorse	**морско конче** (n)	['mɔrskɔ 'kɔntʃə]
oyster	**стрида** (f)	['strida]
shrimp	**скарида** (f)	[ska'rida]
lobster	**омар** (m)	[ɔ'mar]
spiny lobster	**лангуста** (f)	[la'ŋgusta]

219. Amphibians. Reptiles

snake	**змия** (f)	[zmi'jɑ]
venomous (snake)	**отровен**	[ɔt'rɔvɛn]
viper	**усойница** (f)	[u'sɔjnitsa]
cobra	**кобра** (f)	['kɔbra]
python	**питон** (m)	[pi'tɔn]
boa	**боа** (f)	[bɔ'a]
grass snake	**смок** (m)	[smɔk]
rattle snake	**гърмяща змия** (f)	[gɪr'mʲaʃta zmi'jɑ]
anaconda	**анаконда** (f)	[ana'kɔnda]
lizard	**гущер** (m)	['guʃtɛr]
iguana	**игуана** (f)	[igu'ana]
monitor lizard	**варан** (m)	[va'ran]
salamander	**саламандър** (m)	[sala'mandɪr]
chameleon	**хамелеон** (m)	[hamɛlɛ'ɔn]
scorpion	**скорпион** (m)	[skɔrpi'ɔn]
turtle	**костенурка** (f)	[kɔstɛ'nurka]
frog	**жаба** (f)	['ʒaba]
toad	**жаба** (f)	['ʒaba]
crocodile	**крокодил** (m)	[krɔkɔ'dil]

220. Insects

insect, bug	**насекомо** (n)	[nasɛ'kɔmɔ]
butterfly	**пеперуда** (f)	[pɛpɛ'ruda]
ant	**мравка** (f)	['mrafka]
fly	**муха** (f)	[mu'ha]
mosquito	**комар** (m)	[kɔ'mar]
beetle	**бръмбар** (m)	['brɪmbar]
wasp	**оса** (f)	[ɔ'sa]
bee	**пчела** (f)	[ptʃə'la]
bumblebee	**земна пчела** (f)	['zɛmna ptʃə'la]
gadfly	**щръклица** (f), **овод** (m)	['ɕrɪklitsa], ['ɔvɔd]
spider	**паяк** (m)	['pajɑk]
spider's web	**паяжина** (f)	['pajɑʒina]
dragonfly	**водно конче** (n)	['vɔdnɔ 'kɔntʃə]
grasshopper	**скакалец** (m)	[skaka'lɛts]
moth (night butterfly)	**малка пеперуда** (f)	['malka pɛpɛ'ruda]
cockroach	**хлебарка** (f)	[hlɛ'barka]
tick	**кърлеж** (m)	['kɪrlɛʃ]

flea	**бълха** (f)	[bɪl'ha]
midge	**мушица** (f)	[mu'ʃitsa]
locust	**скакалци** (m pl)	[skakal'tsi]
snail	**охлюв** (m)	['ɔhlyf]
cricket	**щурец** (m)	[ʃtu'rɛts]
lightning bug	**светулка** (f)	[svɛ'tulka]
ladybug	**калинка** (f)	[ka'liŋka]
cockchafer	**майски бръмбар** (m)	['majski 'brɪmbar]
leech	**пиявица** (f)	[pi'jɑvitsa]
caterpillar	**гъсеница** (f)	[gɪ'sɛnitsa]
earthworm	**червей** (m)	['ʧərvɛj]
larva	**буба** (f)	['buba]

221. Animals. Body parts

beak	**клюн** (m)	[klyn]
wings	**криле** (pl)	[kri'lɛ]
foot (of bird)	**крак** (f)	[krak]
feathering	**перушина** (f)	[pɛru'ʃina]
feather	**перо** (n)	[pɛ'rɔ]
crest	**качул** (n)	[ka'ʧul]
gill	**хриле** (n)	[hri'lɛ]
spawn	**хайвер** (m)	[haj'vɛr]
larva	**личинка** (f)	['liʧiŋka]
fin	**перка** (f)	['pɛrka]
scales (of fish, reptile)	**люспа** (f)	['lyspa]
fang (canine)	**зъб** (m)	[zɪb]
paw (e.g., cat's ~)	**лапа** (f)	['lapa]
muzzle (snout)	**муцуна** (f)	[mu'tsuna]
mouth (of cat, dog)	**уста** (f)	[us'ta]
tail	**опашка** (f)	[ɔ'paʃka]
whiskers	**мустаци** (m pl)	[mus'tatsi]
hoof	**копито** (n)	[kɔ'pitɔ]
horn	**рог** (m)	[rɔg]
carapace	**черупка** (f)	[ʧə'rupka]
shell (of mollusk)	**мида** (f)	['mida]
eggshell	**черупка** (f)	[ʧə'rupka]
animal's hair (pelage)	**козина** (f)	['kɔzina]
pelt (hide)	**кожа** (f)	['kɔʒa]

222. Actions of animals

to fly (vi)	**летя**	[lɛ'tʲa]
to make circles	**вия се**	['vijɑ sɛ]
to fly away	**отлетя**	[ɔtlɛ'tʲa]
to flap (~ the wings)	**махам**	['maham]
to peck (vi)	**кълва**	[kɪl'va]
to sit on eggs	**излюпвам**	[iz'lypvam]
to hatch out (vi)	**излюпвам се**	[iz'lypvam sɛ]
to build the nest	**вия**	['vijɑ]
to slither, to crawl	**пълзя**	[pɪl'zʲa]
to sting, to bite (insect)	**жиля**	['ʒiʎa]
to bite (ab. animal)	**хапя**	['hapʲa]
to sniff (vt)	**душа**	['duʃʌ]
to bark (vi)	**лая**	['lajɑ]
to hiss (snake)	**съска**	['sɪska]
to scare (vt)	**плаша**	['plaʃʌ]
to attack (vt)	**нападам**	[na'padam]
to gnaw (bone, etc.)	**гриза**	[gri'za]
to scratch (with claws)	**драскам**	['draskam]
to hide (vi)	**крия се**	['krijɑ sɛ]
to play (kittens, etc.)	**играя**	[ig'rajɑ]
to hunt (vi, vt)	**ловувам**	[lɔ'vuvam]
to hibernate (vi)	**изпадам в зимен сън**	[is'padam v 'zimɛn sɪn]
to become extinct	**измра**	[izm'ra]

223. Animals. Habitats

habitat	**среда** (f) **на обитаване**	[srɛ'da na ɔbi'tavanɛ]
migration	**миграция** (f)	[mig'ratsijɑ]
mountain	**планина** (f)	[plani'na]
reef	**риф** (m)	[rif]
cliff	**скала** (f)	[ska'la]
forest	**гора** (f)	[gɔ'ra]
jungle	**джунгла** (f)	['dʒuŋgla]
savanna	**савана** (f)	[sa'vana]
tundra	**тундра** (f)	['tundra]
steppe	**степ** (f)	[stɛp]
desert	**пустиня** (f)	[pus'tiɲa]
oasis	**оазис** (m)	[ɔ'azis]
sea	**море** (n)	[mɔ'rɛ]

lake	**езеро** (n)	['ɛzɛrɔ]
ocean	**океан** (m)	[ɔkɛ'an]
swamp	**блато** (n)	['blatɔ]
freshwater (adj)	**сладководен**	[slatkɔ'vɔdɛn]
pond	**изкуствен вир** (m)	[is'kustvɛn vir]
river	**река** (f)	[rɛ'ka]
den	**бърлога** (f)	[bɪr'lɔga]
nest	**гнездо** (n)	[gnɛz'dɔ]
hollow (in a tree)	**хралупа** (f)	[hra'lupa]
burrow (animal hole)	**дупка** (f)	['dupka]
anthill	**мравуняк** (m)	[mra'vuɲak]

224. Animal care

zoo	**зоологическа градина** (f)	[zɔ:lɔ'gitʃəska gra'dina]
nature preserve	**резерват** (m)	[rɛzɛr'vat]
breeder, breed club	**развъдник** (m)	[raz'vɪdnik]
open-air cage	**волиера** (f)	[vɔli'ɛra]
cage	**клетка** (f)	['klɛtka]
kennel	**кучешка колибка** (f)	['kutʃəʃka kɔ'lipka]
dovecot	**гълъбарник** (m)	[gɪlɪ'barnik]
aquarium	**аквариум** (m)	[ak'varium]
dolphinarium	**делфинариум** (m)	[dɛlfi'narium]
to breed (animals)	**развъждам**	[raz'vɪʒdam]
brood, litter	**потомство** (n)	[pɔ'tɔmstvɔ]
to tame (vt)	**опитомявам**	[ɔpitɔ'mʲavam]
feed (fodder, etc.)	**храна** (f)	[hra'na]
to feed (vt)	**храня**	['hraɲa]
to train (animals)	**дресирам**	[drɛ'siram]
pet store	**зоомагазин** (m)	[zɔ:maga'zin]
muzzle (for dog)	**намордник** (m)	[na'mɔrdnik]
collar	**каишка** (f)	[ka'iʃka]
name (of animal)	**име** (n)	['imɛ]
pedigree (of dog)	**родословие** (n)	[rɔdɔs'lɔviɛ]

225. Animals. Miscellaneous

pack (wolves)	**глутница** (f)	['glutnitsa]
flock (birds)	**ято** (n)	['jatɔ]
shoal (fish)	**пасаж** (m)	[pa'saʒ]
herd of horses	**табун** (m)	[ta'bun]
male (n)	**самец** (m)	[sa'mɛts]

female	**самка** (f)	['samka]
hungry (adj)	**гладен**	['gladɛn]
wild (adj)	**див**	[div]
dangerous (adj)	**опасен**	[ɔ'pasɛn]

226. Horses

horse	**кон** (m)	[kɔn]
breed (race)	**порода** (f)	[pɔ'rɔda]
foal, colt	**жребец** (m)	[ʒrɛ'bɛʦ]
mare	**кобила** (f)	[kɔ'bila]
mustang	**мустанг** (m)	[mus'taŋg]
pony	**пони** (n)	['pɔni]
draft horse	**товарен кон** (m)	[tɔ'varɛn kɔn]
mane	**грива** (f)	['griva]
tail	**опашка** (f)	[ɔ'paʃka]
hoof	**копито** (n)	[kɔ'pitɔ]
horseshoe	**подкова** (f)	[pɔt'kɔva]
to shoe (vt)	**подкова**	[pɔtkɔ'va]
blacksmith	**ковач** (m)	[kɔ'vaʧ]
saddle	**седло** (n)	[sɛd'lɔ]
stirrup	**стреме** (n)	['strɛmɛ]
bridle	**юзда** (f)	[juz'da]
reins	**юзда** (f)	[juz'da]
whip (for riding)	**камшик** (m)	[kam'ʃik]
rider	**ездач** (m)	[ɛz'daʧ]
to break in (horse)	**обяздвам**	[ɔ'bʲazdvam]
to saddle (vt)	**яхна**	['jahna]
to mount a horse	**седна в седло**	['sɛdna f sɛd'lɔ]
gallop	**галоп** (m)	[ga'lɔp]
to gallop (vi)	**галопирам**	[galɔ'piram]
trot (n)	**тръс** (m)	[trɪs]
at a trot (adv)	**в тръс**	[f trɪs]
racehorse	**състезателен кон** (m)	[sɪstɛ'zatɛlɛn kɔn]
horse racing	**конни надбягвания** (n pl)	['kɔɲi nad'bʲagvanija]
stable	**обор** (m)	[ɔ'bɔr]
to feed (vt)	**храня**	['hraɲa]
hay	**сено** (n)	[sɛ'nɔ]
to water (animals)	**поя**	[pɔ'ja]
to wash (horse)	**чистя**	['ʧistʲa]

to hobble (tether)	**спъна кон**	['spɪna kɔn]
to graze (vi)	**паса**	[pa'sa]
to neigh (vi)	**цвиля**	['ʦviʎa]
to kick (horse)	**ритна**	['ritna]

Flora

227. Trees

tree	**дърво** (n)	[dɪr'vɔ]
deciduous (adj)	**широколистно**	[ʃirɔkɔ'listnɔ]
coniferous (adj)	**иглолистно**	[iglɔ'listnɔ]
evergreen (adj)	**вечнозелено**	[vɛʧnɔzɛ'lɛnɔ]
apple tree	**ябълка** (f)	['jabɪlka]
pear tree	**круша** (f)	['kruʃʌ]
sweet cherry tree	**череша** (f)	[ʧə'rɛʃʌ]
sour cherry tree	**вишна** (f)	['viʃna]
plum tree	**слива** (f)	['sliva]
birch	**бреза** (f)	[brɛ'za]
oak	**дъб** (m)	[dɪb]
linden tree	**липа** (f)	[li'pa]
aspen	**трепетлика** (f)	[trɛpɛt'lika]
maple	**клен** (m)	[klɛn]
spruce	**ела** (f)	[ɛ'la]
pine	**бор** (m)	[bɔr]
larch	**лиственица** (f)	['listvɛniʦa]
fir tree	**бяла ела** (f)	['bʲala ɛ'la]
cedar	**кедър** (m)	['kɛdɪr]
poplar	**топола** (f)	[tɔ'pɔla]
rowan	**офика** (f)	[ɔ'fika]
willow	**върба** (f)	[vɪr'ba]
alder	**елша** (f)	[ɛl'ʃʌ]
beech	**бук** (m)	[buk]
elm	**бряст** (m)	[brʲast]
ash (tree)	**ясен** (m)	['jasɛn]
chestnut	**кестен** (m)	['kɛstɛn]
magnolia	**магнолия** (f)	[mag'nɔlija]
palm tree	**палма** (f)	['palma]
cypress	**кипарис** (m)	[kipa'ris]
baobab	**баобаб** (m)	[baɔ'bab]
eucalyptus	**евкалипт** (m)	[ɛfka'lipt]
sequoia	**секвоя** (f)	[sɛk'vɔja]

228. Shrubs

bush	**храст** (m)	[hrast]
shrub	**храсталак** (m)	[hrasta'lak]
grapevine	**грозде** (n)	['grɔzdɛ]
vineyard	**лозе** (n)	['lɔzɛ]
raspberry bush	**малина** (f)	[ma'lina]
redcurrant bush	**червено френско грозде** (n)	[ʧər'vɛnɔ 'frɛnskɔ grɔzdɛ]
gooseberry bush	**цариградско грозде** (n)	[ʦarig'raʦkɔ 'grɔzdɛ]
acacia	**акация** (f)	[a'kaʦijɑ]
barberry	**кисел трън** (m)	['kisel 'trɪn]
jasmine	**жасмин** (m)	[ʒas'min]
juniper	**смрика** (f)	['smrika]
rosebush	**розов храст** (m)	['rɔzɔv hrast]
dog rose	**шипка** (f)	['ʃipka]

229. Mushrooms

mushroom	**гъба** (f)	['gɪba]
edible mushroom	**ядлива гъба** (f)	[jɑd'liva 'gɪba]
toadstool	**отровна гъба** (f)	[ɔt'rɔvna 'gɪba]
cap (of mushroom)	**шапка** (f)	['ʃʌpka]
stipe (of mushroom)	**пънче** (n)	['pɪnʧə]
cep (Boletus edulis)	**манатарка** (f)	[mana'tarka]
orange-cap boletus	**червена брезовка** (f)	[ʧər'vɛna 'brɛzɔfka]
birch bolete	**брезова манатарка** (f)	['brɛzɔva mana'tarka]
chanterelle	**пачи крак** (m)	['paʧi krak]
russula	**гълъбка** (f)	['gɪlɪpka]
morel	**пумпалка** (f)	['pumpalka]
fly agaric	**мухоморка** (f)	[muhɔ'mɔrka]
death cap	**зелена мухоморка** (f)	[zɛ'lɛna mu'hɔmɔrka]

230. Fruits. Berries

fruit	**плод** (m)	[plɔt]
fruits	**плодове** (m pl)	[plɔdɔ'vɛ]
apple	**ябълка** (f)	['jɑbɪlka]
pear	**круша** (f)	['kruʃʌ]
plum	**слива** (f)	['sliva]
strawberry	**ягода** (f)	['jɑgɔda]

sour cherry	**вишна** (f)	['viʃna]
sweet cherry	**череша** (f)	[ʧə'rɛʃʌ]
grape	**грозде** (n)	['grɔzdɛ]
raspberry	**малина** (f)	[ma'lina]
blackcurrant	**черно френско грозде** (n)	['ʧərnɔ 'frɛnskɔ grɔzdɛ]
redcurrant	**червено френско грозде** (n)	[ʧər'vɛnɔ 'frɛnskɔ grɔzdɛ]
gooseberry	**цариградско грозде** (n)	[ʦarig'raʦkɔ 'grɔzdɛ]
cranberry	**клюква** (f)	['klykva]
orange	**портокал** (m)	[pɔrtɔ'kal]
mandarin	**мандарина** (f)	[manda'rina]
pineapple	**ананас** (m)	[ana'nas]
banana	**банан** (m)	[ba'nan]
date	**фурма** (f)	[fur'ma]
lemon	**лимон** (m)	[li'mɔn]
apricot	**кайсия** (f)	[kaj'sijɑ]
peach	**праскова** (f)	['praskɔva]
kiwi	**киви** (n)	['kivi]
grapefruit	**грейпфрут** (m)	['grɛjpfrut]
berry	**горски плод** (m)	['gɔrski plɔt]
berries	**горски плодове** (m pl)	['gɔrski plɔdɔ'vɛ]
cowberry	**червена боровинка** (f)	[ʧər'vɛna bɔrɔ'viŋka]
field strawberry	**горска ягода** (f)	['gɔrska 'jɑgɔda]
bilberry	**боровинки** (f pl)	[bɔrɔ'viŋki]

231. Flowers. Plants

flower	**цвете** (n)	['ʦvɛtɛ]
bouquet (of flowers)	**букет** (m)	[bu'kɛt]
rose (flower)	**роза** (f)	['rɔza]
tulip	**лале** (n)	[la'lɛ]
carnation	**карамфил** (m)	[karam'fil]
gladiolus	**гладиола** (f)	[gladi'ɔla]
cornflower	**метличина** (f)	[mɛtli'ʧina]
bluebell	**камбанка** (f)	[kam'baŋka]
dandelion	**глухарче** (n)	[glu'harʧə]
camomile	**лайка** (f)	['lajka]
aloe	**алое** (n)	[a'lɔɛ]
cactus	**кактус** (m)	['kaktus]
rubber plant, ficus	**фикус** (m)	['fikus]
lily	**лилиум** (m)	['lilium]
geranium	**мушкато** (n)	[muʃ'katɔ]

hyacinth	**зюмбюл** (m)	[zym'byl]
mimosa	**мимоза** (f)	[mi'mɔza]
narcissus	**нарцис** (m)	[nar'ʦis]
nasturtium	**латинка** (f)	[la'tiŋka]
orchid	**орхидея** (f)	[ɔrhi'dɛjɑ]
peony	**божур** (m)	[bɔ'ʒur]
violet	**теменуга** (f)	[tɛmɛ'nuga]
pansy	**трицветна теменуга** (f)	[triʦ'vɛtna tɛmɛ'nuga]
forget-me-not	**незабравка** (f)	[nɛzab'rafka]
daisy	**маргаритка** (f)	[marga'ritka]
poppy	**мак** (m)	[mak]
hemp	**коноп** (m)	[kɔ'nɔp]
mint	**мента** (f)	['mɛnta]
lily of the valley	**момина сълза** (f)	['mɔmina sɪl'za]
snowdrop	**кокиче** (n)	[kɔ'kiʧə]
nettle	**коприва** (f)	[kɔp'riva]
sorrel	**киселец** (m)	['kisɛlɛʦ]
water lily	**водна лилия** (f)	['vɔdna 'lilijɑ]
fern	**папрат** (m)	['paprat]
lichen	**лишей** (m)	['liʃɛj]
tropical greenhouse	**оранжерия** (f)	[ɔran'ʒɛrijɑ]
grass lawn	**тревна площ** (f)	['trɛvna plɔʃt]
flowerbed	**цветна леха** (f)	['ʦvɛtna lɛ'ha]
plant	**растение** (n)	[ras'tɛniɛ]
grass, herb	**трева** (f)	[trɛ'va]
blade of grass	**тревичка** (f)	[trɛ'viʧka]
leaf	**лист** (m)	[list]
petal	**венчелистче** (n)	[vɛnʧə'listʧɛ]
stem	**стъбло** (n)	[stɪb'lɔ]
tuber	**грудка** (f)	['grutka]
young plant (shoot)	**кълн** (m)	[kɪln]
thorn	**бодил** (m)	[bɔ'dil]
to blossom (vi)	**цъфтя**	[ʦɪf'tʲa]
to fade, to wither	**увяхвам**	[u'vʲahvam]
smell (odor)	**мирис** (m)	['miris]
to cut (flowers)	**отрежа**	[ɔt'rɛʒa]
to pick (a flower)	**откъсна**	[ɔt'kɪsna]

232. Cereals, grains

grain	**зърно** (n)	['zɪrnɔ]
cereal crops	**житни култури** (f pl)	['ʒitni kul'turi]

ear (of barley, etc.)	**клас** (m)	[klas]
wheat	**пшеница** (f)	[pʃə'nitsa]
rye	**ръж** (f)	[rɪʒ]
oats	**овес** (m)	[ɔ'vɛs]
millet	**просо** (n)	[prɔ'sɔ]
barley	**ечемик** (m)	[ɛtʃə'mik]
corn	**царевица** (f)	['tsarɛvitsa]
rice	**ориз** (m)	[ɔ'riz]
buckwheat	**елда** (f)	['ɛlda]
pea plant	**грах** (m)	[grah]
kidney bean	**фасул** (m)	[fa'sul]
soy	**соя** (f)	['sɔja]
lentil	**леща** (f)	['lɛʃta]
beans (pulse crops)	**боб** (m)	[bɔb]

233. Vegetables. Greens

vegetables	**зеленчуци** (m pl)	[zɛlɛn'tʃutsi]
greens	**зарзават** (m)	[zarza'vat]
tomato	**домат** (m)	[dɔ'mat]
cucumber	**краставица** (f)	['krastavitsa]
carrot	**морков** (m)	['mɔrkɔf]
potato	**картофи** (pl)	[kar'tɔfi]
onion	**лук** (m)	[luk]
garlic	**чесън** (m)	['tʃəsɪn]
cabbage	**зеле** (n)	['zɛlɛ]
cauliflower	**карфиол** (m)	[karfi'ɔl]
Brussels sprouts	**брюкселско зеле** (n)	['bryksɛlskɔ 'zɛlɛ]
beetroot	**цвекло** (n)	[tsvɛk'lɔ]
eggplant	**патладжан** (m)	[patla'dʒan]
zucchini	**тиквичка** (f)	['tikvitʃka]
pumpkin	**тиква** (f)	['tikva]
turnip	**ряпа** (f)	['rʲapa]
parsley	**магданоз** (m)	[magda'nɔz]
dill	**копър** (m)	['kɔpɪr]
lettuce	**салата** (f)	[sa'lata]
celery	**целина** (f)	['tsəlina]
asparagus	**аспержа** (f)	[as'pɛrʒa]
spinach	**спанак** (m)	[spa'nak]
pea	**грах** (m)	[grah]
beans	**боб** (m)	[bɔb]
corn (maize)	**царевица** (f)	['tsarɛvitsa]
kidney bean	**фасул** (m)	[fa'sul]

pepper	**пипер** (m)	[pi'pɛr]
radish	**репичка** (f)	['rɛpitʃka]
artichoke	**ангинар** (m)	[aŋgi'nar]

REGIONAL GEOGRAPHY

Countries. Nationalities

234. Western Europe

Europe	**Европа**	[ɛv'rɔpa]
European Union	**Европейски Съюз** (m)	[ɛvrɔ'pɛjski sı'juz]
European (n)	**европеец** (m)	[ɛvrɔ'pɛ:ʦ]
European (adj)	**европейски**	[ɛvrɔ'pɛjski]
Austria	**Австрия**	['afstrijɑ]
Austrian (masc.)	**австриец** (m)	[afst'riɛʦ]
Austrian (fem.)	**австрийка** (f)	[afst'rijka]
Austrian (adj)	**австрийски**	[afst'rijski]
Great Britain	**Великобритания**	[vɛlikɔbri'tanijɑ]
England	**Англия**	['aŋglijɑ]
British (masc.)	**англичанин** (m)	[aŋgli'ʧanin]
British (fem.)	**англичанка** (f)	[aŋgli'ʧaŋka]
English, British (adj)	**английски**	[aŋg'lijski]
Belgium	**Белгия**	['bɛlgijɑ]
Belgian (masc.)	**белгиец** (m)	[bɛl'giɛʦ]
Belgian (fem.)	**белгийка** (f)	[bɛl'gijka]
Belgian (adj)	**белгийски**	[bɛl'gijski]
Germany	**Германия**	[gɛr'manijɑ]
German (masc.)	**германец** (m)	[gɛr'manɛʦ]
German (fem.)	**германка** (f)	[gɛr'maŋka]
German (adj)	**немски**	['nɛmski]
Netherlands	**Нидерландия**	[nidɛr'landijɑ]
Holland	**Холандия** (f)	[hɔ'landijɑ]
Dutchman	**холандец** (m)	[hɔ'landɛʦ]
Dutchwoman	**холандка** (f)	[hɔ'lantka]
Dutch (adj)	**холандски**	[hɔ'landski]
Greece	**Гърция**	['gırʦijɑ]
Greek (masc.)	**грък** (m)	[grık]
Greek (fem.)	**гъркиня** (f)	[gır'kiɲa]
Greek (adj)	**гръцки**	['grıʦki]
Denmark	**Дания**	['danijɑ]
Dane (masc.)	**датчанин** (m)	[da'ʧanin]

Dane (fem.)	**датчанка** (f)	[da'ʧaŋka]
Danish (adj)	**датски**	['datski]
Ireland	**Ирландия**	[ir'landijɑ]
Irishman	**ирландец** (m)	[ir'landɛts]
Irishwoman	**ирландка** (f)	[ir'lantka]
Irish (adj)	**ирландски**	[ir'lantski]
Iceland	**Исландия**	[is'landijɑ]
Icelander (masc.)	**исландец** (m)	[is'landɛts]
Icelander (fem.)	**исландка** (f)	[is'lantka]
Icelandic (adj)	**исландски**	[is'lantski]
Spain	**Испания**	[is'panijɑ]
Spaniard (masc.)	**испанец** (m)	[is'panɛts]
Spaniard (fem.)	**испанка** (f)	[is'paŋka]
Spanish (adj)	**испански**	[is'panski]
Italy	**Италия**	[i'talijɑ]
Italian (masc.)	**италианец** (m)	[itali'anɛts]
Italian (fem.)	**италианка** (f)	[itali'aŋka]
Italian (adj)	**италиански**	[itali'anski]
Cyprus	**Кипър**	['kipɪr]
Cypriot (masc.)	**кипърец** (m)	['kipɪrɛts]
Cypriot (fem.)	**кипърка** (f)	['kipɪrka]
Cypriot (adj)	**кипърски**	['kipɪrski]
Malta	**Малта**	['malta]
Maltese (masc.)	**малтиец** (m)	[mal'tiɛts]
Maltese (fem.)	**малтийка** (f)	[mal'tijka]
Maltese (adj)	**малтийски**	[mal'tijski]
Norway	**Норвегия**	[nɔr'vɛgijɑ]
Norwegian (masc.)	**норвежец** (m)	[nɔr'vɛʒɛts]
Norwegian (fem.)	**норвежка** (f)	[nɔr'vɛʃka]
Norwegian (adj)	**норвежки**	[nɔr'vɛʃki]
Portugal	**Португалия**	[pɔrtu'galijɑ]
Portuguese (masc.)	**португалец** (m)	[pɔrtu'galɛts]
Portuguese (fem.)	**португалка** (f)	[pɔrtu'galka]
Portuguese (adj)	**португалски**	[pɔrtu'galski]
Finland	**Финландия**	[fin'landijɑ]
Finn (masc.)	**финландец** (m)	[fin'landɛts]
Finn (fem.)	**финландка** (f)	[fin'lantka]
Finnish (adj)	**фински**	['finski]
France	**Франция**	['frantsijɑ]
Frenchman	**французин** (m)	[fran'tsuzin]
Frenchwoman	**французойка** (f)	[frantsu'zɔjka]
French (adj)	**френски**	['frɛnski]

Sweden	**Швеция**	['ʃvɛtsija]
Swede (masc.)	**швед** (m)	[ʃvɛt]
Swede (fem.)	**шведка** (f)	['ʃvɛtka]
Swedish (adj)	**шведски**	['ʃvɛtski]
Switzerland	**Швейцария**	[ʃvɛj'tsarija]
Swiss (masc.)	**швейцарец** (m)	[ʃvɛj'tsarɛts]
Swiss (fem.)	**швейцарка** (f)	[ʃvɛj'tsarka]
Swiss (adj)	**швейцарски**	[ʃvɛj'tsarski]
Scotland	**Шотландия**	[ʃɔt'landija]
Scottish (masc.)	**шотландец** (m)	[ʃɔt'landɛts]
Scottish (fem.)	**шотландка** (f)	[ʃɔt'lantka]
Scottish (adj)	**шотландски**	[ʃɔt'lantski]
Vatican	**Ватикана**	[vati'kana]
Liechtenstein	**Лихтенщайн**	['lihtɛnʃtajn]
Luxembourg	**Люксембург**	['lyksɛmburg]
Monaco	**Монако**	[mɔ'nakɔ]

235. Central and Eastern Europe

Albania	**Албания**	[al'banija]
Albanian (masc.)	**албанец** (m)	[al'banɛts]
Albanian (fem.)	**албанка** (f)	[al'baŋka]
Albanian (adj)	**албански**	[al'banski]
Bulgaria	**България**	[bɪl'garija]
Bulgarian (masc.)	**българин** (m)	['bɪlgarin]
Bulgarian (fem.)	**българка** (f)	['bɪlgarka]
Bulgarian (adj)	**български**	['bɪlgarski]
Hungary	**Унгария**	[u'ŋgarija]
Hungarian (masc.)	**унгарец** (m)	[u'ŋgarɛts]
Hungarian (fem.)	**унгарка** (f)	[u'ŋgarka]
Hungarian (adj)	**унгарски**	[u'ŋgarski]
Latvia	**Латвия**	['latvija]
Latvian (masc.)	**латвиец** (m)	[lat'viɛts]
Latvian (fem.)	**латвийка** (f)	[lat'vijka]
Latvian (adj)	**латвийски**	[lat'vijski]
Lithuania	**Литва**	['litva]
Lithuanian (masc.)	**литовец** (m)	[li'tɔvɛts]
Lithuanian (fem.)	**литовка** (f)	[li'tɔfka]
Lithuanian (adj)	**литовски**	[li'tɔfski]
Poland	**Полша**	['pɔlʃʌ]
Pole (masc.)	**поляк** (m)	[pɔ'ʎak]
Pole (fem.)	**полякиня** (f)	[pɔʎa'kiɲa]

Polish (adj)	**полски**	['pɔlski]
Romania	**Румъния**	[ru'mınija]
Romanian (masc.)	**румънец** (m)	[ru'mınɛʦ]
Romanian (fem.)	**румънка** (f)	[ru'mıŋka]
Romanian (adj)	**румънски**	[ru'mınski]
Serbia	**Сърбия**	['sırbija]
Serbian (masc.)	**сърбин** (m)	['sırbin]
Serbian (fem.)	**сръбкиня** (f)	[srıp'kiɲa]
Serbian (adj)	**сръбски**	['srıpski]
Slovakia	**Словакия**	[slɔ'vakija]
Slovak (masc.)	**словак** (m)	[slɔ'vak]
Slovak (fem.)	**словачка** (f)	[slɔ'vaʧka]
Slovak (adj)	**словашки**	[slɔ'vaʃki]
Croatia	**Хърватия**	[hır'vatija]
Croatian (masc.)	**хърватин** (m)	[hır'vatin]
Croatian (fem.)	**хърватка** (f)	[hır'vatka]
Croatian (adj)	**хърватски**	[hır'vaʦki]
Czech Republic	**Чехия**	['ʧəhija]
Czech (masc.)	**чех** (m)	[ʧəh]
Czech (fem.)	**чехкиня** (f)	[ʧəh'kiɲa]
Czech (adj)	**чешки**	['ʧəʃki]
Estonia	**Естония**	[ɛs'tɔnija]
Estonian (masc.)	**естонец** (m)	[ɛs'tɔnɛʦ]
Estonian (fem.)	**естонка** (f)	[ɛs'tɔŋka]
Estonian (adj)	**естонски**	[ɛs'tɔnski]
Bosnia-Herzegovina	**Босна и Херцеговина**	['bɔsna i hɛrʦə'gɔvina]
Macedonia	**Македония**	[makɛ'dɔnija]
Slovenia	**Словения**	[slɔ'vɛnija]
Montenegro	**Черна гора**	['ʧərna gɔ'ra]

236. Former USSR countries

Azerbaijan	**Азербайджан**	[azɛrbaj'ʤan]
Azerbaijani (masc.)	**азербайджанец** (m)	[azɛrbaj'ʤanɛʦ]
Azerbaijani (fem.)	**азербайджанка** (f)	[azɛrbaj'ʤaŋka]
Azerbaijani (adj)	**азербайджански**	[azɛrbaj'ʤanski]
Armenia	**Армения**	[ar'mɛnija]
Armenian (masc.)	**арменец** (m)	[ar'mɛnɛʦ]
Armenian (fem.)	**арменка** (f)	[ar'mɛŋka]
Armenian (adj)	**арменски**	[ar'mɛnski]
Belarus	**Беларус**	[bɛla'rus]
Belarusian (masc.)	**беларусин** (m)	[bɛla'rusin]

Belarusian (fem.)	**беларускиня** (f)	[bɛlarus'kiɲa]
Belarusian (adj)	**беларуски**	[bɛla'ruski]
Georgia	**Грузия**	['gruzija]
Georgian (masc.)	**грузинец** (m)	[gru'zinɛʦ]
Georgian (fem.)	**грузинка** (f)	[gru'ziŋka]
Georgian (adj)	**грузински**	[gru'zinski]
Kazakhstan	**Казахстан**	[kazahs'tan]
Kazakh (masc.)	**казах** (m)	[ka'zah]
Kazakh (fem.)	**казашка** (f)	[ka'zaʃka]
Kazakh (adj)	**казахски**	[ka'zahski]
Kirghizia	**Киргизстан**	[kirgis'tan]
Kirghiz (masc.)	**киргиз** (m)	[kir'giz]
Kirghiz (fem.)	**киргизка** (f)	[kir'giska]
Kirghiz (adj)	**киргизки**	[kir'giski]
Moldavia	**Молдова**	[mɔl'dɔva]
Moldavian (masc.)	**молдовец** (m)	[mɔl'dɔvɛʦ]
Moldavian (fem.)	**молдовка** (f)	[mɔldɔ'vaŋka]
Moldavian (adj)	**молдавски**	[mɔl'dafski]
Russia	**Русия**	[ru'sija]
Russian (masc.)	**руснак** (m)	[rus'nak]
Russian (fem.)	**рускиня** (f)	[rus'kiɲa]
Russian (adj)	**руски**	['ruski]
Tajikistan	**Таджикистан**	[taʤikis'tan]
Tajik (masc.)	**таджик** (m)	[ta'ʤik]
Tajik (fem.)	**таджикистанка** (f)	[taʤikis'taŋka]
Tajik (adj)	**таджикски**	[ta'ʤikski]
Turkmenistan	**Туркменистан**	[turkmɛnis'tan]
Turkmen (masc.)	**туркмен** (m)	[turk'mɛn]
Turkmen (fem.)	**туркменка** (f)	[turk'mɛŋka]
Turkmenian (adj)	**туркменски**	[turk'mɛnski]
Uzbekistan	**Узбекистан**	[uzbɛkis'tan]
Uzbek (masc.)	**узбек** (m)	[uz'bɛk]
Uzbek (fem.)	**узбечка** (f)	[uz'bɛʧka]
Uzbek (adj)	**узбекски**	[uz'bɛkski]
Ukraine	**Украйна**	[uk'rajna]
Ukrainian (masc.)	**украинец** (m)	[ukra'inɛʦ]
Ukrainian (fem.)	**украинка** (f)	[ukra'iŋka]
Ukrainian (adj)	**украински**	[ukra'inski]

237. Asia

Asia	**Азия**	['azija]
Asian (adj)	**азиатски**	[azi'aʦki]

Vietnam	**Виетнам**	[viɛt'nam]
Vietnamese (masc.)	**виетнамец** (m)	[viɛt'namɛʦ]
Vietnamese (fem.)	**виетнамка** (f)	[viɛt'namka]
Vietnamese (adj)	**виетнамски**	[viɛt'namski]
India	**Индия**	['indijɑ]
Indian (masc.)	**индиец** (m)	[in'diɛʦ]
Indian (fem.)	**индийка** (f)	[in'dijka]
Indian (adj)	**индийски**	[in'dijski]
Israel	**Израел**	[iz'raɛl]
Israeli (masc.)	**израилтянин** (m)	[izrail'tʲanin]
Israeli (fem.)	**израилтянка** (f)	[izrail'tʲaŋka]
Israeli (adj)	**израелски**	[iz'raɛlski]
Jew (n)	**евреин** (m)	[ɛv'rɛin]
Jewess (n)	**еврейка** (f)	[ɛv'rɛjka]
Jewish (adj)	**еврейски**	[ɛv'rɛjski]
China	**Китай**	[ki'taj]
Chinese (masc.)	**китаец** (m)	[ki'taɛʦ]
Chinese (fem.)	**китайка** (f)	[ki'tajka]
Chinese (adj)	**китайски**	[ki'tajski]
Korean (masc.)	**кореец** (m)	[kɔ'rɛ:ʦ]
Korean (fem.)	**корейка** (f)	[kɔ'rɛjka]
Korean (adj)	**корейски**	[kɔ'rɛjski]
Lebanon	**Ливан**	[li'van]
Lebanese (masc.)	**ливанец** (m)	[li'vanɛʦ]
Lebanese (fem.)	**ливанка** (f)	[li'vaŋka]
Lebanese (adj)	**ливански**	[li'vanski]
Mongolia	**Монголия**	[mɔ'ŋgɔlijɑ]
Mongolian (masc.)	**монголец** (m)	[mɔ'ŋgɔlɛʦ]
Mongolian (fem.)	**монголка** (f)	[mɔ'ŋgɔlka]
Mongolian (adj)	**монголски**	[mɔ'ŋgɔlski]
Malaysia	**Малайзия**	[ma'lajzijɑ]
Malaysian (masc.)	**малайзиец** (m)	[malaj'ziɛʦ]
Malaysian (fem.)	**малайзийка** (f)	[malaj'zijka]
Malaysian (adj)	**малайски**	[ma'lajski]
Pakistan	**Пакистан**	[pakis'tan]
Pakistani (masc.)	**пакистанец** (m)	[pakis'tanɛʦ]
Pakistani (fem.)	**пакистанка** (f)	[pakis'taŋka]
Pakistani (adj)	**пакистански**	[pakis'tanski]
Saudi Arabia	**Саудитска Арабия**	[sau'diʦka a'rabijɑ]
Arab (masc.)	**арабин** (m)	[a'rabin]
Arab (fem.)	**арабка** (f)	[a'rapka]
Arabian (adj)	**арабски**	[a'rapski]

Thailand	**Тайланд**	[taj'land]
Thai (masc.)	**тайландец** (m)	[taj'landɛʦ]
Thai (fem.)	**тайландка** (f)	[taj'lantka]
Thai (adj)	**тайландски**	[taj'lanʦki]
Taiwan	**Тайван**	[taj'van]
Taiwanese (masc.)	**тайванец** (m)	[taj'vanɛʦ]
Taiwanese (fem.)	**тайванка** (f)	[taj'vaŋka]
Taiwanese (adj)	**тайвански**	[taj'vanski]
Turkey	**Турция**	['turʦijɑ]
Turk (masc.)	**турчин** (m)	['turʧin]
Turk (fem.)	**туркиня** (f)	[tur'kiɲa]
Turkish (adj)	**турски**	['turski]
Japan	**Япония**	[jɑ'pɔnijɑ]
Japanese (masc.)	**японец** (m)	[jɑ'pɔnɛʦ]
Japanese (fem.)	**японка** (f)	[jɑ'pɔŋka]
Japanese (adj)	**японски**	[jɑ'pɔnski]
Afghanistan	**Афганистан**	[afganis'tan]
Bangladesh	**Бангладеш**	[baŋgla'dɛʃ]
Indonesia	**Индонезия**	[indɔ'nɛzijɑ]
Jordan	**Йордания**	[jor'danijɑ]
Iraq	**Ирак**	[i'rak]
Iran	**Иран**	[i'ran]
Cambodia	**Камбоджа**	[kam'bɔʤa]
Kuwait	**Кувейт**	[ku'vɛjt]
Laos	**Лаос**	[la'ɔs]
Myanmar	**Мянма**	['mʲanma]
Nepal	**Непал**	[nɛ'pal]
United Arab Emirates	**Обединени арабски емирства**	[ɔbɛdi'nɛni a'rapski ɛ'mirstva]
Syria	**Сирия**	['sirijɑ]
Palestine	**Палестинска автономия**	[palɛs'tinska aftɔ'nɔmijɑ]
South Korea	**Южна Корея**	['juʒna kɔ'rɛjɑ]
North Korea	**Северна Корея**	['sɛvɛrna kɔ'rɛjɑ]

238. North America

United States of America	**Съединени американски щати**	[sɪɛdi'nɛni amɛri'kanski 'ʃtati]
American (masc.)	**американец** (m)	[amɛri'kanɛʦ]
American (fem.)	**американка** (f)	[amɛri'kaŋka]
American (adj)	**американски**	[amɛri'kanski]
Canada	**Канада**	[ka'nada]

Canadian (masc.) **канадец** (m) [ka'nadɛʦ]
Canadian (fem.) **канадка** (f) [ka'natka]
Canadian (adj) **канадски** [ka'naʦki]

Mexico **Мексико** ['mɛksikɔ]
Mexican (masc.) **мексиканец** (m) [mɛksi'kanɛʦ]
Mexican (fem.) **мексиканка** (f) [mɛksi'kaŋka]
Mexican (adj) **мексикански** [mɛksi'kanski]

239. Central and South America

Argentina **Аржентина** [arʒɛn'tina]
Argentinian (masc.) **аржентинец** (m) [arʒɛn'tinɛʦ]
Argentinian (fem.) **аржентинка** (f) [arʒɛn'tiŋka]
Argentinian (adj) **аржентински** [arʒɛn'tinski]

Brazil **Бразилия** [bra'zilijɑ]
Brazilian (masc.) **бразилец** (m) [bra'zilɛʦ]
Brazilian (fem.) **бразилка** (f) [bra'zilka]
Brazilian (adj) **бразилски** [bra'zilski]

Colombia **Колумбия** [kɔ'lumbijɑ]
Colombian (masc.) **колумбиец** (m) [kɔlum'biɛʦ]
Colombian (fem.) **колумбийка** (f) [kɔlum'bijka]
Colombian (adj) **колумбийски** [kɔlum'bijski]

Cuba **Куба** ['kuba]
Cuban (masc.) **кубинец** (m) [ku'binɛʦ]
Cuban (fem.) **кубинка** (f) [ku'biŋka]
Cuban (adj) **кубински** [ku'binski]

Chile **Чили** ['ʧili]
Chilean (masc.) **чилиец** (m) [ʧi'liɛʦ]
Chilean (fem.) **чилийка** (f) [ʧi'lijka]
Chilean (adj) **чилийски** [ʧi'lijski]

Bolivia **Боливия** [bɔ'livijɑ]
Venezuela **Венецуела** [vɛnɛʦu'ɛla]
Paraguay **Парагвай** [parag'vaj]
Peru **Перу** [pɛ'ru]
Suriname **Суринам** [suri'nam]
Uruguay **Уругвай** [urug'vaj]
Ecuador **Еквадор** [ɛkva'dɔr]

The Bahamas **Бахамски острови** [ba'hamski 'ɔstrɔvi]
Haiti **Хаити** [ha'iti]
Dominican Republic **Доминиканска република** [dɔmini'kanska rɛ'publika]

Panama **Панама** [pa'nama]
Jamaica **Ямайка** [jɑ'majka]

240. Africa

Egypt	**Египет**	[ɛ'gipɛt]
Egyptian (masc.)	**египтянин** (m)	[ɛ'giptʲanin]
Egyptian (fem.)	**египтянка** (f)	[ɛ'giptʲaŋka]
Egyptian (adj)	**египетски**	[ɛ'gipɛtski]
Morocco	**Мароко**	[ma'rɔkɔ]
Moroccan (masc.)	**мароканец** (m)	[marɔ'kanɛts]
Moroccan (fem.)	**мароканка** (f)	[marɔ'kaŋka]
Moroccan (adj)	**марокански**	[marɔ'kanski]
Tunisia	**Тунис**	['tunis]
Tunisian (masc.)	**тунисец** (m)	[tu'nisɛts]
Tunisian (fem.)	**туниска** (f)	[tu'niska]
Tunisian (adj)	**туниски**	[tu'niski]
Ghana	**Гана**	['gana]
Zanzibar	**Занзибар**	[zanzi'bar]
Kenya	**Кения**	['kɛnijɑ]
Libya	**Либия**	['libijɑ]
Madagascar	**Мадагаскар**	[madagas'kar]
Namibia	**Намибия**	[na'mibijɑ]
Senegal	**Сенегал**	[sɛnɛ'gal]
Tanzania	**Танзания**	[tan'zanijɑ]
South Africa	**Южноафриканска република**	[juʒnɔafri'kanska rɛ'publika]
African (masc.)	**африканец** (m)	[afri'kanɛts]
African (fem.)	**африканка** (f)	[afri'kaŋka]
African (adj)	**африкански**	[afri'kanski]

241. Australia. Oceania

Australia	**Австралия**	[afst'ralijɑ]
Australian (masc.)	**австралиец** (m)	[afstra'liɛts]
Australian (fem.)	**австралийка** (f)	[afstra'lijka]
Australian (adj)	**австралийски**	[afstra'lijski]
New Zealand	**Нова Зеландия**	['nɔva zɛ'landijɑ]
New Zealander (masc.)	**новозеландец** (m)	[nɔvɔzɛ'landɛts]
New Zealander (fem.)	**новозеландка** (f)	[nɔvɔzɛ'lantka]
New Zealand (as adj)	**новозеландски**	[nɔvɔzɛ'lantski]
Tasmania	**Тасмания**	[tas'manijɑ]
French Polynesia	**Френска Полинезия**	['frɛnska pɔli'nɛzijɑ]

242. Cities

Amsterdam	**Амстердам**	[amstɛr'dam]
Ankara	**Анкара**	['aŋkara]
Athens	**Атина**	['atina]
Baghdad	**Багдад**	[bag'dad]
Bangkok	**Банкок**	[ba'ŋkɔk]
Barcelona	**Барселона**	[barsɛ'lɔna]
Beijing	**Пекин**	[pɛ'kin]
Beirut	**Бейрут**	[bɛj'rut]
Berlin	**Берлин**	[bɛr'lin]
Bombay, Mumbai	**Мумбай**	[mum'baj]
Bonn	**Бон**	[bɔn]
Bordeaux	**Бордо**	[bɔr'dɔ]
Bratislava	**Братислава**	[bratis'lava]
Brussels	**Брюксел**	['bryksɛl]
Bucharest	**Букурещ**	['bukurɛʃt]
Budapest	**Будапеща**	[buda'pɛʃta]
Cairo	**Кайро**	['kajrɔ]
Calcutta	**Калкута**	[kal'kuta]
Chicago	**Чикаго**	[ʧi'kagɔ]
Copenhagen	**Копенхаген**	[kɔpɛn'hagɛn]
Dar-es-Salaam	**Дар ес Салам**	[dar ɛs sa'lam]
Delhi	**Делхи**	['dɛlhi]
Dubai	**Дубай**	[du'baj]
Dublin	**Дъблин**	['dɪblin]
Düsseldorf	**Дюселдорф**	['dysɛldɔrf]
Florence	**Флоренция**	[flɔ'rɛnʦija]
Frankfurt	**Франкфурт**	['fraŋkfurt]
Geneva	**Женева**	[ʒɛ'nɛva]
The Hague	**Хага**	['haga]
Hamburg	**Хамбург**	['hamburg]
Hanoi	**Ханой**	[ha'nɔj]
Havana	**Хавана**	[ha'vana]
Helsinki	**Хелзинки**	['hɛlziŋki]
Hiroshima	**Хирошима**	[hirɔ'ʃima]
Hong Kong	**Хонконг**	[hɔ'ŋkɔŋg]
Istanbul	**Истанбул**	[istan'bul]
Jerusalem	**Ерусалим**	['ɛrusalim]
Kiev	**Киев**	['kiɛv]
Kuala Lumpur	**Куала Лумпур**	[ku'ala lum'pur]
Lisbon	**Лисабон**	[lisa'bɔn]
London	**Лондон**	['lɔndɔn]
Los Angeles	**Лос Анджелис**	[lɔs 'anʤɛlis]

Lyons	**Лион**	[li'ɔn]
Madrid	**Мадрид**	[mad'rid]
Marseille	**Марсилия**	[mar'silijɑ]
Mexico City	**Мексико**	['mɛksikɔ]
Miami	**Маями**	[ma'jɑmi]
Montreal	**Монреал**	[mɔnrɛ'al]
Moscow	**Москва**	[mɔsk'va]
Munich	**Мюнхен**	['mynhɛn]
Nairobi	**Найроби**	[naj'rɔbi]
Naples	**Неапол**	[nɛ'apɔl]
New York	**Ню Йорк**	[ny 'jork]
Nice	**Ница**	['nitsa]
Oslo	**Осло**	['ɔslɔ]
Ottawa	**Отава**	[ɔ'tava]
Paris	**Париж**	[pa'riʒ]
Prague	**Прага**	['praga]
Rio de Janeiro	**Рио де Жанейро**	['riɔ dɛ ʒa'nɛjrɔ]
Rome	**Рим**	[rim]
Saint Petersburg	**Санкт Петербург**	[saŋkt 'pɛtɛrburg]
Seoul	**Сеул**	[sɛ'ul]
Shanghai	**Шанхай**	[ʃʌn'haj]
Singapore	**Сингапур**	[siŋga'pur]
Stockholm	**Стокхолм**	[stɔk'hɔlm]
Sydney	**Сидни**	['sidni]
Taipei	**Тайпе**	[taj'pɛ]
Tokyo	**Токио**	['tɔkiɔ]
Toronto	**Торонто**	[tɔ'rɔntɔ]
Venice	**Венеция**	[vɛ'nɛtsijɑ]
Vienna	**Виена**	[vi'ɛna]
Warsaw	**Варшава**	[var'ʃʌva]
Washington	**Вашингтон**	['vaʃiŋktɔn]

243. Politics. Government. Part 1

politics	**политика** (f)	[pɔli'tika]
political (adj)	**политически**	[pɔli'titʃəski]
politician	**политик** (m)	[pɔli'tik]
state (country)	**държава** (f)	[dır'ʒava]
citizen	**гражданин** (m)	['graʒdanin]
citizenship	**гражданство** (n)	['graʒdanstvɔ]
national emblem	**национален герб** (m)	[natsiɔ'nalɛn gɛrp]
national anthem	**държавен химн** (m)	[dır'ʒavɛn himn]
government	**правителство** (n)	[pra'vitɛlstvɔ]

head of state	**държавен глава** (m)	[dır'ʒavɛn gla'va]
parliament	**парламент** (m)	[parla'mɛnt]
party	**партия** (f)	['partijɑ]
capitalism	**капитализъм** (m)	[kapita'lizım]
capitalist (adj)	**капиталистически**	[kapitalis'titʃəski]
socialism	**социализъм** (m)	[sɔtsia'lizım]
socialist (adj)	**социалистически**	[sɔtsialis'titʃəski]
communism	**комунизъм** (m)	[kɔmu'nizım]
communist (adj)	**комунистически**	[kɔmunis'titʃəski]
communist (n)	**комунист** (m)	[kɔmu'nist]
democracy	**демокрация** (f)	[dɛmɔk'ratsijɑ]
democrat	**демократ** (m)	[dɛmɔk'rat]
democratic (adj)	**демократически**	[dɛmɔkra'titʃəski]
Democratic party	**демократическа партия** (f)	[dɛmɔkra'titʃəska 'partijɑ]
liberal (n)	**либерал** (m)	[libɛ'ral]
liberal (adj)	**либерален**	[libɛ'ralɛn]
conservative (n)	**консерватор** (m)	[kɔnsɛr'vatɔr]
conservative (adj)	**консервативен**	[kɔnsɛrva'tivɛn]
republic (n)	**република** (f)	[rɛ'publika]
republican (n)	**републиканец** (m)	[rɛpubli'kanɛts]
Republican party	**републиканска партия** (f)	[rɛpubli'kanska 'partijɑ]
poll, elections	**избори** (pl)	['izbɔri]
to elect (vt)	**избирам**	[iz'biram]
elector, voter	**избирател** (m)	[izbi'ratɛl]
election campaign	**избирателна кампания** (f)	[izbi'ratɛlna kam'panijɑ]
voting (n)	**гласуване** (n)	[gla'suvanɛ]
to vote (vi)	**гласувам**	[gla'suvam]
suffrage, right to vote	**право** (n) **на глас**	['pravɔ na glas]
candidate	**кандидат** (m)	[kandi'dat]
to be a candidate	**балотирам се**	[balɔ'tiram sɛ]
campaign	**кампания** (f)	[kam'panijɑ]
opposition (as adj)	**опозиционен**	[ɔpɔzitsi'ɔnɛn]
opposition (n)	**опозиция** (f)	[ɔpɔ'zitsijɑ]
visit	**визита** (f)	[vi'zita]
official visit	**официална визита** (f)	[ɔfitsi'alna vi'zita]
international (adj)	**международен**	[mɛʒduna'rɔdɛn]
negotiations	**преговори** (pl)	['prɛgɔvɔri]
to negotiate (vi)	**водя преговори**	['vɔdʲa 'prɛgɔvɔri]

244. Politics. Government. Part 2

society	**общество** (n)	[ɔbʃtɛst'vɔ]
constitution	**конституция** (f)	[kɔnsti'tuʦija]
power (political control)	**власт** (f)	[vlast]
corruption	**корупция** (f)	[kɔ'rupʦija]
law (justice)	**закон** (m)	[za'kɔn]
legal (legitimate)	**законен**	[za'kɔnɛn]
justice (fairness)	**справедливост** (f)	[spravɛd'livɔst]
just (fair)	**справедлив**	[spravɛd'liv]
committee	**комитет** (m)	[kɔmi'tɛt]
bill (draft law)	**законопроект** (m)	[zakɔnɔprɔ'ɛkt]
budget	**бюджет** (m)	[by'ʤɛt]
policy	**политика** (f)	[pɔli'tika]
reform	**реформа** (f)	[rɛ'fɔrma]
radical (adj)	**радикален**	[radi'kalɛn]
power (strength, force)	**сила** (f)	['sila]
powerful (adj)	**силен**	['silɛn]
supporter	**привърженик** (m)	[pri'vɪrʒɛnik]
influence	**влияние** (n)	[vli'janiɛ]
regime (e.g., military ~)	**режим** (m)	[rɛ'ʒim]
conflict	**конфликт** (m)	[kɔnf'likt]
conspiracy (plot)	**заговор** (m)	['zagɔvɔr]
provocation	**провокация** (f)	[prɔvɔ'kaʦija]
to overthrow (regime, etc.)	**сваля**	[sva'ʎa]
overthrow (of government)	**сваляне** (n)	['svaʎanɛ]
revolution	**революция** (f)	[rɛvɔ'lyʦija]
coup d'état	**преврат** (m)	[prɛv'rat]
military coup	**военен преврат** (m)	[vɔ'ɛnɛn prɛv'rat]
crisis	**криза** (f)	['kriza]
economic recession	**икономически спад** (m)	[ikɔnɔ'miʧəski spat]
demonstrator (protester)	**демонстрант** (m)	[dɛmɔnst'rant]
demonstration	**демонстрация** (f)	[dɛmɔnst'raʦija]
martial law	**военно положение** (n)	[vɔ'ɛŋɔ pɔlɔ'ʒɛniɛ]
military base	**база** (f)	['baza]
stability	**стабилност** (f)	[sta'bilnɔst]
stable (adj)	**стабилен**	[sta'bilɛn]
exploitation	**експлоатация** (f)	[ɛksplɔa'taʦija]
to exploit (workers)	**експлоатирам**	[ɛksplɔa'tiram]
racism	**расизъм** (m)	[ra'sizɪm]
racist	**расист** (m)	[ra'sist]

fascism	**фашизъм** (m)	[fa'ʃizɪm]
fascist	**фашист** (m)	[fa'ʃist]

245. Countries. Miscellaneous

foreigner	**чужденец** (m)	[ʧuʒdɛ'nɛʦ]
foreign (adj)	**чуждестранен**	[ʧuʒdɛst'ranɛn]
abroad (adv)	**в чужбина**	[v ʧuʒ'bina]
emigrant	**емигрант** (m)	[ɛmig'rant]
emigration	**емиграция** (f)	[ɛmig'raʦija]
to emigrate (vi)	**емигрирам**	[ɛmig'riram]
the West	**Запад**	['zapad]
the East	**Изток**	['istɔk]
the Far East	**Далечният Изток**	[da'lɛʧnijat 'istɔk]
civilization	**цивилизация** (f)	[ʦivili'zaʦija]
humanity (mankind)	**човечество** (n)	[ʧɔ'vɛʧəstvɔ]
world (earth)	**свят** (m)	[svʲat]
peace	**мир** (m)	[mir]
worldwide (adj)	**световен**	[svɛ'tɔvɛn]
homeland	**родина** (f)	[rɔ'dina]
people (population)	**народ** (m)	[na'rɔd]
population	**население** (n)	[nasɛ'lɛniɛ]
people (a lot of ~)	**хора** (pl)	['hɔra]
nation (people)	**нация** (f)	['naʦija]
generation	**поколение** (n)	[pɔkɔ'lɛniɛ]
territory (area)	**територия** (f)	[tɛri'tɔrija]
region	**регион** (m)	[rɛgi'ɔn]
state (part of a country)	**щат** (m)	[ʃtat]
tradition	**традиция** (f)	[tra'diʦija]
custom (tradition)	**обичай** (m)	[ɔbi'ʧaj]
ecology	**екология** (f)	[ɛkɔ'lɔgija]
Indian (Native American)	**индианец** (m)	[indi'anɛʦ]
Gipsy (masc.)	**циганин** (m)	['ʦiganin]
Gipsy (fem.)	**циганка** (f)	['ʦigaŋka]
Gipsy (adj)	**цигански**	['ʦiganski]
empire	**империя** (f)	[im'pɛrija]
colony	**колония** (f)	[kɔ'lɔnija]
slavery	**робство** (n)	['rɔpstvɔ]
invasion	**нашествие** (n)	[na'ʃɛstviɛ]
famine	**глад** (m)	[glad]

246. Major religious groups. Confessions

religion	**религия** (f)	[rɛ'ligija]
religious (adj)	**религиозен**	[rɛligi'ɔzɛn]
faith, belief	**вяра** (f)	['vʲara]
to believe (in God)	**вярвам**	['vʲarvam]
believer	**вярващ** (m)	['vʲarvaʃt]
atheism	**атеизъм** (m)	[atɛ'izɪm]
atheist	**атеист** (m)	[atɛ'ist]
Christianity	**християнство** (n)	[hristi'janstvɔ]
Christian (n)	**християнин** (m)	[hristi'janin]
Christian (adj)	**християнски**	[hristi'janski]
Catholicism	**Католицизъм** (m)	[katɔli'ʦizɪm]
Catholic (n)	**католик** (m)	[katɔ'lik]
Catholic (adj)	**католически**	[katɔ'litʃəski]
Protestantism	**протестантство** (n)	[prɔtɛs'tanʦtvɔ]
Protestant Church	**протестантска църква** (f)	[prɔtɛs'tanʦka 'ʦɪrkva]
Protestant	**протестант** (m)	[prɔtɛs'tant]
Orthodoxy	**Православие** (n)	[pravɔs'laviɛ]
Orthodox Church	**Православна църква** (f)	[pravɔs'lavna 'ʦɪrkva]
Orthodox	**православен**	[pravɔs'lavɛn]
Presbyterianism	**Презвитерианство** (n)	[prɛzvitɛri'anstvɔ]
Presbyterian Church	**Презвитерианска църква** (f)	[prɛzvitɛri'anska 'ʦɪrkva]
Presbyterian (n)	**презвитерианец** (m)	[prɛzvitɛri'anɛʦ]
Lutheranism	**Лютеранска църква** (f)	[lytɛ'ranska 'ʦɪrkva]
Lutheran (n)	**лютеран** (m)	[lytɛ'ran]
Baptist Church	**Баптизъм** (m)	[bap'tizɪm]
Baptist (n)	**баптист** (m)	[bap'tist]
Anglican Church	**Англиканска църква** (f)	[aŋgli'kanska 'ʦɪrkva]
Anglican (n)	**англиканец** (m)	[aŋgli'kaneʦ]
Mormonism	**мормонство** (n)	[mɔr'mɔnstvɔ]
Mormon (n)	**мормон** (m)	[mɔr'mɔn]
Judaism	**Юдаизъм** (m)	[juda'izɪm]
Jew (n)	**юдей** (m)	[ju'dɛj]
Buddhism	**Будизъм** (m)	[bu'dizɪm]
Buddhist (n)	**будист** (m)	[bu'dist]
Hinduism	**Индуизъм** (m)	[indu'izɪm]

Hindu (n)	**индус** (m)	[in'dus]
Islam	**Ислям** (m)	[is'ʎam]
Muslim (n)	**мюсюлманин** (m)	[mysyl'manin]
Muslim (adj)	**мюсюлмански**	[mysyl'manski]
Shiah Islam	**шиизъм** (m)	[ʃi'izɪm]
Shiite (n)	**шиит** (m)	[ʃi'it]
Sunni Islam	**сунизъм** (m)	[su'nizɪm]
Sunnite (n)	**сунит** (m)	[su'nit]

247. Religions. Priests

priest	**свещеник** (m)	[svɛʃ'tɛnik]
the Pope	**Папа Римски** (m)	['papa 'rimski]
monk, friar	**монах** (m)	[mɔ'nah]
nun	**монахиня** (f)	[mɔna'hiɲa]
pastor	**пастор** (m)	['pastɔr]
abbot	**абат** (m)	[a'bat]
vicar (parish priest)	**викарий** (m)	[vi'karij]
bishop	**епископ** (m)	[ɛpis'kɔp]
cardinal	**кардинал** (m)	[kardi'nal]
preacher	**проповедник** (m)	[prɔpɔ'vɛdnik]
preaching	**проповед** (m)	['prɔpɔvɛd]
parishioners	**енориаши** (pl)	[ɛnɔri'aʃi]
believer	**вярващ** (m)	['vʲarvaʃt]
atheist	**атеист** (m)	[atɛ'ist]

248. Faith. Christianity. Islam

Adam	**Адам**	[a'dam]
Eve	**Ева**	['ɛva]
God	**Бог**	[bɔg]
the Lord	**Господ**	['gɔspɔd]
the Almighty	**Всемогъщ**	[vsɛmɔ'gɪʃt]
sin	**грях** (m)	[grʲah]
to sin (vi)	**греша**	[grɛ'ʃʌ]
sinner (masc.)	**грешник** (m)	['grɛʃnik]
sinner (fem.)	**грешница** (f)	['grɛʃnitsa]
hell	**ад** (m)	[ad]
paradise	**рай** (m)	[raj]
Jesus	**Исус**	[i'sus]

Jesus Christ	**Исус Христос**	[i'sus hris'tɔs]
the Holy Spirit	**Светия Дух**	[svɛ'tija duh]
the Savior	**Спасител**	[spa'sitɛl]
the Virgin Mary	**Богородица**	[bɔgɔ'rɔditsa]
the Devil	**Дявол**	['dʲavɔl]
devil's (adj)	**дяволски**	['dʲavɔlski]
Satan	**Сатана**	[sata'na]
satanic (adj)	**сатанински**	[sata'ninski]
angel	**ангел** (m)	['aŋgɛl]
guardian angel	**ангел-пазител** (m)	['aŋgɛl pa'zitɛl]
angelic (adj)	**ангелски**	['aŋgɛlski]
apostle	**апостол** (m)	[a'pɔstɔl]
archangel	**архангел** (m)	[ar'haŋgɛl]
the Antichrist	**антихрист** (m)	[an'tihrist]
Church	**Църква** (f)	['tsɪrkva]
Bible	**библия** (f)	['biblija]
biblical (adj)	**библейски**	[bib'lɛjski]
Old Testament	**Стария Завет** (m)	['starija za'vɛt]
New Testament	**Новия Завет** (m)	['nɔvija za'vɛt]
Gospel	**Евангелие** (n)	[ɛ'vaŋgɛliɛ]
Holy Scripture	**Свещено Писание** (n)	[svɛʃ'tɛnɔ pi'saniɛ]
heaven	**Небе** (n)	[nɛ'bɛ]
Commandment	**заповед** (f)	['zapɔvɛd]
prophet	**пророк** (m)	[prɔ'rɔk]
prophecy	**пророчество** (n)	[prɔ'rɔtʃəstvɔ]
Allah	**Алах**	[a'lah]
Mohammed	**Мохамед**	[mɔha'mɛd]
the Koran	**Коран**	[kɔ'ran]
mosque	**джамия** (f)	[dʒa'mija]
mullah	**молла** (m)	[mɔl'la]
prayer	**молитва** (f)	[mɔ'litva]
to pray (vi, vt)	**моля се**	['mɔʎa sɛ]
pilgrimage	**поклонничество** (n)	[pɔk'lɔŋitʃəstvɔ]
pilgrim	**поклонник** (m)	[pɔk'lɔŋik]
Mecca	**Мека**	['mɛka]
church	**църква** (f)	['tsɪrkva]
temple	**храм** (m)	[hram]
cathedral	**катедрала** (f)	[katɛd'rala]
Gothic (adj)	**готически**	[gɔ'titʃəski]
synagogue	**синагога** (f)	[sina'gɔga]
mosque	**джамия** (f)	[dʒa'mija]
chapel	**параклис** (m)	[pa'raklis]

abbey	**абатство** (n)	[a'baʦtvɔ]
convent	**манастир** (m)	[manas'tir]
monastery	**манастир** (m)	[manas'tir]
bell (in church)	**камбана** (f)	[kam'bana]
bell tower	**камбанария** (f)	[kambana'rijɑ]
to ring (ab. bells)	**бия**	['bijɑ]
cross	**кръст** (m)	[krɪst]
cupola (roof)	**купол** (m)	['kupɔl]
icon	**икона** (f)	[i'kɔna]
soul	**душа** (f)	[du'ʃʌ]
fate (destiny)	**съдба** (f)	[sɪd'ba]
evil (n)	**зло** (n)	[zlɔ]
good (n)	**добро** (n)	[dɔb'rɔ]
vampire	**вампир** (m)	[vam'pir]
witch (sorceress)	**вещица** (f)	['vɛʃtiʦa]
demon	**демон** (m)	['dɛmɔn]
devil	**дявол** (m)	['dʲavɔl]
spirit	**дух** (m)	[duh]
redemption (giving us ~)	**изкупление** (n)	[iskup'lɛniɛ]
to redeem (vt)	**изкупя**	[is'kupʲa]
church service, mass	**служба** (f)	['sluʒba]
to say mass	**служа**	['sluʒa]
confession	**изповед** (f)	['ispɔvɛd]
to confess (vi)	**изповядвам се**	[ispɔ'vʲadvam sɛ]
saint (n)	**светец** (m)	[svɛ'tɛʦ]
sacred (holy)	**свещен**	[svɛʃ'tɛn]
holy water	**света вода** (f)	[svɛ'ta vɔ'da]
ritual (n)	**ритуал** (m)	[ritu'al]
ritual (adj)	**ритуален**	[ritu'alɛn]
sacrifice	**жертвоприношение** (n)	[ʒɛrtvɔprinɔ'ʃɛniɛ]
superstition	**суеверие** (n)	[suɛ'vɛriɛ]
superstitious (adj)	**суеверен**	[suɛ'vɛrɛn]
afterlife	**задгробен живот** (m)	[zadg'rɔbɛn ʒi'vɔt]
eternal life	**вечен живот** (m)	['vɛʧən ʒi'vɔt]

MISCELLANEOUS

249. Various useful words

background (green ~)	**фон** (m)	[fɔn]
balance (of situation)	**баланс** (m)	[ba'lans]
barrier (obstacle)	**преграда** (f)	[prɛg'rada]
base (basis)	**база** (f)	['baza]
beginning	**начало** (n)	[na'ʧalɔ]
category	**категория** (f)	[katɛ'gɔrija]
cause (reason)	**причина** (f)	[pri'ʧina]
choice	**избор** (m)	['izbɔr]
coincidence	**съвпадение** (n)	[sɪfpa'dɛniɛ]
comfortable (~ chair)	**удобен**	[u'dɔbɛn]
comparison	**сравнение** (n)	[srav'nɛniɛ]
compensation	**компенсация** (f)	[kɔmpɛn'saʦija]
degree (extent, amount)	**степен** (f)	['stɛpɛn]
development	**развитие** (n)	[raz'vitiɛ]
difference	**различие** (n)	[raz'liʧiɛ]
effect (e.g., of drugs)	**ефект** (m)	[ɛ'fɛkt]
effort (exertion)	**усилие** (n)	[u'siliɛ]
element	**елемент** (m)	[ɛlɛ'mɛnt]
end (finish)	**край** (m)	[kraj]
example (illustration)	**пример** (m)	['primɛr]
fact	**факт** (m)	[fakt]
frequent (adj)	**чест**	[ʧəst]
growth (development)	**ръст** (m)	[rɪst]
help	**помощ** (f)	['pɔmɔʃt]
ideal	**идеал** (m)	[idɛ'al]
kind (sort, type)	**вид** (m)	[vid]
labyrinth	**лабиринт** (m)	[labi'rint]
mistake, error	**грешка** (f)	['grɛʃka]
moment	**момент** (m)	[mɔ'mɛnt]
object (thing)	**обект** (m)	[ɔ'bɛkt]
obstacle	**пречка** (f)	['prɛʧka]
original (original copy)	**оригинал** (m)	[ɔrigi'nal]
part (~ of sth)	**част** (f)	[ʧast]
particle, small part	**частица** (f)	[ʧas'tiʦa]
pause (break)	**пауза** (f)	['pauza]

position	**позиция** (f)	[pɔ'zitsija]
principle	**принцип** (m)	['printsip]
problem	**проблем** (m)	[prɔb'lɛm]
process	**процес** (m)	[prɔ'tsəs]
progress	**прогрес** (m)	[prɔg'rɛs]
property (quality)	**свойство** (n)	['svɔjstvɔ]
reaction	**реакция** (f)	[rɛ'aktsija]
risk	**риск** (m)	[risk]
secret	**тайна** (f)	['tajna]
section (sector)	**секция** (f)	['sɛktsija]
series	**серия** (f)	['sɛrija]
shape (outer form)	**форма** (f)	['fɔrma]
situation	**ситуация** (f)	[situ'atsija]
solution	**решение** (n)	[rɛ'ʃɛniɛ]
standard (adj)	**стандартен**	[stan'dartɛn]
standard (level of quality)	**стандарт** (m)	[stan'dart]
stop (pause)	**почивка** (f)	[pɔ'tʃifka]
style	**стил** (m)	[stil]
system	**система** (f)	[sis'tɛma]
table (chart)	**таблица** (f)	['tablitsa]
tempo, rate	**темпо** (n)	['tɛmpɔ]
term (word, expression)	**термин** (m)	['tɛrmin]
thing (object, item)	**вещ** (f)	[vɛʃt]
truth	**истина** (f)	['istina]
turn (please wait your ~)	**ред** (m)	[rɛd]
type (sort, kind)	**тип** (m)	[tip]
urgent (adj)	**срочен**	['srɔtʃən]
urgently (adv)	**срочно**	['srɔtʃnɔ]
utility (usefulness)	**полза** (f)	['pɔlza]
variant (alternative)	**вариант** (m)	[vari'ant]
way (means, method)	**начин** (m)	['natʃin]
zone	**зона** (f)	['zɔna]

250. Modifiers. Adjectives. Part 1

additional (adj)	**допълнителен**	[dɔpɪl'nitɛlɛn]
ancient (~ civilization)	**древен**	['drɛvɛn]
artificial (adj)	**изкуствен**	[is'kustvɛn]
back, rear (adj)	**заден**	['zadɛn]
bad (adj)	**лош**	[lɔʃ]
beautiful (~ palace)	**прекрасен**	[prɛk'rasɛn]
beautiful (person)	**хубав**	['hubav]
big (in size)	**голям**	[gɔ'ʎam]

bitter (taste)	**горчив**	[gɔr'ʧiv]
blind (sightless)	**сляп**	[sʎap]
calm, quiet (adj)	**спокоен**	[spɔ'kɔɛn]
careless (negligent)	**немарлив**	[nɛmar'liv]
caring (~ father)	**грижлив**	[griʒ'liv]
central (adj)	**централен**	[ʦənt'ralɛn]
cheap (adj)	**евтин**	['ɛftin]
cheerful (adj)	**весел**	['vɛsɛl]
children's (adj)	**детски**	['dɛʦki]
civil (~ law)	**граждански**	['graʒdanski]
clandestine (secret)	**нелегален**	[nɛlɛ'galɛn]
clean (free from dirt)	**чист**	[ʧist]
clear (explanation, etc.)	**понятен**	[pɔ'ɲatɛn]
clever (smart)	**умен**	['umɛn]
close (near in space)	**близък**	['blizɪk]
closed (adj)	**затворен**	[zat'vɔrɛn]
cloudless (sky)	**безоблачен**	[bɛ'zɔblaʧən]
cold (drink, weather)	**студен**	[stu'dɛn]
compatible (adj)	**съвместим**	[sɪvmɛs'tim]
contented (adj)	**доволен**	[dɔ'vɔlɛn]
continuous (adj)	**продължителен**	[prɔdɪ'ʒitɛlɛn]
continuous (incessant)	**непрекъснат**	[nɛprɛ'kɪsnat]
convenient (adj)	**пригоден**	[pri'gɔdɛn]
cool (weather)	**прохладен**	[prɔh'ladɛn]
dangerous (adj)	**опасен**	[ɔ'pasɛn]
dark (room)	**тъмен**	['tɪmɛn]
dead (not alive)	**мъртъв**	['mɪrtɪv]
dense (fog, smoke)	**гъст**	[gɪst]
difficult (decision)	**труден**	['trudɛn]
difficult (problem, task)	**сложен**	['slɔʒɛn]
dim, faint (light)	**блед**	[blɛd]
dirty (not clean)	**мръсен**	['mrɪsɛn]
distant (faraway)	**далечен**	[da'lɛʧən]
distant (in space)	**далечен**	[da'lɛʧən]
dry (clothes, etc.)	**сух**	[suh]
easy (not difficult)	**лесен**	['lɛsɛn]
empty (glass, room)	**празен**	['prazɛn]
exact (amount)	**точен**	['tɔʧən]
excellent (adj)	**отличен**	[ɔt'liʧən]
excessive (adj)	**прекален**	[prɛka'lɛn]
expensive (adj)	**скъп**	[skɪp]
exterior (adj)	**външен**	['vɪnʃɛn]
fast (quick)	**бърз**	[bɪrz]

fatty (food)	**мазен**	['mazɛn]
fertile (land, soil)	**плодороден**	[plɔdɔ'rɔdɛn]
flat (~ panel display)	**плосък**	['plɔsɪk]
even (e.g., ~ surface)	**равен**	['ravɛn]
foreign (adj)	**чуждестранен**	[ʧuʒdɛst'ranɛn]
fragile (china, glass)	**крехък**	['krɛhɪk]
free (at no cost)	**безплатен**	[bɛsp'latɛn]
free (unrestricted)	**свободен**	[svɔ'bɔdɛn]
fresh (~ water)	**сладък**	['sladɪk]
fresh (e.g., ~ bread)	**пресен**	['prɛsɛn]
frozen (food)	**замразен**	[zamra'zɛn]
full (completely filled)	**пълен**	['pɪlɛn]
good (book, etc.)	**добър**	[dɔ'bɪr]
good (kindhearted)	**добър**	[dɔ'bɪr]
grateful (adj)	**благодарен**	[blagɔ'darɛn]
happy (adj)	**щастлив**	[ʃtast'liv]
hard (not soft)	**твърд**	[tvɪrd]
heavy (in weight)	**тежък**	['tɛʒɪk]
hostile (adj)	**враждебен**	[vraʒ'dɛbɛn]
hot (adj)	**горещ**	[gɔ'rɛʃt]
huge (adj)	**огромен**	[ɔg'rɔmɛn]
humid (adj)	**влажен**	['vlaʒɛn]
hungry (adj)	**гладен**	['gladɛn]
ill (sick, unwell)	**болен**	['bɔlɛn]
immobile (adj)	**неподвижен**	[nɛpɔd'viʒɛn]
important (adj)	**важен**	['vaʒɛn]
impossible (adj)	**невъзможен**	[nɛvɪz'mɔʒɛn]
incomprehensible	**непонятен**	[nɛpɔ'ɲatɛn]
indispensable (adj)	**необходим**	[nɛɔbhɔ'dim]
inexperienced (adj)	**неопитен**	[nɛ'ɔpitɛn]
insignificant (adj)	**незначителен**	[nɛzna'ʧitɛlɛn]
interior (adj)	**вътрешен**	['vɪtrɛʃɛn]
joint (~ decision)	**съвместен**	[sɪv'mɛstɛn]
last (e.g., ~ week)	**минал**	['minal]
last (final)	**последен**	[pɔs'lɛdɛn]
left (e.g., ~ side)	**ляв**	[ʎav]
legal (legitimate)	**законен**	[za'kɔnɛn]
light (in weight)	**лек**	[lɛk]
light (pale color)	**светъл**	['svɛtɪl]
limited (adj)	**ограничен**	[ɔgrani'ʧən]
liquid (fluid)	**течен**	['tɛʧən]
long (e.g., ~ way)	**дълъг**	['dɪlɪg]
loud (voice, etc.)	**силен**	['silɛn]
low (voice)	**тих**	[tih]

251. Modifiers. Adjectives. Part 2

main (principal)	**главен**	['glavɛn]
matt (paint)	**матов**	['matɔv]
meticulous (job)	**акуратен**	[aku'ratɛn]
mysterious (adj)	**загадъчен**	[za'gadɪʧən]
narrow (street, etc.)	**тесен**	['tɛsɛn]
native (of country)	**роден**	['rɔdɛn]
nearby (adj)	**ближен**	['bliʒɛn]
near-sighted (adj)	**късоглед**	[kɪsɔg'lɛd]
necessary (adj)	**нужен**	['nuʒɛn]
negative (~ response)	**отрицателен**	[ɔtri'ʦatɛlɛn]
neighboring (adj)	**съседен**	[sɪ'sɛdɛn]
nervous (adj)	**нервен**	['nɛrvɛn]
new (adj)	**нов**	[nɔv]
next (e.g., ~ week)	**следващ**	['slɛdvaʃt]
nice (kind)	**мил**	[mil]
nice (voice)	**приятен**	[pri'jatɛn]
normal (adj)	**нормален**	[nɔr'malɛn]
not big (adj)	**неголям**	[nɛgɔ'ʎam]
unclear (adj)	**неясен**	[nɛ'jasɛn]
not difficult (adj)	**лесен**	['lɛsɛn]
obligatory (adj)	**обезателен**	[ɔbɛ'zatɛlɛn]
old (house)	**стар**	[star]
open (adj)	**отворен**	[ɔt'vɔrɛn]
opposite (adj)	**противоположен**	[prɔtivɔpɔ'lɔʒɛn]
ordinary (usual)	**обикновен**	[ɔbiknɔ'vɛn]
original (unusual)	**оригинален**	[ɔrigi'nalɛn]
past (recent)	**минал**	['minal]
permanent (adj)	**постоянен**	[pɔstɔ'janɛn]
personal (adj)	**частен**	['ʧastɛn]
polite (adj)	**вежлив**	[vɛʒ'liv]
poor (not rich)	**беден**	['bɛdɛn]
possible (adj)	**възможен**	[vɪz'mɔʒɛn]
destitute (extremely poor)	**беден**	['bɛdɛn]
present (current)	**настоящ**	[nastɔ'jaʃt]
principal (main)	**основен**	[ɔs'nɔvɛn]
private (~ jet)	**частен**	['ʧastɛn]
probable (adj)	**вероятен**	[vɛrɔ'jatɛn]
public (open to all)	**обществен**	[ɔbʃ'tɛstvɛn]
punctual (person)	**пунктуален**	[puŋktu'alɛn]
quiet (tranquil)	**тих**	[tih]
rare (adj)	**рядък**	['rʲadɪk]

raw (uncooked)	**суров**	[su'rɔf]
right (not left)	**десен**	['dɛsɛn]
right, correct (adj)	**правилен**	['pravilɛn]
ripe (fruit)	**зрял**	[zrʲal]
risky (adj)	**рискован**	[ris'kɔvan]
sad (~ look)	**печален**	[pɛ'ʧalɛn]
sad (depressing)	**тъжен**	['tɪʒɛn]
safe (not dangerous)	**безопасен**	[bɛzɔ'pasɛn]
salty (food)	**солен**	[sɔ'lɛn]
satisfied (customer)	**удовлетворен**	[udɔvlɛtvɔ'rɛn]
second hand (adj)	**употребяван**	[upɔtrɛ'bʲavan]
shallow (water)	**плитък**	['plitɪk]
sharp (blade, etc.)	**остър**	['ɔstɪr]
short (in length)	**къс**	[kɪs]
short, short-lived (adj)	**краткотраен**	[kratkɔt'raɛn]
significant (notable)	**значителен**	[zna'ʧitɛlɛn]
similar (adj)	**приличащ**	[pri'liʧaʃt]
simple (easy)	**лесен**	['lɛsɛn]
skinny	**кльощав**	['klʒʃtaf]
thin (person)	**слаб**	[slap]
small (in size)	**малък**	['malɪk]
smooth (surface)	**гладък**	['gladɪk]
soft (to touch)	**мек**	[mɛk]
solid (~ wall)	**стабилен**	[sta'bilɛn]
somber, gloomy (adj)	**мрачен**	['mraʧən]
sour (flavor, taste)	**кисел**	['kisel]
spacious (house, etc.)	**просторен**	[prɔs'tɔrɛn]
special (adj)	**специален**	[spɛʦi'alɛn]
straight (line, road)	**прав**	[prav]
strong (person)	**силен**	['silɛn]
stupid (foolish)	**глупав**	['glupav]
sunny (day)	**слънчев**	['slɪnʧəv]
superb, perfect (adj)	**превъзходен**	[prɛvɪs'hɔdɛn]
swarthy (adj)	**мургав**	['murgav]
sweet (sugary)	**сладък**	['sladɪk]
tan (adj)	**почернял**	[pɔʧər'ɲal]
tasty (adj)	**вкусен**	['vkusɛn]
tender (affectionate)	**нежен**	['nɛʒɛn]
the highest (adj)	**висш**	[visʃ]
the most important	**най-важен**	[naj 'vaʒɛn]
the nearest	**най-близък**	[naj 'blizɪk]
the same, equal (adj)	**еднакъв**	[ɛd'nakɪv]
thick (e.g., ~ fog)	**гъст**	[gɪst]

thick (wall, slice)	**дебел**	[dɛ'bɛl]
tight (~ shoes)	**тесен**	['tɛsɛn]
tired (exhausted)	**изморен**	[izmɔ'rɛn]
tiring (adj)	**изморителен**	[izmɔ'ritɛlɛn]
transparent (adj)	**бистър**	['bistır]
unique (exceptional)	**уникален**	[uni'kalɛn]
warm (moderately hot)	**топъл**	['tɔpıl]
wet (e.g., ~ clothes)	**мокър**	['mɔkır]
whole (entire, complete)	**цял**	[ʦʲal]
wide (e.g., ~ road)	**широк**	[ʃi'rɔk]
young (adj)	**млад**	[mlad]

MAIN 500 VERBS

252. Verbs A-C

to accompany (vt)	**придружавам**	[pridru'ʒavam]
to accuse (vt)	**обвинявам**	[ɔbvi'ɲavam]
to acknowledge (admit)	**признавам**	[priz'navam]
to act (take action)	**действам**	['dɛjstvam]
to add (supplement)	**добавям**	[dɔ'bavʲam]
to address (speak to)	**обръщам се**	[ɔb'rɪʃtam sɛ]
to admire (vi)	**възхищавам се**	[vɪshiʃ'tavam sɛ]
to advertise (vt)	**рекламирам**	[rɛkla'miram]
to advise (vt)	**съветвам**	[sɪ'vɛtvam]
to affirm (insist)	**утвърждавам**	[utvɪrʒ'davam]
to agree (say yes)	**съгласявам се**	[sɪgla'sʲavam sɛ]
to allow (sb to do sth)	**позволявам**	[pɔzvɔ'ʎavam]
to allude (vi)	**намеквам**	[na'mɛkvam]
to amputate (vt)	**ампутирам**	[ampu'tiram]
to answer (vi, vt)	**отговарям**	[ɔtgɔ'varʲam]
to apologize (vi)	**извинявам се**	[izvi'ɲavam sɛ]
to appear (come into view)	**появявам се**	[pɔja'vʲavam sɛ]
to applaud (vi, vt)	**аплодирам**	[aplɔ'diram]
to appoint (assign)	**назначавам**	[nazna'ʧavam]
to approach (come closer)	**доближавам (се)**	[dɔbli'ʒavam sɛ]
to arrive (ab. train)	**пристигам**	[pris'tigam]
to ask (~ sb to do sth)	**моля**	['mɔʎa]
to aspire to …	**стремя се**	[strɛ'mʲa sɛ]
to assist (help)	**асистирам**	[asis'tiram]
to attack (mil.)	**атакувам**	[ata'kuvam]
to attain (objectives)	**достигам**	[dɔs'tigam]
to revenge (vt)	**отмъщавам**	[ɔtmɪʃ'tavam]
to avoid (danger, task)	**избягвам**	[iz'bʲagvam]
to award (give medal to)	**наградя**	[nagra'dʲa]
to battle (vi)	**сражавам се**	[sra'ʒavam sɛ]
to be (~ on the table)	**лежа**	[lɛ'ʒa]
to be (vi)	**съм, бъда**	[sɪm], ['bɪda]
to be afraid	**страхувам се**	[stra'huvam sɛ]
to be angry (with …)	**сърдя се на …**	['sɪrdʲa sɛ na]

to be at war	**воювам**	[vɔ'juvam]
to be based (on ...)	**базирам се (на ...)**	[ba'ziram sɛ na]
to be bored	**скучая**	[sku'ʧajɑ]
to be convinced	**убеждавам се**	[ubɛʒ'davam sɛ]
to be enough	**стигам**	['stigam]
to be envious	**завиждам**	[za'viʒdam]
to be indignant	**възмущавам се**	[vɪzmuʃ'tavam sɛ]
to be interested in ...	**интересувам се**	[intɛrɛ'suvam sɛ]
to be lying down	**лежа**	[lɛ'ʒa]
to be needed	**трябвам**	['trʲabvam]
to be perplexed	**недоумявам**	[nɛdɔu'mʲavam]
to be preserved	**запазвам се**	[za'pazvam sɛ]
to be required	**трябвам**	['trʲabvam]
to be surprised	**учудвам се**	[u'ʧudvam sɛ]
to be worried	**безпокоя се**	[bɛspɔkɔ'jɑ sɛ]
to beat (dog, person)	**бия**	['bijɑ]
to become (e.g., ~ old)	**ставам**	['stavam]
to become pensive	**замисля се**	[za'misʎa sɛ]
to behave (vi)	**държа се**	[dɪr'ʒa sɛ]
to believe (think)	**вярвам**	['vʲarvam]
to belong to ...	**принадлежа**	[prinadlɛ'ʒa]
to berth (moor)	**акостирам**	[akɔs'tiram]
to blind (other drivers)	**ослепявам**	[ɔslɛ'pʲavam]
to blow (wind)	**надувам**	[na'duvam]
to blush (vi)	**изчервявам се**	[isʧər'vʲavam sɛ]
to boast (vi)	**хваля се**	['hvaʎa sɛ]
to borrow (money)	**взимам на заем**	['vzimam na 'zaɛm]
to break (branch, toy, etc.)	**чупя**	['ʧupʲa]
to breathe (vi)	**дишам**	['diʃʌm]
to bring (sth)	**докарвам**	[dɔ'karvam]
to burn (paper, logs)	**изгарям**	[iz'garʲam]
to buy (purchase)	**купувам**	[ku'puvam]
to call (for help)	**викам**	['vikam]
to call (with one's voice)	**повикам**	[pɔ'vikam]
to calm down (vt)	**успокоявам**	[uspɔkɔ'jɑvam]
can (v aux)	**мога**	['mɔga]
to cancel (call off)	**отменям**	[ɔt'mɛɲam]
to cast off	**отплувам**	[ɔtp'luvam]
to catch (e.g., ~ a ball)	**ловя**	[lɔ'vʲa]
to catch sight (of ...)	**видя**	['vidʲa]
to cause ...	**да бъда причина**	[da 'bɪda pri'ʧina]
to change (~ one's opinion)	**сменям**	['smɛɲam]
to change (exchange)	**сменям**	['smɛɲam]
to charm (vt)	**очаровам**	[ɔʧa'rɔvam]

to choose (select)	**избирам**	[iz'biram]
to chop off (with an ax)	**отсека**	[ɔtsɛ'ka]
to clean (from dirt)	**обелвам**	[ɔ'bɛlvam]
to clean (shoes, etc.)	**пречиствам**	[pɔ'ʧistvam]
to clean (tidy)	**подреждам**	[pɔd'rɛʒdam]
to close (vt)	**затварям**	[zat'varʲam]
to comb one's hair	**сресвам се**	['srɛsvam sɛ]
to come down (the stairs)	**слизам**	['slizam]
to come in (enter)	**влизам**	['vlizam]
to come out (book)	**излизам**	[iz'lizam]
to compare (vt)	**сравнявам**	[srav'ɲavam]
to compensate (vt)	**компенсирам**	[kɔmpɛn'siram]
to compete (vi)	**конкурирам**	[kɔŋku'riram]
to compile (~ a list)	**съставям**	[sɪs'tavʲam]
to complain (vi, vt)	**оплаквам се**	[ɔp'lakvam sɛ]
to complicate (vt)	**усложнявам**	[uslɔʒ'ɲavam]
to compose (music, etc.)	**съчинявам**	[sɪʧi'ɲavam]
to compromise (reputation)	**компрометирам**	[kɔmprɔmɛ'tiram]
to concentrate (vi)	**концентрирам се**	[kɔntsənt'riram sɛ]
to confess (criminal)	**признавам се**	[priz'navam sɛ]
to confuse (mix up)	**объркввам**	[ɔ'bɪrkvam]
to congratulate (vt)	**поздравявам**	[pɔzdra'vʲavam]
to consult (doctor, expert)	**консултирам се с ...**	[kɔnsul'tiram sɛ s]
to continue (~ to do sth)	**продължавам**	[prɔdɪ'ʒavam]
to control (vt)	**контролирам**	[kɔntrɔ'liram]
to convince (vt)	**убеждавам**	[ubɛʒ'davam]
to cooperate (vi)	**сътруднича**	[sɪt'rudniʧa]
to coordinate (vt)	**координирам**	[kɔ:rdi'niram]
to correct (an error)	**поправям**	[pɔp'ravʲam]
to cost (vt)	**струвам**	['struvam]
to count (money, etc.)	**броя**	[brɔ'jɑ]
to count on ...	**разчитам на ...**	[ras'ʧitam na]
to crack (ceiling, wall)	**напуквам се**	[na'pukvam sɛ]
to create (vt)	**създам**	[sɪz'dam]
to cry (weep)	**плача**	['plaʧa]
to cut off (with a knife)	**отрязвам**	[ɔt'rʲazvam]

253. Verbs D-G

to dare (~ to do sth)	**осмелявам се**	[ɔsmɛ'ʎavam sɛ]
to date from ...	**датирам се**	[da'tiram sɛ]
to deceive (vi, vt)	**лъжа**	['lɪʒa]

to decide (~ to do sth)	**решавам**	[rɛ'ʃʌvam]
to decorate (tree, street)	**украсявам**	[ukra'sʲavam]
to dedicate (book, etc.)	**посвещавам**	[pɔsvɛʃ'tavam]
to defend (a country, etc.)	**защитавам**	[zaʃti'tavam]
to defend oneself	**защищавам се**	[zaʃtiʃ'tavam sɛ]
to demand (request firmly)	**изисквам**	[i'ziskvam]
to denounce (vt)	**доносничa**	[dɔ'nɔsnitʃa]
to deny (vt)	**отричам**	[ɔt'ritʃam]
to depend on ...	**завися (от ...)**	[za'visʲa ɔt]
to deprive (vt)	**лишавам**	[li'ʃʌvam]
to deserve (vt)	**заслужавам**	[zaslu'ʒavam]
to design (machine, etc.)	**проектирам**	[prɔɛk'tiram]
to desire (want, wish)	**желая**	[ʒɛ'laja]
to despise (vt)	**презирам**	[prɛ'ziram]
to destroy (documents, etc.)	**унищожавам**	[uniʃtɔ'ʒavam]
to differ (from sth)	**отличавам се**	[ɔtli'tʃavam sɛ]
to dig (tunnel, etc.)	**ровя**	['rɔvʲa]
to direct (point the way)	**направлявам**	[naprav'ʎavam]
to disappear (vi)	**изчезна**	[iz'tʃəzna]
to discover (new land, etc.)	**откривам**	[ɔtk'rivam]
to discuss (vt)	**обсъждам**	[ɔb'sɪʒdam]
to distribute (leaflets, etc.)	**разпространявам**	[rasprɔstra'ɲavam]
to disturb (vt)	**безпокоя**	[bɛspɔkɔ'ja]
to dive (vi)	**гмуркам се**	['gmurkam sɛ]
to divide (math)	**деля**	[dɛ'ʎa]
to do (vt)	**правя**	['pravʲa]
to do the laundry	**пера**	[pɛ'ra]
to double (increase)	**удвоявам**	[udvɔ'javam]
to doubt (have doubts)	**съмнявам се**	[sɪm'ɲavam sɛ]
to draw a conclusion	**правя заключение**	['pravʲa zakly'tʃəniɛ]
to dream (daydream)	**мечтая**	[mɛtʃ'taja]
to dream (in sleep)	**сънувам**	[sɪ'nuvam]
to drink (vi, vt)	**пия**	['pija]
to drive a car	**карам кола**	['karam kɔ'la]
to drive away (scare away)	**изгоня**	[iz'gɔɲa]
to drop (let fall)	**изтървавам**	[istɪr'vavam]
to drown (ab. person)	**давя се**	['davʲa sɛ]
to dry (clothes, hair)	**суша**	[su'ʃʌ]
to eat (vi, vt)	**ям**	[jam]
to eavesdrop (vi)	**подслушвам**	[pɔts'luʃvam]
to emit (give out - odor, etc.)	**разпространявам**	[rasprɔstra'ɲavam]
to enter (on the list)	**вписвам**	['fpisvam]

to entertain (amuse)	**забавлявам**	[za'bavʎavam]
to equip (fit out)	**оборудвам**	[ɔbɔ'rudvam]
to examine (proposal)	**разгледам**	[razg'lɛdam]
to exchange (sth)	**разменям си**	[raz'mɛɲam si]
to exclude, to expel	**изключвам**	[isk'lytʃvam]
to excuse (forgive)	**извинявам**	[izvi'ɲavam]
to exist (vi)	**съществувам**	[sɪʃtɛst'vuvam]
to expect (anticipate)	**очаквам**	[ɔ'tʃakvam]
to expect (foresee)	**предвиждам**	[prɛd'viʒdam]
to explain (vt)	**обяснявам**	[ɔbʲas'ɲavam]
to express (vt)	**изразявам**	[izra'zʲavam]
to extinguish (a fire)	**загасявам**	[zaga'sʲavam]
to fall in love (with …)	**влюбя се**	['vlybʲa sɛ]
to feed (provide food)	**храня**	['hraɲa]
to fight (against the enemy)	**боря се**	['bɔrʲa sɛ]
to fight (vi)	**бия се**	['bija sɛ]
to fill (glass, bottle)	**напълвам**	[na'pɪlvam]
to find (~ lost items)	**намирам**	[na'miram]
to finish (vt)	**приключвам**	[prik'lytʃvam]
to fish (angle)	**ловя риба**	[lɔ'vʲa 'riba]
to fit (ab. dress, etc.)	**подхождам**	[pɔd'hɔʒdam]
to flatter (vt)	**подмазвам се**	[pɔd'mazvam sɛ]
to fly (bird, plane)	**летя**	[lɛ'tʲa]
to follow … (come after)	**вървя след …**	[var'vʲa sled]
to forbid (vt)	**забранявам**	[zabra'ɲavam]
to force (compel)	**принуждавам**	[prinuʒ'davam]
to forget (vi, vt)	**забравям**	[zab'ravʲam]
to forgive (pardon)	**прощавам**	[prɔʃ'tavam]
to form (constitute)	**образовам**	[ɔbra'zɔvam]
to get dirty (vi)	**изцапам се**	[is'tsapam sɛ]
to get infected (with …)	**заразя се**	[zara'zʲa sɛ]
to get irritated	**дразня се**	['drazɲa sɛ]
to get married	**женя се**	['ʒɛɲa sɛ]
to get rid of …	**избавям се от …**	[iz'bavʲam sɛ ɔt]
to get tired	**уморявам се**	[umɔ'rʲavam sɛ]
to get up (arise from bed)	**ставам**	['stavam]
to give a bath	**къпя**	['kɪpʲa]
to give a hug, to hug (vt)	**прегръщам**	[prɛg'rɪʃtam]
to give in (yield to)	**отстъпвам**	[ɔts'tɪpvam]
to go (by car, etc.)	**пътувам**	[pɪ'tuvam]
to go (on foot)	**вървя**	[vɪr'vʲa]
to go for a swim	**къпя се**	['kɪpʲa sɛ]

to go out (for dinner, etc.)	**излизам**	[iz'lizam]
to go to bed	**лягам да спя**	['ʎagam da spʲa]
to greet (vt)	**приветствувам**	[pri'vɛtstvuvam]
to grow (plants)	**отглеждам**	[ɔtg'lɛʒdam]
to guarantee (vt)	**гарантирам**	[garan'tiram]
to guess right	**отгатна**	[ɔt'gatna]

254. Verbs H-M

to hand out (distribute)	**раздам**	[raz'dam]
to hang (curtains, etc.)	**закачам**	[za'katʃam]
to have (vt)	**имам**	['imam]
to have a try	**опитам се**	[ɔ'pitam sɛ]
to have breakfast	**закусвам**	[za'kusvam]
to have dinner	**вечерям**	[vɛ'tʃərʲam]
to have fun	**веселя се**	[vɛsɛ'ʎa sɛ]
to have lunch	**обядвам**	[ɔ'bʲadvam]
to head (group, etc.)	**оглавявам**	[ɔgla'vʲavam]
to hear (vt)	**чувам**	['tʃuvam]
to heat (vt)	**нагрявам**	[nag'rʲavam]
to help (vt)	**помагам**	[pɔ'magam]
to hide (vt)	**крия**	['krijɑ]
to hire (e.g., ~ a boat)	**наемам**	[na'ɛmam]
to hire (staff)	**наемам**	[na'ɛmam]
to hope (vi, vt)	**надявам се**	[na'dʲavam sɛ]
to hunt (for food, sport)	**ловувам**	[lɔ'vuvam]
to hurry (sb)	**карам ... да бърза**	['karam da 'bɪrza]
to hurry (vi)	**бързам**	['bɪrzam]
to imagine (to picture)	**представям си**	[prɛts'tavʲam si]
to imitate (vt)	**имитирам**	[imi'tiram]
to implore (vt)	**умолявам**	[umɔ'ʎavam]
to import (vt)	**внасям**	['vnasʲam]
to increase (vi)	**увеличавам се**	[uvɛli'tʃavam sɛ]
to increase (vt)	**увеличавам**	[uvɛli'tʃavam]
to infect (vt)	**заразявам**	[zara'zʲavam]
to influence (vt)	**влияя**	[vli'jajɑ]
to inform (~ sb about ...)	**съобщавам**	[sɪɔbʃ'tavam]
to inform (vt)	**информирам**	[infɔr'miram]
to inherit (vt)	**наследявам**	[naslɛ'dʲavam]
to inquire (about ...)	**научавам**	[nau'tʃavam]
to insist (vi, vt)	**настоявам**	[nastɔ'jɑvam]
to inspire (vt)	**въодушевявам**	[vɪɔduʃɛ'vʲavam]
to instruct (teach)	**инструктирам**	[instruk'tiram]

to insult (offend)	**оскърбявам**	[ɔskır'bʲavam]
to interest (vt)	**интересувам**	[intɛrɛ'suvam]
to intervene (vi)	**намесвам се**	[na'mɛsvam sɛ]
to introduce (present)	**запознавам**	[zapɔz'navam]
to invent (machine, etc.)	**изобретявам**	[izɔbrɛ'tʲavam]
to invite (vt)	**каня**	['kaɲa]
to iron (laundry)	**гладя**	['gladʲa]
to irritate (annoy)	**дразня**	['drazɲa]
to isolate (vt)	**изолирам**	[izɔ'liram]
to join (political party, etc.)	**присъединявам се**	[prisıɛdi'ɲavam sɛ]
to joke (be kidding)	**шегувам се**	[ʃɛ'guvam sɛ]
to keep (old letters, etc.)	**съхранявам**	[sıhra'ɲavam]
to keep silent	**мълча**	[mıl'ʧa]
to kill (vt)	**убивам**	[u'bivam]
to knock (at the door)	**чукам (на врата)**	['ʧukam na vra'ta]
to know (sb)	**познавам**	[pɔz'navam]
to know (sth)	**знам**	[znam]
to laugh (vi)	**смея се**	['smɛjɑ sɛ]
to launch (start up)	**пускам, стартирам**	['puskam], [star'tiram]
to leave (~ for Mexico)	**заминавам**	[zami'navam]
to leave (spouse)	**изоставям**	[ɔs'tavʲam]
to leave behind (forget)	**забравям**	[zab'ravʲam]
to liberate (city, etc.)	**освобождавам**	[ɔsvɔbɔʒ'davam]
to lie (tell untruth)	**лъжа**	['lıʒa]
to light (campfire, etc.)	**запалвам**	[za'palvam]
to light up (illuminate)	**осветявам**	[ɔsvɛ'tʲavam]
to love (e.g., ~ dancing)	**обичам**	[ɔ'biʧam]
to like (I like ...)	**харесвам**	[ha'rɛsvam]
to limit (vt)	**ограничавам**	[ɔgrani'ʧavam]
to listen (vi)	**слушам**	['sluʃʌm]
to live (~ in France)	**живея**	[ʒi'vɛjɑ]
to live (exist)	**живея**	[ʒi'vɛjɑ]
to load (gun)	**зареждам**	[za'rɛʒdam]
to load (vehicle, etc.)	**натоварвам**	[natɔ'varvam]
to look (I'm just ~ing)	**гледам**	['glɛdam]
to look for ... (search)	**търся**	['tırsʲa]
to look like (resemble)	**приличам**	[pri'liʧam]
to lose (umbrella, etc.)	**губя**	['gubʲa]
to love (sb)	**обичам**	[ɔ'biʧam]
to lower (blind, head)	**спускам**	['spuskam]
to make (~ dinner)	**готвя**	['gɔtvʲa]
to make a mistake	**греша**	[grɛ'ʃʌ]
to make angry	**сърдя**	['sırdʲa]

to make copies	**размножавам**	[razmnɔ'ʒavam]
to make easier	**облекча**	[ɔblɛk'ʧa]
to make the acquaintance	**запознавам се**	[zapɔz'navam sɛ]
to make use (of ...)	**ползвам**	['pɔlzvam]
to manage, to run	**ръководя**	[rɪkɔ'vɔdʲa]
to mark (make a mark)	**отбелязвам**	[ɔtbɛ'ʎazvam]
to mean (signify)	**знача**	['znaʧa]
to memorize (vt)	**запомням**	[za'pɔmɲam]
to mention (talk about)	**споменавам**	[spɔmɛ'navam]
to miss (school, etc.)	**пропускам**	[prɔ'puskam]
to mix (combine, blend)	**смесвам**	['smɛsvam]
to mock (make fun of)	**присмивам се**	[pris'mivam sɛ]
to move (to shift)	**премествам**	[prɛ'mɛstvam]
to multiply (math)	**умножавам**	[umnɔ'ʒavam]
must (v aux)	**дължа**	[dɪ'lʒa]

255. Verbs N-S

to name, to call (vt)	**наричам**	[na'riʧam]
to negotiate (vi)	**водя преговори**	['vɔdʲa 'prɛgɔvɔri]
to note (write down)	**отбележа**	[ɔtbɛ'lɛʒa]
to notice (see)	**забелязвам**	[zabɛ'ʎazvam]
to obey (vi, vt)	**подчинявам се**	[pɔdʧi'ɲavam sɛ]
to object (vi, vt)	**възразявам**	[vɪzra'zʲavam]
to observe (see)	**наблюдавам**	[nably'davam]
to offend (vt)	**обиждам**	[ɔ'biʒdam]
to omit (word, phrase)	**пропускам**	[prɔ'puskam]
to open (vt)	**отварям**	[ɔt'varʲam]
to order (in restaurant)	**поръчвам**	[pɔ'rɪʧvam]
to order (mil.)	**заповядвам**	[zapɔ'vʲadvam]
to organize (concert, party)	**организирам**	[ɔrgani'ziram]
to overestimate (vt)	**надценявам**	[naʦsə'ɲavam]
to own (possess)	**владея**	[vla'dɛjɑ]
to participate (vi)	**участвам**	[u'ʧastvam]
to pass (go beyond)	**минавам**	[mi'navam]
to pay (vi, vt)	**плащам**	['plaʃtam]
to peep, spy on	**надниквам**	[nad'nikvam]
to penetrate (vt)	**прониквам**	[prɔ'nikvam]
to permit (vt)	**разрешавам**	[razrɛ'ʃʌvam]
to pick (flowers)	**късам**	['kɪsam]
to place (put, set)	**нареждам**	[na'rɛʒdam]
to plan (~ to do sth)	**планирам**	[pla'niram]
to play (actor)	**играя**	[ig'rajɑ]

to play (children)	**играя**	[ig'rajɑ]
to point (~ the way)	**посочвам**	[pɔ'sɔtʃvam]
to pour (liquid)	**наливам**	[na'livam]
to pray (vi, vt)	**моля се**	['mɔʎa sɛ]
to predominate (vi)	**преобладавам**	[prɛɔbla'davam]
to prefer (vt)	**предпочитам**	[prɛtpɔ'tʃitam]
to prepare (~ a plan)	**подготвя**	[pɔd'gɔtvʲa]
to present (sb to sb)	**представлявам**	[prɛtstav'ʎavam]
to preserve (peace, life)	**съхранявам**	[sɪhra'ɲavam]
to progress (move forward)	**напредвам**	[nap'rɛdvam]
to promise (vt)	**обещавам**	[ɔbɛʃ'tavam]
to pronounce (vt)	**произнасям**	[prɔiz'nasʲam]
to propose (vt)	**предлагам**	[prɛd'lagam]
to protect (e.g., ~ nature)	**опазвам**	[ɔ'pazvam]
to protest (vi)	**протестирам**	[prɔtɛs'tiram]
to prove (vt)	**доказвам**	[dɔ'kazvam]
to provoke (vt)	**провокирам**	[prɔvɔ'kiram]
to pull (~ the rope)	**дърпам**	['dɪrpam]
to punish (vt)	**наказвам**	[na'kazvam]
to push (~ the door)	**блъскам**	['blɪskam]
to put away (vt)	**скривам**	['skrivam]
to put in (insert)	**слагам**	['slagam]
to put in order	**подреждам**	[pɔd'rɛʒdam]
to put, to place	**слагам**	['slagam]
to quote (cite)	**цитирам**	[tsi'tiram]
to reach (arrive at)	**стигам**	['stigam]
to read (vi, vt)	**чета**	[tʃə'tɪ]
to realize (a dream)	**осъществявам**	[ɔsɪʃtɛst'vʲavam]
to recall (~ one's name)	**спомням**	['spɔmɲam]
to recognize (identify sb)	**опознавам**	[ɔpɔz'navam]
to recommend (vt)	**съветвам**	[sɪ'vɛtvam]
to recover (~ from flu)	**оздравявам**	[ɔzdra'vʲavam]
to redo (do again)	**преправям**	[prɛp'ravʲam]
to reduce (speed, etc.)	**намалявам**	[nama'ʎavam]
to refuse (~ sb)	**отказвам**	[ɔt'kazvam]
to regret (be sorry)	**съжалявам**	[sɪʒa'ʎavam]
to reinforce (vt)	**укрепвам**	[uk'rɛpvam]
to remember (vt)	**помня**	['pɔmɲa]
to remind of ...	**напомням**	[na'pɔmɲam]
to remove (~ a stain)	**премахвам**	[prɛ'mahvam]
to remove (~ an obstacle)	**отстранявам**	[ɔtstra'ɲavam]
to rent (sth from sb)	**наемам**	[na'ɛmam]

to repair (mend)	**поправям**	[pɔp'ravʲam]
to repeat (say again)	**повтарям**	[pɔf'tarʲam]
to report (make a report)	**докладвам**	[dɔk'ladvam]
to reproach (vt)	**упреквам**	[up'rɛkvam]
to reserve, to book	**резервирам**	[rɛzɛr'viram]
to restrain (hold back)	**удържам**	[u'dɪrʒam]
to return (come back)	**завръщам се**	[zav'rɪʃtam sɛ]
to risk, to take a risk	**рискувам**	[ris'kuvam]
to rub off (erase)	**изтрия**	[ist'rijɑ]
to run (move fast)	**бягам**	['bʲagam]
to satisfy (please)	**удовлетворявам**	[udɔvlɛtvɔ'rʲavam]
to save (rescue)	**спасявам**	[spa'sʲavam]
to say (~ thank you)	**кажа**	['kaʒa]
to scold (vt)	**ругая**	[ru'gajɑ]
to scratch (with claws)	**драскам**	['draskam]
to select (to pick)	**избера**	[izbɛ'ra]
to sell (goods)	**продавам**	[prɔ'davam]
to send (a letter)	**изпращам**	[isp'raʃtam]
to send back (vt)	**върна обратно**	['vɪrna ɔb'ratnɔ]
to sense (danger)	**чувствам**	['ʧuvstvam]
to sentence (vt)	**осъждам**	[ɔ'sɪʒdam]
to serve (in restaurant)	**обслужвам**	[ɔbs'luʒvam]
to settle (a conflict)	**уреждам**	[u'rɛʒdam]
to shake (vt)	**треса**	[trɛ'sa]
to shave (vi)	**бръсна се**	['brɪsna sɛ]
to shiver (with cold)	**треперя**	[trɛ'pɛrʲa]
to shoot (vi)	**стрелям**	['strɛʎam]
to shout (vi)	**викам**	['vikam]
to show (to display)	**показвам**	[pɔ'kazvam]
to shudder (vi)	**трепвам**	['trɛpvam]
to sigh (vi)	**въздъхна**	[vɪz'dɪhna]
to sign (document)	**подписвам**	[pɔt'pisvam]
to signify (mean)	**означавам**	[ɔzna'ʧavam]
to simplify (vt)	**опрощавам**	[ɔprɔʃ'tavam]
to sin (vi)	**греша**	[grɛ'ʃʌ]
to sit (be sitting)	**седя**	[sɛ'dʲa]
to sit down (vi)	**сядам**	['sʲadam]
to smash (~ a bug)	**смачкам**	['smaʧkam]
to smell (scent)	**мириша**	[mi'riʃʌ]
to smell (sniff at)	**мириша**	[mi'riʃʌ]
to smile (vi)	**усмихвам се**	[us'mihvam sɛ]
to snap (vi, ab. rope)	**скъсам се**	['skɪsam sɛ]
to solve (problem)	**реша**	[rɛ'ʃʌ]

to sow (seed, crop)	**сея**	['sɛja]
to spill (liquid)	**проливам**	[prɔ'livam]
to spit (vi)	**плюя**	['plyja]
to stand (toothache, cold)	**търпя**	[tɪr'pʲa]
to start (begin)	**започвам**	[za'pɔʧvam]
to steal (money, etc.)	**крада**	[kra'da]
to stop (please ~ calling me)	**прекратявам**	[prɛkra'tʲavam]
to stop (for pause, etc.)	**спирам се**	['spiram sɛ]
to stop talking	**замълча**	[zamɪl'ʧa]
to stroke (caress)	**галя**	['gaʎa]
to study (vt)	**изучавам**	[izu'ʧavam]
to suffer (feel pain)	**страдам**	['stradam]
to support (cause, idea)	**подкрепям**	[pɔtkrɛ'pʲam]
to suppose (assume)	**предполагам**	[prɛtpɔ'lagam]
to surface (ab. submarine)	**изплувам**	[isp'luvam]
to surprise (amaze)	**удивлявам**	[udiv'ʎavam]
to suspect (vt)	**подозирам**	[pɔdɔ'ziram]
to swim (vi)	**плувам**	['pluvam]
to turn on (computer, etc.)	**включвам**	['vklyʧvam]

256. Verbs T-W

to take (get hold of)	**взимам**	['vzimam]
to take a bath	**мия се**	['mija sɛ]
to take a rest	**почивам**	[pɔ'ʧivam]
to take aim (at ...)	**целя се в ...**	['ʦɐʎa sɛ v]
to take away	**отнасям**	[ɔt'nasʲam]
to take off (airplane)	**излитам**	[iz'litam]
to take off (remove)	**свалям**	['svaʎam]
to take pictures	**снимам**	['snimam]
to talk to ...	**говоря с ...**	[gɔ'vɔrʲa s]
to teach (give lessons)	**обучавам**	[ɔbu'ʧavam]
to tear off (vt)	**откъсна**	[ɔt'kɪsna]
to tell (story, joke)	**разказвам**	[ras'kazvam]
to thank (vt)	**благодаря**	[blagɔda'rʲa]
to think (believe)	**смятам**	['smʲatam]
to think (vi, vt)	**мисля**	['misʎa]
to threaten (vt)	**заплашвам**	[zap'laʃvam]
to throw (stone)	**хвърлям**	['hvɪrʎam]
to tie to ...	**завързвам**	[za'vɪrzvam]
to tie up (prisoner)	**свързвам**	['svɪrzvam]

to tire (make tired)	**уморявам**	[umɔ'rʲavam]
to touch (one's arm, etc.)	**докосвам се**	[dɔ'kɔsvam sɛ]
to tower (over ...)	**възвисявам се**	[vɪzvi'sʲavam sɛ]
to train (animals)	**дресирам**	[drɛ'siram]
to train (sb)	**тренирам**	[trɛ'niram]
to train (vi)	**тренирам се**	[trɛ'niram sɛ]
to transform (vt)	**трансформирам**	[transfɔr'miram]
to translate (vt)	**превеждам**	[prɛ'vɛʒdam]
to treat (patient, illness)	**лекувам**	[lɛ'kuvam]
to trust (vt)	**доверявам**	[dɔvɛ'rʲavam]
to try (attempt)	**опитвам се**	[ɔ'pitvam sɛ]
to turn (~ to the left)	**завивам**	[za'vivam]
to turn away (vi)	**обръщам се**	[ɔb'rɪʃtam sɛ]
to turn off (the light)	**изключвам**	[isk'lyʧvam]
to turn over (stone, etc.)	**обърна**	[ɔ'bɪrna]
to underestimate (vt)	**недооценявам**	[nɛdɔ:ʦə'ɲavam]
to underline (vt)	**подчертая**	[pɔdʧər'tajɑ]
to understand (vt)	**разбирам**	[raz'biram]
to undertake (vt)	**предприемам**	[prɛtpri'ɛmam]
to unite (vt)	**обединявам**	[ɔbɛdi'ɲavam]
to untie (vt)	**отвързвам**	[ɔt'vɪrzvam]
to use (phrase, word)	**употребявам**	[upɔtrɛ'bʲavam]
to vaccinate (vt)	**ваксинирам**	[vaksi'niram]
to vote (vi)	**гласувам**	[gla'suvam]
to wait (vt)	**чакам**	['ʧakam]
to wake (sb)	**събуждам**	[sɪ'buʒdam]
to want (wish, desire)	**искам**	['iskam]
to warn (of the danger)	**предупреждавам**	[prɛduprɛʒ'davam]
to wash (clean)	**мия**	['mijɑ]
to water (plants)	**поливам**	[pɔ'livam]
to wave (the hand)	**махам**	['maham]
to weigh (have weight)	**тежа**	[tɛ'ʒa]
to work (vi)	**работя**	[ra'bɔtʲa]
to worry (make anxious)	**безпокоя**	[bɛspɔkɔ'jɑ]
to worry (vi)	**вълнувам се**	[vɪl'nuvam sɛ]
to wrap (parcel, etc.)	**опаковам**	[ɔpa'kɔvam]
to wrestle (sport)	**боря се**	['bɔrʲa sɛ]
to write (vt)	**пиша**	['piʃʌ]
to write down	**записвам**	[za'pisvam]

Made in the USA
Lexington, KY
31 August 2014